THE DISCOVERY OF
FRANCE

Graham Robb

THE DISCOVERY OF
FRANCE

PICADOR

First published 2007 by Picador
an imprint of Pan Macmillan Ltd
Pan Macmillan, 20 New Wharf Road, London N1 9RR
Basingstoke and Oxford
Associated companies throughout the world
www.panmacmillan.com

ISBN 978-0-330-42760-9

Typeset by SetSystems Ltd, Saffron Walden, Essex
Printed and bound in Great Britain by
Mackays of Chatham plc, Chatham, Kent

For Margaret

Contents

Contents

List of Illustrations

SECTION TWO

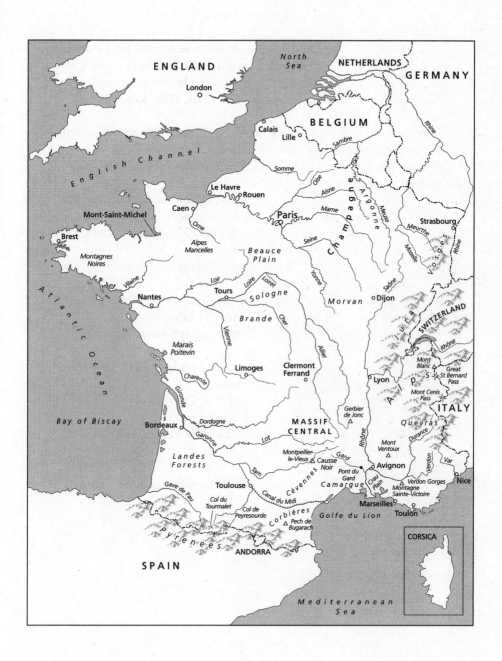

Artois

Flandre

Picardie

Normandie

Ile-de-France

Lorraine

Champagne

Alsace

Bretagne

Maine

Orléanais

Belfort

Anjou

Touraine

Nivernais

Franche-
Comté

Poitou

Berry

Bourgogne

Aunis

Bourbonnais

Saintonge

Marche

Lyonnais

Savoie

Angoumois

Limousin

Auvergne

Dauphiné

Guyenne et Gascogne

Languedoc

Comtat
Venaissin

Nice

Provence

Béarn

Languedoc

Foix

Roussillon

Corse

PROVINCES, pre-Revolution

DÉPARTEMENTS IN 1790

Itinerary

TEN YEARS AGO, I began to explore the country on which I was supposed to be an authority. For some time, it had been obvious that the France whose literature and history I taught and studied was just a fraction of the vast land I had seen on holidays, research trips and adventures. My professional knowledge of the country reflected the metropolitan view of writers like Balzac and Baudelaire, for whom the outer boulevards of Paris marked the edge of the civilized world. My accidental experience was slightly broader. I had lived in a small town in Provence and a hamlet in Brittany next door to people whose first language was not French but Provençal or Breton, and I first became superficially fluent in French, while working in a garage in a Paris suburb, thanks to an Algerian Berber from the mountains of Kabylie. Without him, the Parisian dialect of the foreman would have been completely incomprehensible.

In the periods of history where I made my intellectual home, the gap between knowledge and experience was even wider. There was the familiar France of monarchy and republic, pieced together from medieval provinces, reorganized by the Revolution and Napoleon, and modernized by railways, industry and war. But there was also a France in which, just over a hundred years ago, French was a foreign language to the majority of the population. It was a country that had still not been accurately mapped in its entirety. A little further back in time, sober accounts described a land of ancient tribal divisions, prehistoric communication networks and pre-Christian beliefs. Historians and anthropologists had referred to this country, without irony, as 'Gaul' and quoted Julius Caesar as a useful source of information on the inhabitants of the uncharted interior.

I owed my first real inklings of this other France to a rediscovery of the miraculous machine that opened up the country to millions of people at the end of the nineteenth century. Once or twice a year, I travelled through France with the dedicatee of this book at the speed of a nineteenth-century stagecoach. Cycling not only makes it possible to conduct exhaustive research into local produce, it also creates an enormous appetite for information. Certain configurations of field, road, weather and smell imprint themselves on the cycling brain with inexplicable clarity and return sometimes years later to pose their nebulous questions. A bicycle unrolls a 360-degree panorama of the land, allows the rider to register its gradual changes in gear ratios and muscle tension, and makes it hard to miss a single inch of it, from the tyre-lacerating suburbs of Paris to the Mistral-blasted plains of Provence. The itinerary of a cyclist recreates, as if by chance, much older journeys: transhumance trails, Gallo-Roman trade routes, pilgrim paths, river confluences that have disappeared in industrial wasteland, valleys and ridge roads that used to be busy with pedlars and migrants. Cycling also makes conversation easy and inevitable – with children, nomads, people who are lost, local amateur historians and, of course, dogs, whose behaviour collectively characterizes the outlook of certain regions as clearly as human behaviour once did.

Each journey became a complex puzzle in four dimensions. I wanted to know what I was missing and what I would have seen a century or two before. At first, the solution seemed to be to carry a miniaturized library of modern histories, ancient guidebooks and travellers' accounts, printed on thin paper in a tiny typeface. For example, a set of the reports written by the Prefects who were sent out by Napoleon after the Revolution to chart and describe the unknown provinces could be made to weigh less than a spare inner-tube. It soon became apparent, however, that the *terra incognita* extended much further than I had realized and that far more time would have to be devoted to the more physically demanding task of sedentary research.

This book is the result of fourteen thousand miles in the saddle and four years in the library. It describes the lives of the inhabitants of France – wherever possible, through their own eyes – and the exploration and colonization of their land by foreigners and natives, from the late seventeenth century to the early twentieth. It follows a roughly chronological route, from the end of the reign of Louis XIV to the outbreak of the First World War, with occasional detours through pre-Roman Gaul and present-day France.

Part One describes the populations of France, their languages, beliefs and daily lives, their travels and discoveries, and the other creatures with whom they shared the land. In Part Two, the land is mapped, colonized by rulers and tourists, refashioned politically and physically, and turned into a modern state. The difference between the two parts, broadly speaking, is the difference between ethnology and history: the world that was always the same and the world that was always changing. I have tried to give a sense of the orrery of disparate, concurrent spheres, to show a land in which mule trains coincided with railway trains, and where witches and explorers were still gainfully employed when Gustave Eiffel was changing the skyline of Paris. Readers who are better acquainted with the direct route of political history may wish to take their bearings from the list of events at the back of the book.

This was supposed to be the historical guidebook I wanted to read when setting out to discover France, a book in which the inhabitants were not airlifted from the land for statistical processing, in which 'France' and 'the French' would mean something more than Paris and a few powerful individuals, and in which the past was not a refuge from the present but a means of understanding and enjoying it. It can be read as a social and geographical history, as a collection of tales and *tableaux*, or as a complement to a guidebook. It offers a sample itinerary, not a definitive account. Each chapter could easily have become a separate volume, but the book is already too large to justify its inclusion in the panniers. It was an adventure to write and I hope it shows how much remains to be discovered.

PART ONE

1

The Undiscovered Continent

ONE SUMMER IN THE EARLY 1740s, on the last day of his life, a young man from Paris became the first modern cartographer to see the mountain called Le Gerbier de Jonc. This weird volcanic cone juts out of an empty landscape of pastures and ravines, blasted by a freezing wind called the *burle*. Three hundred and fifty miles south of Paris, at a point on the map diametrically opposed to the capital, it stands on the watershed that divides the Atlantic from the Mediterranean. On its western slope, at a wooden trough where animals once came to drink, the river Loire begins its six-hundred-and-forty-mile journey, flowing north then west in a wide arc through the mudflats of Touraine to the borders of Brittany and the Atlantic Ocean. Thirty miles to the east, the busy river Rhône carried passengers and cargo down to the Mediterranean ports, but it would have taken more than three days to reach it across a sparsely populated chaos of ancient lava-flows and gorges.

If the traveller had scaled the peak of phonolithic rock – so called because of the xylophonic sound the stones make as they slide away under a climber's feet – he would have seen a magnificent panorama: to the east, the long white curtain of the Alps, from the Mont Blanc massif to the bulk of Mont Ventoux looking down over the plains of Provence; to the north, the wooded ridges of the Forez and the mists descending from the Jura to the plains beyond Lyon; to the west, the wild Cévennes, the Cantal plateau and the whole volcanic range of the upper Auvergne. It was a geometer's dream – almost one-thirteenth of the land surface of France spread out like a map.

From the summit, he could take in at a glance several small regions whose inhabitants barely knew of each other's existence. To walk in any direction for a day was to become incomprehensible, for the Mézenc range to which the mountain belonged was also a watershed of languages. The people who saw the sun set behind the Gerbier de Jonc spoke one group of dialects; the people on the evening side spoke another. Forty miles to the north, the wine growers and silk-weavers of the Lyonnais spoke a different language altogether, which had yet to be identified and named by scholars. Yet another language was spoken in the region the traveller had left the day before, and though his own mother tongue, French, was a dialect of that language, he would have found it hard to understand the peasants who saw him pass.

The traveller in question (his name has not survived) belonged to an expedition that was to lay the groundwork for the first complete and reliable map of France. A team of young geometers had been assembled by the astronomer Jacques Cassini, instructed in the new science of cartography and equipped with specially made portable instruments. Cassini's father had studied the rings of Saturn and measured the size of the solar system. His map of the Moon was more precise than many maps of France, which still contained several uncharted regions. Now, for the first time, France would be revealed in all its detail as if from a great height above the Earth.

One part of the expedition had followed the river Loire as far as it could go. Roads and byways came and went with the seasons and often passed through forests where no sightings could be taken, and so the river was the only certain guide to the interior. But south of Roanne, the Loire was a truculent stream that ran through narrow gorges. In parts, it could hardly be followed, let alone used for transport. The vast plateau of the Massif Central was still the fortress it had been when the Arverni tribes held out against the Romans. Its rivers were unnavigable and its links to the rest of France practically non-existent. The mail coach from Paris stopped at Clermont. A branch service struggled on as far as Le Puy, two days to the south-east. After Le Puy, there was nothing but mule-tracks and open country. Asking for directions was a waste of time. Even a century later, few people could walk far from their place of birth without getting lost.

By the time the geometer reached the foot of the Mézenc range, he was two days from the nearest road. The only noticeable settlement for miles around was a village of black lava-stone hovels. According to one map, Les Estables should have been several miles to the south-west. In fact, it lay on a track that led towards the summit of the Mézenc. A small tower would make observations easy if the weather stayed fine, and there might be a French-speaking priest to identify remote hamlets and to give the names of woods and rivers. In any case, there was nowhere else to spend the night.

The appearance of a stranger in the landscape was a notable event. To isolated villagers, a man in foreign clothes who pointed inexplicable instruments at barren rocks was up to no good. It had been noticed that after the appearance of one of these sorcerers, life became harder. Crops withered; animals went lame or died of disease; sheep were found on hillsides, torn apart by something more savage than a wolf; and, for reasons that remained obscure, taxes increased.

Even a century later, this was still a remote and dangerous part of France. A nineteenth-century geographer recommended viewing the Mézenc region from a balloon, but 'only if the aeronaut can remain out of range of a rifle'. In 1854, Murray's *Handbook for Travellers in France* warned tourists and amateur geologists who left the coach at Pradelles and struck out across country in search of 'wild and singular views' not to expect a warm welcome. 'There is scarcely any accommodation on this route, which can hardly be performed in a day; and the people are rude and forbidding.' The handbook, perhaps deliberately, said nothing of Les Estables, which lay on the route, nor did it mention the only occasion on which the village earned itself a place in history – a summer's day in the early 1740s when a young geometer on the Cassini expedition was hacked to death by the natives.

*

AS FAR AS WE KNOW, the villagers of Les Estables were never punished for the murder of Cassini's geometer. To judge by similar incidents elsewhere in France, his death was the result of a collective decision taken by people who lived by their own unwritten laws. Outside interference of any kind was perceived as an evil intrusion. In many parts of France, even in the early twentieth century, a common prayer asked for deliverance from Satan, sorcerers, rabid dogs and 'Justice'.

The people of the Mézenc, like the inhabitants of many others towns and villages in France, would not have considered themselves 'French' in any case. Few would have been able to say exactly what the word meant. They knew what they had to know to survive from one season to the next. Some of them travelled south in search of work. They traded with their neighbours and leased their land to shepherds who brought huge, three-mile-long flocks of sheep to graze on their pastures in summer. But these movements were regulated by tradition and confined to ancient routes that never varied. When the writer George Sand ventured into the region in 1859, she was amazed to discover that 'the locals are no more familiar with the area than strangers'. Her native guide was unable to tell her the name of the mountain (the Mézenc) 'which has been staring him in the face since the day he was born'.

Revelling in the ignorance of peasants was a favourite pastime of the tiny, educated elite, before and after the Revolution of 1789. Reports of half-human savages and grovelling troglodytes lurking in thickets and holes in the ground gave the civilized minority a sense of its own sophistication. But the ignorance was mutual. Forty years after the young geometer's death, the few people who could afford the Cassini charts or who saw them in a private collection might have imagined that the hills and gorges of the Mézenc region were no longer *terra incognita*. They could locate Les Estables near the southeastern edge of the ancient plateau where most of the major river systems rise, on a line from Bordeaux in the west to a mountain in the foothills of the Alps which the charts called 'Mont Inaccessible'. But the little cottages and turrets that represented human settlements on the map were deceptively precise. Many of these places had only been glimpsed by the map-makers from the tops of trees and towers.

A modern historian who leaves behind the quiet towns and almost deserted main roads of eighteenth- and nineteenth-century France has more to learn from George Sand's illiterate guide than from the famous tourist herself. In many respects, the more accurate the map, the more misleading the impression. Most official, political definitions of the country are quite useless for describing the world of its inhabitants. For someone who sets out across the country, they serve mainly as distant landmarks, and create the comforting impression of knowing where the road is supposed to lead.

Provisionally, then, pre-Revolutionary France can be described as a nation composed of several feudal provinces or '*généralités*'. Some of these provinces, known as '*pays d'état*', had their own regional parliaments and imposed their own taxes. Others, known as '*pays d'élection*', were taxed directly by the state. Many of them have been a part of France for less than four hundred years (see Chronology, p. 359). To historians who tried to describe the entire kingdom, the chaotic effects of the division of Charlemagne's empire in 843, and even the tribal divisions described by Julius Caesar, were still apparent in the maze of internal customs barriers and legal discrepancies.

This jumble of old fiefdoms was, however, controlled by an ambitious and increasingly powerful monarchy. Roman Gaul had looked to the Mediterranean. Now, economic and political power was firmly centred in the north. In 1682, Louis XIV moved his court to the edge of a hunting forest twelve miles south-west of Paris. The avenues of Versailles and the boulevards of Paris were gradually extended across a kingdom that seemed to educated people to be the work of divine providence. Nearly all the frontiers of France were natural: the Atlantic Ocean to the west; the Pyrenees and the Medi-terranean to the south; the Alps, the Jura and the Rhine to the east; the English Channel to the north. Only the flat north-eastern frontier was open, but it was consolidated by the conquest of Artois and Flanders. Later, the annexation of Lorraine would give the kingdom its satisfying, providential shape. A guide for foreign and domestic travellers published in 1687 painted a familiar, reassuring picture of a nation 'joined and united in all its parts and provinces', 'seated in the middle of Europe', 'almost round and like an oval'.

The seventeenth-century guidebook went on to describe France as a densely populated nation with barely an acre of uncultivated land, a high-speed transport system and an extensive network of comfortable, moderately priced hotels. This was the sort of glorious mirage that might have appeared in summer skies above the manicured forest of

Versailles. It will be our last sight for some time to come of an ordered and comprehensible country.

*

A HUNDRED AND FIFTY YEARS had passed since Louis XIV's chief minister, Colbert, had dreamt of a road system that would unite and energize the kingdom, yet, in June 1837, when Henri Beyle – later known as Stendhal – stepped out of the public coach to stretch his legs at a tiny staging-post called Rousselan, thirteen miles from the city of Bourges, he was struck by a sense of *'complete isolation'*. (This was a man who had trudged across the endless Russian steppes with Napoleon's retreating army.) Apart from the post-house itself and the towers of Bourges cathedral on the edge of the wooded plain, there were no signs of human life. A few hours later, beyond a marshy belt of cabbage fields, in Bourges itself, the only faces to be seen were those of a group of soldiers and a sleepy servant in the hotel.

The city at the geographical centre of France seemed to be quite dead. And in the town Stendhal had left that morning, La Charité-sur-Loire, there was so little traffic that everyone had known where he was going and why he was forced to stop there (a broken axle) before he had spoken to a soul. Ahead of him lay an eight-hour journey on the overnight diligence to Châteauroux, forty miles to the west. He left Bourges at 9 p.m. At midnight he was in Issoudun, a proudly somnolent town which had won a battle to maintain its economic and social stagnation by forcing the Paris–Toulouse road to be built twelve miles to the west. Napoleon had paid it the compliment of using it as a place of internal exile. Five hours later, Stendhal's coach rattled into Châteauroux, the capital of the Indre *département* and the biggest town in the former province of Berry.

Stendhal's discovery of solitude was not unusual. To travellers stunned by hours of monotony and desolation, a small provincial town like Châteauroux was an oasis of noise and colourful inconvenience. Later tourists in search of picturesque isolation would be amazed by the din of tiny places, putting up their bulwarks of noise against the surrounding silence: bells ringing on the slightest pretext, unoiled pump handles screeching, and normal conversations being carried on at a volume that would now seem deliberately offensive.

At the gates of Châteauroux began a region of marshes and moors known as the Brande. Some of the younger inhabitants of the Brande had never seen a paved road, let alone a four-wheeled carriage lurching through the countryside like an enchanted house. Renegade priests who had marooned themselves in the Brande during the Revolution had freely given themselves up after a few days.

Beyond the squares, the monuments and the rooms of state that form the backdrop of most French history lay a world of ancient tribes and huge vacant spaces. Anyone heading north on the Paris–Toulouse road had to spend at least eleven hours crossing a pestilential, undrained region of stagnant ponds and stunted woods called the Sologne: 'a desolate country, on a difficult, sandy, deserted road; not a single château, farm or village in the distance, just a few lonely, wretched hovels'. The main road east from Paris to Strasbourg and Germany passed through the almost featureless plains of the Champagne, where settlements were so rare that single hawthorn bushes were preserved as precious landmarks.

When the Romantic poet Alfred de Vigny expressed the seemingly un-Romantic wish 'Never leave me alone with Nature', he was writing as a man who had travelled widely in France. The words 'Sologne', 'Champagne', 'Dombes', 'Double', 'Brenne' and 'Landes' aroused as much horror in travellers as the wilder passes of the Alps and the Pyrenees. Even the most garrulous writers struggled to find something to say about these forlorn regions. 'Nothing of note' was a common remark in guidebooks and travellers' accounts.

From the red, stony wastes of the Esterel in south-eastern Provence, to the ocean of gorse, broom and heather that covered much of Brittany, France was a land of deserts. The greatest of these was the Landes (the name means 'moorland' or 'waste'). In the south-west of France, three thousand square miles of scrub, pine plantations and black sand occupied a triangle bounded by the river Garonne, the foothills of the Pyrenees and the gigantic, land-devouring sand dunes or 'walking mountains' of Mimizan and Arcachon. The zone of silence, where birdsong was never heard, began just south of Bordeaux and continued for two days until the swathe of sinking sand that passed for a road reached the outskirts of Bayonne. Travellers sometimes reported seeing tall, spidery figures passing over the horizon, a few ancient tile-kilns and ramshackle huts of wood and clay, and very little else.

As late as 1867, after more than a century of agricultural improvements, a national census estimated that 43 per cent of land that could be cultivated was 'dominated by the forces of nature': grasslands, forests and moors. Wolves were still a threat in several central regions, including the Dordogne, at the end of the nineteenth century. In 1789, when the Revolutionary parliament discussed the division of the old provinces into *départements* and *communes*, there was some concern that they were creating phantom districts in which a hypothetical population would be governed by a non-existent mayor.

This disconcertingly spacious world, whose inhabitants will begin to emerge in the following chapter, is almost unimaginable without a drastic recalibration of the scale of populousness and isolation. The two hundred thousand square miles of Europe's biggest country were still magnified by medieval time. On the eve of the French Revolution, France was three weeks long (Dunkirk to Perpignan) and three weeks wide (Strasbourg to Brest). Journey times had barely changed since the days of the Romans, when wine-merchants could reach the English Channel from the Mediterranean ports in less than a month. When speeds increased in the late eighteenth century, they did so only for a handful of rich people, and luck still played a big role. Marseille was less than two weeks from Paris, but only if certain conditions were met: perfect weather, a recently repaired road, a modern coach with full suspension, healthy horses, and a fast but careful driver who was never thirsty and never had an accident. These times, moreover, refer only to the transport of human beings. Goods transport was even slower and less predictable. In 1811, overseas produce entering France through the port of Nantes would not be expected in Paris for another three weeks. A merchant in Lyon would be surprised to receive it in under a month.

France was, in effect, a vast continent that had yet to be fully colonized. No one who crossed the country on minor roads would have found it hard to believe that Julius Caesar had been able to march an army for several days through Gaul without being spotted by the enemy. Fugitives made journeys that now seem incredible. In 1755, during the official persecution of Protestants in Languedoc, the pastor Paul Rabaut, who was one of the most wanted men in France, travelled from Nîmes to Paris and then to L'Isle-Adam for a secret interview with the Prince de Conti. He returned to the south without being captured or seen. During the royalist reprisals known as the White Terror, a republican lawyer fleeing for his life left the Paris–Lyon road and walked into the hills and forests to the west of the Rhône. From there, he made his way safely back to Paris on the main road from the Auvergne. His route would have taken him through the forest of Bauzon, which was practically a separate principality, ruled for several centuries by a succession of robber kings known as the 'capitaines de Bauzon'.

The appalling isolation in which some feral human beings managed to exist gives some idea of how lonely a remote area could be. In the wooded hills of the Aveyron, where only an occasional column of smoke might betray a human presence, the boy who came to be known as Victor de l'Aveyron lived alone for several years before he was captured by peasants in 1799 and put on display as a freak of nature. The 'wild girl' of the Issaux forest, south of Mauléon in the Basque Country, had been playing with friends when she got lost in the snow. She wandered in the gloom of the green desert for eight years before she was discovered by shepherds in 1730, alive but speechless. Further west, on the edge of the Iraty forest, a naked, hairy man who could run like a deer, and who was later thought to be the remnant of a Neanderthal colony, was spotted several times in 1774, indulging in his favourite pastime: scattering flocks of sheep. On the last occasion, when the shepherds tried to catch him, he ran away, giggling, and was never seen again.

Even in apparently civilized parts, it was possible to cover large distances undetected. In the mid-eighteenth century, the bandit Louis Mandrin and his three-hundred-strong band of smugglers roamed over an area one-fifth the size of France, from the Auvergne to the Franche-Comté, attacking large towns and successfully evading three regiments for a year and a half. He was eventually captured only because his mistress betrayed him. For years after the Revolution, banditry remained a problem in the Somme *département*. Until the 1830s, even the relatively industrialized northern *départements* were a thieves' paradise.

Tales of isolation and ignorance tend to be associated with spectacular exceptions and with regions that lie beyond what some French historians have termed 'an enlarged Paris Basin', which accounts for more than one-third of the country – an enormous parallelogram stretching from Lille to Clermont-Ferrand and from Lyon to Le Mans, where 'men, ideas and merchandise', all identifiably and self-consciously French, had supposedly been pumping through the system since the Ancien Régime. In this view, modern France existed long ago, in a virtual form, as an enormous Parisian suburb, and was simply waiting for the bicycle, the steam engine, and the automobile to bring it to life.

If a mischievous muse of History deposited a group of these historians by the side of a *route nationale* at any time between 1851 and 1891, they would see, on average, fewer than ten vehicles an hour, travelling at speeds between 3 and 13 mph. Further back in time, the influence of those radiant towns and cities would be almost imperceptible. Accurate traffic censuses are unavailable for earlier periods, but since only a few hundred private vehicles were using the national road system at the end of the eighteenth century, it can hardly have been prone to traffic jams.

In 1787 and 1788, the English farmer Arthur Young was amazed to find 'the wastes, the deserts, the heath, ling, furze, broom, and bog that I have passed for three hundred miles' continuing to 'within three miles of the great commercial city of Nantes!' The outskirts of Toulouse were just as empty: 'not more persons than if it were a hundred miles from any town.' Surely, he thought, the capital itself, 'where so many great roads join', would prove that, if the body was sluggish, at least the heart was beating. But on a May morning, for the first ten miles of the great road south to Orléans, the total count was two mail-coaches and 'very few' sedan chairs. And when he drew near to Paris on the northern road from Chantilly, 'eagerly on the watch for that throng of carriages which near London impede the traveller, I watched in vain; for the road, quite to the gates, is, on comparison, a perfect desert.'

*

THE SEEMINGLY RIDICULOUS QUESTION then arises: where was the population of Europe's most populous country?

Despite the impression of many travellers, most French people did not live in towns. At the time of the French Revolution, almost four-fifths of the population was rural. Over half a century later, more than three-quarters still lived in a *commune* of fewer than two thousand inhabitants. (This was the definition of 'rural' in 1846.) But these people were not necessarily aware of each other's existence. A *'commune'* is not a village or a town but the area controlled by a mayor and a council.* Some, like the *commune* of Arles in the Camargue plain, stretched across large, sparsely populated regions. Others, like Verdelot, forty miles east of Paris in the Brie, contained dozens of tiny settlements, none of which could be described as a town or even a large village.

After the Revolution, almost a third of the population (about ten million people) lived in isolated farms and cottages or in hamlets with fewer than thirty-five inhabitants and often no more than eight. A peasant girl who went to work in Paris might, when looking through the scullery window at the street, see more people at a glance than she had known in her entire previous life. Many recruits from the Dordogne in 1830 were unable to give the recruiting sergeant their surnames because they had never had to use them. Until the invention of cheap bicycles, the known universe, for many people, had a radius of less than fifteen miles and a population that could easily fit into a small barn.

The distinction between 'urban' and 'rural' might suggest that some citizens at least were connected to the rest of the world. In reality, most towns were half-dissolved into the surrounding countryside. Before the gates were locked at night, people and animals came and went from field to street. Mud carpeted the cobbles and created its own miniature geography of hills and ravines. Agriculture resided in the city in the form of vineyards, vegetable plots, pigsties, paddocks and mounds of manure.

---

* A *commune* is the smallest of the administrative divisions introduced in 1790. Today, there are 36,565 *communes*, 3,876 *cantons*, 329 *arrondissements*, 96 *départements* (including 4 overseas) and 22 *régions*.

In many minds, the clearest demographic distinction was not 'urban' and 'rural' but 'Parisian' and 'provincial'. Travelling through France in 1807 'by a route never before performed', Lieutenant-Colonel Ninian Pinkney of the North American Native Rangers found himself back on the frontier as soon as he left Paris ('as retired as in the most remote corner of England') and subsequently discovered that 'there are absolutely no interior towns in France like Norwich, Manchester, and Birmingham'. French towns were confined and corseted by their customs barriers, and the population remained almost static from the early nineteenth century until after the First World War.

Even before it became the goal of most internal migrants, Paris seemed to drain the country. In 1801, more people lived in Paris (just under 550,000) than in the next six biggest cities combined (Marseille, Lyon, Bordeaux, Rouen, Nantes and Lille). In 1856, Paris could have swallowed up the next eight biggest cities, and in 1886, the next sixteen. Yet Paris accounted for less than 3 per cent of the population until 1852 and, until 1860, covered an area of only 3,402 hectares (thirteen square miles), which is not even twice the size of the Eurodisney site.

The hidden population of France was obviously not to be found simply by looking through a carriage window. Tax collectors, missionaries, and early ethnologists had to branch off onto tracks that no coach would ever follow. Even then, without the panoramic, X-ray vision of a statistician or a poet, vital signs might be scarce. Victor Hugo's description of the west of France might look like science-fiction anthropology, but Hugo had covered more miles on foot than any historian of France and he knew how to read a landscape:

> It is difficult to picture those Breton forests as they really were. They were towns. Nothing could be more secret, silent and savage than those inextricable entanglements of thorns and branches. In those vast thickets, stillness and quietness made their lair. No desert ever appeared more deathlike and sepulchral. Yet if those trees could have been felled at a single blow, as if by a flash of lightning, there would have stood revealed in those shades a swarming mass of men.
>
> Some curious statistics make it possible to comprehend the powerful organization of the great peasant revolt. In Ille-et-Vilaine, in the forest

of Le Pertre . . . there was no sign of human life, and six thousand men were there under the leadership of Focard. In Morbihan, in the forest of Molac, not a soul could be seen, and there were eight thousand men. Those two forests are not among the largest in Brittany.

Hugo's fantastic vision of a densely populated desert is confirmed by the map (p. 16). The population predictably appears to be densest along the main corridors of trade: the Rhône valley and the Rhineland, Flanders and the Channel coast, Paris and its zone of supply, a few Mediterranean ports and the fertile valley of the Garonne from Toulouse to Bordeaux. But there are also some curiously high concentrations in areas that seemed to many travellers to be almost uninhabited.

It was quite possible to pass through some densely populated regions, close enough to smell the pigs, without seeing a single human being. Jacques Cambry, who explored Brittany in 1794–95 ('for no one, I believe, has ever gone to Brittany in order to study it or to satisfy their curiosity'), claimed that only a few hunters had ever seen 'those houses that lie hidden behind ditches, in tangles of trees or bushes, and always in the lowest parts so that water will collect and help to rot the straw, scrub and gorse that they use for manure'. Settlements could be isolated by mud and thorn as effectively as by canyons and cliffs.

South of the Loire, in the Vendée, unmapped tracks ran for hundreds of miles through deep tunnels of vegetation. An aerial view would have shown a typical bocage landscape of fields marked off by trees and bushes. On the ground, it was a muddy labyrinth sunk in a limitless wood. On a sunny day, a traveller could walk for hours and emerge from the bocage as pale as a ghost. Openings in the hedgerow were closed with hurdles made from the same material as the hedge. A peasant could slip into his field, close the leafy door, and leave no trace of his passing.

In the Vendée, a hundred and seventy thousand people lived in groups with an average size of fifteen. There were twenty thousand tiny places in the Ille-et-Vilaine *département*, the same number in the Sarthe, and twenty-five thousand in Finistère. In the hills of the Cévennes, some parishes had more than a hundred hamlets. This

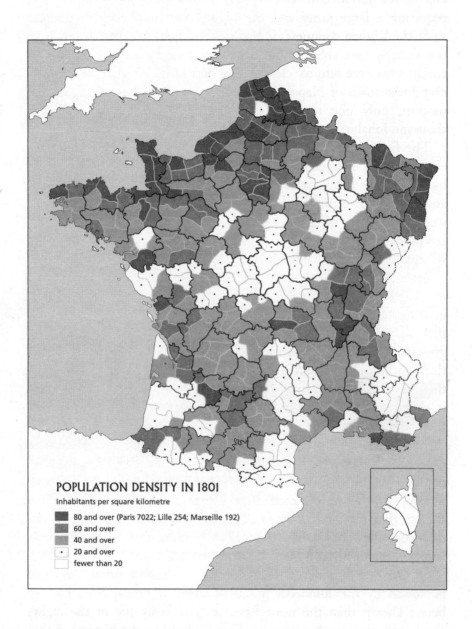

POPULATION DENSITY IN 1801

Inhabitants per square kilometre

- 80 and over (Paris 7022; Lille 254; Marseille 192)
- 60 and over
- 40 and over
- 20 and over
- fewer than 20

explains why the extermination of Protestants in the Cévennes at the end of the seventeenth century was such a long and arduous task, requiring a large army and the biggest road-building programme since the Roman conquest. It also explains how the royalist rebels in the Vendée were able to hold out for so long against the republican troops who were sent to 'cleanse' the west of France. Until the bleak, rectilinear town of Napoléon-Vendée was created as an imperialist outpost, only one town in the *département* had more than five thousand inhabitants.

The faceless millions who lived in this vast and largely undiscovered country belonged to an earlier stage of civilization than the three hundred or so people who make up the usual cast list of eighteenth- and nineteenth-century French history. Their patterns of settlement were a guarantee of ignorance and illiteracy, since a scattered population was just as difficult to educate as it was to conquer. But they were, after all, the inhabitants of France.

Even today, the labourers, land-owning peasants, artisans, and uncategorized women and children who made up the 'rural' three-quarters of the population are often described collectively as though they were proto-French beings, too remote and nebulous to feel the gravitational forces of centralization. They received historical rather than anthropological attention only when they began to think of themselves as French, when they heard about Paris and wanted to see it, or when they asserted regional identities and separatist desires and thus acknowledged the effective primacy of Parisian France. One of the quotations most frequently used to evoke this mass of population is Jean de La Bruyère's depiction in 1688 of the 'wild animals that one sees in the countryside' – sun-blackened beasts, both male and female, 'attached to the earth that they stubbornly dig': 'They make sounds that resemble articulate speech, and when they rise up on their feet, they show a human face ... At night they creep away into lairs where they live on black bread, water and roots.'

Similar descriptions of the ignoble savages of modern Gaul can be found by the hundred. Some of these picturesque insults are better known than the most basic facts of daily life in the eighteenth and nineteenth centuries. They belong to the history of that internecine racism that still plays a major role in French society.

These administratively inconvenient millions belong to French history as much as American Indians belong to the history of America. Not all of them were mud-caked field-hands. They were provincial aristocrats and tribal chiefs, mayors and councillors, migrant workers, merchants, magicians, hermits, and even local historians.

When they murdered the young geometer on Cassini's expedition, the people of Les Estables were acting ignorantly but not irrationally. They were defending themselves against an act of war. If a local sorcerer had shown them on the surface of a pond or in the flames of a bonfire their home as it would appear in the twenty-first century – a second-rate Nordic ski resort 'on the confines of three attractive regions', 'thirty kilometres from the nearest hospital', 'waiting to seduce you with its hospitality and its customs' – they would have been amazed at the mysterious forms that their punishment had taken.

2

The Tribes of France, I

At the southern end of one of the lovely flat valleys that spread out from the Pyrenees like the rays of the sun, when the cloud is not too low, the hamlet of Goust can be seen on a rocky platform fifteen hundred feet above the chilly spa of Eaux-Chaudes. Until the early twentieth century, it was considered to be an autonomous republic. The smallest undeclared nation in Europe consisted of twelve granite houses and about seventy people, who were ruled by a council of old men. There were no beggars, no servants, and, to the envious delight of the travellers who discovered this spartan Shangri-la, no tax-payers.

The hamlet-nation of Goust had been known to the outside world since at least the fifteenth century, but the people were left to their own happy devices, 'an entirely isolated tribe, which has conserved its simple, primitive customs'. The frighteningly steep, rubble-strewn road that leads up to the hamlet was built less than forty years ago. In 2005, Nathalie Barou, the great-granddaughter of one of the women in the photograph of 1889 (figure 1), showed me the medieval door-lintel that bears the original name of her family: Baron. A Baron of Goust is known to have existed in the sixteenth century. One of his ancestors, impoverished by the crusades, may have sold the land to his serfs, who never saw the need to join the confederations that would one day form the province of Béarn and eventually become part of France.

The people of Goust had no church and no cemetery. When someone died, the coffin was attached to ropes and lowered to the valley below. In fine weather, the living clambered down the mountain to sell milk and vegetables, to have their children baptized or to look at the ladies who came to take the waters at Eaux-Chaudes. When a road was dynamited through the gorge below the hamlet in 1850 and the skimpy wooden 'Bridge of Hell' was rebuilt in stone, Goust became a picturesque excursion for a few bored invalids and travel writers. Without them, it might have passed into oblivion like the hundreds of other 'autonomous republics' that once existed within the borders of France.

Goust was an exception mainly because it was relatively well known and because geographical force majeure held it in its patriarchal pose well into the steam age. Compared to other small, remote places, it was really quite well connected to the outside world. Its seventy inhabitants, some of whom were said to have celebrated their hundredth birthday, could hardly have thrived in total seclusion. Their communal treasury contained wool from Barèges and ribbons from Spain, and their genes too must have contained mementos of trips to the world beyond. Even the dead of Goust were comparatively well travelled. Their counterparts in high Alpine villages, if they gave up the ghost during the six or seven months of isolation, were stored on the family roof under a blanket of snow until spring thawed the ground, releasing the body to the grave and allowing a priest to reach the village.

Spectacular sites like Goust came to play a vital role in the creation of a French national identity. For the postcard-buying public with return tickets to modern civilization, tribes belonged to remote places – the further from the city, the further back in time. Teetering on the rocky perimeter of France, villages like Goust in the Pyrenees or Saint-Véran in the Alps were the national parks and reservations of the educated imagination. The truth was soon forgotten when cheap travel and national newspapers had telescoped the country and erased the old tribal divisions. Goust was in many respects a normal community in eighteenth- and early nineteenth-century France. As the economist Michel Chevalier told the readers of a Parisian journal in 1837 after a visit to the eastern Pyrenees and Andorra:

Each valley is still a little world which differs from the neighbouring world as Mercury does from Uranus. Each village is a clan, a kind of state with its own form of patriotism. There are different types and characters at every step, different opinions, prejudices and customs.

If Chevalier had travelled from Paris on foot, instead of taking a high-speed coach on a modern road, he might have found that his description fitted most of the country.

Visiting these clans and tiny states involves a long journey into undiscovered France, from towns and villages to hamlets and other forms of settlement that are not so easily defined. France itself will begin to look like an almost arbitrary division of Western Europe. Later, nationwide patterns will appear and the inhabitants will turn out to have something more than geographical proximity in common, but if the historical road signs of later generations were allowed to dictate the journey from start to finish, most of the country and its inhabitants would remain as obscure as the origins of Goust.

*

BEFORE THE RAILWAYS blurred the landscape and reduced its inhabitants to faces on a platform and figures in a field, travellers were often bemused by sudden changes in the population. On fording a stream or turning at a crossroads, the occupants of a carriage could find themselves among people of radically different appearance, with their own style of dress and architecture, their own language and their own peculiar concept of hospitality. The colour of eyes and hair, the shape of heads and faces and even the manner of watching a coach go by could change more abruptly than the vegetation.

When the differences were exaggerated by speed, tribal frontiers were often startlingly obvious. On the left bank of the river Adour, in the Chalosse region east of Bayonne, the natives were said to be tall, strong, well fed and welcoming. On the right bank, they were skinny, miserable and suspicious. Climate, water and diet, ancient and modern migrations, clan rivalries and all the inexplicable variations of habit and tradition could turn the smallest area into a maze of unmarked borders. Even supposedly civilized regions were carved up like provinces after the fall of an empire. In Burgundy, according to Restif de la Bretonne, the neighbouring villages of Nitry and Sacy were so dissimilar (respectively courteous and brutish) that a certain

Comte de S* 'chose them especially so that he could see a lot of country without travelling very far [about three miles] and thus produce an abbreviated description of rural life throughout the entire kingdom.' Restif's own mother was always treated as an outsider in Nitry because she came from a village on the other side of the river Cure, ten miles to the west. 'According to custom, her children-in-law disliked her, and no one took her side in the village because she was foreign.'

It is easy to imagine the bewilderment of wealthy urban travellers who set out to discover their country only to find a crazed human landscape of tribes and clans. Even a brief journey through northern France could make it impossible to form a clear impression of 'the French'. At Dieppe, the Polletais or Poltese fisher-folk spoke a dialect that was barely recognizable as a form of French. Cross-Channel tourists, who bought their ivory carvings and gawped at the women in their bunched-up petticoats and knee-length skirts, wondered why they looked so different from the rest of the population. (No one knows to this day.) Further up the coast, at Boulogne-sur-Mer, the suburb of Le Portel had a separate population numbering about four thousand, remarkable for its height and its handsome, vigorous appearance. In 1866, an anthropologist suggested that the people of Le Portel were of Andalusian origin, but his study of the heads, hands, feet and breasts of the female population (the male population was out at sea) proved inconclusive. Thirty miles inland, at Saint-Omer, the 'floating islands' to the east of town were farmed by a community which had its own laws, customs and language. They lived in the low canal houses in the suburbs of Hautpont and Lysel, which still look like a Flemish enclave in a French town.

To many travellers, the various populations of France seemed to have little in common but their humanity. There were doubts even about this. Even at the end of the nineteenth century, there were reports of distinct, autonomous tribes on the borders of Brittany and Normandy. On the Côte d'Azur in the hills behind Cannes and Saint-Tropez, wild people were said to descend into market towns wearing goatskins and speaking their own incomprehensible language. In 1880, in the forest around Villers-Cotterêts (Alexandre Dumas's birthplace, forty-five miles north-east of Paris), an anthropologist discovered 'some out-of-the-way villages whose inhabitants are of a completely different type than those of the surrounding villages and who seem to bear the mark of a particular race, predating the Cimmerian invasions with which our historical era begins'.

Now that another century has passed and the Villers-Cotterêts forest is a well-publicized excursion for Parisians, forty-five minutes from the Gare du Nord, its 'prehistoric' population will remain forever mysterious. As far as French anthropology is concerned, prehistory did not end until the Revolution. Before then, the state took no interest in the cultural and ethnic diversity of the masses. Statistics are scarce until Napoleon and unreliable even then. Sciences that made it possible to analyse populations according to physical and cultural traits evolved only when the tribes they hoped to study were turning into modern French citizens. But the troubling question was at least asked by inquisitive travellers: who were the inhabitants of France?

*

IN POLITICAL HISTORY, the answer seems quite simple. The people of Dieppe, Boulogne, Goust and Saint-Véran all belonged to the same nation. They were answerable to provincial *parlements* and ultimately to the King. Most of them paid taxes – in money, labour (maintaining roads and bridges) and eventually, when systematic conscription was introduced at the end of the eighteenth century, in human life. They had locally appointed officials – an agent to collect taxes and a guard to police the community. But laws, especially those relating to inheritance, were widely ignored and direct contact with the central power was extremely limited. The state was perceived as a dangerous nuisance: its emissaries were soldiers who had to be fed and housed, bailiffs who seized property and lawyers who settled property disputes and took most of the proceeds. Being French was not a source of personal pride, let alone the basis of a common identity. Before the mid-nineteenth century, few people had seen a map of France and few had heard of Charlemagne and Joan of Arc. France was effectively a land of foreigners. According to a peasant novelist from the Bourbonnais, this was just as true in the 1840s as it was before the Revolution:

We had not the slightest notion of the outside world. Beyond the limits of the canton, and beyond the known distances, lay mysterious lands that were thought to be dangerous and inhabited by barbarians.

The great cathedrals of France and their numberless flock of parish churches might appear to represent a more powerful common bond. Almost 98 per cent of the population was Catholic. In fact, religious practice varied wildly. (This will become quite obvious later on.) Heavenly beings were no more cosmopolitan than their worshippers. The graven saint or Virgin Mary of one village was not considered to be the same as the saint or the Virgin down the road. Beliefs and practices centred on prehistoric stones and magic wells bore only the faintest resemblance to Christianity. The local priest might be useful as a literate man, but as a religious authority he had to prove his worth in competition with healers, fortune-tellers, exorcists and people who could apparently change the weather and resuscitate dead children. Morality and religious feeling were independent of Church dogma. The fact that the Church retained the right to impose taxes until the Revolution was of far greater significance to most people than its ineffectual ban on birth-control.

The smaller divisions of the kingdom paint a different picture of the population that turns out, however, to be just as unreliable. For a long time, the provinces of France were widely thought to be the key to understanding the national identity. The idea was that these historical, political divisions corresponded to certain human traits, like the segments of a phrenologist's head.

There are some good examples of this geo-personal approach in the travel accounts of François Marlin, a Cherbourg merchant who treated the naval-supplies business as an excuse to explore his native land and covered more than twenty thousand miles between 1775 and 1807: 'The people of Périgord are lively, alert and sensible. The people of Limousin are more sluggish and constricted in their movements.' Commercial travellers supping at the tavern in Auch could easily be told apart like different breeds of dog:

The *Lyonnais* acts high and mighty, talks in a clear and sonorous voice, is witty but also arrogant and has a filthy, impudent mouth. The *Languedocien* is gentle and courteous and has an open face. The

Normand spends more time listening than speaking. He is suspicious of other people and makes them suspicious of him.*

However, as Marlin discovered, even if the assumptions were flattering, most people refused to be identified with such large areas. They belonged to a town, a suburb, a village or a family, not to a nation or a province. The common cultural heritage of certain regions was more obvious to outsiders than to the people themselves. Brittany would have to be subdivided several times before an area could be found that meant something to the people who lived there. Bretons in the east spoke a dialect of French called Gallo or Gallot; Bretons in the west spoke various forms of Breton. The two groups almost never intermarried. In the west, the people of Armor ('the Land by the Sea') had little to do with the people of Argoat ('the Land of Forests'). And in Armor alone, there were sub-populations so diverse and antagonistic that they were assumed by various writers to have their origins far beyond the granite coast, in Semitic tribes, in ancient Greece or Phoenicia, in Persia, Mongolia, China or Tibet.

*

SINCE FRANCE HAD BEEN pieced together by treaties and con-quests, and since two-thirds of the territory had been French for less than three hundred and fifty years, it is not surprising that there was no deep-rooted sense of national identity. Before the Revolution, the name 'France' was often reserved for the small mushroom-shaped province centred on Paris. In Gascony and Provence, anyone from the north was a 'Franchiman' or a 'Franciot'. Neither term was registered by the official dictionary of the Académie Française. How-ever, there was little sense of regional identity either. The Breton, Catalan, Flemish and Provençal populations of France developed their political identities only much later, in reaction to the national

---

* These moral maps of France are still quite popular today, and even more implausible than they were in the eighteenth century. For example, in the 1997 *Guide Bleu*: 'The Norman's measured replies are perhaps an effect of the unpredict-able climate'; 'The Bretons once wore round hats [an allusion to an insulting song], and they are still hard-headed'; 'In the land of bullfights and rugby [Languedoc], passions always have the last word'.

identity that was imposed on them. Only the Basques seem to have been united against the outside world, but the figures of hate in their public *masquerades* were not Frenchmen or Spaniards but gypsies, tinkers, doctors and lawyers. Inter-regional games of pelota aroused greater passions than the victories and defeats of Napoleon.

The propaganda of French national unity has been broadcast continuously since the Revolution, and it takes a while to notice that the tribal divisions of France were almost totally unrelated to administrative boundaries. There was no obvious reason why these people should have formed a single nation. As Hervé Le Bras and Emmanuel Todd wrote in 1981, referring to the extreme variety of family structures in France, 'from an anthropological point of view, France ought not to exist'. Ethnically, its existence was just as unlikely. The Celtic and Germanic tribes who invaded ancient Gaul and the Frankish tribes who attacked the ailing Roman province had almost as many different origins as the population of modern France. The only coherent, indigenous group that a historically sound National Front party could claim to represent would be the very first wandering band of pre-human primates that occupied this section of the Western European isthmus.

The Cherbourg merchant, François Marlin, eventually found that the best answer to the question, 'Who are the inhabitants of France?' was no answer at all. He wanted his travel accounts to be an antidote to all the useless guidebooks written by armchair plagiarists and so tried simply to observe the physical differences that mirrored the changing landscape. If his observations were combined with those of other travellers, the result would be an unpublishable map of France divided into zones of ugliness and beauty. Basque women were 'all clean and pretty'. 'All the cripples, one-eyed people and hunchbacks seem to have been shut up in Orléans.' 'Pretty women are rare in France, and especially here in the Auvergne; but one does see a lot of robust women.' 'The most beautiful eyes in the provinces can be found in Brest, but the mouths are less attractive: the sea-air and a great deal of neglect in that department soon tarnish the enamel of the teeth.'

This would hardly satisfy a historical anthropologist, and it gives only the vaguest idea of the social geography of France. No one could tell whether these physical differences were signs of ancient ancestry or simply an effect of the trades people practised and the food they ate. But at least Marlin had seen the population (or the part of the population that lived near a road) with his own eyes:

> I quite like the way in which women and children come running up to see a traveller pass. This enables a curious man to see all the beauties of a place, and I could tell you exactly how many pretty women there are in Couvin.

In Marlin's mind, this was the kind of eye-witness description that could usefully be kept in the leather pockets of the diligence. The other guides, with their bogus erudition, could be left under the flapping canvas on top of the coach to be soaked by the rain and blown away by the wind.

*

AN EXPEDITION INTO tribal France could begin almost anywhere and at almost any time. A hilltop in the Aveyron, for instance, where the limestone plateaux of the Causses turn into a crumpled map of rocks and gorges. The year is 1884. The priest of Montclar has found an exciting diversion from the monotony of life in a small town. His telescope is trained on a battlefield in the valley below. An army of men, women and children, wielding cudgels and lugging baskets of stones, is advancing on the village of Roquecezière. But scouts have been posted. Another army has already emerged from the village and is preparing to defend its territory.

On the bare rock that towers above the village, turning its back to the battle, is a colossal cast-iron statue of the Virgin Mary. The statue has been funded by public subscription – something of a miracle in this impoverished region – and has recently been placed on the rock to commemorate a successful mission.

Incensed to see the sacred effigy pointing its bottom at their village, the invaders have come to turn it around. The battle rages for hours. Several people are seriously injured. At last, the Roquecezièrain lines are breached and the statue is worked around to face the other village. To prevent a full-scale war, the Church authorities find a compromise. The Virgin is rotated ninety degrees, supposedly so that each village can see half of her face. However, she now looks east-north-east, towards Saint-Crépin, which contributed more than half the cost of the statue, and still has her back turned to the little clutch of houses at her foot.

The Battle of Roquecezière, like thousands of other tiny conflicts, is not mentioned in any history of France. Village wars had no perceptible effect on national security and their causes were often ancient and obscure. Yet they were a normal part of life for many people well into the nineteenth century. A 'very fat filc' in the archives of the Lot *département* describes village brawls between 1816 and 1847: 'bloody scenes, combats, disorders, serious wounds, treaties of peace and rumours of war'. Villagers settled their differences in pitched battles rather than waste their time and money in court. Half-forgotten insults and territorial disputes culminated in raids on neighbouring villages to steal the corn or to carry off the church bells. Sometimes, champions were appointed and their battles entered local legend. Usually, a single battle was not enough. The Limousin villages of Lavignac, Flavignac and Texon were at war for more than forty years. Texon ceased to exist as a *commune* in 1806, but this bureaucratic technicality did not prevent it from behaving as an independent state.

Caesar's famous description of Gaul as a country 'divided into three parts' must have struck many travellers as a breezy over-simplification. Caesar, however, went on to observe that Gaul was also subdivided into innumerable tiny regions: 'Not only every tribe, canton, and subdivision of a canton, but almost every family is divided into rival factions.' The basic division was the *pagus*, the area controlled by a tribe. Two thousand years after the conquest of Gaul, the *pays* (pronounced *pay-ee*) was still a recognizable reality. The word *pays* – usually translated as 'country' – referred, not to the abstract nation, but to the tangible, ancestral region that people thought of as their home. A *pays* was the area in which everything was familiar: the sound of the human voice, the orchestra of birds and insects, the choreography of winds and the mysterious configurations of trees, rocks and magic wells.

To someone with little experience of the world, the *pays* could be measured in fields and furrows. To a person far from home, it might be a whole province. The term has since acquired a more precise and picturesque meaning. It was revived in the 1960s to promote local development and tourism: 'Pays de la Loire', 'Pays de Caux', 'Pays de Bray', etc. These geographical areas are larger versions of the 'Petites Régions Agricoles' which were devised in 1956 to serve as a basis for agricultural statistics. The National Institute of Statistics currently lists 712 of them. The Brie, for instance, is divided into 'wooded', 'central', 'Champagne' (three zones, distinguished by postcode), 'eastern', 'French' (two zones) and 'humid'. The part of Champagne once known as 'pouilleuse' (flea-bitten or beggarly) no longer officially exists.

This was the puzzle of micro-provinces that General de Gaulle had in mind when he asked, 'How can one be expected to govern a country that has two hundred and forty-six different kinds of cheese?' This famous phrase, now usually inflated to 'one cheese for every day of the year', has become part of an unofficial catechism of national pride. It is often recited to foreign visitors, even in regions that are dominated by a single, economically buoyant cheese. But it was a puzzle that any modern-day marketing-board official could easily solve. In earlier days, no one could have put a figure on the *pays* of France. Even in 1937, when publishing a very long list of *pays* in his nine-volume *Manual of Contemporary French Folklore*, Arnold van Gennep warned that the list was incomplete because 'some *pays* are still unknown'. Throughout the nineteenth century, functionaries at every level complained of this fragmentation of the territory with no trace of irony. The *pays* rather than the state was the fatherland of the benighted peasant.

Secret army reports of the 1860s and 70s show that 'patriotism' on a national level meant very little to natives of a *pays*. In most of the Auvergne, the army could obtain help only 'by payment, requisition or threats' (1873). In a town near Angers, the men would fight only if they were close to home: 'They are still Angevin, not French' (1859). 'The peasants of the Brie are timorous and have little guile, and all resistance on their part would be easily put down' (1860). Spies returning to Caesar's camp on the banks of the Saône in 58 BC must have delivered very similar reports.

*

WITH DIFFERENT MAPS and sensors, it is still possible to explore the labyrinth of tiny regions without getting lost. At certain times of day, even if the boundaries are invisible, the approximate limits of a *pays* can be detected by a walker or a cyclist. The area in which a church bell can be heard more distinctly than those of other villages in the region is likely to be an area whose inhabitants had the same customs and language, the same memories and fears, and the same local saint.

Bells marked the tribal territory and gave it a voice. When the bell was being cast by a travelling founder, villagers added heirlooms to the metal – old plates, coins and candlesticks – and turned it into the beloved embodiment of the village soul. It told the time of day and announced annual events: the beginning and end of harvest, the departure of flocks for the high pastures. It warned of incursions and threats. In the 1790s, recruiting sergeants marched across the Sologne through overlapping circles of sound to find, when they arrived in each village, that all the young men had disappeared. Bells were thought to dispel the thunder and hailstorms that destroyed the crops, which explains why so many people were electrocuted at the end of a bell-rope. They chased away the witches who piloted storm clouds and summoned angels so that prayers said while the bell was ringing – as in Millet's painting *L'Angélus* – were more effective than at other times. In foggy weather, rescue bells were rung to guide travellers who might be lost.

The number of bells and the size of the bell tower often give a fairly accurate measure of population density. Hardly anyone complained about excessive ringing, but there were countless complaints about bells that were too faint to be heard in the outlying fields. When migrants talked nostalgically of their distant native *clocher*, they were referring not only to the architectural presence of a steeple in the landscape but also to its aural domain.

A map of these spheres of audible influence would show the tiny size of tribal domains far more accurately than a map of *communes*. A study of *communes* in nineteenth-century Morbihan (southern Brittany) appears to show that the population was quite adventurous. By 1876, more than half the married people in Saint-André had been born in a different *commune*. In almost every case, however, the *commune* in question was adjacent. According to the study, 'sentimental determinants' (love) might have played a role, but most people married in order to consolidate inherited land rights, even if it meant marrying a first cousin. The choice of partners was guided by the ancient system of hamlets whose frontiers – banks of earth, ditches and streams – have either disappeared or become unnoticeable. Official boundaries were scarcely more significant than garden fences in the territories of birds.

The same agoraphobic settlement of the open spaces of France can be seen all over the country. As late as 1886, over four-fifths of the population were still described as 'almost stationary' (living in the *département* where they were born). Over three-fifths had remained in their native *commune*. But even the expatriates in other *départements* had not necessarily strayed from the local group of hamlets: the neighbouring hamlet may simply have lain on the other side of a departmental boundary.

Some communities were forced by low numbers or by local feuds to look further afield, but even they were unlikely to travel far. The widowed ploughman in George Sand's *The Devil's Pond* (1846) is appalled at the thought of finding a new wife three leagues (eight miles) away in 'a new *pays*'. In an extreme case, the persecuted cagots, most of whom lived in scattered hamlets (see p. 43), might find a husband or a wife more than a day's walk from home, but this was very unusual. Records of six hundred and seventy-nine cagot couples from 1700 to 1759 show that almost two-thirds of the brides came from within shouting distance of the bridegroom. The others were close enough to cause little inconvenience to the wedding guests. In Saint-Jean-Pied-de-Port, all but four of the fifty-seven women had married less than five miles from home. Only two of the six hundred and seventy-nine were described as 'foreign'. This was not a reference to another land. It meant simply, 'not from the region'.

*

EVEN WITH STATISTICS and a proper sense of scale, descending into the land of a thousand *pays* is a disconcerting experience. The broader patterns that will eventually appear are not much in evidence, but nor is the expected anarchy. Many places turn out to be fully functioning jurisdictions with their own parliaments and unwritten constitutions. Nearly every village had a formal assembly of some kind, especially in *pays d'état* such as Burgundy, Brittany and Provence, where royal influence had always been weak. In the south, where taxation was based on land, the need to measure and record holdings had given rise to some quite sophisticated village institutions that not only regulated the use of common land but also managed assets and ran a budget. When agents of the Revolution came to administer the kiss of life to the supposedly moribund towns and villages of provincial France, they found the body in surprisingly good health.

Some of these towns and villages were flourishing democracies when France was still an absolute monarchy. François Marlin ran into such a place on his journey through Picardy in 1789. The conspicuously clean and tidy village of Salency, he learned, was governed by an old priest. The children were never sent away to become servants, and they were not allowed to marry outside the parish. There were six hundred people with only three surnames between them. All were considered equal, and everyone worked the land, using spades instead of ploughs. As a result, their harvests were abundant, their children – even the girls – were taught to read and write by a salaried schoolmaster and his wife, and everyone was healthy, peaceful and attractive. 'The very notion of crime is unknown to them ... The story of a girl who sinned against modesty would sound to them like a tale invented by a liar.'

This is a fairly typical account of a self-governing village. The chief, as in Salency, was often a priest, acting as an administrator rather than as an agent of the Catholic Church. On the Breton islands of Hoedic and Houat, the priest, mayor, judge, customs officer, postal director, tithe collector, teacher, doctor and midwife were all the same man. The arrival of two deputy mayors in the 1880s – one for each island – made no difference whatsoever. Some places were run by councils that were perfect miniatures of a national administration. The town of La Bresse, in a valley of the western Vosges, had its own legislature and judiciary until the Revolution. According to a geographer writing in 1832, 'the judges of this town, though clumsy and common in appearance, showed a great deal of common sense'. A visiting lawyer who quoted in Latin in his speech for the defence was fined by the court 'for taking it into your head to address us in an unknown tongue' and was ordered to learn the law of La Bresse within a fortnight.

Some village states covered many square miles. A clan called Pignou occupied several villages near Thiers in the northern Auvergne. They even had their own town, which apparently boasted all the comforts of modern civilization. A leader was elected by all the men over twenty years of age and titled 'Maître Pignou'. Everyone else was known by their Christian name. If the Maître Pignou proved inept, he was replaced. There was no private property, and all the children were brought up by a woman known as the Laitière because she also ran the communal dairy. Girls never worked in the fields but were sent instead to a convent at common expense. People who married outside the clan were banished forever, though they all eventually begged to be readmitted.

If so many tiny places declared independence at the time of the Revolution, it was because they were already partly independent. Their aim was not to develop the local economy and become part of a larger society. Change of any kind generally meant disaster or the threat of starvation. The dream of most communities was to sever ties, to insulate the town or village, which is partly why measures varied from one village to the next: standardization would have made it easier for outsiders to compete with local producers.* They wanted to refine and purify the group. The boast that no one ever married outside the tribe was as common in France as it is in most tribal societies. Local legends often referred to a special dispensation granted by the Pope (or, more likely, the local bishop) that allowed them to marry close relatives. Prudent management of village

---

* Even after the introduction of the decimal system in 1790, a '*pinte*' was just over a litre in one Limousin village and well over two litres in another. The Nord *département* had thirty-five different measures of capacity, all bearing the same name. Travellers from the north found their 'leagues' getting longer as they headed south. Some parts had still not adopted the older systems that the decimal system was supposed to replace. In 1807, Champollion, the decipherer of Egyptian hieroglyphics, found that the country people of the Isère 'have retained the custom of using Roman numerals'.

resources could prevent the population from abandoning the tiny fatherland. Sometimes, daughters as well as sons were paid to remain. The 'Chizerot' tribe on the banks of the Saône in Burgundy had a communal fund that was used to give poor girls a dowry so that they would not have to look for a husband elsewhere.

Self-government was not an idle dream. It was the unavoidable reality of daily life. People who rarely saw a policeman or a judge had good reasons to devise their own systems of justice. Hard-pressed provincial governors had equally good reasons to turn a blind eye. By most accounts, local justice was an effective blend of psychological manipulation and force. In Pyrenean villages from the Atlantic to the Mediterranean, claims were settled in a series of three meetings, at the first of which both parties had to remain silent. Cases rarely reached the third meeting. In Mandeure, near the Swiss border, when something had been stolen, a meeting was called on the main square. The two mayors held a stick at either end and the entire population of several hundred people would pass underneath to prove their innocence. No thief had ever dared to pass under the stick. 'Had he done so, and was later found out ... he would have been shunned like a wild animal and the dishonour would have redounded on his family.'

*

THESE LOCAL SYSTEMS of justice might explain the apparently bizarre fact that, according to some nineteenth-century criminal statistics, France had an almost entirely law-abiding population. Crime in some *départements* seemed to have died out altogether. Sometimes there were 'white sessions', when courts sat but heard no cases. In 1865, in the Aveyron *département*, where the Battle of Roquecezière took place, there were eight convictions for crimes against the person and thirteen for crimes against property. In the Cher *département* (population: 336,613), the figures were three and zero. Nationally, excluding Paris, the 1865 figures suggest that it took eighteen thousand people to produce one criminal.

It does not take a cynic to suspect that most descriptions of village republics are a misty image of the truth. Thieves, murderers and rapists did, of course, exist. François Marlin had picked his way through too many dung-obstructed, priest-forsaken places not to be impressed by Salency, but its cleanliness and the absence of crime were the public face of a necessarily despotic government. The self-proclaimed virtue of the people of Salency must have wrecked the lives of many people – 'foreigners', homosexuals, 'witches' and, perhaps more than any other category of undesirable, unmarried mothers. About ten times as many illegitimate children were born in Paris than anywhere else, not because Parisians were more promiscuous but because girls who 'sinned against modesty' were often forced to leave their *pays*.

Village justice was not always benign or fair. Slight deviations from the norm – a man or a woman who married a younger person or who married for a second time, anyone who married a stranger, a man who beat his wife or allowed himself to be beaten by her – was likely to be punished with a 'charivari': a noisy, humiliating and often bloody serenade or procession. According to an anthropologist, adulterers in Brittany were 'the object of insulting vegetable bombardments'. A cart containing the victim would make the rounds of neighbouring villages, turning him into an object of ridicule throughout the known universe. Bad roads prevented produce from leaving the region, but they also prevented fear and envy from evaporating into a wider world.

In the eyes of the educated minority, there was no real difference between village justice and mob rule. When a 'witch' was burned to death in 1835 at Beaumont-en-Cambrésis, in the industrial Nord department, with the collusion of the local authorities, it seemed as though the Middle Ages had never ended. But to people who lived their whole lives in a small town or village, French imperial justice could be just as shocking and incongruous as it was to the people of colonial North Africa.

3

The Tribes of France, II

THE SENSE OF IDENTITY attached to these little *pays* was more potent than any later sense of being French. The *paysans* had no flags or written histories, but they expressed their local patriotism in much the same way as nations: by denigrating their neighbours and celebrating their own nobility.

The vast and vulgar repertoire of village nicknames is the best surviving evidence of this sub-national pride. A few flattering names have been officially adopted, like Colombey-les-Belles – now said to refer to the local women but perhaps originally applied to cows. But if all the nicknames had been adopted, the map of France would now be covered with obscenities and incomprehensible jokes. In one small part of Lorraine, there were the 'wolves' of Lupcourt, whose local saint was Saint Loup, the 'greencoats' of Réméréville, whose tailor had once produced a batch of jackets in green cloth that never wore out, and the 'big pockets' of Saint-Remimont, whose tailor cut his coats much longer than anyone else. There were the 'shit-arses' (*culs crottés*) of Moncel-sur-Seille, whose mud was unusually clingy, the 'hoity-toitys' (*haut-la-queue*) of Art-sur-Meurthe, who lived near the big city of Nancy, and the 'sleepers' of Buissoncourt-en-France, who dug a mighty moat around their village and lived in happy seclusion behind a drawbridge.

Some names referred to famous events in village history: the '*rôtisseurs*' ('roast-meat sellers') of Ludres, who had once turned out en masse to watch their adulterous priest being burned at the stake, or the '*poussais*' ('chasers') of Vigneulles, who took up pitchforks and routed their neighbours from Barbonville when they came to steal their miracle-working statue of the Virgin. Most names were deliberately offensive. The '*oua-oua*' (pronounced 'wa-wa') of Rosières-aux-Salines had a speech defect, caused by a local thyroid condition, which was considered hilarious. Some nicknames lasted into the twentieth century. The most insulting were probably never recorded except, when education had reached the village, in the form of graffiti. 'Les mangeurs de merde [shit-eaters] de Lautenbach' was inscribed in a Lauten bach bus-shelter at the foot of the Grand Ballon mountain in Alsace in 2004.

In a world where filth stayed close to home and the subterranean odysseys of today's human waste were unimaginable, coprophilia was a common theme. The people of Saint-Nicolas-de-Port were known as 'loudmouths'. Their neighbours at Varangéville across the river liked to assemble on the banks of the Meurthe to bombard them with a chorus of

> Booyaî d'Senn'Colais,
> Tend tet ghieule quand je . . .*

While insults were the language of village foreign policy, domestic propaganda proclaimed the unsullied honour of the tribe. Many communities claimed prestigious forebears. The powerful Pignou clan of Thiers traced itself back to a single omniscient ancestor who, in the year 1100, had set down all the rules by which they still lived. (The actual date was probably 1730.) In Mandeure, which boasts a Roman amphitheatre, the dominant group believed itself to be descended from a Roman general. They had the carved lintels and the mosaics to prove it. Outsiders who tried to settle on their territory were repulsed as barbarians. Claims to ancient nobility were also made by a visibly distinct part of Issoudun's population, as Balzac explained in *The Two Brothers* (1841):

> The suburb is called 'Faubourg de Rome'. Its inhabitants, whose race, blood and physiognomy are indeed distinctive, claim to be descended from the Romans. Almost all are wine growers and remarkably strict in their morals, no doubt because of their origin, and perhaps too because of their victory over the Cottereaux and the Routiers,† whom they exterminated in the plain of Charost in the twelfth century.

---

* 'Loudmouths of St Nicks, / Open your gob when I'm taking a . . .' (in the local Lorrain dialect).
† An assortment of adventurers and bandits employed by Henry II of England.

Some of these claims to ethnic distinction were based on historical truth. The Foratin people of the Berry were descendants of Scottish mercenaries who were given forest land between Moulins and Bourges in the fifteenth century by Charles VII. (Some nineteenth-century visitors claimed to detect a slight accent.) A hamlet, a château and a forest clearing called 'Les Écossais' still exist, and the town of Aubigny-sur-Nère hosts an annual 'Franco-Scottish' festival on Bastille Day. The Gavaches or Marotins were a separate sub-population in the Gironde, east of Bordeaux, numbering about eight thousand in the late 1880s. They had been brought from Poitou and Anjou in the sixteenth century to repopulate a region devastated by plague and retained their separate identity into the twentieth century.

Most claims – especially those relating to the Romans – were pure fantasy. The blood of the Romans would not have filtered down unmixed through fifty generations. 'Romans' were the aristocrats of the common imagination, the lost rulers who had clearly been far better than the local lord. Some of their bridges were still in use and their buildings were often the most impressive in town. Many villages in the south named their local officials 'consuls' in imitation of the Romans. It was partly thanks to this genealogical conceit that the Roman remains of Orange, Nîmes and Arles were preserved at a time when ancient monuments were treated as a handy source of building material. History in the usual sense had very little to do with it. In the Tarn, 'the Romans' were widely confused with 'the English', and in parts of the Auvergne, people talked about 'le bon César', not realizing that 'good old Caesar' had tortured and massacred their Gallic ancestors. Other groups – the people of Sens, the marsh dwellers of Poitou and the royal house of Savoy – went further and traced their roots to Gallic tribes who had never surrendered to the Romans.

Even if this was oral tradition, the tradition was unlikely to be very old. Local tales rarely date back more than two or three generations. Town and village legends had a rough, home-made quality, quite different from the rich, erudite heritage that was later bestowed on provincial France. Most historical information supplied by modern tourist offices would be unrecognizable to natives of the eighteenth and nineteenth centuries. After a four-year expedition to Brittany, a folklorist returned to Paris in 1881 to report – no doubt to the disappointment of Romantic lovers of the misty Armorican peninsula – that not a single Breton peasant had ever heard of bards and Druids.

*

THESE LOCAL LEGENDS began to disappear just when they were most likely to be written down. A region that could be reached by tourists and ethnologists could also be reached by education and newspapers, which homogenized most people's sense of the past and made the old tales sound ridiculously local. This is why the voice of tribal history could only be heard in relatively remote regions with a tradition of hostility to governments and friendliness to strangers.

A long stretch of the French Atlantic coast, in the former provinces of Aunis, Saintonge and Poitou, is still a midge-infested wilderness of partially drained marshes. Two hundred years ago, the Marais Poitevin was known to the outside world as a bleak backwater with a population of criminals, misfits and deserters from Napoleon's armies who had headed west, marooned themselves in the reeds in decaying boats, and never returned to civilization. A few visitors who braved the fevers that came off the marshes were surprised, therefore, to see signs of a lively and well-organized society: livestock floating serenely across the flat horizon and families setting off for church in plank boats light enough to be carried under the arm. They found children whose long-legged beds were lapped by the water at high tide and who learned to sail almost before they could talk. Most surprising of all, these people, who called themselves Colliberts, seemed to be happy with their watery homes and refused to be moved when the canal-builders offered them homes 'in the plain'.

The Colliberts were also known, disparagingly, as 'Huttiers' (hut-dwellers) because they lived in shacks that looked like half-submerged islands in the swamp. The musky smoke of sun-dried dung filtered through a roof of reeds. Tables and chairs were made from bundles of reeds and bulrushes. A network of channels connected the marshes to dry land and the open sea. Many of the Colliberts made a living by selling fish at Les Sables-d'Olonne. There were more of them than anyone supposed. In the early twentieth century, the fleet on the Poitou swamp still numbered almost ten thousand.

Detailed descriptions of the Colliberts' life are sadly scarce, but we do know that they had their own history and traditions. An educated Collibert called Pierre told the tribal story to a visitor in the 1820s. Pierre or his interviewer may have added some Romantic, Ossianic touches, but the elements of the tale are convincingly typical.

> I was born a Collibert. This is the name that is given to a class of men who are born, live and die in their boats. They approach dry land only to sell their catch and to buy the bare necessities.
>
> We are a separate race and our origins go back to the first days of the world. When Julius Caesar appeared on the upper reaches of the Dive and the Sèvre, our ancestors, the Agesinates Cambolectri, who were allies of the Pictavi, occupied the territory that would later form part of Bas-Poitou and which is now known to everyone as the Vendée.
>
> The Roman conqueror, not daring to set foot in our forests, considered us defeated and passed on his way.

According to Collibert lore, Goths and Scythians who fought in Roman legions married the more civilized Agesinates, who had taken to farming the land.

> To rid themselves of the earlier inhabitants, who still led a nomadic existence in their midst, they hunted them out of the Bocage and drove them back into the swamps along the Ocean, trapping them between dry land and the stormy sea. . . .
>
> We were given the name Collibert, which means 'free head'. Having robbed us of our forests, our conquerors left us our freedom . . . Yet as they wandered on the shores and in the swamps, our fathers ever had before their eyes the land they had lost. This painful sight gave the sad Colliberts an implacable hatred for the human race. . . .
>
> Such is the race into which I was born. Our ways have not changed since the first days of our exile. As they were in the fourth century, so are they now, and our close marriages have perpetuated in almost all their purity the unhappy remains of the ancient Agesinates Cambolectri.

The loss of land and exile, the radical distinction from the world beyond, pride in unchanged ways and the ancient purity of the race – all this is typical of tribal lore. The origins were invariably dated to the dawn of time, and sometimes still are.* These legends were usually patched together from old tales and scraps of historical information gleaned from almanacs or picked up from travellers. The tale of the Agesinates comes from Pliny the Elder, not from collective memory. In reality, the Colliberts were probably freed serfs who farmed the first drained marshes of the Poitou in the thirteenth century.

The waterlands still exist, but the local people no longer define themselves as Colliberts nor trace their origins to a prehistoric tribe.

*

IF EVERY TRIBAL TALE had survived, a complete history of the French people as they saw themselves would form a vast encyclopedia of micro-civilizations. In most cases, only the bare bones remain. Hundreds of sub-populations were probably never described. Nearly all the places mentioned in this chapter lay close to major trade and tourist routes. Further into France, in parts that were untouched by roads or canals, the spaces are almost blank.

These groups should not be considered backward simply because their form of civilization was about to change. They were not formless planetoids waiting to be swallowed by a giant state. Like Goust, they were not extreme cases. The real extreme was something almost unrecognizable as a community, though it was common enough to form a significant percentage of the population. The improvised hamlets called *lieux-dits* (from the phrase 'the place known as . . .') are still quite numerous today. Some are entirely rural; others look like isolated sections of a shanty-town. Some seem to wander over small parts of the landscape from one map to the next. Many have names like Californie, Canada, Cayenne or Le Nouveau Monde ('The New World') – far-flung outposts of tiny empires, founded by paupers, foreigners, misanthropes or outcasts who tried to scratch a living on the edge of a wood or a swamp.

In many cases, all that remains of their identity is a name, which is often grimly literal or ironic. A place called Loin-du-bruit ('Far-

---

* A man in the Basque province of Soule told me in 2002, 'Once upon a time the sea covered the land as far as San-Sebastián, and when the sea went out, there were the Basques.'

from-the-noise') is a tiny zone of immobilized caravans and metal shelters that cringes beside the screaming torrent of trucks heading for La Rochelle on the N137. There are still dozens of Tout-y-faut ('Everything is lacking'), Pain perdu ('Lost bread'), Malcontent, Gâtebourse ('Purse's ruin') and Gâtefer ('Wreck-iron' – referring to the effect of stony ground on a ploughshare). About thirty places are called Perte-de-temps ('Waste-of-time'), many of them not surprisingly now deserted. These precarious communities are a reminder that modern France is not just the result of continuous traditions; it was also formed from disappearances and extinctions.

Tribal histories briefly written on the landscape are barely decipherable, but their worlds can still be sensed. *Lieux-dits* are often encountered in significantly unpleasant circumstances – when the wind suddenly blows cold or the countryside turns ugly. Sometimes, their names appear on small blue signs in the roadside grass or on complicated panels which travellers have to memorize like magic spells before venturing into the maze of lanes. Often, they sound like warnings, laments or weather forecasts: Le Loup-garou ('Werewolf'), Prends-toi-garde ('Watch Out'), La Sibérie ('Siberia'), Pied-Mouillé ('Wetfoot'), Parapluie ('Umbrella'), 'Mauvais-vent' ('Badwind') or La Nuaz ('Cloud') – a literally invisible hamlet that sits in the Beaufortain Alps at an altitude to which the cloud-layer usually descends.

*

IT WOULD BE HARD to venture any further into *la France profonde* without completely running out of information. The time has almost come to return to Paris and the relative comfort of bureaucratic control. But a sense of being lost in tribal France is an opportunity not to be missed. Anyone who avoids the main highways is likely to discover older itineraries by accident: pilgrim paths, drove roads, tiny river valleys, routes taken by saints or by their relics, arrow-straight 'Roman roads' that were cut across the landscape long before the Romans. Sites of no apparent interest begin to form a pattern: a place on the outskirts of a town where no one would stop unless they had to, a copse at the end of a lane that goes nowhere, the shady side of a stream or a windy patch of thorn and rubble where a cottage or a Gaulish house once stood.

It was in places such as these that one of the largest tribes of France used to live, scattered over a vast area that stretches from north-western Spain to the English Channel. This tribe will return us by an unexpected route to a more familiar world.

The earliest record of the people known as cagots dates from the year 1000. For over nine hundred years, they were found in small communities throughout the west of France under various names: 'agotac' in the Basque Country, 'gahets' or 'gafets' in Gascony, 'capots' in parts of Languedoc and Anjou, 'caqueux' or 'cacous' in Brittany. There were cagots in murky suburbs of Bordeaux and Toulouse, Rennes and Quimper, and on the edge of almost every town and village in south-western France. There were also a few isolated communities across the border in north-western Navarre.

Traces of the cagots survive today in place names, in worn stone faces carved into door lintels, and in tiny doors and fonts in about sixty churches from Biarritz to the western side of the Col de Peyresourde. Most cagot doors are found to the left of the porch: the cagots were supposed to slip into church and sit on benches along the cold north wall.* They were not allowed to sit with the rest of the congregation. At communion, they received the host on the end of a stick. They were forbidden to walk barefoot in public and to touch the parapet of a bridge with their bare hands. Until the seventeenth century, they paid no taxes because their money was considered unclean and they were excused military service because they were not allowed to carry arms.

The only trades that male cagots were allowed to practise were carpentry and rope-making. A trace of this enforced specialization can still be found in the town of Hagetmau, which was once the focal point of several cagot communities, where almost half the population

---

* These doors are often said to have been made unusually low to humiliate the cagots, but the surviving examples (Duhort, Monein, Navarrenx, etc.) are well above the average height of the population, then and now. There is no sign of any attempt to conceal the prejudice. At Monein, the cagot section is marked by a dwarfish figure at the base of a column on the north side (see illustrations). An almost featureless stone head, not much bigger than a tennis ball, can be seen under a window-sill in the Pyrenean village of Bielle. Another cagot head survived in Hagetmau until 2004, when a clump of semi-derelict old houses known as the Quartier des Cagots was pulled down.

works in the chair industry. Many of the women worked as midwives and were thought to know secret remedies and spells. Since the cagots were skilled carpenters, they were treated as a valuable workforce by some nobles and educated people who found the prejudice absurd. In 1681, the parliament of Rennes made it illegal to persecute anyone on the grounds that they were a cagot. This made little difference to their daily lives. In the early eighteenth century, a wealthy cagot in the Landes was seen taking water from the font for 'clean' people. His hand was sliced off by a soldier and nailed to the church door. In 1741, a cagot from Moumour who had dared to cultivate the soil had his feet pierced with red-hot iron spikes.

Other prejudices and persecutions came and went. The church at Navarrenx was Catholic, then Protestant, then Catholic again, but the cagot door remained. On the eve of the Revolution, some priests were still refusing to admit cagots into the body of the church or to bury them with other Christians. The curé of Lurbe forced them to use a trough as their font and tried to prosecute his elder brother for marrying a cagot girl. This was in 1788, by which time they were becoming harder to find in urban areas, though Brest still had a separate cagot community in 1810. Local persecution continued for generations. In the 1840s, a historian searching for the 'cursed races' of France and Spain found about a hundred and fifty towns and villages where people identified as cagots were living. At Borce, a cagot mayor was forced out of office in 1830; at Aramits, cagot fathers had difficulty finding good husbands for their daughters; at Dognen and Castetbon, cagots were still being buried in separate graveyards in 1847, and many other cagot cemeteries were reserved for outsiders who died in the *commune*. A baker at Hennebont in southern Brittany lost all his working-class customers when he married a *cacouse*. In 1964, a teacher in Salies-de-Béarn, where the Pyrenean foothills begin to flatten out towards the Landes, found that some families were still being mocked as descendants of cagots.

No one knows – and no one knew – why the cagots were ostracized and persecuted. Birth certificates and other legal documents identified them as cagots simply because their parents had also been cagots. Strange genetic features were reported, as late as the 1890s, and linked with events in the misty past: missing earlobes, in-growing nails, bright blue or olive eyes, yellowish skin, webbed hands and feet, baby-hair on adult heads. In the south-west, it was widely believed that their ancestors were Visigoths defeated by King Clovis in the sixth century. Their name was said to derive from the Bearnese or Latin for 'Goth dog', though it is more likely to be related to a word for excrement. A group of cagots who sent a petition to Pope Léon X in the sixteenth century claimed to be the descendants of Cathar heretics who were exterminated in the Albigensian crusades in the thirteenth century. But the cagots predate the Cathars and there is no sign that their religion was unorthodox. A similar theory held that they were the first Christian converts in Gaul (one of their names was '*chrestiens*') and that when the rest of the country was Christianized, the old pagan prejudice survived. In some periods and places, they were confused with lepers, though leper colonies existed in France several centuries before the first known 'cagoteries', and early edicts mention lepers and cagots as separate categories of undesirable.*

Nearly all the old and modern theories are unsatisfactory: Roman legionaries with leprosy who were sent to spas in Gaul, crusaders returning to France with the disease, Saracens who collaborated with Charlemagne and fled to France after the defeat at Roncevaux. It finally became apparent that the real 'mystery of the cagots' was the fact that they had no distinguishing features at all. They spoke whichever dialect was spoken in the region and their family names were not peculiar to the cagots. They did not, as many Bretons believed, bleed from the navel on Good Friday. The only real difference was that, after eight centuries of persecution, they tended to be more skilful and resourceful than the surrounding populations, and more likely to emigrate to America. They were feared because they were persecuted and might therefore seek revenge. Songs and sayings about the cagots never bothered to justify the prejudice:

---

* E.g. the Parlement de Bordeaux, judgement of 14 May 1578: The 'officers and consuls of Casteljaloux and all other places' are instructed to force 'ladres and lépreux' (lepers) and 'capots and gahets' (cagots) to wear 'the marks and tokens they have always worn in the past: for the former, a rattle; for the latter, a red sign on the breast in the form of a duck's foot.'

A baig dounc la Cagoutaille!	Down with the Cagots,
Destruisiam tous lous Cagots,	Let's destroy them all!
Destruisiam la cagoutaille,	Let's destroy the Cagots,
A baig dounc tous lous Cagots!	And down with them all!*

The most promising theory about their origin is still being tested, but it may eventually provide a good explanation. Many cagot communities lay on the main pilgrim routes to Compostela. Their incidence increases as the various routes converge in the south-west. The red webbed-foot symbol that cagots were sometimes forced to wear may have been the trademark of a carpenters' guild which became powerful during the medieval building boom on the Compostela route. The intense tribal loyalties of certain guilds are well attested until the late nineteenth century, and the curiously wide spread of cagots over culturally and geographically distinct regions is reminiscent of the trans-national networks of itinerant apprentices. A semi-nomadic, alien population known for its mysterious skills and which employed local forest-dwellers would certainly have been perceived as a threat. Something of this unease can still be seen on lonely sections of the Compostela route in Roussillon, in villages with no willing interest in the outside world, where signs forbidding 'Camping sauvage' compete with signs advertising the 'Routes de Saint Jacques'. Pilgrims and other strangers are watched from windows and encouraged to keep moving by the free-range village dogs.

The problem with any theory is that the distribution of cagots is not primarily a population pattern but the footprint of a prejudice. The fact that the cagot zone of the south-west so closely follows the historical borders of Gascony suggests that official tolerance of the prejudice played a bigger role in determining the distribution of cagots than the movements of a particular group of people.

The only certainty is that cagots were identified as a separate group and forced to live in cheerless hamlets and suburbs. Nearly everything that is known about them relates to persecution. There is very little information on their lives and practices, though they do appear to have had a strong collective identity. A group of cagots in Toulouse

---

* In Béarnais. Recorded near Oloron-Sainte-Marie, c. 1844.

in 1600 called for their blood to be examined to prove that they were just like other people. When the Revolution came, cagots stormed municipal buildings to destroy their birth records. Unfortunately, local memory was enough to keep the tradition alive. Some very long rhyming songs preserved the names of cagots for future generations as effectively as a bureaucrat's card index.

An autobiographical song written in Basque by a young cagot shepherd-poet in 1783 suggests a long apprenticeship in the ironies of persecution. His sweetheart, a shepherdess, 'her beautiful eyes full of tears', has come to tell him that her father has moved her to a different pasture. Someone has told the family that her fiancé is an 'agot' (Basque for 'cagot'). In this part of the song, the girl is the first to speak:

'Jentetan den ederrena ümen düzü agota:
Bilho holli, larrü churi eta begi ñabarra.
Nik ikhusi artzaiñetan zü zira ederrena:
Eder izateko aments agot izan behar da?'

'So' izü nuntik ezagützen dien zuiñ den agota:
Lehen sua egiten zaio hari beharriala;
Bata handiago dizü, eta aldiz bestia
Biribil et'orotarik bilhoz üngüratia.'

'Hori hala balimbada haietarik etzira,
Ezi zure beharriak alkhar üdüri dira.
Agot denak chipiago badü beharri bata,
Aitari erranen diot biak bardin tüzüla.'

'The agot, they say, is the handsomest of men;
Fair hair, white skin and eyes of blue.
You are the handsomest shepherd I know:
In order to be handsome, must one be an agot?'

'By this can you recognize an agot:
First look for clues in the ear;
He has one ear too large, and the other
Is round and covered all over with hair.'

'If that is so, you are not one of those folk,
For your ears are a perfect match.
If agots always have one ear too small,
I'll tell my father that yours are both alike.'

*

A PERSECUTED TRIBE that wanted to destroy its own tribal identity was not a relic of a barbarian age. The mysterious cagots were modern French citizens, harbingers of a state in which justice would be stronger than tradition. One day, as the end of the song suggests, economic development would eradicate the difference: 'If, like you, I had been rich, your father would not have said that I was a cagot.'

Even so, tribal identities would prove remarkably immune to legislation, wealth and passing time. They survived industrialization, migration to cities and even, in some parts, half a century of television and autoroutes. The Welche community along the ridge of the Vosges, whose Romance dialect once formed a linguistic island in a Germanic sea, still operates a clan system to find employment for the young and to prevent the community from flowing away into the Alsatian plain. The watery suburbs of Saint-Omer are still inhabited by descendants of the Hautponnais and Lyselar. Even the caste of cagots seems to be unconsciously perpetuating itself. Tracing their lineage from legal documents, an anthropologist has recently discovered that families descended from cagots still tend to intermarry and practise the same traditional trades, though they have never heard of cagots.

It would take something more powerful than political will to forge this swarming continent of microscopic kingdoms into a single nation. Discrimination was the life-blood of tribal France. But it was also one of the means by which the modern nation would consolidate its identity. When François Marlin happened upon a large pariah community in the city of Metz in 1780, he could not have known that he was looking into the distant future:

> They have been piled up here in a little street where they are locked up each night like convicts in a jail. So that they can be told apart from other people, these wretches are forced to wear a black coat and white bands. They can also be recognized by their beards and by the air of reproof that is imprinted on their faces, not by the crime they are supposed to have committed, but by the degraded state in which they live.

Beyond the Rhineland, the Jewish population of France was tiny and, in some *départements*, non-existent. Yet the Dreyfus Affair would divide the nation as effectively as the Virgin of Roquecezière divided one Aveyron village from another.

In the absence of a Jewish population, and in regions where cagots were unknown, one of the commonest terms of tribal abuse was 'Saracen'. It was applied to dozens of different groups, from the Pas-de-Calais to the Loire Valley and the Auvergne, and from the tip of the Gironde peninsula to the Alps of Savoy. The Burhin and Chizerot tribes on either bank of the Saône in Burgundy were thought to be Saracen because they were short and dark and because they treated illnesses with a special form of 'oriental' massage. (Reports that they wore turbans and Turkish trousers and swore by Allah are not entirely reliable.) The dark-eyed, dark-haired people of the spacious Val d'Ajol near Plombières-les-Bains were also said to be Saracen. One of the clans was famous for treating broken bones and dislocated limbs. Their children were sometimes seen on doorsteps, playing with dismantled skeletons.

Arab colonies along the eighth-century invasion routes may have contributed physical features, words and even skills to the local population, but when all the 'Saracen' tribes of France are plotted on a map, it becomes apparent that they existed almost everywhere except where one would expect to find a strong Arab influence.

Local identity consisted ultimately, not in ethnic origins, but in the fact that a community happened to be where it was rather than somewhere else. On this local level, the river of history is a sluggish stream full of counter-currents and hidden chasms. In the summer of 2004, rock faces on the road that climbs steeply out of the Val d'Ajol to the north were covered with political posters urging a population once thought to be Saracen to say '*Non à l'Islamisation de la France*'. For some of its inhabitants, tribal France is still a dangerous, divided land.

4

O Òc Sí Bai Ya Win Oui
Oyi Awè Jo Ja Oua

ON THE SIXTEENTH DAY of Prairial in Year II of the 'one and indivisible' French Republic (4 June 1794), the representative of the Loir-et-Cher *département* was making his way to the National Convention through a city that was being torn apart by something worse than tribal war. On that day, Citizen Robespierre was to be elected President of the Convention. For the next seven weeks, France would be governed by the guillotine. But the Abbé Henri Grégoire had more serious matters on his mind. Four years before, he had sent a questionnaire to town halls all over France on the subject of patois. ('Patois' was the derogatory term for dialects other than the official state idiom in its standard form. According to the *Encyclopédie*, it meant 'Corrupt language as spoken in almost all the provinces. . . . "Language" proper is spoken only in the capital.') The key questions were these: Did the people of the region have their own patois? Could it be used to express intellectual concepts or was it riddled with obscenities and oaths? Were the country people patriotic? and, most importantly of all, How could their patois be destroyed?

The Abbé Grégoire was not a linguistic terrorist. He had campaigned for the abolition of slavery and the death penalty; he called for Jews to be given full citizenship and tried to save national treasures from revolutionary 'vandalism' (the word 'vandalism' was his invention). He wanted to cover the country with libraries and schools, but none of this would be possible, he believed, without a common tongue. Without a national language, there could be no nation.

Grégoire himself came from a poor family in Lorraine. He knew that an ignorant, divided population was easily exploited. To his ears, patois was the voice of superstition and subservience. As a fellow revolutionary put it, linguistic diversity was 'one of the sturdiest flying-buttresses of despotism'. The government had already spent a small fortune having its decrees translated into Catalan, Basque, Breton, Provençal and Alsatian, but the only lasting solution, in Grégoire's mind, was to silence those ancient tongues for good.

Replies to the questionnaire had straggled in from representatives, mayors, lawyers, clerics and a semi-literate farmer from Brittany. From some regions – Picardy, the centre of France, much of the Auvergne and most of Brittany – there was no response, either because no one had the necessary information or because no one cared about the incomprehensible jabbering of peasants. But there was enough to give the Abbé Grégoire a clearer view of the fragmented nation than anyone before.

The Abbé Grégoire's report on 'The Necessity and Means of Exterminating Patois and Universalizing the Use of the French Language' painted an alarming picture of a land that was still festering in medieval ignorance. The fringes of France were already known to be dominated by languages quite different from French: Basque, Breton, Flemish and Alsatian. But the two Romanic languages that covered most of the country – French in the north, Occitan in the south – also turned out to be a muddle of incomprehensible dialects. In many parts, the dialect changed at the village boundary. Several respondents claimed that differences were perceptible at a distance of one league (less than three miles) and sometimes just a few feet, as the writer from Périgueux explained: 'The patois's reign ends at the river Nizonne. It is amazing to cross this little stream and to hear an entirely different patois, which sounds more like French.' In the Jura, there were 'almost as many different patois as there are villages'. Even plants and stars had their own local names, as if each little region lived under a different sky.

The reports confirmed the Abbé's fears. Peasants in the Armagnac were 'too ignorant to be patriotic'. News of important events and government decrees left the capital on the broad river of French only to run aground in the muddy creeks of patois. A landowner from Montauban found the same startling ignorance in the Quercy: the peasants might talk of Revolution and the Constitution, but when they are asked whose cause they support, 'they answer without hesitation, "the King's".' If there were people who thought that the King was still alive and on the throne, how could they be taught the principles of liberty and equality?

As the replies came in, the republican vision of a united country began to look like the fantasy of a small Parisian elite. Large parts of France were barely French at all. Foreign visitors often claimed to find Latin more useful than French. On the borders, speakers of Spanish and Italian had never bothered to learn French because their own languages were easily understood by their neighbours. Further north, in areas like the Limousin, where two major language groups coincide – French and Occitan – a muddled lingua franca had evolved. 'French-speaking' peasants had to be persuaded to revert to patois for the sake of clarity. 'Such disorder reigns that the prayer recited by fathers when the family is together at evening can be understood only by the Supreme Being.'

Worse still, it appeared that 'patois' was not confined to the countryside and was not spoken only by peasants. The town of Salins (now Salins-les-Bains) was divided into north and south by a language barrier. The city of Lyon was a hive of micro-dialects: 'The river people, the butchers, the silk-workers, the fish-wives and the herb-sellers each have a language all their own.' In some southern regions, rich people, priests, scholars, lawyers and tradesmen all spoke the local dialect and 'felt ill at ease' when speaking French. If certain *quartiers* of Paris had been included in the questionnaire, the Abbé might have added the communities of migrant workers who lived in the capital and whose dialects had a noticeable effect on the speech of Parisian workers.

The information was uneven and incomplete, but there was enough to show – or so it seemed to the Abbé – that the nation was in a fragile state. The land of liberty appeared to be a body composed of ancient, decaying limbs with feeble connections to the brain. The Ordinances of Villers-Cotterêts in 1539 had made the dialect of Paris and the Île-de-France, now known as French, the language of official documents. Other forms of French that had once been dominant –

Normand, Picard and Champenois – were relegated to the status of dialects. Similar decrees were enacted after the annexation of various territories: Flanders, Alsace, Roussillon, Lorraine and Corsica. But no one had ever tried to change the language of the masses. The Abbé's survey was a revelation. According to his estimate, more than six million French citizens were completely ignorant of the national language. Another six million could barely conduct a conversation in it. While French was the language of civilized Europe, France itself had no more than three million 'pure' French-speakers (11 per cent of the population), and many of them were unable to write it correctly. The official idiom of the French Republic was a minority language. 'In liberty, we are the advance-guard of nations. In language, we are still at the Tower of Babel.'

Compared to later linguistic purges (see p. 325), the Abbé Grégoire's proposals for flattening the Tower of Babel were remarkably gentle: hasten the processes by which people were induced to learn French (build more roads and canals, and disseminate news and agricultural advice); pay particular attention to the Celtic and 'barbarian' fringes where counter-revolution was rife (the Basque Country, Brittany and Alsace); above all, simplify the French language and abolish irregular verbs – a measure that would have rescued countless schoolchildren from the despotism of pernickety pedagogues.

With the Revolution burning its way into the ancient forest of languages, it must have seemed that the whole nation would soon be speaking with one voice. But the biggest surprises were yet to come. The Abbé's figures are almost certainly an underestimate. Seventy years later, when official statistics treated a few days at school or the merest smattering of French as evidence of an ability to speak the language, many or most of the *communes* in fifty-three out of eighty-nine *départements* were said to be non-French-speaking. In 1880, the number of people who felt comfortable speaking French was estimated to be about eight million (just over one-fifth of the population). In some parts, prefects, doctors, priests and policemen were like colonial officials, baffled by the natives and forced to use interpreters.

The Abbé Grégoire would have been appalled, but he might have

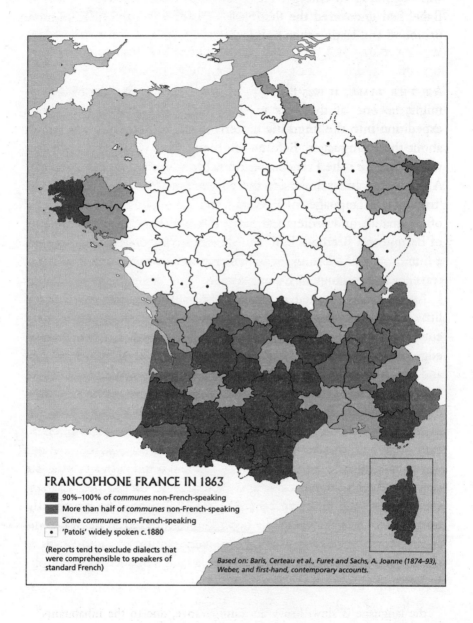

FRANCOPHONE FRANCE IN 1863

- ■ 90%–100% of *communes* non-French-speaking
- ■ More than half of *communes* non-French-speaking
- ▨ Some *communes* non-French-speaking
- • 'Patois' widely spoken c.1880

(Reports tend to exclude dialects that
were comprehensible to speakers of
standard French)

Based on: Baris, Certeau et al., Furet and Sachs, A. Joanne (1874–93),
Weber, and first-hand, contemporary accounts.

been consoled or at least intrigued by the more complex truth that was beginning to emerge. His attempt to undermine the Tower of Babel had uncovered the first clear signs of a cultural division more profound and lasting than political unity.

*

AT THE TIME, it was far from obvious that the muddle of dialects might be one of the keys to the identity of France. The Abbé's expedition into the linguistic hinterland shows how little was known about these languages. Before – and long after – his report, dialects were treated by the French-speaking elite as deviant forms of French. A few poets and scholars treasured them as historical curios – the 'troubadour' languages of Provence and Languedoc, the 'old French' of Normandy and proletarian Paris, the 'prehistoric' mother-tongues of Basque and Breton – but to most educated people, dialect was just a humorous or irritating inconvenience, a peasant's ruse to cheat the traveller and to laugh at his expense.

As the Abbé pointed out, the National Convention itself was a little Babel of regional accents. However, the representatives were educated men who owed their advancement in part to their knowledge of French. Any other dialect was likely to be seen as a corrupt and ancient idiom. Standard French had been tamed and regulated, notably by the French Academy. The size of the Academy's official dictionary (about fifteen thousand words, compared to forty thousand in Furetière's dictionary of 1690) showed its determination to eradicate the rabble of synonyms, onomatopoeias and vulgarities. French was supposed to be a product of the rational mind, a beautiful estate carved out of a jungle of strange sounds and obscenities. Dialects were seen as natural excrescences of the landscape. The nineteenth-century Larousse encyclopedia described the Limousin dialect as the audible form of peasant apathy (too many diminutives and words of one syllable). The Poitevin dialect had 'a rough quality, like the soil'. In Bourg d'Oisans, in the Alpine Écrins massif,

> the language is slow, heavy and unfigurative, due to the inhabitants'
> physical and moral ill health and the nature of the country, which is
> covered with high, barren mountains.

Words for 'gibberish' still reflect this political-linguistic geography: *charabia* (from *charabiat*, a migrant worker from the Auvergne), *baragouin* (from the Breton *bara*, 'bread', and *gwin*, 'wine') or '*parler comme une vache espagnole*' (the 'cow' was originally a 'Basque').

By the time of the Revolution, most dialects had no written form. For those that did, spelling was largely a matter of individual choice. Dictionaries of regional languages were rarely taken seriously, even by their authors. Until the mid-nineteenth century, they were presented as manuals for provincials who wanted to speak correctly and not sound ridiculous when they went to Paris. A bilingual French–Comtois dictionary (the language of Besançon and the Franche-Comté) was written in 1753 by Marie-Marguerite Brun 'to help my compatriots to reform their language'. A popular work on the language of Lyon (fourth edition, 1810) was titled *Bad Language* and addressed to those 'who are not fortunate enough to live in a select society'. Even the great French–Languedocian dictionary compiled by Boissier de Sauvages (1785) advertised itself as 'A Collection of the Principal Errors Made in Diction and in French Pronunciation by the Inhabitants of the Southern Provinces'.

Though the words themselves proved the wealth and vitality of 'patois' and the impoverishment of official, academic French, they were treated as a natural resource to be plundered by the dominant language. Dialect terms such as '*affender*' (to share a meal with an unexpected visitor), '*aranteler*' (to sweep away spiders' webs), '*carioler*' (to cry out while giving birth), '*carquet*' (a secret place between breast and corset), '*river*' (to strip off leaves by running one's hand along a branch) and a thousand other useful gems were like trophies brought back from foreign parts and cleansed of their original context. None of them were admitted to the dictionary of the French Academy. When linguistically omnivorous writers like Balzac used dialect words in their published works, they were accused of sullying the language of civilization.

The world to which these words belonged would not be fully charted until the twentieth century. In most people's minds – if they gave the matter any thought – the map of languages had more blank spaces than contemporary maps of Africa. Educated travellers were constantly amazed to find that their French was quite useless.

I was never able to make myself understood by the peasants I met along the way. I spoke to them in French; I used the patois of my region; I tried speaking to them in Latin, but all in vain. Finally, when I was tired of talking without being understood, they spoke to me in turn using a language which I found completely incomprehensible.

This was written by a priest from the Provençal Alps travelling in the Limagne region of the Auvergne in the late 1770s. Similar accounts can be found from the Ancien Régime to the First World War. The disorientation of Jean Racine, when he found himself linguistically stranded in Provence in 1661, was a common experience in some parts of France even two centuries later. Racine wrote to his friend La Fontaine about a trip to his uncle's home in Uzès, fifteen miles north of Nîmes. (This was several years before he wrote the plays that would be hailed as the purest expression of classical French.)

By the time I reached Lyon, the local language was already becoming incomprehensible, and so was I. This misfortune increased at Valence, and God so willed it that when I asked a maid for a chamber-pot, she put a warming-pan in my bed. But it's even worse in this *pays*. I swear to you that I need an interpreter as much as a Muscovite would need one in Paris.

A few days later, he told another correspondent, 'I cannot understand the French of this region and no one can understand mine.'

If an educated man with relatives in Provence was unable to order a chamber-pot in Valence, was effectively illiterate further south and failed even to identify the language he was hearing, it is no wonder that 'France' sometimes seemed a rather abstract concept.

*

WITH A TWENTY-FIRST-CENTURY satellite image of the languages of France, it is easy to see that the language Racine heard at his uncle's home was not a form of French at all. Long before reaching Uzès, he had crossed the great divide between the northern *oïl* or French languages and the southern Oc or Occitan languages (so named in the Middle Ages after the words for 'yes'). It was not until 1873 that a heroic two-man expedition began to trace the

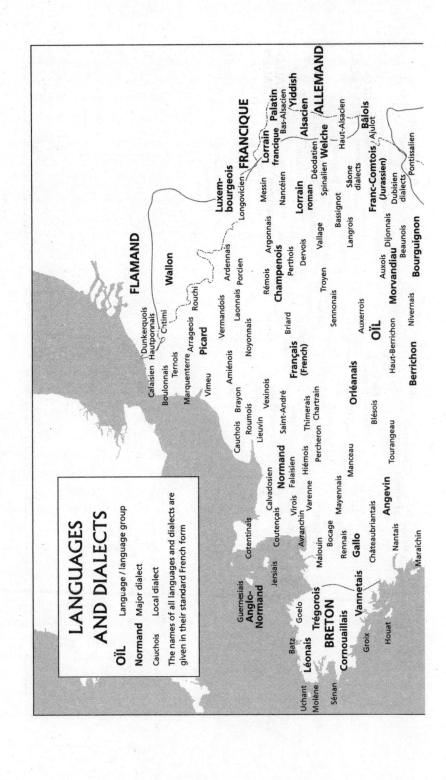

LANGUAGES AND DIALECTS

OÏL Language / language group

Normand Major dialect

Cauchois Local dialect

The names of all languages and dialects are given in their standard French form

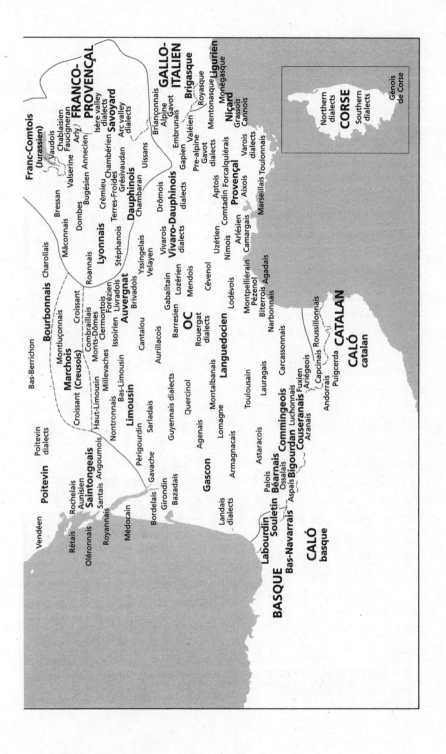

frontier of Oïl and Oc by interviewing hundreds of people in tiny villages. It covered one-third of the distance from the Atlantic to the Alps before one of the explorers died and the other lost an eye. Until then, the line was commonly supposed to follow the river Loire. In fact, it runs much further south, from the tip of the Gironde estuary, along the northern edge of the Massif Central, through a narrow mixed zone known as the 'Croissant' (crescent), which includes Limoges, Guéret and Vichy. About forty-five miles before the Rhône valley, Oc and Oïl are separated by a third Romanic group of dialects known, confusingly, as Francoprovençal. (Provençal itself belongs to the Occitan group.) The languages of Oïl, Oc and Francoprovençal together account for about 94 per cent of the territory.*

At his uncle's home in Uzès, Racine found himself four branches away from French. He was in the realm of Occitan, in the area dominated by Provençal – specifically, Rhodanian (Rhône) Provençal, comprising five main dialects, one of which was the dialect spoken in Uzès.

This much was known, at least to scholars, by the end of the nineteenth century. About fifty-five major dialects and hundreds of sub-dialects had been identified, belonging to four distinct language groups: Romanic (French, Occitan, Francoprovençal, Catalan and the Italic languages spoken in Corsica and along the Italian border); Germanic (Flemish, Frankish and Alsatian); Celtic (Breton); and an isolated group, Euskaric (Basque). Many more were unknown or unrecognized. Shuadit or Judeo-Provençal was a separate language spoken by Jews in the Papal enclave of Vaucluse. It became extinct in 1977 and survives only in liturgical texts. Zarphatic or Judeo-French was spoken in the Moselle and the Rhineland until the Second World War. The last speakers died in concentration camps. The Iberian gypsy language Caló had two main forms in France – Basque and

---

* The 'discovery' of Francoprovençal is always attributed to the Italian linguist G.-I. Ascoli, who described it in 1873. However, 'a patois that is neither the language of Oc nor the language of Oïl' was known in the 1820s to a travelling cabinet-maker, Agricol Perdiguier, and presumably to most other itinerant artisans and traders. Perdiguier called it 'Allobroge', from the tribe that once occupied the region of Geneva, Grenoble and Vienne.

Catalonian – but little was known about the people, let alone their language.

Even if a place was known to outsiders, its language might remain a secret. The Pyrenean village of Aas, at the foot of the Col d'Aubisque, above the spa town of Eax-Bonnes, had its own whistling language which was unknown even in the neighbouring valleys until it was mentioned on a television programme in 1959. Shepherds who spent the summer months in lonely cabins had evolved an ear-splitting, hundred-decibel language that could be understood at a distance of up to two miles. It was also used by the women who worked in the surrounding fields and was apparently versatile enough in the early twentieth century to convey the contents of the local newspaper. Its last known use was during the Nazi Occupation, when shepherds helped Jewish refugees, Résistants and stranded pilots to cross the border into Spain. A few people in Aas today remember hearing the language, but no one can reproduce the sounds and no recordings were ever made. If such a remarkable language escaped detection, many other quieter dialects must have died out before they could be identified.

*

THE KNOWN DIALECTS of France can all be placed precisely on the tree of languages – even the whistling language of Aas, which was based on the local Bearnese dialect. Naturally, to a cross-country traveller who leapt from one branch to the next, the effect was obscurity and chaos. The title of this chapter lists some of the major forms of 'yes' in clockwise order, starting with Provence and ending with Savoy. But even this is a simplification. In mid-nineteenth-century Brittany, a person who walked the five miles from Carnac to Erdeven could hear three distinct pronunciations of the word *ya* ('yes'): *iè*, *ia* and *io*. Along the Côte d'Azur, from Menton to Mons (west of Grasse), fathers ten miles apart were called *païre*, *père*, *pa*, *pèro* and *papo*. As the sun travelled over the Franche-Comté, it changed its name to *souleil*, *soulet*, *soulot*, *s'lot*, *soulu*, *sélu*, *slu*, *séleu*, *soureil*, *soureuil*, *sereil*, *s'reil* and *seroille*.

Writers of travel accounts and official reports revelled in the blur of local words and the incomprehensibility of peasants. Just as

Romantic engravers surrounded their steeples with bats and birds of prey, they darkened the Dark Continent with tales of ignorance and isolation. Later, the impressions of the monolingual elite would be confirmed by professional linguists who identified variant forms of sub-dialects in tiny areas, sometimes in a single village and, in one case, in a single family. But these erudite descriptions gave only the faintest impression of what was after all a means of communication.

The language landscape as it appeared to the speakers themselves was harder to describe, though some of its contours and vistas can be seen even in the earliest surveys. The Abbé Grégoire's questionnaire was just the first of many reports from the linguistic frontier. In 1807, Napoleon's Minister of the Interior ordered the prefects of every *département* to supply him with translations of the parable of the Prodigal Son into the local patois. (The story of a swineherd who returns to civilization must have seemed appropriate.) The results, in ninety different patois, predictably showed huge differences, even within the same group of dialects. The sample sequence below follows the arc of the Mediterranean, staying within forty miles of the coast, from the eastern Pyrenees to Marseille. The average distance between each phrase is forty-six miles.

> Un home tingue dos fills. Y digue lo mes jove de ells al pare: Pare,
> daii me la part de be que me pertoca. (Catalonian Pyrenees)*
> Un hommé abio dous mainachés. Et lé pus joubé diguec à soun païré:
> Moùn païré, dounatz-mé la partido dal bé qué mé rébén.
> (Carcassonne)
> Un home abio dous éfans. Lous pus jouine diguet à soun péra:
> Moun péra, douna me la part de bostre bianda que me coumpeta.
> (Lodève)
> Un ome avié dous efans. Lou mendre li diguet: Paire, bailo-mi ce que
> deu mi reveni de toun be. (Lasalle)
> Un homé avié dous garçouns. Et lou cadè dighé à soun péro: Moun
> péro, beïla-mé la par que deou me révéni de vastè ben. (Nîmes)
> Un homo avié dous eufans. Lou plus jouîné diguet à soun péro:
> Moun péro, douna mi ce que deou mé revenir de vouestre ben.
> (Marseille)

* 'A certain man had two sons. And the younger of them said to his father, Father, give me the portion of goods that falleth to me.' (Luke 15:11–12)

The fact that would have been obvious to the speakers of these dialects is that the similarities outnumber the differences. Mutual comprehensibility rather than isolation was the norm. The effective range of some dialects was astonishing. The 'Friends of the Constitution' who wrote to the Abbé Grégoire from Carcassonne noted the 'infinite number' of dialects in villages and towns, but they also pointed out that a person could travel twenty or thirty leagues (fifty-six or eighty-three miles) 'and understand this multiplicity of dialects despite knowing only one of them'. In the Landes, though forms of Landais or 'Gascon noir' still differ from town to town, a writer from Mont-de-Marsan assured the Abbé that 'all Gascons understand one another without interpreters, from Bayonne to deepest Languedoc', which suggests a range of about two hundred and fifty miles.

Even mountains and gorges were not insuperable barriers. An isolated village that was forced to find resources in the world beyond was more likely to be bilingual than a community that could feed itself. Travelling teachers in the Dauphiné and Provence who walked among the livestock at fairs with an ink-bottle tied to their buttonhole crying '*Maître d'école!*' traditionally came from the mountainous area around Briançon, where seasonal migration had produced a population of polyglots. The Provençal shepherds who walked two hundred miles from Arles to the Oisans could converse with locals all along the route and, when they arrived in the Alps, negotiate the rental of summer pastures with people who, from a linguist's point of view, spoke a different language.

*

THE NOTION THAT French rapidly became the common tongue and supplanted other languages is only partly true. Before the Revolution, in the centre, but not the suburbs, of commercial cities like Bordeaux and Marseille, people from all walks of life could converse with French-speaking strangers from the north. In the Périgord, speaking French (once known derisively as '*francimander*') was no longer considered a silly affectation, though many people refused to speak it in case they made mistakes and sounded foolish. In the Provençal Alps, where French was of little practical use in daily life, speaking the national language was the equivalent of putting on one's

Sunday best, just as speaking Latin must have been several centuries before.

At the same time, some of the other languages of France, far from being smothered by French, were thriving. Improved communications spread the use of French, but they also gave some dialects a wider range than they had ever had before. The Abbé Grégoire would have been dismayed to learn that French-speaking town-dwellers in Brittany were learning Breton. According to the farmer who wrote to him from Tréguier, Breton had 'become necessary to the inhabitants of towns who have to deal with peasants every day to buy their produce'. Breton was 'now more familiar to townspeople than French'. At Avignon and Carpentras, according to an official report in 1808, 'wealthy, educated people' were 'obliged to know and all too often to speak patois' in order to communicate effectively with workers, tradesmen and servants. Priests delivered sermons and magistrates heard witnesses in Provençal. (For the same reason, presumably, when she revealed herself to Bernadette Soubirous in 1858, the Virgin Mary used the local dialect of Lourdes.) 'It follows from this', said the report, 'that the French that is spoken in this region, and even the French that is taught, is not only inelegant, it is not even correct.' French itself, in other words, was not imported to the provinces like a crate of merchandise. It was acclimatized and hybridized like a plant. About twenty regional varieties of French are still recognized today as distinct dialects.

In northern France, where statistics seem to show the gradual retreat of Flemish before the tide of French, many French-speakers were just as keen as Flemish-speakers to acquire the second language. In towns and cities bordering the realm of Flemish – Lille, Douai, Cambrai and Avesnes – almost everyone was bilingual. In the Lys *département*, which was created in 1795 from part of Belgium, a language-learning programme had been in operation since before the Revolution. Farmers and tradesmen exchanged their children when they were eight to ten years old. 'The aim is to familiarize one group of children with French and the other with Flemish. These emigrations last only a few years, after which each child returns to his own country.' The same practice was reported after the Revolution in Alsace and Lorraine.

Private arrangements like these would not have appeared in official statistics, which are extremely sketchy in any case until the twentieth century. The use of minority languages was certainly under-reported, as it still is today. Even now, there are French people who speak a language other than French without knowing it. An elderly innkeeper in Villard at the foot of the Little Saint Bernard Pass told me that he and his friend had been punished at school in the early 1940s for not speaking proper French, but he was uncertain whether the idiom they used was Savoyard or a patois form of French.

Modern figures vary wildly, but even the lowest estimates suggest that, in certain situations, a large minority of people still use the languages that were thought to be dying out in the nineteenth century: the various forms of Occitan have at least two million speakers; Alsatian has 1.5 million; Breton 500,000; Corsican 280,000; Basque and Flemish 80,000 each (in France); Francoprovençal 70,000. Figures for major dialects like Auvergnat, Norman and Picard are unavailable, though they can still be heard in daily use.

Two centuries ago, these languages and dialects cohabited with French and often lived quite happily without it. As late as 1863, a quarter of all army recruits were said to speak 'patois' and nothing else. French itself seemed to be declining in certain areas. School inspectors found that children in the Lauragais south-east of Tou-louse forgot what little French they knew as soon as they left school: 'French leaves no more trace in their minds than Latin does in the minds of college students.' In the Cerdagne, in the eastern Pyrenees, language teachers inadvertently created a bizarre school pidgin com-posed of Latin, French and Catalan. Men returning from the army quickly reverted to their native tongue. A man who came home to Cellefrouin near Angoulême in 1850 after seven years in the army and thirty years in America was speaking the patois of his boyhood again within a few days. Conscription spread the national language but it could also preserve the older forms of patois, and some recruits never learned French at all. There are several reports of Breton soldiers being shot by their comrades in the First World War because they were mistaken for Germans or because they failed to obey incomprehensible orders.

Many people who were recorded in statistics as French-speakers would have spoken the language only during a certain phase of life, when they were serving an apprenticeship, travelling to markets or working in a town. The dormancy of the local language could create the impression – often a false impression – that it was disappearing. For the last hundred and fifty years, examples of 'pure' patois have been collected from people invariably described as 'old', as if a separate, senescent species somehow propagates itself and its language without ever growing young. Generation after generation, countless people said the same thing: that the old language was spoken now only by the old people. A woman in the small Alsatian town of Thann told me this (in French) in 2004. She was probably born in the early 1970s. It turned out, however, that when she talked to her little daughter at home, she used Alsatian. The younger woman who was with her was introduced – and introduced herself – as an example of the generation that has almost forgotten the language and will see the last speakers of it die away. Yet she, too, spoke Alsatian with her mother and grandmother. She also took many of her school classes in Alsatian. She could easily have told me in Alsatian that Alsatian was dying out.

*

THE BELIEF THAT the proliferation of different dialects is related to the economic and cultural backwardness of a region is no longer tenable. President Pompidou's statement, in 1972, that 'There is no place for regional languages in a France that is destined to set its mark on Europe' now seems to belong to a distant age. Mountainous areas, like the remote Cantal where Pompidou was born, might have swarmed with micro-dialects, but so did some of the more vibrant and industrialized parts of France: Normandy, Flanders, Alsace and parts of the Mediterranean coast.

The Abbé Grégoire and all the later politicians and teachers who tried to eradicate 'patois' wanted to impose a single language. They were bound to see French as the language of authority and everything else as a sign of chaos, barbarism or rebellion. But official surveys revealed a picture of unexpected order. Far from being a blank slate on which the modern principles of liberty and equality could be inscribed, France appeared to have been divided up long before, not by kings and armies, but by ancient, inscrutable processes that would not easily be changed by act of parliament. The Revolution created a new nation and a new calendar, but it also discovered a country – or countries – that had been taking shape even before the nation had a name and the Christian calendar had been invented.

Something like a fault-line ran across the land. The Abbé Grégoire saw only part of this rift – the division of the languages of Oc and Oïl – and blamed it on 'the former feudal domination'. The curiously sharp division of Oc and Oïl does appear to follow the boundaries of medieval provinces for part of its course, but it also matches several other ancient divisions. North of the line, roofs usually have a slope of forty-five degrees and are made of flat tiles or slate; to the south, they slope at thirty degrees and are made of rounded tiles. North of the line, agricultural practice – three plantings a year and use of the plough – differed from practice in the south: biennial plantings and use of the *araire* (a primitive, wheel-less plough that could easily be dismantled). Customary law prevailed in the north and Roman law in the south.

No one knows exactly why this divide exists. It may reflect the influence of Frankish peoples from the north and Burgundians from the east, or it may reflect the more lasting establishment of Roman rule in the south. (Occitan is closer than French to Latin.)* It may even be evidence of much older tribal territories. Later studies showed that eyes and hair were generally darker south of the line. They also suggested that southerners were less educated and more likely to refuse to fight for their country.

A study of aerial photographs and place names has identified a possible frontier zone comparable to the Welsh Marches, covering most of the former province of La Marche and corresponding to the 'Croissant' where dialects have elements of both Oc and Oïl. This *limes* may once have separated Ligurian tribes from Celtic invaders and, later, Romans from barbarians. A major Roman road, the Via

---

* For example:

English	bird	horse	water	pear	ripe
Latin	aucellus	caballus	aqua	pera	maturum
Occitan	aucel	caval	aiga	pera	madur
French	oiseau	cheval	eau	poire	mûr

Agrippa, from Lyon to Bordeaux via Clermont and Limoges, follows the language divide quite closely. Like most Roman roads, it was almost certainly built on a much earlier route.

This line can still be followed on the ground. In 2005, I cycled along sections of the Oc–Oïl–Croissant frontier for a total of about fifty miles, between towns and villages identified as linguistically distinct by the 1873 expedition. For almost twenty miles, the line follows a narrow ridge on a road that is barely used by modern traffic but forms an obvious route through the landscape. Elsewhere, the Oc–Oïl divide runs through areas that are still unpopulated or covered by forests on treacherous, marshy terrain used mainly for military training. Curiously, where the two languages once came together, in linguistic 'islands' of mixed Oc and Oïl along the valleys of the Dronne and the Vienne, there is now a noticeable preponderance of bilingual Franco-British towns and villages (notably Aubeterre), in which local forms of pidgin French are evolving.

By using the 1873 data, it is possible to find the point at which Oc, Oïl and Croissant intersected. This watershed of three language groups is one of the most obscure and significant locations in the historical geography of France. It lies on a tiny road north-east of Angoulême where the Braconne Forest ends abruptly and opens out onto the plains and valley of the Charente. By chance, the landscape has arranged itself in a textbook illustration of the north–south divide: the Croissant is marked by the forest, the northern, Oïl side by a wheat field, and the southern, Oc side by a vineyard.

*

SUCCESSIVE GOVERNMENTS would try to erase this north–south line or rather, pretend that it didn't exist. One of the lasting innovations of the Revolution, in January 1790, was to carve the country into *départements*. The *départements* were to be of roughly equal size so that everyone would be able to reach the legal and administrative centre in a day. Nearly all the *départements* were named after physical features: mountains (Basses-Alpes, Cantal, Vosges, etc.), rivers (Dordogne, Haut-Rhin, Vendée, etc.), or geographical location (Nord and Côtes-du-Nord). Later, as the empire grew, southern Savoy became 'Mont-Blanc', the Swiss Jura became 'Mont Terrible' and Luxembourg became 'Forêts'. Only one city had a *département* to itself: Paris, which was described in the parliamentary debate on *départements* as 'the most beautiful city in the world', 'the fatherland of arts and sciences', 'the capital of the French empire'.

The idea was that timeless, natural logic should prevail over the old feudal and tribal divisions. Tyrants came and went but the Alps would last forever. In this way, 'prejudices, habits and barbaric institutions consolidated by fourteen centuries of existence' would be swept away. Language barriers were explicitly ignored, despite objections from some councils – like that of Saint-Malo on the borders of Brittany – that they would be forced to work with people who spoke 'languages predating Caesar's conquest'.

A seemingly small but important complaint about the new *départements* was that people would lose their collective names. Bretons, Burgundians, Gascons and Normans would officially cease to exist and be left with nothing but a national identity. The new names were too brutally descriptive to be used for individuals. No one would try to call themselves a Bouches-du-Rhônien or a Mont-Blancois.

The success of the Revolution's egalitarian reinvention of France lay, ironically, in the rise of the urban middle class, which was less attached to ancient boundaries and local identities. The historical divisions of France came to be associated with quaint provincials and primitive peasants. For all its practical virtues, the division of France into *départements* helped to accelerate a process that can best be described as the opposite of discovery. Ignorance of daily life beyond the well-connected cities and familiarity with the monuments and personalities of Paris would be signs of enlightened modernity. The provinces would be recreated as the great domain of the unconscious mind – *la France profonde*, a source of fairy tales, natural wonders and threats to civilization.

The commemoration of national anniversaries that is still a notable feature of French public life is also an obliteration of events and cultures that are not to be remembered. This process of forgetting was one of the great social forces in the formation of modern France. Middle-class children would forget the provincial languages they learned from nurses and servants, or remember them only as a picturesque remnant of the past. Peasant children would be thrashed and mocked for speaking the language of their parents at school. Most of the descendants of those benighted millions in the Abbé Grégoire's 'eradication' report would lose the tribal speech of their *pays* and acquire a highly codified and formal foreign language known as French – a language which, according to many French-speakers, almost no one speaks correctly. In the land of a thousand tongues, monolingualism became the mark of the educated person.

5

Living in France, I:
The Face in the Museum

ALMOST EVERY TOWN IN FRANCE now has a museum of 'daily
life' or of 'popular arts and traditions'. Most of them are stocked
with artefacts that would otherwise have disappeared or turned into
expensive accessories in homes and restaurants. The roughly decorated chests, the butter churns and baskets, the wooden tables with
smooth, saucer-shaped depressions into which the soup was poured,
bear witness to the resilience of their owners. They have the dignity
of objects that shared a human life. Each one contains the ghost of a
gesture that was performed a million times. They make it easy to
imagine a life of hard work and habit.

Naturally, the artefacts are the best examples available: the hefty
cradle, the expensive plough with metal parts and a manufacturer's
name, the embroidered smock that was kept in a chest as part of
someone's trousseau and never saw the pigsty or the field. As survivors, they tell a heartening tale of endurance. Other companions of
daily life – the rotting bed, the treasured dung heap, the stench-laden
fug of human and animal breath that could extinguish a burning
candle – are impossible to display.

Sometimes, the person who was survived by her possessions
appears in their midst and the purposeful display is belied by the
photograph of a face scoured by hardship. The expression is often
one of faint suspicion, dread or simply dull fatigue. It makes imag-
ining the life that belonged to these objects seem a blundering
intrusion. It seems to say that daily existence is harder to fathom
than the obsolete tools and kitchen utensils, and that, if it could be
recreated, the staple diet of a past life, with its habits, sensations and

smells, would have a stranger taste than the most exotic regional dish.

Written descriptions of daily life inevitably convey the same bright sense of purpose and progress. They pass through years of lived experience like carefree travellers, telescoping the changes that only a long memory could have perceived. Occasionally, however, a simple fact has the same effect as the photograph in the museum. At the end of the eighteenth century, doctors from urban Alsace to rural Brittany found that high death rates were not caused primarily by famine and disease. The problem was that, as soon as they became ill, people took to their beds and hoped to die. In 1750, the Marquis d'Argenson noticed that the peasants who farmed his land in the Touraine were 'trying not to multiply': 'They wish only for death'. Even in times of plenty, old people who could no longer wield a spade or hold a needle were keen to die as soon as possible. 'Lasting too long' was one of the great fears of life. Invalids were habitually hated by their carers. It took a special government grant, instituted in 1850 in the Seine and Loiret *départements*, to persuade poor families to keep their ailing relatives at home instead of sending them to that bare waiting room of the graveyard, the municipal hospice.

When there was just enough food for the living, the mouth of a dying person was an obscenity. In the relatively harmonious household of the 1840s described by the peasant novelist Émile Guillaumin, the family members speculate openly in front of Émile's bed-ridden grandmother (who has not lost her hearing): '"I wish we knew how long it's going to last." And another would reply, "Not long, I hope."' As soon as the burden expired, any water kept in pans or basins was thrown out (since the soul might have washed itself – or, if bound for Hell, tried to extinguish itself – as it left the house), and then life went on as before.

'Happy as a corpse' was a saying in the Alps. Visitors to villages in the Savoy Alps, the central Pyrenees, Alsace and Lorraine, and parts of the Massif Central were often horrified to find silent populations of cretins with hideous thyroid deformities. (The link between goitre and lack of iodine in the water was not widely recognized until the early nineteenth century.) The Alpine explorer Saussure, who asked in vain for directions in a village in the Aosta Valley when most of the villagers were out in the fields, imagined that 'an evil spirit had turned the inhabitants of the unhappy village into dumb animals, leaving them with just enough human face to show that they had once been men'.

The infirmity that seemed a curse to Saussure was a blessing to the natives. The birth of a cretinous baby was believed to bring good luck to the family. The idiot child would never have to work and would never have to leave home to earn money to pay the tax-collector. These hideous, blank creatures were already half-cured of life. Even the death of a normal child could be a consolation. If the baby had lived long enough to be baptized, or if a clever witch revived the corpse for an instant to sprinkle it with holy water, its soul would pray for the family in heaven.

*

LIKE THE FACE in the museum, these desperate situations seem to contradict the material improvements that typify many histories of the period. One reason is that nearly every autobiographical account of ordinary life in eighteenth- and nineteenth-century France comes from the early chapters of memoirs written by exceptional men who rose through the ranks of the army or the Church, who wrote their way to fame or who were plucked from obscurity by a patron, a lover or, eventually, an electorate. Few men and even fewer women had the means or the desire to write a book on 'How I failed to overcome my humble origins'. Apart from the countless riches-to-riches tales written by aristocrats, almost all the lives that we know about follow the same untypical upward trend: the farmer's son Restif de la Bretonne, the cutler's son Diderot, the watchmaker's son Rousseau, the Corsican cadet Napoleone Buonaparte.

These spectacular successes are more typical of long-term trends than of individual lives. Categorical terms like 'peasants', 'artisans' and 'the poor' reduce the majority of the population to smudges in a crowd scene that no degree of magnification could resolve into a group of faces. They suggest a large and luckless contingent that filled in the background of important events and participated in the nation's historical development by suffering and engaging in a semblance of economic activity.

Even with a short-term view, these categories turn out to be misleading. Rich people could fall into poverty and peasants could be rich and powerful. Many peasants lived in towns and commuted to the fields. Many were also craftsmen, traders and local officials, just as many so-called aristocrats were semi-literate farmers. Statistics based on a mixture of surveys, censuses and guesswork give what seems a balanced view of the whole population. In 1789, three-quarters were described as 'agricultural'. A century later, the agricultural population had fallen to about 48 per cent, while 25 per cent worked in industry, 14 per cent in commerce and transport, 4 per cent in public services and administration and 3 per cent in the liberal professions, and 6 per cent were independently wealthy. But for reasons that will become clear, these figures always exaggerate the tidy divisions of the population and underestimate the number of people who tried to live off the land.

In the following scenes of daily life, and throughout the remainder of this part of the book, the people of France will gradually discover their own land, including real and imaginary domains that would never be charted by historians and administrators. But they should first be pictured in their unhistorical stillness, in the shadows of winter and the silence of towns and fields. Though nothing much will appear to happen in the next few pages, this is still just a brief glimpse of what for many people was half of human existence. The practical problem is that a social history in which the length of chapters matched the amount of time spent on each activity would be intolerably though accurately tedious. Ninety-nine per cent of all human activity described in this and other accounts took place between late spring and early autumn.

*

WHEN STARS AND PLANETS were still a noticeable source of illumination and cloudy, moonless nights were as black as abandoned coal mines, travellers at certain times of the year could take their bearings from fires lit on hilltops. From the Vosges to the Pyrenees and from the English Channel to the Alps, bonfires marked the two big moments of the calendar. In some parts, the fires were lit at Mid-summer and at Christmas, in other parts during Carnival and Lent.

These celebrations of what scholars called the solstice were associated with various magical effects, especially with the fertility of fields, animals and people. They became much less common in the mid- to late-nineteenth century, when they were replaced by fireworks and secular holidays like Bastille Day and the Saint-Napoléon, doused by incredulity, fire regulations and perhaps, above all, by the fact that the year was no longer clearly divided into two.

For the millions of people who danced around the bonfires and scattered the ashes on their fields, the year consisted of twelve months and two seasons. There was the season of labour when even the longest days were too short, and the season of inactivity when time slowed to a crawl and seemed in danger of stopping altogether. As they said in the Alpine Queyras, 'Seven months of winter [November to May], five months of hell [June to October]'. In the eastern Pyrenees, when snow was falling or when the rain had settled in, 'men were as idle as marmots'. (The marmot is the large and floppy mountain rodent that sleeps in a burrow and was harvested rather than hunted, tossed into a rucksack and sometimes boiled while still asleep.) The man who compared his compatriots to marmots was writing in the 1880s, almost a century after the abolition of the monarchy but several decades before technology, in the form of roads, lighting and the amazing luxury of coal and gas heating, had undermined the tyranny of the weather.

The tradition of seasonal sloth was ancient and pervasive. Mountain regions closed down in the late autumn. Entire Pyrenean villages of wood, like Barèges on the western side of the Col du Tourmalet, were abandoned to the snow and reclaimed from the avalanches in late spring. Other populations in the Alps and the Pyrenees simply entombed themselves until March or April, with a hay-loft above, a stable to one side and the mountain slope behind. According to a geographer writing in 1909, 'the inhabitants re-emerge in spring, dishevelled and anaemic'. But hibernation was not peculiar to high altitudes. More temperate regions, too, retreated into a fortress of sleep. Idleness and torpor cast an eerie pall over the well-cultivated parts of the Berry, where seasonal variations are slight and the temperature rarely falls below freezing. George Sand's normally phlegmatic husband felt 'something like fear' when he saw a tidy land that seemed to be farmed by ghosts. The fields of Flanders were deserted for much of the year. An official report on the Nièvre in 1844 described the strange mutation of the Burgundian day-labourer once the harvest was in and the vine stocks had been burned:

> After making the necessary repairs to their tools, these vigorous men will now spend their days in bed, packing their bodies tightly together in order to stay warm and to eat less food. They weaken themselves deliberately.

Human hibernation was a physical and economic necessity. Lowering the metabolic rate prevented hunger from exhausting supplies. In Normandy, according to the diary of Jules Renard, 'the peasant at home moves little more than the sloth' (1889); 'in winter, they pass their lives asleep, corked up like snails' (1908). People trudged and dawdled, even in summer. They ate more slowly than modern people. Life expectancy at birth now seems depressingly low: in 1865, it was a few months over forty years in only twenty *départements*; in Paris and Finistère, it was under thirty; the national average was thirty-seven years two months. Life expectancy at five was fifty-one. Despite this, complaints about the brevity of life are far less common than complaints about its inordinate length. Slowness was not an attempt to savour the moment. A ploughman who took hours to reach a field beyond the town was not necessarily admiring the effect of morning mist on the furrows and the steaming cattle against the rising sun, he was trying to make a small amount of strength last for the working day, like a cartload of manure spread over a large field.

A visitor to a château in the country might see the sun rise earlier over the fields and the leafing of trees and the stirring of animals without noticing much difference in the world of human beings. After the Revolution, in Alsace and the Pas-de-Calais, officials complained that wine-growers and independent farmers, instead of undertaking 'some peaceful and sedentary industry' in the quieter seasons, 'abandon themselves to dumb idleness'. Modern conveniences – in this case, more efficient ploughs – were blamed for turning the stout yeomanry of France into human vegetables. Income actually seemed to act as a deterrent. At Beaucaire on the lower Rhône, the biggest fair in Europe was held every summer from 22 July to 1 August. In those eleven days, the local people made enough money to spend the rest of the year in idleness while their vast, deserted fairground slowly fell to pieces around them: 'For the remaining months, the Beaucairiens smoke, play cards, hunt and sleep.'

These season-long siestas dismayed economists and bureaucrats who looked enviously at the industrial power-house of Britain. They were especially horrified by the troglodytic dwellings that seemed to embody the sleepiness of France. In the Dordogne, the Tarn, the Loire Valley and the limestone and sandstone belt that stretches from the Ardennes to Alsace, thousands of people lived in cliff faces like swallows or in caves and chalk pits like prehistoric tribes. Whole villages of troglodytes lined the banks of the Loire and its tributary the Loir. From Anjou to Poitou, thin columns of smoke rose from the fields like the plumes of Lilliputian volcanoes. Quarries were dug into vineyards and then excavated laterally beneath the vines. Some of these subterranean apartment blocks had several floors and were home to hundreds of people.

In Arras and other towns in Flanders, up to one-third of the population – artisans as well as labourers – lived in underground cities carved into medieval quarries. These *'boves'* (an old French word for 'cavern') were later used as sanctuaries, bomb-shelters, secret routes to the front in the First World War and eventually as candle-lit restaurants and tourist attractions. Little is said or known today about their use as normal residential areas. People whose lives were not divided by the seasons found these living arrangements unproductive and lugubrious:

> The vital air is constantly contaminated by the breath of eight to ten individuals who are piled up there in a tiny dwelling for twelve to fifteen hours a day with only one air-hole between them.

To the writer of this report in 1807, this bleary half-life was a sign of moral deficiency: the artisans of Arras were 'not very enterprising' and the day-labourers were 'apathetic'. But the people who lived safely underground in the sleep-inducing gloom were trying to survive, not to promote economic growth. Many of them could afford to move house, but preferred to stay where the summers were cool and the winters warm. When the workers of Lille were moved by philanthropic reformers from their 'unhygienic' cellars, they found the long trek up six flights of stairs to their attic rooms as depressing as the descent to a dungeon.

*

MEN AND WOMEN who did almost nothing for a large part of the year tend not to figure prominently in history books. Studies and museums naturally highlight enterprise and undervalue the art of remaining idle for months on end. They make those parts of France where winter lasted longest appear to have been impressively busy. In the twenty-first century, 'traditional' low-season industries make a big contribution to many local economies. Handcrafted briar-wood pipes can be bought in the Jura, wooden toys in the Queyras, esparto sandals in the Basque Pyrenees, leather gloves in the Aveyron, knives in the Aubrac and clogs almost everywhere from Brittany to the Vosges.

Some of these industries are practised today with an intensity and expertise that would have amazed the original craftsmen. It is not uncommon to find a flourishing potter or basket-weaver who left a well-paid job in Paris for a troglodyte's cave in the provinces. Many 'lost skills' never existed in the first place and were never the basis of a thriving economy. In most of these regions, only a few people remained busy all year round. In the late 1900s, when Alpine tourists were creating a new market for wooden toys, the Queyras still had just a handful of toy-makers. Most felt safer cocooned in idleness. As the son of a Pyrenean peasant in the 1880s explained, 'They had hardly any spirit of enterprise and were loath to make life more complicated when it was already hard enough to bear.'

Economists who wondered at this waste of human capital ignored the fact that the impetus for trade was not usually a desire to amass wealth. Otherwise, a peasant who spent several days taking a basket of eggs to a distant market and who did not include time in the calculation of profit would have to be seen as a remarkably dull-witted businessman rather than someone who had learned to match his footsteps to the rhythm of life.

Until the late nineteenth century, money itself was scarce in France and little used by people who owned no land and paid no tax. Apart from salt and iron, everything could be paid for in kind, and there was little reason to work more than was strictly necessary. Even though its workers were highly specialized and connected to an international network of buyers and retailers, the cottage clock-making industry in the Rhineland and the Alps was not just a forerunner of full-scale production: creating and tinkering with tiny mechanisms for six or seven months of the year made time pass less slowly. Some men and women simply found clock-making more appealing than endless games of cards. The clocks, moreover, proved that time was indeed passing. It may be no coincidence that some of the main clock-making regions were those where pagan festivals still marked the moment when, after a hundred days of darkness, the sun returned to the deepest valleys.

A sensitive economic barometer might register these activities as contributions to the gross national product, but it would give a false impression of the producers' mentality. In parts of the Auvergne, women got together in the evening, sometimes until after midnight, to sew and knit clothes that they sold to travelling merchants for a pittance. In a technical sense, this was a form of industrial enterprise, but the main reason for the sewing was not to create a surplus. The idea was simply to make enough money to pay for the lamp oil that allowed them to get together in the first place.

Boredom was as powerful a force as economic need. It helps to explain so many aspects of daily life, at all times of the year, that it could form the basis of an academic discipline: cottage industries and hibernation, bizarre beliefs and legends, sexual experiment, local politics, migration and even social aspiration. In small, suspicious communities where neighbour competed with neighbour, boredom was one of the main elements of social cohesion. It brought people together and counteracted the effects of poverty and class rivalry. Even in the insanely energetic universe of Balzac's novels, boredom is one of the great guiding principles of French society, from the gilded tedium of Paris apartments to the cloistral silence of provincial towns:

> Life and movement are so quiet there that a stranger might have
> thought those houses uninhabited had his eyes not suddenly met the

pale, cold expression of a motionless figure whose half-monastic face leaned over the window-sill at the sound of an unknown step.

*

TWO MONTHS BEFORE the fall of the Bastille, in the quiet towns of Balzac's Touraine and in the black basalt hovels where the women of the Auvergne sewed to keep the lamps alight, there was, for once, a new topic of conversation. A rare conjunction of historical time and daily life had occurred. On 5 May 1789, at a meeting of the States-General,* the towns and parishes of France were invited to list their grievances. The very idea that it might be possible to alter the conditions of life was a revolution in itself. For the first time, suffering seemed to have an audience and literacy had a point.

The sixty thousand or so 'Cahiers de Doléances' were, of course, written by literate or semi-literate people, often by the local lawyer. Crudely drafted lists of grievances were passed to larger committees who prepared more politely abstract reports for the States-General. But enough of the humbler Cahiers have survived to construct a detailed panorama of daily life in France.

Most of the Cahiers list the same grievances: taxation, the *corvée* (road-repairing duty), impassable roads and broken bridges, hospitals that no one could reach though they paid for them in taxes, the billeting of troops and their hungry horses, lack of representation and arbitrary or unaffordable justice, ineffective policing, the proliferation of con men, uncertified surgeons and beggars – either local people who were starving to death or aggressive intruders – and, of course, ecclesiastical and seigneurial privilege. Hunting rights were the sorest point: to see a furry feast scampering across a field and to know that catching it might mean death by hanging was more than a hungry peasant could bear. If the local lord spent all his time in a city or was not very keen on hunting, the area might be overrun by deer, boars, hares, rabbits and pigeóns. To many foreign travellers, the character-istic sound of the French Revolution was the constant crepitation of

---

* The États-Généraux: the disjointed predecessor of a national parliament, com-posed of the three 'estates': clergy, nobles and commons.

muskets in the countryside exterminating the animals that had once enjoyed aristocratic immunity.

In the Cahiers that were drafted by small parish committees, one complaint dominates all the others: the pain and botheration of living in the natural world. The desire of most people was not to have their human rights enshrined in a glorious constitution. They wanted freedom from poor soil and bad weather, from gales, hailstorms, fire and flood, from wolves, cold and famine. Many towns and villages described their predicament as though they were island states cut off from the outside world.

> This community is situated in the most atrocious and abominable corner of the world. Its only possessions – if they can be called that – are rugged rocks and mountains that are almost inaccessible.... It is ten mortal hours on foot from the neighbouring towns of Cahors and Figeac. The paths that lead there are impassable on horseback let alone on foot. (Cabrerets, Lot *département*)

> On one side, the deadly winds of north and west lay waste to it by sand and storm from which it has no shelter but the islands of Jersey and Guernsey. On the other side, countless rabbits devour the various products of the soil. The parish is further afflicted by the voracious pigeons of three dove-cotes which seem to band together to devour every kind of seed.... This parish has no woods, next to no plants, no pasture and no trade. (Rozel, Manche *département*)

The man who wrote directly to the King from Catus in the Quercy ('a town of whose very existence, Sire, you are no doubt unaware') suggested, with some justification, that 'to know our little town is to know the province of Quercy and all of France'. In misery, the kingdom was united:

> *If only the King knew!*, we cried a thousand times from the depths of our abyss. Today, the King knows, and Hope, like a healing balm, is already coursing through our veins.... Our only desire is to preserve the bare essentials for our decrepit fathers, our groaning wives and our tender children.

Eight miles from the King's palace at Versailles, in a region where more than half the population owned no land, the parish of Saint-Forget was the twin in misery of Catus. The people were often reduced to 'the most extreme poverty' by a momentary lack of work, a fall of snow, a spell of rain or a few days of illness. They could not afford a schoolteacher and the land lay fallow because farmers were 'discouraged'. In bad years, they starved; in good years, they went hungry because their produce was taxed but could not be transported and sold.

The wealth of evidence in the Cahiers de Doléances is not completely reliable. Some places hoped to avoid tax by depicting their land as an arid desert, a festering flood-plain or a fruitless confusion of rocks and torrents ravaged by weeds and wild animals. If they could prove that the land could not be farmed, it would not be liable to tax. The village of Sexey-les-Bois (Meurthe-et-Moselle) claimed that two-thirds of its inhabitants were widows and that all the able-bodied people, who were taxed at 20 per cent, had 'sold their meagre furniture and gone to live in the woods'. Some villages tried to shift the tax burden onto supposedly more fortunate neighbours. The Cahiers from the Quercy province make it sound as though all the soil of the region around Cahors had long since been washed away. The village of Escamps described its predicament in terms almost identical to those of many other Cahiers:

> Poor old people whom age and the burden of work have robbed of the strength to go running off to beg alms from charitable souls can be seen groaning with hunger. Every day, a multitude of little children can be seen groaning with hunger despite the vigility [sic] of their father and mother. Such is the sorry state of this unhappy community which can be called without the slightest hesitation the most wretched that exists and that ever could have existed.

A slightly callous view of past suffering has emphasized the suspiciously repetitive nature of these Cahiers. Set phrases were suggested by central committees and copied down by local committees. One village found an adequate expression of its suffering and others repeated the impressive details: children eating grass, tears moistening bread, farmers feeling envious of their animals, and so on. But those grass-eating children were clearly not a figure of speech: the harvest of 1788 had been worse than usual, and the Cahiers were drawn up in the dangerously hollow months when last year's supplies were running low and next year's corn had yet to ripen. The relatively prosperous town of Espère obviously had nothing to gain when it applied the phrase to its neighbours:

> We have not yet seen our children munching grass like those of our neighbours, and our old people, happier than many of those in the surrounding region, almost all survived the rigours of last January. Only once did we have the affliction of seeing one of our own people die of hunger.

If some of these accounts sound unconvincing, it is partly because they represent hours of intellectual labour. Their writers were struggling to find the right words, dressing up their misery in stiff, incongruous clothes for a trip to the city. Exaggeration was not a miserly ruse, it was a means of survival. Tax inspectors came to villages with armed dragoons on the lookout for signs of recent income: poultry feathers on a doorstep, a new suit of clothes, fresh repairs to rotting barns and crumbling walls. The collectors themselves were recruited locally and often barely numerate. They could be sent to prison if they failed to collect the prescribed amount.

Even for prosperous peasants, disaster always loomed. Few lives were free from sudden setbacks. Every year, several villages and urban districts went up in smoke. An English traveller, crossing the Jura from Salins to Pontarlier in 1738, was told that 'there is scarce a Village in all this Tract that does not perish by Flames once at least in 10 Years'. Salins itself was almost totally destroyed in 1825 by a fire that burned for three days. The city of Rennes disappeared in 1720 and much of Limoges in 1864. Thatch was cheap (gleaned from harvested fields in October), but it harboured huge populations of insects and caught fire easily unless it was completely covered by a layer of clay, quicklime, horse manure and sand. (In some parts, thatch was outlawed in new buildings in the mid-nineteenth century and replaced by the red corrugated iron that was thought to add a pleasant touch of colour to the landscape.) Many people burned to death in their homes or were killed when their house suddenly fell on them. The spontaneous combustion of dung heaps and haystacks was a surprisingly common cause of destitution and was often blamed on jealous neighbours and pyromaniac witches.

Frosts, floods and livestock disease were the most frequent calamities after fire, but the greatest natural disasters were caused by hail. A ten-minute hailstorm could wipe out the work of a generation, demolishing roofs, stripping trees, flattening crops and covering the ground with a carpet of twigs, leaves and small dead birds. In 1789, the town of Pompey near Nancy was still recovering from the effects of a hailstorm that had decimated its harvest twelve years before. In 1900, forty years after a hailstorm swept through a valley in the Bourbonnais, some houses still had roofs that were half tile and half slate, because the local supply of tiles had been exhausted. Failure to prevent hailstorms was, understandably, one of the commonest causes of disenchantment with the local priest (see p. 127). More progressive towns and villages relied on the dubious effects of 'anti-hail' cannon, which were fired at the sky when dark battalions of storm clouds massed above the fields.

These disasters affected all but a tiny minority of people. In a land of small, vulnerable *pays*, the section of the population comfortably referred to as 'the poor' could suddenly swell to enormous proportions. At the time of the Revolution, almost half the population of France could be described as poor or indigent. Depending on the region, between half and nine-tenths of families were unable to support themselves with the land they owned and were forced to sell their labour or fall into the stairless pit of debt. Hippolyte Taine's image of the common people in his *Origins of Contemporary France* (1879) might seem melodramatic when compared to the steady march of economic progress, but it matches the simple evidence of daily life in every part of France:

> The people are like a man walking through a pond with water up to his chin. At the slightest dip in the ground, at the merest ripple, he loses his footing, sinks and suffocates. Old-fashioned charity and new-fangled humanity try to help him out, but the water is too high. Until the level falls and the pond finds an outlet, the wretched man can only snatch an occasional gulp of air and at every instant he runs the risk of drowning.

Taine's alarming picture of a population sinking into destitution referred to the late eighteenth century but it could just as well have referred to much later periods.

*

EVEN IF THEY WERE enterprising and intelligent and managed to acquire an education, and even if they were born in the more buoyant nineteenth century, life for most people was a game of snakes-and-ladders with very short ladders and very long snakes. The Breton peasant Jean-Marie Déguignet (1834–1905) wrote his memoirs because he had never read about anyone like himself, except in novels. In the Quimper public library, he saw a tiny part of French life brilliantly illuminated by a handful of egos while the mass of humanity was left in the dark. The bare facts of his own life are refreshingly unremarkable:

1834, July. Born at Guengat in Lower Brittany. Poor harvests and sick livestock force his father, a tenant farmer, to leave for the city.

1834, September. At the age of two months, moves to Quimper with some planks and straw, a cracked cauldron, eight bowls and eight wooden spoons. His earliest memory: watching his mother pluck fleas from his dead sister's head.

1840. Lives in the village of Ergué-Gabéric. Is kicked in the head by a horse and badly disfigured. For several years, suffers from a repulsive suppuration.

1843–44. Is taught to read Breton by an old seamstress and learns the 'noble profession' of begging.

1848–54. Works as a cowherd, as a field-hand on a government-sponsored model farm and as a servant to the Mayor of Kerfeunteun, a suburb of Quimper. Learns to read the newspaper in French.

1854–68. After enlisting in the army, serves in the Crimea, Algeria and Mexico.

1868–79. Returns to Brittany, marries a young girl and rents some land from the owner of the château at Toulven. Despite opposition to his 'new-fangled' farming techniques (draining the barnyard and disinfecting the house, subscribing to an agricultural journal and ignoring the phases of the moon and his mother-in-law's advice), he creates a highly successful farm.

1879. The farmhouse burns down, and the landowner refuses to renew the lease. 'Another fifteen years of my life wasted. After working so hard to improve that farm, now I had to leave it.'

1880–82. Crushed by a cart and left half-crippled, he finds work as a fire-insurance salesman. His alcoholic wife is sent to the asylum.

1883–92. Obtains a licence to sell tobacco in Pluguffan near Quimper. Rents a field and begins to rebuild his fortune. He supports himself and his three children.

1892–1902. Forced to sell his tobacco shop and disowned by his children, he lives in slums and garrets, becomes progressively poorer and writes his memoirs 'when the weather permits'.

1902. Evicted from his rented 'hole' because of complaints about the filth. Suffers from paranoid delusions and attempts suicide. Committed to the mental hospital at Quimper. Dies at the age of seventy-one in 1905.

As a literate, atheist Breton peasant with a passion for agricultural innovation, Déguignet was not entirely typical, but the world that wore him down was familiar to thousands of people: the precariousness of hard-won fortune and the weakness of family ties in the face of hardship. The modern edition of Déguignet's memoirs appeals to a muddled sense of rustic nostalgia and suggests that the subject of the book is 'The Waning of Rural France'. It describes him as a witness to 'the start of the breakdown of traditional Breton society'. In fact, his memoirs describe the exact opposite. The society into which he was born was always on the verge of collapse – not just because of war or anarchy but also because of hunger, disease, bad weather, bad luck, ignorance and migration. Poverty pushed his family onto the road; fear and envy turned his neighbours into enemies; fire and feudal privilege destroyed his livelihood.

There is something beautifully appropriate in Déguignet's circular career. The boy who began his professional life as a beggar and ended it as an insurance salesman is a better symbol of his age than all the famous parvenus who left their place of birth and returned – if they returned at all – decades later, as a bust in the town hall or a statue in the square. As a beggar boy, Déguignet worked for a single mistress, lived from day to day and exploited the superstitions of his clients: they gave him the customary measure of oats or buckwheat flour because 'they were convinced that they would get it back a hundredfold', not in heaven, but quite literally, in the next few weeks or months. As a fire-insurance salesman, he worked for a company with offices in a city, followed set procedures and exploited his clients' rational fears.

It was thanks to innovations like insurance that families were able to plan for the future and to treat the next generation as something more precious than a source of cheap labour. In 'traditional' society, fairy tales presented child labour as something normal and necessary. In 'The Three Spinners', a father quite rightly decides to get rid of his daughter because 'she ate [crêpes] but did no work'. Tearful tales of devoted children and family reunions were popular with bourgeois readers because they reflected aspirations, not because they were true to life. In Burgundy, until the eve of the First World War, relations between parents and children were distinctly unsentimental, according to a local historian: 'The son was usually treated as a servant, minus the wages.' Until the Second World War, peasant photograph albums almost never contained pictures of children.

Déguignet was fortunate in having parents who wanted to keep him. Thousands of children – like Tom Thumb in the French fairy tale – were abandoned every year. At Provins, between 1854 and 1859, 1,258 children were deposited in the rotating barrel built into the wall of the general hospital. (It can now be seen in the local museum.) These *tours d'abandon*, which contained a straw bed and some blankets, made it possible for mothers to abandon their babies anonymously and safely. They were outlawed as a public disgrace in 1861, which simply meant that more babies than before were left to die on doorsteps. In 1869, over 7 per cent of births in France were illegitimate, and one-third of those children were abandoned. Each year, fifty thousand human beings started life in France without a parent. Many were sent to the enterprising women known as 'angel-makers' who performed what can most kindly be described as post-natal abortions. A report on the hospice at Rennes defined them as 'women who have no milk and who – doubtless for a fee – feloniously take care of several children at the same time. The children perish almost immediately.'

Before 1779, the nuns who ran the foundling hospital in Paris were obliged by law to take the infant overflow from the provinces. This emergency regulation produced one of the strangest sights on the main roads of France. Long-distance donkeys carrying panniers stuffed with babies came to the capital from as far away as Brittany, Lorraine and the Auvergne. The carters set out on their two-hundred-and-fifty-mile journeys with four or five babies to a basket, but in towns and villages along the route they struck deals with midwives and parents. For a small fee, they would push in a few extra babies. To make the load more tractable and easier on the ears, the babies were given wine instead of milk. Those that died were dumped at the roadside like rotten apples. In Paris, the carters were paid by the head and evidently delivered enough to make it worth their while. But for every ten living babies that reached the capital, only one survived more than three days.

These tiny, drunken creatures made epic journeys that dwarfed the journeys of most adults. The part they played in the history of France is microscopic and immense. Some of the few that survived would have joined the army of vagrants and labourers that eventually swelled the suburbs of industrial cities and helped to fuel a more stable French economy. Life for these landless servants of industry would be even more precarious than it had been for their parents in the fields.

6

Living in France, II: A Simple Life

THE FEW TRAVELLERS who explored this suffering land of fragmented village states inevitably came to wonder how the geographical entity known as France could function as a political and economic unit. Perhaps, after all, things were not as bad as they seemed? As French historians have been pointing out ever since the English farmer Arthur Young made his agricultural tours of France in 1787, 1788 and 1789, not everyone was drowning in poverty. Not all French towns were full of 'crooked, dirty, stinking streets' (Brive) and 'excrementitious lanes' (Clermont-Ferrand). Some of them, as Young observed, had 'foot-pavements' or *trottoirs* (Dijon and Tours). Not every tavern toilet was a 'temple of abomination' and not every serving-girl a 'walking dung-hill'. Sometimes the traveller was spared the agony of eating his meal on a straight-backed, straw-bottomed chair, and sometimes a glimpse of the greasy, dog-fouled kitchen did not instantly remove his appetite. Many rural houses had windows, quite a few peasants wore shoes and stockings, and if the women of Languedoc went barefoot, at least they had the 'superb consolation' of walking on magnificent new roads.

The lasting value of Arthur Young's accounts, which were translated into French and widely read, lay in the fact that he confronted his agronomic theories with the evidence of his senses. The discovery of France by educated people made it possible to place the fragile existence of the majority in a wider picture, though the colour of individual lives was often lost in the landscape of economic abstraction. Those 'walking dung-hills' were, after all, human beings. They lived by the habits and beliefs of a particular society which had, however implausibly, survived for centuries. This society may not have matched the aspirations and convictions of middle-class observers, but it had a logic and efficiency of its own. The population of France was never a shapeless mass of human raw material, waiting to be processed by the huge, mutating machine of political interference and turned into the people conveniently known as 'the French'.

*

IT WAS UNFORTUNATE for his reputation in France that Arthur Young happened to choose the Château de Combourg in Brittany as a prime example of ignorance and waste. He could not have known that the boy who grew up in the castle towers would become one of France's greatest Romantic writers, François-René de Chateaubriand:

> SEPTEMBER 1 [1788]. To Combourg. The country has a savage aspect; husbandry not much further advanced, at least in skill, than among the Hurons, which appears incredible amidst enclosures; the people almost as wild as their country, and their town of Combourg one of the most brutal filthy places that can be seen; mud houses, no windows, and a pavement so broken as to impede all passengers, but ease none – yet here is a chateau, and inhabited; who is this Monsieur de Chateaubriant, the owner, that has nerves strung for a residence amidst such filth and poverty?

Years later, Chateaubriand commented on this passage in his memoirs: 'This M. de Chateaubriand was my father. The retreat that seemed so hideous to the ill-tempered agronomist was a fine and noble dwelling, albeit dark and solemn.' He said nothing, however, about Young's description of the town.

This was not just a matter of personal pride. The underlying problem was that France, like other countries, came to be judged by the degree to which it met the standards of the middle class. It was as if the nation could have no adult identity until it cleaned its streets and citizens and enjoyed the benefits of international trade. Until then, the masses would be more vegetable than human:

> Each family is almost self-sufficient, producing on its own plot of land the greater part of its requirements, and thus providing itself with the necessaries of life through an interchange with nature rather than by

means of intercourse with society. [. . .] The great mass of the French nation is formed by the simple addition of like entities, much as a sack of potatoes consists of a lot of potatoes huddled into a sack.
(Karl Marx, *The Eighteenth Brumaire of Louis-Napoléon*)

Arthur Young was a perceptive man with good, practical knowledge of his subject. On the castle lawn at Nangis, he showed the Marquis de Guerchy how to make a proper haystack. His faults were those of most observers, both French and foreign, who mistook the obscure logic of daily life for ignorance and exaggerated the plight of the common people in order to show how much they had to gain from civilization. They observed, without always knowing what they saw.

Wealthy men from northern cities pitied the half of France where the prehistoric plough was little better than a hoe – but indispensable on thin and rocky ground. They pitied the huddled masses whose windows were holes in the wall or panes of oil-soaked paper – though many in the warmer south felt no need of glass and spared themselves the cost of window tax and wafery panes that were shattered by wind and hail. They patronized the toothless, stunted peasants of the 'Chestnut Belt' who preferred the meaty fruit of their useful forests to the tasteless, warty potato, and who lived in smoky hovels, cheek by jowl with livestock – who provided them with companionship and warmth. They felt a sense of patriotic shame when they saw their compatriots carrying their shoes on a string around their neck on the way to church or market, and ploughmen who preferred the supple leather of bare feet to the abrasive weight of a mud-caked clog.

This was simplicity rather than deprivation, and even a kind of inoculation against true poverty. Most people lived in prudent anticipation of misfortune. Sayings of the 'knowing my luck' variety warned against the folly of trying too hard and expecting too much:

'No fine day without a cloud.'
'If the he-wolf doesn't get you, the she-wolf will.'
'Weeds never die.'
(Vosges)

'Illness comes on horseback and leaves on foot.'
(Flanders)

'Poor people's bread always burns in the oven.'
'When you've made a good soup, the Devil comes and shits in it.'
(Franche-Comté)

'If only God was a decent man.'
(Auvergne)

Compared to the moral marquetry of Parisian epigrammatists, these proverbs are rough-hewn blocks, but they express the experience of a whole nation, not just the neuroses of a tiny elite. Even the elite was not immune from the Devil's tricks. Two years after Arthur Young's last tour of France, one summer night in 1791, a large green coach trundled out of Paris by the eastern gate. It was carrying a valet who called himself M. Durand, some women and children and an extraordinary amount of luggage. After a night and a day, it reached the little town of Sainte-Menehould on the edge of the Argonne forest. While the horses were being changed, the postmaster's son peered through the window at the occupants of the carriage. Then he looked at the coin in his hand and recognized the face. Twenty miles further on, at Varennes, the coach was stopped and the royal family was escorted back to Paris.

The meteoric fall of King Louis XVI and Marie-Antoinette came to be seen as a horrible exception in French history. Their little son, the Dauphin, was imprisoned in the Temple in Paris, mistreated by his jailers and died in wretched obscurity. Yet the tale of his martyrdom became a national myth, not because it was so out of the ordinary but because it expressed a common fear and a common reality. Anyone, even a royal prince, could be reduced to prison rations and wiped from the face of the earth.

*

As LONG AS HISTORIANS were unwilling to sacrifice the grand view from Paris for the humbler horizons of their native town or village, the mystery would remain unsolved and, for that matter, unnoticed: how, in these conditions, did a society that was recognizably French survive and, eventually, prosper? Perhaps the question should have been: did it survive, or is the continuity of French society – rather than Breton, Burgundian, Mediterranean or Alpine society – a historical illusion?

Even ignoring the tribal loyalties of the population, their different languages and the continental size of the land, the political basis of the union was remarkably fragile. Civil order broke down altogether in the west of France during the Revolution, in parts of Provence during the 1832–35 cholera epidemic and in Paris itself at almost regular intervals. Lyon rebelled in 1831 and 1834 and had to be subdued by government troops. In 1841, a census created rumours that everything from furniture to unborn babies was to be taxed. Riots ensued, and for several weeks large parts of the country from Lille to Toulouse were out of control. In 1871, Paris became a separate people's republic and the country was governed from Bordeaux while seven other cities declared their independence.

The Revolution itself was not a storm that came and went but an earthquake that followed long-established fault-lines. In 1793, when the nation was in danger of collapsing into anarchy, the cities of Arras, Brest, Lyon, Marseille and Nantes had to be recaptured by the republican army and were treated as rebel colonies:

DECREE OF THE NATIONAL CONVENTION
[Paris, 12 October 1793]

The city of Lyon shall be destroyed. . . .

. . . The collection of dwellings remaining in existence shall henceforth be called Ville-Affranchie [Freed-Town].

There shall be erected above the ruins of Lyon a column announcing to posterity the crime and punishment of that city and bearing the inscription,

'Lyon made war on liberty. Lyon no longer exists.'

The nation's most successful foreign ruler, Napoleon Bonaparte, did not see 'France' as a foregone conclusion. When he crossed the country as a prisoner of the Allies in 1814, he was cheered as far as Nevers, booed at Moulins, cheered again at Lyon and almost lynched in Provence, where he disguised himself as an English lord and then as an Austrian officer. In Napoleon's view, the restored king, Louis XVIII, should rule the country as a conquering despot, 'or he'll never be able to do anything with it'. Something called French society might have existed, but its features are hard to distinguish in the history of the state.

A more convincing definition of French identity might be found by settling in a French town or village when it comes to life again in spring, watching the comings and goings of the people and listening to their conversations.

At first, the process of selecting a particular place would only emphasize the confusion. Rural France can be divided roughly into three zones: the open-field country of the north and north-west where cultivated strips of land radiate from the compact village; the patchwork bocage of the west and centre, where the fields are enclosed by hedges and paths; and the stony tracts and sparse settlements of the south and south-east. But within each zone, there are many different shapes of town and village. It might be a wine-growing town like Riquewihr in Alsace, walled in by its vineyards and hoarding shade for its cellars; a Provençal village like Bédoin, curled up like an ear against the shock-wave of the mistral; or a 'street village' like Aliermont, whose houses line the former main road from Neufchâtel to Dieppe for ten miles to catch the passing trade like fishermen on a riverbank. If the settler had time to become acquainted with the peculiar geometry of the place, he might choose one of the silent outposts of the Beauce, a patch of brown roof tiles in the plain, where farmyards alternate with houses and sudden glimpses of vast fields beyond; or even one of the scattered colonies of the Forez and the eastern Auvergne, where the separate parts of the village seem to have sprouted in ancient forest clearings and are still more closely tied to the field at the door than to the arbitrary church and indifferent town hall.

These various types of settlement imply different, but not profoundly different, ways of life. All are moulded by the immediate countryside and only marginally by their nearest trading partners. Many still have a defensive air, though their sphere of activity now extends far beyond what were once the concentric rings of the customs barriers, the perimeter zone of gardens and cornfields and the forested horizon. Today, the only traces of defence, apart from restored town gates and fortifications, are barking dogs, speed-bumps and signs asking drivers not to kill the local children. Nearly all these places have become porous and suburban. Between seven and nine o'clock, Aliermont is emptied out by Dieppe and the local engineering factory; the tourist 'Route des Vins' on which Riquewihr stands is thick with traffic bound for Colmar and Mulhouse; Bédoin's schoolchildren migrate for the day to Carpentras on a high-speed coach that tears along the back roads. Two centuries ago, most of the traffic came from the other direction, on market days, with tiny loads of vegetables or fuel, an animal to sell and a thirst for news and gossip. The morning rush-hour began before dawn. At Mars-la-Tour, on the road to Metz, Arthur Young heard the village herdsman sound his horn at four in the morning, 'and it was droll to see every door vomiting out its hogs or sheep, and some a few goats, the flock collecting as it advances'.

Whenever he saw the swarms of market-goers entering a town with their 'trifling burthens' – a basket of apples, a tray of grubby cheeses or a lone cabbage – Arthur Young knew that he was looking at the effects of the national disease: 'a minute and vicious division of the soil'. Yet this fragmentation of the land was also its unifying feature. Even after the Revolution had taught these tiny worlds that they belonged to the same fatherland, this 'vicious division of the soil' might prove to be their salvation.

*

PERHAPS THE BEST PLACE in which to observe the effects of fragmentation – because the creator of the place intended it to be typical – would be a small market town on the eastern borders of Normandy. Yonville-l'Abbaye, in Gustave Flaubert's novel of 'provincial life', *Madame Bovary*, lies along its little river 'like a cowherd taking a siesta'. It has a tiny conurbation of thatched cottages and courtyards cluttered with cider presses, cart sheds and straggly fruit trees. The town centre has a smithy, a wheelwright's workshop, a white house with a circle of lawn ('this is the notary's house, the finest in the *pays*'), a musty church, a town hall 'designed by a Paris architect', a tiled roof on pillars that serves as a market hall, the Golden Lion inn and a few shops. The draper and the chemist have pretensions to elegance; the other businesses are probably little more than workshops and doorsteps.

The new doctor lives in 'one of the most comfortable houses in Yonville': it has its own wash-house, a kitchen with a pantry, a sitting room, an apple loft and an arbour at the foot of the garden. The person who designed this remarkable residence was a Polish doctor with 'extravagant' ideas who ran away and was never seen again. The new doctor's wife, Emma Bovary, is the granddaughter of a shepherd and the daughter of a farmer, but her convent education has given her ideas above her station and she finds the house small and depressing.

Since 1835, Yonville has been joined to the outside world by a road. Carters who ply the route from the port of Rouen to Flanders sometimes use it as a short cut. There is even a daily coach to Rouen – a 'yellow trunk' slung on huge wheels that spoil the view and spatter the passengers with mud. The driver of 'L'Hirondelle' ('The Swallow') supplements his wages by running a rudimentary freight service from the city: he brings rolls of leather for the cobbler, hats for the draper, iron for the blacksmith and herrings for his mistress. Despite these signs of progress, the town is still a willing prisoner of its setting. It lies between arable land and pasture,

> [but] instead of improving the ploughland, they cling to the pasture, however depreciated its value, and the lazy little town has turned its back on the plain and continued its natural growth towards the river.

A progressive bourgeois like the town chemist, M. Homais, who is not directly dependent on the land, can afford to revel in the stupidity of peasants: 'Would to heaven our farmers were trained chemists or at least lent a more attentive ear to the counsels of science!' But improving land is expensive and animals are a comfort. A peasant might invest in fertilizer and increase the yield of grain, but why should she risk her livelihood in a volatile market? Grain prices are even less reliable than the weather. A pig in the paddock is worth more than the promise of a merchant in the city.

Only people who have more than one source of food would use the expression 'stuck in their ways' as an insult. The smallholders of Yonville had good reason to be cautious. At about the time when the novel takes place, in the little market town of Ry, which Flaubert appears to have used as a model for Yonville-l'Abbaye, a woman complained to the authorities that she and her children were starving to death.

If Yonville or Ry had been better connected to the city of Rouen, which in turn was connected by the river Seine to Paris and the Channel ports, they would have suffered more from shortages and unrest. In troubled times, towns and villages that lay within the supply zone of cities were sucked dry by military commissioners and the civilian population. Agricultural progress might create a surplus and encourage investment, but it could also create excessive demand and a transport network that could quickly pump out the region's produce. Wheat growers and wine growers were more worldly but also more vulnerable to change. In the poorer parts of southern France, where the staple crop, the chestnut, was expensive to transport and not much in demand, winter supplies remained safely in the region. Townships in isolated areas like the Gâtine in Poitou were not as idiotic as they seemed to government officials when they came to rebuild their infrastructure after the Revolution and found that, 'as soon as a *bourgade* [a large village] and even a town felt itself under threat, it destroyed all its bridges'.

Until the advent of the railways, economic isolation was both a weakness and a strength. The fragmented, tribal state of the country allowed it to survive its partial, periodic disintegration. Flaubert himself lived in a grand house in Croisset by the banks of the Seine, three miles downstream from Rouen. Croisset lay on one of the major highways of European history. It had seen Christian missionaries, Viking invaders and Norman pirates. It saw the ship that returned Napoleon's ashes to France in 1840. From his riverside pavilion, Flaubert could watch tourist boats on the Seine and the steamships and barges bound for Paris and Le Havre. And one day in the winter of 1870, he saw 'the spike of a Prussian helmet glittering in the sun on the towpath at Croisset'. For a month and a half, Prussian soldiers occupied his house, drank his wine and read his books. For Flaubert, the Franco-Prussian War was a personal and financial disaster. He ended his life almost bankrupt, having lent most of his inheritance to the husband of his niece, a Rouen timber importer whose business suffered badly from the war.

Meanwhile, in the little town of Ry, life went on much the same as before. By the time Flaubert's home was invaded by Prussians, Ry had a post office, a small cotton mill and a *bureau de bienfaisance* for distributing alms to the poor. It even had a 'Rural Institution', founded by the local chemist, M. Jouanne, where local children were taught the rudiments of agriculture: 'The man of the fields knows nothing of the composition of fertilizer', declared M. Jouanne in a progressive social science journal. 'The most elementary notions of agricultural physics and chemistry are completely foreign to him.' But progress would leave the little town in peace. There would always be people like the old peasant woman in *Madame Bovary* who could look back on more than half a century's service on the same farm and whose idea of a wise investment was giving money to the curé to say masses for her soul.

*

NOW THAT MANY small communities are trying to protect themselves from the effects of global trade and economic migration, there is nothing obviously implausible about the idea that France was held together by the ant-like activity of smallholders rather than by the grand schemes of Napoleon Bonaparte, Napoleon III or François Mitterrand. Long before the lofty reclamation projects of the Second Empire (p. 268), the land was being cleared and colonized, step by step, by the majority of the population who lived as farmers, share-croppers, hired hands and gleaners.

The millions of people who seemed so stubbornly inefficient to administrators were engaged in the mysterious activity known as 'muddling through'. The closest economic term is probably 'cross-subsidizing'. Few people, apart from blacksmiths, could earn a living from just one trade. A farmer might own a plot of land but also work as a day-labourer for someone else. A wine grower might also be a weaver. In the Alps, a single peasant, working on small plots at different altitudes at different times of year, could be a market gardener, a fruit farmer, a wine grower, a sheep farmer, a timber merchant and a dealer in hides and horns. Shepherds and shepherd-esses had time for all sorts of other industries: making cheese (as some still do), weaving straw hats, knitting clothes, carving wood, hunting, smuggling, dog-breeding, searching for precious stones, serving as a guide to soldiers, explorers and tourists, making up songs and stories, playing musical instruments (which 'amuses the sheep and keeps away the wolves') and, like Joan of Arc and Bernadette of Lourdes, acting as messengers between this world and the next.

Every town and village was a living encyclopedia of crafts and trades. In 1886, most of the eight hundred and twenty-four inhabitants of the little town of Saint-Étienne-d'Orthe, on a low hill near the river Adour, were farmers and their dependents. Of the active population of two hundred and eleven, sixty-two had another trade: there were thirty-three seamstresses and weavers, six carpenters, five fishermen, four innkeepers, three cobblers, two shepherds, two blacksmiths, two millers, two masons, one baker, one *rempailleur* (upholsterer or chair-bottomer) and one witch (potentially useful in the absence of a doctor), but no butcher and no storekeeper other than two grocers. In addition to the local industries and the services provided by itinerant traders (see p. 146), most places also had snake collectors, rat catchers with trained ferrets and mole catchers who either set traps or lay in wait with a spade. There were *rebilhous*, who called out the hours of the night, 'cinderellas', who collected and sold ashes used for laundering clothes, men called *tétaires*, who performed the function of a breast-pump by sucking mothers' breasts to start the flow of milk, and all the other specialists that the census listed under 'trades unknown' and 'without trade', which usually meant gypsies, prostitutes and beggars.

As the Breton peasant Déguignet discovered to other people's cost, begging was a profession in its own right. Beggar women sold their silence to respectable people by making lewd and compromising remarks about them in the street. They borrowed children who were diseased or deformed. They manufactured realistic sores from egg yolk and dried blood, working the yolk into a scratch to produce the full crusty effect. A judge at Rennes in 1787 reported 'a bogus old man with a fake hump and a club foot, another man who succeeded in blacking out one eye to give a terrible, dramatic impression of blindness, and yet another who could mimic all the symptoms of epilepsy. 'Idle beggar' was a contradiction in terms. As Déguignet insisted in his memoirs, it was no simple task to hide behind a hedgerow and to fabricate a stump or 'a hideously swollen leg covered with rotten flesh'.

These rustic trades were also found in cities. In the 1850s, one of the first amateur anthropologists of Paris, the Caribbean writer Privat d'Anglemont, set out to explain how seventy thousand Parisians began the day without knowing how they would survive 'and yet somehow end up managing to eat, more or less'. The result was a valuable compendium of little-known trades. He found a man who bred maggots for anglers by collecting dead cats and dogs in his attic, women who worked as human alarm clocks (a speedy woman in a densely populated *quartier* could serve up to twenty clients), 'guardian angels' who were paid by restaurants to guide their drunken clients home, a former bear-hunter from the Pyrenees who exterminated cats, and a goatherd from the Limousin who kept a herd of goats on the fifth floor of a tenement in the Latin Quarter.

Once people were asked to define their profession on a birth certificate or a census form, they began to look like members of an organized, efficient population, highly specialized and distributing their efforts according to need. But this would have implied a degree of economic cohesion that barely existed before the First World War. The proliferation of trades could indicate a thriving market town, but it could also indicate a need to produce everything locally and an inability to pay tax except by selling manufactured goods. Large-scale industry was confined to a few regions and coal-blackened valleys (see p. 265). Until the late nineteenth century, French travellers who saw the hellish industrial conurbations of Britain felt that they were travelling on a different planet. Most factories in mid-nineteenth-century France were run by families, most ironworks were located in villages, and most textile manufacture was manual. Even in the 1860s, craftsmen outnumbered factory workers by about three to one.

The truth is more chaotic than the census forms suggest. 'Muddling through' involved a great deal of bungling, improvisation, bluffing and deceit. A history teacher who explored his own *département*, the Aveyron, in 1799, found that the art of the potter was still 'in its infancy'. People wove cloth but could barely be described as weavers. Builders were jacks-of-all-trades who were good at nothing. There were carpenters who had never seen a rasp or a mortise chisel, black-smiths who hobbled mules with heavy shoes and who tried to mend clocks, shepherds who marked their sheep with indelible tar, and cooks whose only recipe was salt, spices and as much meat as possible.

These trades, like most farm labours, were not practised at the rhythm of a production line. Deadlines were imposed by daylight and the seasons. At harvest time, a field hand might work for fifteen hours a day, but eight hours or less at other times. In the Indre, during the growing season, the fields were busy from six in the morning until seven at night, but empty for three hours in the middle of the day. Siestas were not peculiar to the sunny south. Relentless hard work was rare and, for most people, to judge by their diets (see p. 297), physically impossible.

A calendar of weeks, months and years was not a prison wall with tiny windows of relief. Farm work usually took up no more than two hundred days a year. Factory workers rarely worked more than two hundred and sixty days. A typical year included several religious holidays (Holy Week, Easter Week, Midsummer Day, All Saints' Day, Christmas, New Year and three days of carnival), an annual pilgrimage-picnic, the local saint's 'day', which could last for several days, the saint's day of the neighbouring village, markets and fairs about once a week and a dozen or so family get-togethers. In most parts of France, according to superstition, Friday was the day when it was safer to do nothing: starting the harvest or a new building, doing business, sowing seed, slaughtering a pig, adding a new animal to the herd, cleaning a stable, digging a grave, changing sheets, washing clothes, baking, leaving on a journey, laughing or giving birth – doing any of these on a Friday was asking for trouble. The shirt that was laundered on a Friday would become a shroud. Sunday, of course, was a day of complete rest. If a man went fishing on a Sunday, his children might be born with the heads of fish.

A rhyme heard at Matignon in Brittany suggests that, with the right combination of excuses and at the right time of year, the entire working week could vanish like a thief:

Lundi et mardi, fête;	Monday, Tuesday: holiday;
Mercredi, je n'pourrai y être;	Wednesday, I can't be there;
Jeudi, l'jour Saint-Thomas;	Thursday is St Thomas' day;
Vendredi, je n'y serai pas;	Friday too I'll stay away;
Samedi, la foire à Plénée:	Saturday is the Plénée fair,
Et v'là toute ma pauv' semaine passée!	And that's the whole week gone!

*

To the inhabitants of a particular *pays*, much of this book would have sounded like a history of the world in which their village happened to make a fleeting appearance. But if an inhabitant of the twenty-first century were deposited in a certain *pays* at a particular time before the First World War, he might experience the same disorientation.

A modern traveller who sat down to rest on the edge of a field and woke up two hundred years ago would see a very similar landscape, apparently suffering from long neglect. The crops would be shorter, cluttered with stubble and weeds, and busy with birds and insects. The road would be a rutted track between ditches, roughly aimed at the nearest steeple but hard to distinguish from all the other tracks that wandered across the fields. There would be fewer tidy parallelograms of forest and a more chaotic arrangement of hedges, ponds and hamlets. The scene might suggest a housekeeper's attention to small spaces and a greater vulnerability to the elements. Without the large-scale geometry of water towers, silos, power lines and vapour trails, human habitation would seem to cower in the landscape.

The lone tractor would be replaced by earth-coloured figures working at the rhythm of a herd. On closer inspection, the human machines would seem to be in a poor state of repair. Guessing their age would be impossible. In the mid-nineteenth century, over a quarter of the young men who stood naked in front of military recruitment boards were found to be unfit for service because of 'infirmity', which included 'weak constitution', a useless or missing limb, partial blindness and eye disease, hernias and genital complaints, deafness, goitre, scrofula and respiratory and chest complaints. In a typical contingent of two hundred and thirty thousand, about one thousand were found to be mentally defective or insane, two thousand were hunchbacks and almost three thousand had bow legs or club feet. A further 5 per cent were too short (under five feet), and about 4 per cent suffered from unspecified complaints which probably included dysentery and virulent infestations of lice. For obvious reasons, people suffering from infectious diseases were not examined and do not appear in the figures.

This was the healthiest section of the population – young men in their early twenties. The physical condition of everyone else might give the traveller serious doubts about information culled from books, museums and paintings – even if the painters belonged to the Realist school. Jean-François Millet's 'Sower' is an Olympian athlete and his 'Man with a Hoe', slumped over his tool, is tired rather than incapacitated. Jules Breton's working women all have well-turned ankles, shapely breasts and laundered skirts. Gustave Courbet's beautifully tattered 'Stone-Breakers' have not been blinded by chips of stone, their joints have survived the hours of jarring blows and they work in a dust-free environment. Painted peasants are nearly always up to the task. There are no crippled ploughmen, no puny blacksmiths and no myopic seamstresses. Naturally, the stench of sweat and wet wool, of cheese and rotting cabbage, is also missing, as is the whole topography of fresh and fetid odours that allowed a blind man to find his way to the nearest village and to know when he wandered from his *pays*.

At first sight, the figures in the field are more impressive than the figures in the paintings. They have hips that can push against the haunches of a cow, and arms and neck muscles that can carry seventy or eighty pounds. (In the Alps, it was said that two women could carry the load of one mule.) But their sturdiness is deceptive. This is strength born of habit and the repetition of a small number of gestures. The faces tell a different tale. If one of the living figures turned around, the traveller might find himself looking at what Lieutenant-Colonel Pinkney unkindly called 'a Venus with the face of an old monkey'.

To judge by the reactions of contemporary travellers, the biggest surprise would be the preponderance of women in the fields. Until the mid- to late-nineteenth century, almost everywhere in France, apart from the Provençal coast (but not the hinterland), the north-east and a narrow region from Poitou to Burgundy, at least half the people working in the open air were women. In many parts, women appeared to do the lion's share of the work.

This simple fact was soon erased from histories of France by writers who either never saw the countryside or thought it futile to make distinctions between the potatoes in a sack (p. 91). From the Loire Valley to the Alps and Corsica, women ploughed, sowed, reaped, winnowed, threshed, gleaned and gathered firewood, tended the animals, baked bread, fed it to the men and children, kept house ('badly', according to a report on southern Normandy in 1802) and gave birth to more hungry mouths. Housekeeping was the least of their labours. Significantly, it was mainly in Provence, where a greater number of women worked as housewives, that houses were haunted by nimble spirits that did the washing up, made the beds and emptied the chamber pots.* The spirit world left outdoor work to humans. All along the Atlantic coast, women were seen ploughing the fields, slaughtering animals and sawing wood while the men stretched out on piles of heather in the sun. In the Auvergne, in order to clear the snow, milk the cows, feed the pig, fetch the water, make the cheese, peel and boil the chestnuts and spin the cloth, women rose earlier and went to bed later than men.

Some tasks, like fetching water, were considered exclusively female. Very little was considered exclusively male. At Granville on the Cotentin peninsula, women fished, repaired boats and worked as stevedores and carpenters. In the Alps, they were yoked to asses and hitched to ploughs, and sometimes lent to other farmers. Before the snow had melted, they could be seen scattering black earth on the snow to hasten the thaw, and lugging baskets of soil up to fields so steep that the animals sometimes toppled over in a strong wind.

The report on southern Normandy cruelly suggested that women were treated as beasts of burden because hard work had robbed them of their beauty: a sun-baked, arthritic creature was hardly an ornament and might as well be put to work. In parts like the southern Auvergne, where society was patriarchal, women seemed to belong to a different caste. Tribal justice has left little trace in official records, but anecdotal evidence suggests that a woman born in the Velay, the Vivarais or the Gévaudan was more likely than women elsewhere to be beaten and raped with impunity, and more likely to be sold into marital slavery for the sake of consolidating farmland. Further north, women's status was reflected in terms of address – the husband called his animals, children and wife '*tu*', while she addressed him formally

---

* In 1887, a priest near Toulon recommended, as a practical form of exorcism, spilling lentils on the floor and leaving them overnight. Apparently, picking up lentils was too tedious even for a supernatural being.

as '*vous*'. In many parts, while guns were fired and church bells tolled for the birth of a baby boy, the appearance of a girl was considered an embarrassing non-event.

Hundreds of misogynistic proverbs from all parts of France seemed to confirm the impression that this was a barbaric society of sarcastic, sponging bullies:

'Oats to goats and wine to women is wasted wealth.'
(Vosges)

'Marry your daughter far away and keep your dung heap close to home.'
(Vexin, Normandy)

'A dead wife, a living horse, a wealthy man.'
(Brittany)

'A man has but two good days in life:
The day of his wedding and the day he buries his wife.'
(Provence, Languedoc, Gascony, Basque Country)

No female equivalents of those misogynistic sayings have survived. However, given the fact that nearly all of them were recorded by men, this is hardly surprising. And there are other proverbs that imply a certain unease at female solidarity: 'At the well, the mill, the oven and the wash-house, women leave nothing unsaid'; 'When a woman comes back from the stream [where the laundry is done], she could eat her man alive.'

Any of those women in the fields might have explained that none of this exactly matched the truth. The women worked because the men were in the high summer pastures, or out at sea, or on a seven-month tour of France, selling trinkets from a wicker basket. When the men returned to the harbour or the mountains, the women were naturally in charge. They organized the farm, repaired the buildings, negotiated with landowners and officials and struck deals with traders. Often, the women were the first to migrate to the city or the plain, and the first to create an industrial economy by selling their wares to travelling merchants. Many of them had no particular reason to wait for the men's return. Women in France are still automatically associated, in magazines, advertisements and casual conversation, with husbands and children. Yet nineteenth-century censuses show that over a third of all women were single, and that 12 per cent of women over fifty had never married.

The casual use of '*les hommes*' to refer to the whole population is blatantly inappropriate. It is no exaggeration to say that the predominantly rural economy of France was supported and to a large extent run by women. This might explain why, despite earning half a man's wages for the same work, women in France were often thought to have too much power and why the anti-feminist reforms of Napoleon and the Restoration government were so draconian. The Code Civil of 1804 denied married women the right to control their own property. The Code Pénal of 1811 effectively made a wife's adultery an excuse for murder. Not surprisingly, many working women never married their partner and many communities took a lenient view of pre-marital sex. 'No house was ever shamed by a girl who let her skirts be lifted.' (Savoy)

Misinterpretations were inevitable. Bourgeois observers saw dungy creatures grubbing in fields with their bottoms higher than their heads and, blind to the beauty of robustness, compared them to their own upright, fragrant wives. They found it odd that courting couples expressed affection by punching and throwing stones at one another, and they would have laughed at their terms of endearment. In a rare surviving love note, written on a postcard in the 1900s in almost indecipherable spelling, a Vendée peasant told his fiancée, 'You're so fresh and lovely the only thing I can compare you to is fields of young cabbages before the caterpillars have got to them.'*

Patriotic observers blamed the apparent mistreatment of women on foreign influences, just as many people in France today imagine that most violence against women is perpetrated by immigrants. In everything they saw, they were hampered by ignorance of daily life in their own land. If Breton women stood while their husbands ate, it was not because they were slaves but because buckwheat crêpes make an even more dismal meal when deposited all at once on the table. And if women spent the evenings working together in a barn, it was

* '[. . .] d'ine si baëlle fraichur qu'y paeu ja meille t'quimparerr qu'à t'chié chimps d'junes chaoux avin qu'les ch'neuilles y seillejin passerr.' (Maraîchin sub-dialect of Poitevin.)

not because they were segregated but because they preferred each other's company and efficiency. According to the Breton writer Pierre-Jakez Hélias, who grew up among the Bigouden people of Finistère, a woman who walked behind her husband in the street, carrying the bags and wielding an umbrella, was not a servant following her master but a cowherd making sure that the animal stayed on the path instead of wandering off to join its friends at the watering hole.

The Breton peasant Déguignet witnessed scenes all over patriarchal Brittany that suggest quite strongly that not all women were submissive and abused. At the time of year when the fields were busy and 'the best men were about', the women played a game called 'putting the *coz* and the *goaskerez* to the big fellows'. At midday, when the men were asleep, four or five women would find a man on his own, pin him down and stuff his pants with mud or cow dung.

> This was called *laka ar c'hoz* (putting the muck in), and it did the victim no great harm. But the other trick was worse. In this one, the woman left free would split the end of a thick stick, then with her two hands she would pry it apart the way you open a trap, and fit it onto the *organis generationis ex pace per hominis*. This was called *lakad ar woaskeres* (putting on pressure). It was done in full daylight and right out in the fields in front of everyone, in front of gangs of children clapping and screaming with laughter.

If convention had allowed painters to depict a group of women 'putting on pressure', museums of daily life might have a less melancholy air.

*

SCENES LIKE THESE are a happy reminder that chance encounters can be more revealing than a thousand statistics and written reports. Unfortunately, nearly all the distant figures mentioned in travellers' accounts, who might have dispelled false impressions with a few words and gestures, are just dots in the landscape. But sometimes, one of those figures comes close enough to be seen and heard.

A certain nameless woman is known to us only from a brief conversation and a description of her face. But we also know the time and the place: a long hill near the small town of Dombasle, near the Argonne forest, in the early summer of 1789. This is one of the natural internal frontiers of France, where the Champagne plateau slopes away to Lorraine and slices down towards the valley of the Rhône. The Argonne once divided the lands of one Gallic tribe from those of its neighbours. Later, it marked the western edge of the kingdom of Lotharingia, which was carved out of Charlemagne's empire by the Treaty of Verdun in 843. Now, at the end of the eighteenth century, parts of the ancient forest have been cleared and drained by glass makers, charcoal burners, sawyers and tilers, but its giant trenches and embankments still form a barrier ten miles wide between France and its enemies in the east.

The woman in question comes from the part of Champagne known as 'pouilleuse'. Her only education was probably the catechism and a few prayers and legends learned from an old woman who lived on her neighbours' charity. From the age of seven, she would have looked after the animals on her parents' small farm. She might be nineteen before she was ready to bear children and pregnant before she was twenty.

Some women never marry. Many live with a man who is a husband in all but name. Weddings and official documents are costly, and a girl can spend ten years in bondage trying to amass a small trousseau of furniture, linen and a few silver coins. Country girls have gone to town and lived in attics, cellars and even cupboards, and returned with a fatherless baby. Some employers send the maid away before the year's wages are due in the autumn. Pregnant girls are often questioned about the missing father by the magistrate when the pain of labour is likely to produce the truth.

For these and other reasons, she marries, with very little to her name. On her wedding night, the young people of her husband's village break down the door, in the traditional manner, and make the couple drink mulled wine from a chamber pot and inspect the sheets for signs that the marriage will be blessed. A child is born before the wedding bouquet of thorns and fruit has turned to dust. As the proverb says, 'Women give birth after three months, but only the first time.'

For the rest of her life, she lives in a low, dark house of white stone. It has a wide tiled roof and a hawthorn bush to ward off lightning. Outdoors, she wears a full green flannel skirt and a pointy hood. She is more prolific than the fields, which produce a crop of barley or rye only once every two years. Like most women, she tries to limit the effects of her husband's lovemaking, but only one reliable method exists, and anyone who has come home after dark on the back road by the pond has heard the sad croaking of the Night Washerwomen who are condemned to wash the shrouds and corpses of the children that they killed.

When the local lord increases the rent on the field, she leaves for Verdun and returns with the baby of a bourgeoise. For the next four years, she will be a mother to someone else's child. If one of her own babies is found at her breast, she will lose the money and her husband will be fined by the courts as much as he could earn in twenty days at harvest time.

One day, walking up the long hill near her home, she sees a gentleman on the road ahead and quickens her step. A stranger's tale is always welcome. It can be spun out later on in the long evenings when the women sit around shelling peas, carding wool or sewing white dresses for the village fête. The man is well dressed, in the clothes of another country, but travelling on his own without a carriage. He holds the bridle of a mare that clops along the chalky road. The horse is tired and half-blind but taller than the local breed and evidently well treated since the gentleman has dismounted to spare her on the climb.

She walks alongside him to the brow of the hill. From there, the heavy undulations of the Argonne massif roll away to the forests in the west and descend on the other side to the valley of the Meuse and the bridge at Verdun. The latest description of the route, in the *Complete Itinerary of France* (1788), describes the spot: 'Steep climb. Crossing of the great primitive chain that separates the basins of the sea and the rivers.'

'A sad country,' she says, 'and difficult times.' The gentleman is pleasantly inquisitive and asks the reasons for her complaint. In the clear Champenois dialect, she explains that her husband owns very little: 'a morsel of land, one cow, and a poor little horse'. She has seven children, and 'the cow's milk helps to make the soup'.

'But why, instead of a horse, do not you keep another cow?'

'Oh, my husband could not carry his produce so well without a horse; and asses are little used in the country.'

A few weeks before, she would have had little to add, but the command to draw up a list of grievances and the rumours that travel along the road from Paris have made an impression. Recently, she has heard that 'something is to be done by some great folks for such poor ones, but I don't know who nor how; but God send us better, for we are crushed by tithes and taxes'.

Her face confirms the truth of what she says in all but one respect. That evening, at Mars-la-Tour, the traveller remembers her face when he writes his account: 'It speaks, at the first sight, hard and severe labour. I am inclined to think that they work harder than the men.' 'This woman, at no great distance, might have been taken for sixty or seventy, her figure was so bent and her face so furrowed and hardened by labour, – but she said she was only twenty-eight.'

He dates the entry in his diary: 12 July 1789. Two days later, the Bastille in Paris is stormed by a mob and destroyed. News reaches the Argonne a few days later and the postmaster or a coachman explains what the Bastille is and what it means. The foreign gentleman, Arthur Young, hears the news when he arrives at the inn in Strasbourg on 20 July: 'The absolute overthrow of the old government!' 'It will be a great spectacle for the world to view, in this enlightened age, the representatives of twenty-five millions of people sitting on the construction of a new and better order and fabric of liberty than Europe has yet offered.'

From Paris, where the new National Assembly sits, the 'great folks' send out proclamations and the rumours turn into a river of news. There is no longer any need to wait for the mail coach from Paris. The news is shouted from field to field as it was in the days before the road was built. One day, ten miles to the north, the King and Queen are arrested and taken back to Paris. Though the town gates are closed, people on the other side of Verdun hear the incredible report before sunset. Along the road that runs through Dombasle, men and women stand on their doorsteps, eyeing passers-by and comparing them to faces they have seen in almanacs, wondering about signs in the sky.

When the great estates of châteaux and monasteries are sold off, her husband acquires another morsel of land. But 'citizens', as they must now be called, are still 'crushed by tithes and taxes'. A field that might once have been rented from a lord or an abbey is now liable to tax, and, as people say, 'money is expensive'. Some of their neighbours are poorer as landowners than they were as labourers.

Twenty years later, her husband is dead and her life seems very long. Napoleon's armies have passed through the Argonne, followed by the Prussians and the Austrians and the hungry Cossacks, and she has fewer children to farm the land. Some have died in battle, others have gone to work in cloth mills in the west. People at the market sometimes talk of change, which usually means that the people in Paris are fighting each other again. But the lord has returned to his château, and the mayor, who owns the biggest vineyard in the region, has founded a dynasty of his own. Some of the common land is closed off and there are regulations about the quantities of wood and dead leaves that can be taken from the forest.

The fields change more than the people. Now, there are potatoes (unknown when she was a child), artichokes for the animals, beetroot, rape and a few vines for money, and clover, which means less time lugging baskets of manure up the long hill. Her children will have luxuries. Her son plays billiards at the cafe in Dombasle and smokes a pipe. Her daughter wears a crinoline dress and spends all day indoors.

One day, in old age, she is sitting in front of her house, staring at a figure with a large black hood pulled over his head. He may be one of the first ethnologists to explore and record the towns and villages of the Argonne, or a photographer from Paris in search of 'typical' peasants. A face as eloquent as a landscape appears on the lens. Its furrows will survive the chemical decomposition of the albumen.

When she dies, the bed of straw on which she lay is burned. She is wrapped in a sheet and placed between rough planks that are good only for a coffin. For reasons that no one can remember, her hand is closed over a coin. She is buried in the churchyard where her neighbours will come on All Souls' Day to picnic and pray for the dead.

The photograph survives. A century later, restored and magnified, she appears in a museum of daily life, representing all her compatriots like a local saint or like a chance encounter on the road.

7

Fairies, Virgins, Gods and Priests

SOME FRENCH LANDSCAPES have barely changed in two thousand years. The rosary of lagoons on the Golfe du Lion and the
salt delta of the Camargue would not surprise a Roman sailor, though
he might find that he had been navigating by the chimneys of a
cement factory or a seaside apartment block rather than by the
beacon towers of the Massiliotes tribe. Beyond the marshes, east of
Arles, the Grande Crau is still the 'stony plain' seen by Pliny the
Elder, strewn with the giant boulders that Zeus hurled at the enemies
of Hercules. Pushing up the valley of the Rhodanus against the Black
Boreas (the mistral) towards the Cemmenus Mountain (the Cévennes), the geographer Strabo would still find that 'the olive-planted
and fig-bearing country ends, [and that] the vine, as you thus proceed,
does not easily bring its fruit to maturity'.

To see even the best-preserved landscape as it appeared to its
earlier inhabitants would of course require a complete telepathic
transfer. Scanned with the mind of a native, the area perceived as a
'view' would be a small world of secret passages and strange but
familiar creatures. The perception of space would be vertical rather
than horizontal, measured by density rather than distance. The hills
on the horizon might be nameless but the immediate environment
would be teeming with more places than appear on a modern road
map of France.

Some people discovered the land on epic seasonal journeys that
followed long-established routes (Chapter Eight), but the earliest
voyages of discovery were always undertaken in the little *pays* that
rarely extended for more than half a day's walk in any direction.

Native perceptions of these worlds were often dismissed as superstitious fantasies or cited as proof that the religion of the Druids had never died out. But these primitive beliefs were not the worm-eaten legacy of a prehistoric age, nor were they peculiar to peasants and the countryside. They were the means by which most people discovered, explained and even enjoyed their world.

*

ONE MORNING IN THE late winter of 1858, a fourteen-year-old girl left the dirty, slum-ridden Pyrenean town where she had grown up and set off along the torrential river called the Gave de Pau. Despite her chronic asthma, she walked for ten miles, past slimy limestone caverns, watermills and chapels, a hamlet built by a colony of cagots, and the nail-makers' forges at Saint-Pé. At last, she came to an ivy-covered bridge. On the other side were a vast grey church and a wood that was occupied by a permanent fair. A noisy, festive crowd was buying cakes and rosaries, singing songs, staring at gaudy pictures of the blessed Virgin, evil Jews and Roman soldiers, and half-listening to gesticulating priests who harangued them in Bearnese. For the girl, the shrine at Bétharram lay at the outer limits of the world. She had just enough time to pray at the shrine, buy a rosary and return home before dark.

Like the thousands of other pilgrims who went to Bétharram every year – many of them, like the girl, on foot and in rags, but some in gorgeous clothes and carriages – she was hoping for a miracle. Her father had lost an eye while roughening up a millstone with a chisel, and then the new owner of the mill had turned them out. A year before Bernadette's visit to Bétharram, her father had been accused of stealing two bags of flour. Winter work was hard to find and the family had been forced to move from the district where the cagots once lived, to the medieval prison that was now used to house the indigent. They were cold, hungry and desperate. There were other shrines much closer to home, but the Bétharram Virgin was known to be more potent and prolific than all the others.

The caves of Bétharram had been a holy site long before cults of the Virgin Mary began to appear in the Pyrenees in the Middle Ages, but its national fame dated from the early sixteenth century, when two shepherds saw a light in some bushes and found the tiny statue of a woman. For the first twenty-two years, the statue had performed more than twenty miracles a year. The name, 'Beth-Arram' ('beautiful branch'), referred to the branch that miraculously appeared when a shepherdess fell into the river. Bernadette Soubirous, the girl who visited the shrine that day in February, was also a shepherdess, and it was reasonable to expect a special favour from the Virgin.

A few days later, Bernadette, her sister and a friend were gathering firewood and bones by the river between the forest and the town. Here, the water had created a network of caverns and strange stalactitic formations. The caverns were associated with oracles and demons. Carved stones, arrowheads and even human bones had been found there. But they also attracted tourists in search of natural wonders. George Sand had visited them in 1825:

> The entrance to these grottos is admirable. I went ahead on my own and was thrilled to find myself in a magnificent hall supported by enormous masses of rock that looked like Gothic pillars.

The scenic grottos of Lourdes were a valuable resource for the scruffy little town. Lourdes lay on the pilgrim route to Bétharram and on the tourist route to the spas. The local chemist had been noted in guidebooks since the time of Napoleon for his delicious syrups and chocolate confectionery. But Lourdes's only other attraction was a gloomy fortress. It had no healing waters to attract wealthy invalids, and its rival, Argelès, had won the battle to become the administrative centre of the region.

The three girls reached the part of the river where it was joined by a small canal, at the cave called Massabielle, which means 'Old Rock'. This was common land, where poor people gathered fuel and swineherds brought their pigs. As she was removing her stockings to cross the canal, Bernadette heard a sudden gust of wind coming from the cave. Looking up, a few feet above the entrance, she saw a tiny figure dressed in white. It was no taller than herself (four foot seven inches). It wore a blue sash and a yellow rose on each foot. She later described it as '*uo pétito damisèla*' (in French, *une petite demoiselle*). The figure reminded her of a twelve-year-old girl she knew who often wore a white dress.

As usual when a Virgin appeared, there was great excitement in the region. Over the next six weeks, followed by an ever larger crowd, Bernadette saw the *demoiselle* another seventeen times. She revealed to her the existence of a spring in the cavern floor and told her that a chapel should be built on the spot. On the sixteenth visit, she was persuaded to ask the figure what she was. She told her, in the local dialect, '*Que soy era immaculada councepciou.*' She had no idea what the mysterious words meant, though she would have heard them when she was taught the catechism. (This was in 1858. The doctrine of the Immaculate Conception had been proclaimed in 1854 by Pope Pius IX and promulgated in Lourdes in 1855.)

Some people thought that they knew better than the girl herself what she had seen. The local newspaper called the apparition a 'lady', which led some to suppose that the little pauper had been impressed by an elegant tourist or one of the local beauties – perhaps the newspaper editor's fiancée or the chemist's wife, who was known as 'la Belle Chocolatière' because she bought her clothes in Paris. But Bernadette had a very different creature in mind. Later, she became quite angry when painters and sculptors depicted the tiny, child-like apparition as a tall, well-fed lady in corsets and crinolines, well past puberty and more likely to be at home in a Paris salon than in a damp provincial cave.

To Bernadette and the local people, '*damisèla*' had a particular connotation. *Demoiselles* were forest fairies, who dressed in white and disappeared if anyone came too close. Flowers grew at their feet. They could conjure up a sudden wind and calm it just as quickly. They lived in caves and grottos and were associated with springs and running water. They were also known to be on the side of the poor and could be quite violent when an injustice had been done. In neighbouring parts of the Pyrenees, when the Forest Code of 1827 placed restrictions on the food and fuel that could be gleaned from what had once been common land, forest guards and industrial charcoal burners had been terrorised by ghostly white figures. Their huts were set on fire and they were threatened with mutilation. The 'War of the Demoiselles' was at its height in the early 1830s but continued sporadically until the 1870s. The *demoiselles* of this rural Résistance turned out to be local men dressed up as fairies but they modelled their behaviour on supernatural spirits that were believed to exist as late as the 1950s.

The events at Lourdes came to be seen as a battle between sceptics and believers, but there was a much older and deeper division between the authorities and the common people. The peasant mind was quite at home with mysteries and contradictions. The apparition was the Virgin Mary and she was also a pagan spirit. In folk tales told in many parts of France, the Virgin and the local fairy were inter-changeable. Four centuries before, Joan of Arc and the children of her village had danced around the 'Fairy Tree' and woven wreaths for the statue of the Virgin. The vital point was not the metaphysical status of the being but her actions and sympathies.

Like the forest fairies and most of the other Pyrenean Virgins, the Lourdes Virgin appeared on common land. She was kind to the poor but also quite capable of humiliating doubters and had to be appeased with offerings. Above all, she was not a creature of the Catholic Church. As usual in such cases, the Church authorities were sceptical. Like the local Prefect, they were also concerned about the threat to law and order. In their view, Bernadette was a simple-minded peasant, and the twenty thousand people who deposited candles and offerings at the cave were a nuisance and a public health hazard.

Twelve years before, on a lonely mountainside at La Salette in the diocese of Grenoble, the Virgin had appeared to two shepherds – a sullen girl and a boy with such a short attention span that he started throwing stones while the Virgin was still delivering her message. The Virgin of La Salette was a far more questionable apparition than the Virgin of Lourdes but popular enthusiasm had forced the Church to validate the miraculous cures she performed.

Four years passed before Bernadette's vision was ratified by the Church, but by then her family and the town had been saved. Soon, Lourdes had more visitors than the grandest Pyrenean spas. Proper-ties on the road to the shrine soared in value and shops sprang up like flowers at the feet of a fairy. 'Here the relations of the celebrated child contrive to make money out of the connection by advertising in large letters above their shops, "Bernadette's Aunt", etc.' (Henry Blackburn, *The Pyrenees: a Description of Summer Life at French Watering Places*, 1881). Whatever educated people chose to believe, this was not cynical opportunism. The little people had won a great victory, and it was right and proper, in their view, that they should profit from the Virgin's gift. The *demoiselle* had chosen Lourdes, not Bétharram or Argelès. One day, Lourdes would have more hotels than anywhere but Paris, and Bétharram would be deserted. As Henry Blackburn's landlady at Argelès remarked a little sourly, 'It's a stroke of good luck for Lourdes.'

*

THE EVENTS IN LOURDES were spectacular but not exceptional. They belonged to an ancient tale that can be traced back to the days of Roman Gaul, and even further, beyond the birth of Christ, into unrecorded history.

Some of the early parts of this tale can be deciphered with a map of France and a list of place names. If all the places named after a saint are marked on the map, a distinct pattern appears: a concentration of 'Saints' (or the earlier 'Dam-' and 'Dom-', from *dominus*) in the centre and the west, and large areas with relatively few 'Saints' in the north, the north-east and the far south-west. This pattern reflects varying degrees of settlement and stability in the early Middle Ages: a town or village that was already well established when the new religion came was less likely to be renamed after a saint than a scattered settlement that only later coalesced around a church. Even at this distance in time, smaller details are also visible. Places called Saint-Martin (the Roman soldier who became Bishop of Tours and evangelized Gaul in the fourth century) tend to occur along the lines of Roman roads and perhaps reveal the routes by which the new religion spread. Places called Saint-Bonnet – excluding the 'Bonnets' that were derived from the name of the Celtic god Belenos – draw an erratic line across the country from Savoy to the Gironde, and appear to trace the route that was taken by Saint Bonitus. (Bonitus died in the seventh century while returning to Clermont-Ferrand from Rome, and then continued in a disembodied state or was carried in a reliquary until he reached the Atlantic Ocean.)

The pattern of saints' names is curiously reminiscent of a long-term trend that is known to geographers and historians as the Saint-Malo–Geneva line (p. 318). This imaginary line runs diagonally across

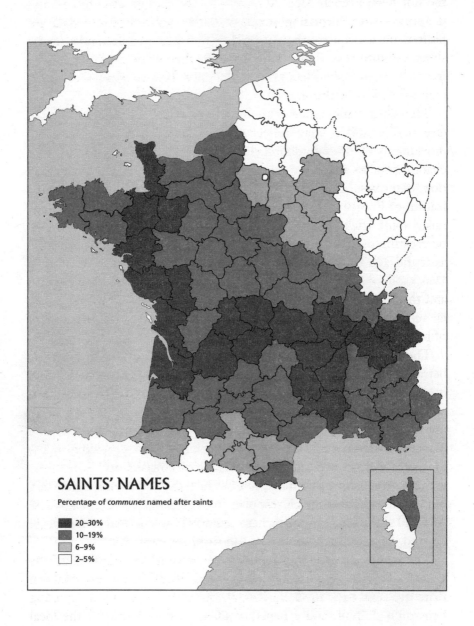

SAINTS' NAMES

Percentage of *communes* named after saints

- 20–30%
- 10–19%
- 6–9%
- 2–5%

the country from the Cotentin peninsula in the English Channel to the northern French Alps. At least until the late nineteenth century, it appears with surprising regularity when various sets of data are plotted on a map: south and west of the line, people tended to be shorter and to have darker hair and eyes; they were less literate, lived in smaller places, had less taxable income and were more likely to be employed in agriculture.

The Saint-Malo–Geneva line may predate the north–south divide (see p. 67), and it may reflect ancient and otherwise untraceable movements of the population. It may be the 'strange attractor' of a chaotic process involving geology and climate, invasion and migration, enterprise and inertia. It does at least suggest that the Christianization of France was subordinate to other realities and trends, and it raises some tricky questions. Did the Church consolidate the nation by creating parishes and dioceses, or was it simply implanting itself – as it did at Lourdes – on societies and beliefs that already existed? Was modern Gaul created or only conquered by the Roman Empire and the Roman Catholic Church? And were 'superstition' and popular religion just the jumbled bones of Druidism or a coherent system of belief?

The nervous reaction of the Church to Bernadette's vision in 1858 betrayed a fear of insignificance that was almost as old as the Church itself. Since the fourth or fifth centuries, the Church had been eradicating and commandeering pagan sites. Sometimes, saints were invented to replace the old gods. Saint Minerve took the place of Minerva, Mars became Saint Mard or Saint Maurice. Ancient religious sites were converted to a semblance of Christianity. Saint Anne is the patron saint of Brittany, not because she ever went to Brittany, but because she was the closest plausible match for the Celtic goddess Ana and the sacred swamps where this world was joined to the world beyond. (*Ana* or *anam* was a Gaulish word for swamp.)

The names changed but the holy sites were rarely abandoned. The chapel of Saint Agathe in the valley of the Vilaine in southern Brittany dates back to Gallo-Roman times. It has a fresco depicting Eros on a dolphin and a naked woman – either Venus or the local fairy – combing her hair beside the water. Before the ninth century, the chapel was rededicated to a certain male 'Saint Venus' who later became Saint Vénier. In the eighteenth century, when the old miracle-working saints were replaced with the saints of the Catholic Reformation, the Sicilian saint Agatha was imported as a replacement for Saint Vénier, who had always enjoyed the reputation of making sterile women pregnant.

Thirty years after Bernadette's vision, the Church was still planting crosses on sacred sites. The aim of this cuckoo-like activity was 'to give the cross the benefit of the respect and religious thoughts that were attached to the site'. Prayers to the local deity would be intercepted by the cross and redirected to Christian heaven. Supposedly absurd beliefs and practices would die out and the people would be persuaded to abandon their fetishistic cults and to worship a god whose son was born of a virgin.

There is plenty of evidence on the back roads of France that this spiritual war was being fought quite recently. Crosses commemorating missions at the end of the nineteenth century often stand at crossroads next to modern road signs, electricity substations and communal rubbish containers. Sometimes, a map-maker's triangulation mark is embedded in the stone pediment of the cross. It is not usually obvious that these crosses are monuments to an ancient struggle. They are often assumed to have something to do with the 'dechristianization' of France by the Revolution and its subsequent reconversion to Catholicism. They seem to be a simple declaration of the fact that France is a Christian country, just as the whole road system seems to be oriented on the great Gothic cathedrals.*

The roadside crosses belong to the same long tale that leads to Lourdes. They usually occupy ancient sacred sites that belong to a different religious tradition with its own decaying network of monuments. The prehistoric 'nail-stone' at Laon Cathedral, which proved a man's innocence if he could drive a nail into it, was sacrificed to urban improvements in the early nineteenth century, but a large menhir still leans against the cathedral of Le Mans like a stubborn

* Since 1768, all distances have been measured from a point in the square in front of Notre-Dame in Paris. The octagonal brass plaque that now marks 'Point Zéro' replaced an earlier triangular stone with a post bearing the arms of Notre-Dame of Paris.

old relative ensconced in a corner of her daughter's grand drawing room. Most of the monuments, brutalized by time and a continual process of desecration and reconsecration, are found in out-of-the-way places that hardly seem to be places at all. They stand along older routes that now exist only in a vestigial, disconnected state, interrupted by roads and railways and too erratic to be of use to high-speed travellers.

The stones themselves appear suddenly in the corner of the eye like figures in a landscape that seemed a moment before to be empty. On a small, muddy road near Flers in Normandy stands a prehistoric stone that was carved on all four sides into the shape of a Christian cross about three centuries ago. This is a typical 'prehistoric' site: the area is deserted but shows recent signs of picnics and more intimate activities. A concrete culvert suggests a spring or a small underground stream. Two tall oak trees stand next to the stone, about four feet apart. The oak was sacred to the Druids, and even in the nineteenth century, passing between two trees or through the hole in a trunk was thought to have magical effects, usually associated with fertility. Since trees on sacred sites were often replanted when they died, the two oaks beside the stone are probably living on the site of their prehistoric ancestors.

Stones like this have survived – when they were not smashed up and used for road-building – not because they were preserved by government commissions but because, until quite recently, they were objects of greater popular devotion than churches and cathedrals. They were associated with stories that were more familiar to most people than the Gospels. The carved stone near Flers is probably related to the bigger standing-stone five miles to the east on the other side of the village of Sainte-Opportune. This slightly stooping block of granite, which lies next to a willow and a boggy spring, was said to be the sharpening-stone used by the Devil or Gargantua in a ploughing competition with Saint Peter. According to another version, Gargantua fell asleep when he should have been mowing the field and when Saint Opportuna came and kicked him, he peevishly threw away his stone.

These religious monuments – even the enormous megalithic alignments of Carnac – did not appear on maps until the twentieth century, though the map-makers often used prehistoric sites for their geodesic measurements and propped their instruments on the stones. By then, many of them had been vandalized by passing strangers and disturbed by treasure-seekers. Most are still undervalued as national treasures and some are still not shown on maps. One of the biggest dolmens in Europe, at Bagneux in the Loire Valley, was once used for feasting and dancing. It has since been engulfed by the suburbs of Saumur and was on sale in 2006 as part of a plot which includes two apartments and the cafe-bar 'Le Dolmen'.

*

THESE OBSTINATE STONES may provide clues to the prehistoric past, but they can also be used as signposts to a more recent world.

A day east of Lourdes – thirty miles as the crow flies or fifty miles by road – a cluster of hamlets lies just off the trans-Pyrenean road near the Col de Peyresourde, which is best known today as a regular obstacle on the Tour de France cycle race and as the pseudo-Himalayan setting for a James Bond film.

A group of stones stands on the hills around the hamlets. Some were brought by glaciers and landslides, others were placed there deliberately to complete a circle or a line. Above the village of Poubeau, a road spirals up and a track leads off through the remains of a wood to an open field. At this point, the village below is invisible and there is a magnificent view of the mountains. A six-foot-tall lump of granite stands in the field. It was known as the 'Cailhaou d'Arriba-Pardin' (the Stone that Came from God) and could be made to tremble very slightly. Next to it there was once a smaller stone, about three feet tall, in the shape of a penis, now buried in the earth. Girls and women would sit astride the phallic stone or kneel on a slab placed in front of it. This was quite a common activity in many parts of France and perhaps very common indeed, depending on the interpretation of phrases in official reports such as 'too disgusting to describe'. On the eve of Mardi Gras, a fire was lit next to the stone and there were 'obscene' dances.

'Fertility rites' were still being performed in Poubeau in 1875 when an anthropologist came to investigate with a local guide:

The spirit who inhabits the stone does not enjoy an immaculate reputation in the region but the inhabitants think none the less of it. So many happy unions consecrated by marriage and by the birth of numerous children began with meetings at the stone that young and old alike have very pleasant memories of it. They love the stone and are quite prepared to defend it if need be.

When an iron cross was embedded in the stone in the 1810s, the cross was destroyed by lightning, which enhanced the stone's prestige. When workmen came to remove it in 1835, they were attacked by villagers. Later, unexplained accidents occurred. A local priest was killed by a falling rock. Finally, in 1871, another priest erected the cross that is still rusting away on top of the stone. The villagers then supposedly abandoned the cult and merely processed to the stone on Rogation Sunday to ask it for a good harvest. However, blushing girls interviewed by the anthropologist in 1875 hinted that the stone was still not entirely celibate.

The Cailhaou Arriba-Pardin and its neighbours were the archivists and storytellers of the community. As well as the Cailhaou, there was the 'peyre-hita', which was still being 'touched in a certain manner' by local women in 1877. There was the group of stones on the pass where, some years before, Jesus had asked a shepherd for some food and was so annoyed by the man's refusal that he turned him, his dog and his sheep to stone. There was also the 'waltzing-stone' near a bone-filled cave which once had a phallic appendage, the enormous 'fire-stone' by Peyrelade where the summer solstice was celebrated, and the amazing talking-stone just above Jurvielle at the source of a stream.

The talking-stone was the home of an *incantada*, which entered and exited by a door carved in the granite. Its whispered messages could be heard if one placed one's ear on a little cavity. *Incantadas* were angels who, when war broke out between Good and Evil, had declared themselves neutral. In those days, God was merciful but wanted to keep his mercy a secret for the time being, and so he banished the angels to Earth. They had to keep washing themselves until they were clean enough to be allowed back into heaven. This was a particularly good place to do the washing. Clothes washed at the talking-stone came out whiter than white.

These cherished stones were not the numinous objects admired by neo-Druids. There was no 'stone cult', as priests and Romantic anthropologists believed. The stones were a normal part of daily life, marking the boundaries of the *pays* and embodying the life of the community: seasonal celebrations, storytelling, laundry, sex, and defiance of the authorities. They were spirits of the land who gave life to the landscape and made the physical world more interesting. The stones were a greater threat to the Catholic Church than the French Revolution: it was thanks to the spirits – but not the Church – that the local people had somewhere to dance, somewhere to celebrate the old festivals and somewhere secret where young people could find their way to the other side of virginity, watched only by the snowy peaks.

*

MONUMENTS LIKE THE STONES at the Col de Peyresourde marked the smallest of the concentric spheres within which people explored their world. Most spirits belonged, not to a *pays*, but to a particular site, and their influence rarely extended more than a few feet. In these tiny, magical universes, the intercontinental world of theological doctrine was meaningless. In 1890, at Bérou in Normandy, when a missionary preacher told his flock that there was only one Virgin Mary, a woman was heard to mutter, 'Old fool! As if everyone didn't know that the daughter's here and the mother's at Revercourt' (two miles away).

Popular saints did not like to travel. Statues and figurines that were moved to a church from the place where they were miraculously discovered – a pond, a ditch or a tree trunk that had grown up around a woody niche and concealed the statue until the tree was felled – invariably returned by mysterious means to the place of discovery. These silent acts of resistance were the saints' way of demanding a chapel of their own, even if it was inconvenient for mortal beings. According to a story that was still being told at the end of the nineteenth century, the people of Six-Fours, Reynier and Toulon tried to entice their Virgin with beautiful shrines but she rejected them all and had to be enshrined on top of the Sicié hill with a lovely view of the Côte d'Azur. Until recently, it was impossible to visit her except on foot. Other Provençal Virgins made themselves so heavy while they were being moved that their human bearers had to give up the struggle and leave them where they had first been found.

The social and political development of France owes a great deal to the supernatural acts of inanimate objects. By stubbornly remaining on common ground, the saints not only helped safeguard gleaning and grazing rights, they also acted as a link between communities. And while the saints were rooted to the spot, their mortal devotees travelled great distances to seek their help and advice. A pilgrimage could bring together the inhabitants of a whole group of villages or of two divided valleys. In the hilly diocese of Le Puy-en-Velay in the Haute-Loire *département*, sixty-three statues of the Virgin Mary are still the objects of large annual pilgrimages. The diocesan guide talks appropriately of particular Marys 'draining' a particular region. Many of them occupy key geographical positions. They are often found along the line of watersheds, with splendid views in all directions.

The souvenir shops, the tour buses and the blundering amateur army of camper vans that now seem to spoil the high passes of the Alps and the Pyrenees are just a faint reflection of the pilgrim shanty-towns that sprang up every year. The pilgrimage to Notre-Dame de Héas in a desolate part of the Pyrenees once attracted twelve thousand people at a time. The pilgrims arrived on foot, camped in fetid shacks, drank all night and told tales of Our Lady of Héas and how the masons who built the chapel were sustained by the milk of goats that mysteriously ran away before they could be eaten. At daybreak, mass was held and the priest's assistant would beat the surging crowd away from the altar with a stick. Meanwhile, other pilgrims swarmed over the rock where the Virgin had appeared, hammering away like blacksmiths to dislodge a sacred fragment that would later be ground to dust and swallowed with holy water.

Many attempts were made to end these rowdy festivals. A righteous holiday crowd that could fill a small town was an obvious threat to order. Three times, between 1798 and 1800, policemen and soldiers came to stop up the sacred well of Saint Clotilde, which was built on the site of a dolmen at Les Andelys on the Seine. Every year, on 2 June, the town was invaded by a 'savage horde' of pilgrims from all over Normandy. They took off their clothes and slithered into the water, holding onto their baskets and umbrellas – because Saint Clotilde also attracted thieves. After bathing, they snatched flaming branches from a bonfire and were sometimes badly burned. Children had been known to die after falling into the freezing waters of the healing spring. On the final attempt to close the shrine, two thousand stone-wielding bathers made the soldiers run away and then unplugged the well and wallowed in the water 'with frenzied cries of triumph'.

Whatever their therapeutic value, these pilgrimages were vital to the wealth and happiness of many regions. While fairs were primarily attended by men, pilgrimages involved whole communities. They were a chance to exchange news, to see another place and to take a holiday, which is partly why the people of Lourdes always went somewhere else to be healed by the Virgin Mary. Before bicycles and railways, pilgrimages expanded and consolidated areas of trade, which might explain why so many Virgins appeared between regions that offered different kinds of agricultural produce. Just as fairs made it possible to improve livestock, pilgrimages – which some observers crudely described as 'orgies' – had a similar effect on the human stock. At the pilgrimage to Sainte-Baume in southern Provence, each village had its own defensive encampment in the woods, but lovers came in the night and the saint's reputation for making marriages was never seriously threatened.

A pilgrimage was above all a rite of passage and something to look back on with pride. In Restif de la Bretonne's part of Burgundy, a boy who had never gone to Mont-Saint-Michel (three hundred miles away) 'was considered a coward', and a girl who had never visited the tomb of Sainte Reine (forty miles to the east) 'seemed to lack modesty'. It might be the only long journey a person ever made. On many of the Provençal mountains, these voyages of a lifetime had been marked for countless centuries by little piles of stones and votive offerings that littered the otherwise deserted land. Now that most pilgrim sites have been tidied up, the best place to see the poignant, personal effect of these offerings is on the lunar upper slopes of Mont Ventoux, where, all summer long, a stream of quietly exhilarated cyclists deposits water bottles, inner tubes and stones at the foot of the memorial to the British rider Tom Simpson who collapsed and died there during the 1967 Tour de France. The jersey he was wearing at the time can be seen with other relics at a chapel in the Armagnac dedicated to Notre-Dame des Cyclistes.

*

VISITORS TO THIS LAND of independent saints and pilgrims might reasonably have asked: Where was the Church in all of this? Where was that religious golden age when humble peasants looked to the priest for guidance and salvation?

The beloved village priest, that staple figure of Romantic fiction, was a very rare breed. In most people's minds, the man in black was supposed to be useful, like a doctor, a snake-catcher or a witch. He should be willing to write inaccurate letters of recommendation, to read the newspaper and to explain government decrees. He should also be able to pull strings in the spirit world, influence the weather and cure people and animals of rabies. (This partly explains the godlike status of Louis Pasteur, who developed a vaccine for rabies in 1885.) Naturally, this put the priest in a tricky position. If he refused to ring the bells to prevent a hailstorm, he was useless. If he rang the bells and it hailed anyway, he was inept. In 1874, the curé of the Limousin village of Burgnac refused to join a 'pagan' harvest procession. It duly hailed, the harvest was lost, and the curé had to be rescued from an angry crowd. To the poor sharecropper who led the crowd, this sort of behaviour made no sense at all: 'Why would a priest who preaches religion try to do away with it?'

If his magic powers were weak, the priest would be seen as a busybody and a kill-joy. No one took kindly to an outsider who tried to stop people feasting in the cemetery, chatting and walking about during mass and bringing their animals into church to be blessed. The curé of Ars, Jean-Marie Vianney (1786–1859), who became the object of a pilgrimage, is the only priest who managed to make his parishioners give up dancing and drinking. He did not become the patron saint of parish priests because he was typical. Most other priests who won the hearts of their parishioners did so by reaching a quiet compromise with the pagan world. Since the majority of priests were the sons of artisans and peasants, many of them shared the fears and visions of their flock. In the 1770s, a curé near Auch was heard to call out before mass, 'Sorcerers and sorceresses, wizards and witches, leave thou the Church ere the Holy Sacrifice commence!' – at which some of the congregation stood up and went out.

No one can say exactly what the Church meant to people who lived in fear of evil spirits, lit candles to their saint and sprinkled holy water on their fields. Statistical maps of the spiritual life of France seem to show a persistent pattern. In 1790, priests were required to swear an oath declaring their loyalty to the Constitution and acknowledging that they were first and foremost employees of the state. Over half of all parish priests swore the oath, but in some parts, over three-quarters refused, presumably with the support of their flock. The areas of greatest resistance – the west of France from the Vendée to Calvados, the north and north-east, the southern Massif Central and much of the south – are also the areas where, a hundred years later, church attendance was highest.

The implications for the Church, however, are far from obvious. Simply attending a service was no more proof of religious fervour than it is today. In the Var, in south-eastern Provence, many priests swore allegiance to the state, and church attendance was poor, but attendance at popular festivals and pilgrimages was very high. In the neighbouring *département*, the Basses-Alpes, church attendance was high but, considering the congregations' behaviour, only the most optimistic bishop could interpret this as a sign of popular devotion to the Church. In 1759, a chaplain at Ribiers threatened his flock with excommunication if they failed to cooperate with a police investigation. Women in the congregation stormed the altar, tore off his wig, destroyed the processional crosses and beat him with the broken pieces. Apparently, they were concerned, not about their eternal souls, but about the possible effect of this priestly magic on the harvest. Not all anti-clerical violence was perpetrated by atheist revolutionaries.

The only certainty seems to be that France was a Catholic country, in the sense that it was not a Protestant country. Even this distinction is not as illuminating as it sounds.* The military campaign against the

---

* About 2.2 per cent of the population of France was Protestant in the mid-nineteenth century – just over 833,000 people, four-fifths of whom were concentrated

Protestants of the Cévennes after the Revocation of the Edict of Nantes (1685) had some popular support, and at the time of the Revolution there were people in the regions of Toulouse and Nîmes who believed that the Edict of Toleration (1787) and the oath to the Constitution (1790–91) were part of a Protestant plot. Fifty years later, in Nîmes and Montpellier, particularly among the bourgeoisie, the old religious divide was reflected in political allegiance, place of residence and choice of wife or husband. But there are just as many signs of religious tolerance and indifference. In the early 1800s, priests in the Bordelais and the Périgord were distressed to see Catholics and Protestants 'showing mutual affection'. 'Mixed' churches in Alsace, where the choir was reserved for Catholics and closed off with a curtain or a grille during the Protestant service, were still in use in the 1860s. Several Catholic communities in the Auvergne, the Limousin and the Périgord converted to Protestantism overnight when the Church became too demanding, meddlesome and expensive.

The history of persecution has dates and memorable scenes. The history of indifference is harder to trace, except through the occasional observations of outsiders. In 1878, Robert Louis Stevenson arrived with his donkey at Florac (Lozère), which had been a frontier town in the days of Protestant persecution. Coming from a land where sectarian violence was common, he found the combination of long memories and religious tolerance extraordinary:

> I observed that Protestant and Catholic intermingled in a very easy manner; and it surprised me to see what a lively memory still subsisted of the religious war . . .
>
> Later in the day one of the Protestant pastors was so good as to visit me . . . Florac, he told me, is part Protestant, part Catholic; and the difference in religion is usually doubled by a difference in politics. You may judge of my surprise . . . when I learned that the population lived together on very quiet terms; and there was even an exchange of hospitalities between households thus doubly separated. . . . They had all been sabring and shooting, burning, pillaging, and murdering, their

---

in Alsace and around Montbéliard (Lutheran), in the region of Nîmes and western Provence, and in a narrow crescent from Montpellier to La Rochelle and Poitou (Calvinist or 'Huguenot').

hearts hot with indignant passion; and here, after a hundred and seventy years, Protestant is still Protestant, Catholic still Catholic, in mutual toleration and mild amity of life.

*

MANY OF THE MISSIONARIES who set out to 'reconvert' the population, in the early Middle Ages or the early twentieth century, did not automatically assume that France was a Christian country. The religion known as Druidism had been eradicated, at least in its established form, by the Romans, but 'pagan' gods – the gods of a *pagus* or a *pays* – seemed to carry on much as before. Even in Brittany, which was supposed to be a bastion of Catholicism, the Church was important in the same way that a shopping mall is important to shoppers: the customers were not especially interested in the creator and owner of the mall; they came to see the saints, who sold their wares in little chapels around the nave. New saints were still being created in the nineteenth century in total disregard of Church dogma: the well-preserved corpse of a long-suffering wife, a victim of the Chouan rebellion who had died on a suicide mission, a hairy hermit living in a tree and even some popular priests on whose tombstones sick children were laid. Even more recently, the ruined prehistoric chamber advertised to tourists as 'Merlin's Tomb' in the Paimpont forest in Brittany has become a religious site. Prayers to Merlin the Enchanter, written on paper, are regularly deposited around the tomb and inserted in a cleft in the rock.

These beliefs thrived on the established Church like mistletoe on an oak. They had no religious institutions of their own, but they were consistent enough, throughout France and much of Western Europe, to be described as a form of religion. The nameless faith borrowed elements of Christianity but dispensed with most of its moral and theological foundations, and reorganized the hierarchy of sacred beings. The Virgin Mary was always more important than God. Like his son, God offered neither redemption nor forgiveness. He had been known to destroy towns and to cause serious road accidents just to make his point. He was no more popular than a bishop. In 1872, a woman in Chartres who was standing in the way of a church procession was asked to make way for '*le bon Dieu*'. She retorted, 'Huh! I didn't come here for *him*, I came for *her*' (pointing at the Virgin).

The Devil was almost as powerful as God and far more accommodating. Not all of the forty-nine 'Devil's Bridges' in France should provoke a feeling of satanic dread. Any stroke of luck – finding buried treasure, coming into an inheritance, not losing livestock to an epidemic, or a rockfall that conveniently bridged a torrent – was probably the Devil's work. Despite his power, the Devil, who usually looked like a gentleman or a wealthy farmer, was notoriously gullible and had sometimes been tricked into building churches and abbeys. He built most of his bridges on the understanding that he would be given the first soul to cross the bridge, only to be fobbed off with a cat.

Jesus Christ was a relatively minor figure. In the not-so-distant past, he had walked the land dispensing practical advice. He was known to have been a beggar, which explained his resourcefulness and cunning. In pseudo-Gospel stories – told as though they were local events – Jesus would try to beat some sense into his muddle-headed sidekick, Saint Peter: 'You fool! You never blab about an animal's faults at the fair before selling it and getting your hands on the money!'

God, the Devil and Jesus, like Gargantua and the fairy Mélusine, were the protagonists of folk tales who had been active in the recent past. They were the stuff of *veillées* and *chambrées* – the informal assemblies where villagers got together to frighten each other, or to conjure away the fear of night, with tales of weird beings: the heavenly hunt that passed overhead in the evening sky with strange cries; werewolves, the Devil's Cow, the *vouivre* (a flying snake with a carbuncle for an eye), the *lupeux* (a gnarly creature often seen sitting on a twisted tree trunk), hornèd men who stole young girls because there were no hornèd women, mermen who broke fishing nets and green men who were harmless, and of course the Beast of the Gévaudan, which really existed.* The main difference between the Christian figures and the

---

* The Bête du Gévaudan was an unusually fierce and daring wolf, which roamed over a sparsely populated area of about nine hundred square miles, claiming at least twenty lives in two years (1764–65) and giving rise to two pilgrimages. The Beast

pagan fairies is that the fairies were generally expected to return in the next century or as soon as Christianity came to an end.

These legendary or part-legendary figures were spectacularly out-numbered and out-performed by saints. Unlike God and the fairies, saints belonged to everyday life. On his own ground, a saint was more effective than God. As the curé of Étaples near Le Touquet reported to his bishop, referring to the local miracle-working saint, 'There are two "dear Lords" at Étaples: the real one and Saint Josse, and I'm not at all sure that Saint Josse isn't number one.'

Saints were associated with solid facts like an attribute or a name. Saint Anthony is often depicted with the pig of gluttony, which made him popular with swineherds; John the Baptist held the Lamb of God and was the favourite saint of shepherds. Saint Pissoux was supposed to be good for urinary infections, Saint Bavard ('chatty') for mutes and Saint Clair ('clear') for the short-sighted. Where no suitable name existed, a new saint was created. 'Saint Sourdeau' cared for the deaf, 'Saint Plouradou' dealt with crying children and 'Saint Sequayre' (as in *sec*) caused one's enemies to shrivel up and die. In Normandy, reciting the service of the Toussaint (All Saints' Day) was thought to be good for people with a cold because *Toussaint* sounds like *tousser* (to cough).

The great advantage of the saints was that they actually existed in the material world. Some of them can still be seen in churches, where they often have a dual audience: a parishioner or a pilgrim com-municating with a real being, and a tourist looking at an example of religious art. A saint was not a theological concept or an artistic representation. The statue or figurine *was* the saint. This is why people were so upset when their curé tried to replace a filthy, shapeless and sometimes partially incinerated lump of wood with a shiny new saint fresh from the factory. The new Saint Aygulf at Notre-Dame de Brusc near Grasse (a Christianized pagan deity who could make it rain and whose petitioners always carried umbrellas when they came to pray) had a golden crosier, a coat and a lily and

---

now makes an important contribution to the tourist economy of the southern Auvergne and is responsible for the controlled reintroduction of wolves to the Gévaudan.

pink complexion and was completely useless. The new Black Virgin at Le Puy-en-Velay was known to perform fewer miracles than the old one, despite the fact that the latter had been denounced as a statue of Isis brought back from the Crusades.

The life of the saint was determined, logically, by the physical composition of the effigy. A certain Saint Greluchon started life as the funerary statue of a lord at Bourbon-l'Archambault. (Other Greluchons or Guerlichons – from a word for a little boy's penis – were popular throughout the Berry and the Bourbonnais.) Infertile women came to scratch away his genitals and drink the dust in a little white wine. The more determined women, who wanted twins, came with rasps and knives. When the genitals had gone, they started on his chin, and by the time he was placed in the local museum in 1880, he was just a mutilated bust. A museum employee was later sacked for scraping at the replacement chin.

Concrete evidence of these local cults can be found in hundreds of devoutly mutilated stone figures. The effects of centuries of rubbing and scraping are usually quite easy to distinguish from vandalism, though many churches blame the damage on the French Revolution. The parts most often atrophied or missing are the nose, the hands and the feet. At Le Vigeant, in the valley of the Vienne, the figure of a knight has lost most of its feet to mothers who put the dust in their toddlers' shoes to help them learn to walk.

The saints performed miraculous cures, but they had to be cajoled and bullied like lazy public servants. In Tréguier, according to Ernest Renan, prayers to Saint Yves took the form of a challenge: 'You were a just man when you were alive; prove to me that you still are.' In this way, 'one could be sure that one's enemy would be dead within the year.' When he was a child, Renan's father had been taken to the chapel of the saint who cured fever.

> A blacksmith came too, with his forge, his nails and his tongs. He lit the forge, heated the tongs and held a red-hot horseshoe in the saint's face, saying as he did so, 'Take away this child's fever or I'll shoe you like a horse.' The saint immediately did as he was told.

If the saint refused to cooperate, he was liable to be punished. In Haudiomont, when the vines froze on Saint Urban's day (25 May), his effigy was dragged through the nettles that grew around the church. When the phylloxera epidemic wiped out their vines, the people of Mouzon in the Ardennes threw the statue of their saint into the river Meuse. Even in some religious communities, saints were humiliated if they failed to answer prayers. In 1887, a visitor to a convent in a large Provençal town noticed that Saint Joseph had been turned to face the wall. It was explained that Saint Joseph was 'doing penance' for having failed to persuade a landowner to leave a certain piece of land to the convent in his will. If he failed again, he would be taken down to the cellar and thrashed.

The Virgin of Lourdes was never treated in this way, but even she had to pass a test. On the Virgin's second appearance, Bernadette threw holy water at the figure until the bottle was empty, saying, 'If you come from God, you can stay; if not, go away.' Since the Virgin appeared high up on the cave wall, this was not a gentle, ritual sprinkling. It was a sensible experiment conducted by a girl who lived in a world where spirits were as real as policemen, priests and debt collectors.

*

PAGAN SAINT-WORSHIPPERS did not suddenly die out and disappear like fairies. They turned into the population of modern France. It is worth remembering that while the Catholic Church in the nineteenth century always took the side of authoritarian regimes, the governments that are supposed to have secularized France were democratically elected. They represented a population whose concerns were overwhelmingly practical and whose beliefs had a firmer basis in reality than upper-class infatuations with mesmerism, astrology and Ouija boards.

Common experience showed that prayer had no effect on the physical world. Sickness was real and demanded a real remedy. 'Miraculous' cures were based on notions that were a better mental preparation for the scientific age than the airy abstractions of theology, which many priests, let alone parishioners, found impossible to fathom. Everything was believed to have a particular cause, which was either known or knowable. The cure itself nearly always involved a physical activity or a real substance. This is why quack doctors and their customers adapted so easily to the new world of scientific medicine and why education so quickly eradicated misconceptions without plunging the population into an abyss of religious doubt. The difference between the generations that swallowed saints' dust and the generations that visited a qualified doctor was not mental capacity but information.

Of course, an endless list of ridiculous beliefs could be drawn up. Many thought that sick people should not wear clean clothes and that lice helped children to grow. Hedgehogs were burned to death in Brittany because they were thought to suck the milk from cows and to eat ducks. Sacrificing animals to cure an illness was a common practice, which shows that magic remedies were not used only by the poor. A popular cure for pneumonia was still being tried in some upper-class households at the end of the nineteenth century: slice a living white dove down the middle and place the two palpitating halves on the patient's chest. Cruelty to humans was just as common. A belief in magic was often an excuse for persecuting strangers and eccentrics. After 1862, there are no more reports of witches being burned to death, but there were still attempts to prosecute people who supposedly blighted cattle with the evil eye. The combination of misery and ignorance was also a gold mine for swindlers. A pedlar could make a fortune selling useless secrets, such as how to find the magic luminescent herb which prevented its possessor from ever being fooled.

Yet there was more sense in 'magic' than met the educated eye. By 1876, there was one doctor for every 2,700 people in France, but most doctors had to be paid in money rather than in produce, and medicines were expensive. Since many people called the doctor only as a last resort, this tended to confirm the belief that doctors brought death. In the circumstances, gullibility had a therapeutic value. Some cures clearly had a beneficial, psychosomatic effect. Two scholars who are compiling a list of every folk remedy used in France in the nineteenth century expect to find between twenty and thirty thousand different remedies. If most fatal poisons were excluded by a process of elimination, some of these remedies were bound to be either effective or harmless enough to allow wishful thinking to work its wonders. The more violent cures, such as scraping the mouth of a paralysed person with a razor and rubbing it with salt, would at least have rooted out the malingerers and hypochondriacs.

Faith in magic was not always misplaced, even by scientific standards. The healers of the Auvergne known as *rabouteurs* (bone-setters) and *metzes* (doctors or magicians) had an excellent grasp of basic medicine. They could heal burns, extract bullets and stop haemorrhaging (a common problem when vines were being pruned). Some were able to diagnose illness by inspecting urine. Unlike most doctors, they did not always ask for payment. Many were also blacksmiths – a trade traditionally associated with magic – and ran antenatal clinics. Some women found childbirth less painful after regular sessions in the smithy, lying on a vibrating anvil while the blacksmith swung his hammer and sparks flew about. Terrified neurotics were released from evil curses and found themselves for a time the centre of attention. At the end of the nineteenth century, eight thousand people a year were still arriving at Aumont railway station to visit a road-mender at Nasbinals who performed miraculous cures in his spare time.

Away from the noisy, carnage-strewn main roads of French history, the picture is unexpectedly calm. It suggests compromise and tolerance rather than hatred and fear: priests led pilgrimages to Gallo-Roman shrines, parishioners performed pagan rites under the eyes of the village priest. The best-known images of French religious history are bloody and violent: the Saint Bartholomew Day's massacre, the smashing of the west facade of Notre-Dame, the guillotining of priests and the removal of the word 'saint' from every street and town in France. A thousand other images, too quaint and unlike modern times to be easily remembered, give a more truthful impression of the recent pagan past: a milkless mother in Clermont d'Excideuil (Dordogne) holding a soft cheese to her breast while the curé reads a Gospel passage, and then leaving the cheese as payment; rheumatic pilgrims at the church of Darnac in the Limousin throwing balls of wool at a saint behind an iron cage, trying to hit the part of the saint that corresponded to the rheumatic limb, and the priest of Darnac gathering up the wool and knitting himself some warm clothes for the winter.

The lasting changes to the world of saints and fairies came when people were no longer exposed to the frightening, isolated little worlds where unknown creatures lived complex lives of their own. The great symbol of secularized France is not the operating theatre or the ballot box but the vast megalithic alignments of autoroutes that bypass towns and villages and offer just an occasional glimpse of a cathedral spire fleeing across the landscape. New, high-speed roads erased the pagan spirits by removing knowledge of the spaces where they lived. The spaces themselves are still there, and when the small road on the map turns into a track and the sky defies the weather forecast, it takes an act of faith to believe that their sacred inhabitants never existed.

8

Migrants and Commuters

EVEN THREE OR FOUR DECADES after the Revolution of 1789, the empty spaces and silent towns with which this book began seemed to represent the normal state of affairs. Returning from Madrid to Paris in 1826, the economist Adolphe Blanqui passed through cities where life was either 'languishing for lack of momentum or actually going backwards': Angoulême, with its paltry river that only small boats could negotiate, Poitiers, with its twisted medieval streets, and Tours, where convents and seminaries outnumbered factories. The only real signs of life, as far as Blanqui could tell, were 'in the centre, by which I mean Paris, and at a few points on the perimeter': Rouen, Bordeaux and Marseille. All the other towns were like tiny asteroidal systems in the early universe:

> At Blois as in many other places . . . either nobody changes place or else they feel compelled to orbit the planet sent from Paris. The rural policeman revolves around the mayor, who revolves around the sub-prefect, who revolves around the prefect. These various bodies each have a considerable number of satellites. The result is monotony such as anyone accustomed to life in Paris can scarcely comprehend.

Forms of life that are more recognizably modern will dominate the second part of this book. The towns of France will stir with new activity. The advent of compulsory education, industrial investment, canals, railways and roads that remained open for most of the year produced changes so dramatic that the older France seems by comparison to have been almost entirely inert, waiting in its mud-clogged villages and unmapped wastes for administrators, doctors, teachers and busybodies to hack their way through the thicket and release it from an ancient spell. Soon, it would be hard for city-dwellers to believe that there was once a time when the bourgeoisie was almost stationary, rooted in its bourgs and walled into its houses, 'like Robinson Crusoe on his island', while large numbers of peasants and workers moved about the land.

*

SOME OF THE LARGE minority that ranged over the uncharted country has already been seen in passing: the unstoppable pilgrims, the pedlars, beggars and bandits. Many more remain invisible. Their movements are hard to detect with sensors that were devised for a later world, when all roads led to Paris, when trade followed routes that could be found on maps and when almost no one travelled without a ticket.

Standing by a main road and waiting for these migrants and commuters to appear in a statistically convenient form would be a long and fruitless task. A better starting point can be found in the common surprises of a traveller's life, especially in those that seem either inexplicable or unimportant. Two facts in particular come to mind. The first concerns the curiously novelistic nature of pre-twentieth-century travel.

In the autumn of 1834 (to take one example among many), the art critic Auguste Jal was sitting with his wife in a public coach, bumping and swaying down the valley of the Rhône towards Marseille. It was raining, but the summer drought had just ended and the river was still too low for the steamboat, which was faster and more comfort-able than the coach. Five other people were crammed into the coach: a member of the Académie de Marseille, a lawyer from Paris and his two young friends who were going to visit the dockyards at Toulon, and a simple-minded dealer in silks who, 'from 11 to 13 October – the time it took to travel from Lyon to Marseille – returned a little too often to his favourite subject: the vat in which the scarves are dyed'. For much of the journey, the road was deserted except for 'a few peasant carts pulled by an ox or a cow in horse's harness'.

In Orange, Jal was appalled by the botched restoration of the Roman arch. He wrote in his diary, referring to the new government inspector of historic monuments, Mérimée, and the polymath historian and critic, Claude Fauriel: 'What must be the opinion of M. Prosper Mérimée, who has just passed us in the stagecoach, chatting with M. Fauriel?'

The significance of this trivial encounter is its triviality. Jal thought nothing of seeing two familiar faces passing in a carriage window, four hundred and fifty miles from Paris. He mentioned it only because he happened to be thinking of historic monuments. The coincidences that novelists devised to stitch together their plots and sub-plots were not necessarily implausible to their original readers: coincidences were a normal part of life. While the average peasant's world rarely had a diameter of more than a dozen miles – about twice the size of nineteenth-century Paris – the world of a wealthy traveller was, in effect, not much bigger. A peasant might move in circles, radiating from a single point. A bourgeois – if he moved at all – was more likely to move in straight lines along fixed corridors. If he wanted to disappear, he could simply leave the system of corridors and slip away into a different dimension.

The second fact of life on the road is harder to explain. Long before railways and the modern telegraph (p. 252), news of important events could spread across the country at amazing speeds. The usual speed for an earth-shattering piece of news travelling over a hundred miles was between 4 and 7 mph. Le Havre heard about the fall of the Bastille (late afternoon, 14 July 1789) in the early hours of 17 July. In good conditions, Brest, at the tip of the Breton peninsula, was fifty-four horse-hours from Paris. Average speeds fell drastically on longer journeys, even on post roads, where horses and riders were relayed. Béziers – five hundred and twenty miles on post roads from Paris – heard about the fall of the Bastille almost seven days after the event (an average speed of less than 4 mph). Smaller towns might be closer in space but further away in time, unless a local inhabitant happened to bring the news. Vitteaux – a hundred and sixty-five miles from Paris in the Auxois region east of Dijon – heard about the Bastille from a local tailor who travelled without stopping for two days and two nights at an average speed of 3½ mph. Even the high-speed messengers employed by groups of traders averaged only 7 mph over long distances.

Despite this, there are several well-attested examples of news travelling at much higher speeds. The arrest of the royal family at Varennes in the Argonne was known on the other side of France in Quimper at 7 a.m. on 24 June 1791. On post-roads, Quimper was five hundred and forty miles from Varennes, which means that the news reached this remote and poorly served part of France at an average speed of almost 11 mph, maintained for two days and two nights. This is faster even than the news of the Battle of Waterloo brought by fleeing soldiers. At Villers-Cotterêts, the young Alexandre Dumas found their speed of a league and a half an hour (just over 4 mph) quite extraordinary: 'It seems that the messengers of misfortune have wings.'

The century's greatest expert on gossip and pre-industrial telecommunications, Honoré de Balzac, suggested that rumour could travel at about 9 mph. The following passage from *Les Marana* refers to the sleepy provincial island in the heart of Paris, whose silence was preserved by toll bridges until the mid-nineteenth century:

> Do not ask after the whereabouts of that mysterious telegraph which transmits to all places at once, in the wink of an eye, a story, a scandal or a piece of news. Ask not who operates the telegraph. An observer can merely note its effects. That telegraph is a social mystery. Some incredible examples can be cited. One will suffice: the murder of the Duc de Berry, who was struck down at the Opéra [in 1820], was reported, ten minutes after the crime, in the depths of the Île Saint-Louis.

These speeds were effectively unattainable by conventional transport over long distances. Until the mid-nineteenth century, long-distance speeds over 10 mph usually indicate some form of remote transmission, such as the pigeons used by a few stock-market speculators to transmit share prices, or the stationary messengers who shouted the news of Caesar's victory at Cenabum (Orléans) all the way to the land of the Arverni, a hundred and fifty miles away – a speed in excess of 12 mph. (An experiment conducted in the nineteenth century showed that, using this method, only three hundred and fifty-two people were needed to transmit a message from Orléans to the frontiers of the Auvergne.)

With an inexhaustible supply of data, logical explanations could be found for exceptional speeds. To bring the news of the King's arrest to Quimper, a fast rider must have set off from Paris as soon as word came from Varennes. He must have ridden through the night twice or been relayed by other night-riders. The roads, for once, were presumably all passable and all the bridges intact. Relay horses other than the small Breton breeds must have been available, fed and harnessed at every stage.

This is not beyond the bounds of possibility. The truly remarkable thing about the dissemination of news is its unpredictability and its apparent independence from known transport networks. In 1932, Georges Lefebvre studied the spread of the 'Great Fear' that gripped two-thirds of the country in late July and early August 1789. The Revolution sparked rumours in half a dozen places of invading foreign troops and bandits paid by vengeful aristocrats to destroy the harvest. It was the sort of panic that could – and did – make a rational person mistake a herd of cows for a marauding gang of cut-throats. When Lefebvre charted the course of each rumour, he exposed the previously unsuspected arteries of a gigantic ants' nest.

Maps of the Great Fear seem to show a communication system that was strangely unreliant on any infrastructure. Paris played no role in the rumour network, nor did natural routes like the valleys of the Rhône and the Garonne. Even the road system was irrelevant. In the Languedoc hills, on a single day, the same rumour appeared in places twenty miles apart that were unconnected by road. The Great Fear spread through the Vendée and Normandy, through Picardy and Champagne with the same inexplicable speed. Riots broke out and châteaux were burned to the ground. Leaving the region of Troyes, the rumours ignored the river Saône and entered the Franche-Comté instead by the mountains of the Jura. The Vercors, perched on its plateau like a Lost World, a blank on the map of human migration, suddenly seemed to have lively connections with the outside world.

Higher ground slowed the rumours but did not stop them. The lofty Massif Central, bypassed by travelling apprentices, kings and theatre companies on tour, Napoleon Bonaparte, several epidemics and, until 1951, the Tour de France, was infiltrated from the north,

1. The ladies of Goust, a self-governing hamlet-republic in the Pyrenees, photographed by an American tourist in 1889: 'They know of no taxes of any kind to pay; they always marry within the village, except where the patriarchs may grant a dispensation with an outsider.' (Edwin Dix, *A Midsummer Drive Through the Pyrenees*.)

2. A cagot (the persecuted caste found in Brittany, Gascony and the Basque Country), at the foot of a column by the north wall of the church at Monein (Pyrénées-Atlantiques).

3. The menhir near Dol-de-Bretagne, at Champ Dolent (Field of Woe or Wailing – a local name for 'abattoir'). Local legends associated the stone with Gargantua, the Devil, two warring brothers and Julius Caesar. Romantic scholars associated it with the Druids. The Church often 'converted' the stones by carving them into the shape of a cross or by inserting a crucifix.

4. A bear handler (orsalher) with his wife, baby, bear and baboon by a railway line in a Paris suburb. Most orsalhers and their bears came from the central Pyrenees. There was a school for performing bears at Ercé. When this postcard photograph was taken in the 1900s, the Pyrenean brown bear was on the verge of extinction. This one had probably been imported from Russia or the Balkans.

908. Les petits métiers de Paris
Le montreur d'ours   J. H.

5. 'Intérieur dans les Landes (lou pachedeuy)'. Oxen were a source of traction, fertilizer, warmth and company. '*Pachedeuy*' was a mixture of hay and bran used as forage.

6. Chimney-sweeps on the banks of the Seine in central Paris. Photograph by Charles Nègre, c. 1851.

7. 'A sombre desert where the cicada sings and the bird is silent, where all human habitation disappears' (V. Hugo). Shepherds in the Landes, at La Mouleyre, near Commensacq, on one of the few surviving patches of the original Landes. The encroaching forest of oak and pine can just be seen on the horizon. A shepherd on stilts could travel at the speed of a trotting horse.

8. Road-building in the Oisans (French Alps), c. 1918. The first surfaced road to cross the region (by the Col du Lautaret) was completed in 1862. The slopes had already been cleared by soil erosion and avalanches. Most of these roads were built for the tourist trade by Italian workers.

105. Lib. Poupin, Mortagne

Le PÈRE JEAN habite la commune de Moulins, près Châtillon (Deux-Sèvres), dans une vieille masure au toit à moitié effondré. Il possède bien au moins 30 pantalons, gilets, paletots, chapeaux et cravates ; le tout, jeté pêle-mêle dans un désordre extraordinaire, produit un effet indescriptible. Le père Jean est superstitieux ; il a un cauchemar continuel (ça revient la nuit chez lui, dit-il). Mais, malgré ce fâcheux contretemps, il en prend son parti et vit en véritable philosophe, sans souci du lendemain. C'est un type unique qu'il faut voir.

9. A Vendée peasant dressed up as a royalist rebel. The caption explains that 'Old Jean' lives in a tumbledown cottage at Moulins near Châtillon (now Mauléon), with his indescribably chaotic collection of old clothes. 'Old Jean is superstitious' but 'takes a philosophical view of the future. He is one of a kind and must be seen to be believed.' The Chouan guerrillas had fought the republican government in the west of France in the days of this man's great-great-grandfather.

4   TYPES D'AUVERGNE. — La Bourrée. — LL.   25 – 1.910

10. 'Types d'Auvergne. La Bourrée'. The bourrée was a lively dance from the Auvergne. It was sometimes fashionable, in less boisterous forms, in Paris. The Church associated it with pagan revelry. When this scene was staged, c. 1905, few people agile enough to dance it could remember the steps. The violinist and his sheet music have replaced the hurdy-gurdy man. The unidentified town in the valley is the spa of La Bourboule.

11. Shanty town in Belleville, in the eastern suburbs of Paris, previously an area of vineyards and quarries. Photograph by Charles Marville, c. 1865.

12. An assistant of the anthropologist Hippolyte Müller, founder of the Musée dauphinois in Grenoble, collecting ethnological artefacts in 1917. Müller cycled all over the region seeking out prehistoric sites to 'connect the earliest inhabitants of a *pays* with those who live there now'. This photograph was taken in July 1917 at Le Coin (6,600 feet), one of the hamlets of Molines-en-Queyras in the Alps.

the east and the west. From one day to the next, a rumour that the King of Sardinia had launched an invasion left Briançon and crossed the 8,000-foot Col d'Izoard into the Queyras and the Ubaye before rushing down into Mediterranean Provence and, incredibly, across the tight, plunging valleys to the west. The rumours died out only when faced with the combined passive force of sparse population and difficult terrain (the Plateau de Millevaches, some of the highest Alpine massifs, the Sologne, the Dombes and the Landes).

This mysteriously efficient network was still functioning after the fall of Napoleon. In 1816, the deposed emperor was rumoured to have escaped from St Helena and returned to Paris. One such rumour sprang up – simultaneously, it seemed – in Nemours and parts of Burgundy and the Bourbonnais. The authorities understandably suspected a well-organized plot. Agents provocateurs were active, but not necessarily in this case. News that spread like a stain instead of travelling from A to B could cover vast areas in very little time. The scattered sources of rumours reaching the little market town of Charlieu, in the hills between the Forez and the Beaujolais (reported at a public meeting on 28 July 1789), indicate a rumour catchment area of three thousand square miles. This particular area included five or six major dialects and the three main language groups of France. No pigeon, horse or locomotive could have disseminated news so quickly.

*

A PARTIAL EXPLANATION of these coincidences and connections could be found by following some of the thousands of migrant workers who ranged across the land.

The aspect of their world that now seems most conspicuously exotic was not officially discovered and described until the early nineteenth century. When Napoleon's statisticians first surveyed the westernmost Breton *département*, Finistère, they were startled to find that almost one-fifth of the total surface was taken up by 'roads and byways' – ruts, paths, cartways and great trampled swathes of land that were lost to agriculture and often unusable even as tracks. Paradoxically, this inaccessible part of France was riddled with routes. Further studies confirmed the incredible figures. Finistère was an extreme case, but many other *départements* turned out to be crazed with tiny roads: 12 per cent of the Bas-Rhin, 4 per cent of the Vienne, 3 per cent of the Nord, just under 2 per cent of the Haute-Marne, 1.4 per cent of the Pas-de-Calais. The effect can still be pictured in some parts of France. So many different roads once ran from Beauvais to Amiens that six of them still exist, all more or less the same length (thirty-five to thirty-nine miles) and sometimes close enough for a person on one road to wave to someone on the other.

The huge discrepancy between the trifling amount of traffic on main roads and the quantities of goods delivered to markets and ports suggests that three-quarters of all trade in the early nineteenth century passed through this all-encompassing web. This was the system of fragile capillaries that carried the rumours and news. Many of these paths had no visible existence, even to a person standing on one. The French word *route*, which means both 'route' and 'road', preserves the ambiguity. Some *routes*, like smugglers' paths in Brittany and the Basque Country, were little more than memories passed on from one generation to the next. A featureless meadow on the high plains of Provence where a stranger would see nothing but grass blowing in the wind might be a major European crossroads between the Alps, the Mediterranean, the Rhône Valley and northern Italy. When he was trudging south through the Cévennes from Le Monastier to Saint-Jean-du-Gard in 1878, Robert Louis Stevenson imagined himself a hundred miles from civilization:

> My road lay through one of the most beggarly countries in the world.
> It was like the worst of the Scottish Highlands, only worse; cold,
> naked, and ignoble, scant of wood, scant of heather, scant of life.
> A road and some fences broke the unvarying waste, and the line of
> the road was marked by upright pillars, to serve in time of snow.

In fact, much of the 'Stevenson Trail', as it is now known, runs along the 140-mile route known, for part of its length, as the Voie Regordane (the origin of the name is obscure). This had been a major north–south route since pre-human times, when a fault line opened up a succession of passes linking the Massif Central with the Mediterranean. In the mid-eighteenth century, a hundred mule drivers regularly plied the Voie Regordane with their clanging mule trains, taking metals and materials down to the inland port of Saint-Gilles and returning with produce for the Auvergne and the main road to Paris in baskets and goatskins. In some of those desolate highland towns, Stevenson could have bought wine, olive oil, salted fish, almonds, oranges, figs and raisins, not to mention salt, soap, paper and a proper packsaddle for his donkey.

Stevenson actually saw a relatively dynamic part of the Auvergne. He was able to pay for things with money and stayed in inns that had ticking clocks. He enjoyed luxurious breakfasts of chocolate, brandy and cigarettes. When he walked along the road, he heard the sound of the wind in telegraph wires. Bands of harvesters watched him pass as they walked across the fields. On the high road, for the twelve miles between Le Bouchet-St-Nicolas and Pradelles, the only other travellers he saw were 'a cavalcade of stride-legged ladies and a pair of post-runners', but he also saw some of the million tendrils of the other network that carried most of the traffic:

> The little green and stony cattle-tracks wandered in and out of one another, split into three or four, died away in marshy hollows, and began again sporadically on hillsides or at the borders of a wood.
>
> There was no direct road to Cheylard, and it was no easy affair to make a passage in this uneven country and through this intermittent labyrinth of tracks.

This labyrinth is the reason why the towns and villages of France were both cut off and connected. Wares and produce travelled through the system of tracks and tiny roads by something akin to Brownian motion, changing hands slowly over great distances. When the main roads were improved and railways were built, trade was drained from the capillary network, links were broken, and a large part of the population suddenly found itself more isolated than before. Many regions today are experiencing the same effect because of the TGV railway system.

*

IT WOULD TAKE a thousand separate maps to show the movements of the migrant population through this labyrinth of tracks, but an excellent overall view can be gained from any large-scale relief map or satellite photograph.

At this height above the land, a diagonal line can be seen running from the western Pyrenees to the Vosges, marking off the highest ground and dividing the country roughly into two. Migrants originating south and east of the line flowed from the highlands like melting snow while transhumant animals headed for the mountains. A saying in western Languedoc described it nicely: '*Crabas amont, filhas aval*' ('Goats go up and girls go down'). In this half of France, the main watershed was the ancient collapsed volcano called the Cantal. It covers an area of almost a thousand square miles, which makes it the largest volcanic structure in Europe. From the *département* to which the Cantal gave its name, thousands of men, women and children descended every year to the plains of Gascony and Spain, to the Mediterranean and Marseille, to Lyon and the Rhône valley and to Poitou and the Paris Basin.

This was the zone of long-distance migration. North and west of the line, seasonal migration tended to be shorter. In this half of France, people were more likely to die within sight of their village steeple, and their knowledge of the outside world was more likely to be passive. They heard about events from the semi-nomadic individuals who moved about the country: bell-founders, knife-grinders, distillers and pedlars; wine- and corn-brokers; wandering singers, circus acts and quack doctors; hair-harvesters who collected raw material for wig-makers, clog-makers who set up temporary villages in forests, and beggars who made themselves welcome by bringing news and gossip and sometimes love letters. Some of these short-range nomads were listed in an army handbook of 1884 as a vital source of information on a region:

> Deserters, strangers passing through, homeless people arrested by the police . . . hunters, poachers, shepherds, charcoal burners, woodcutters . . . It is best to take several and to question them separately. . . . Smugglers and pedlars make particularly good spies.

Mass movements in this lowland half of the country were comparatively modest, though they were still great odysseys to the people who undertook them. In spring, long processions of young girls followed by pack donkeys carrying luggage and the weary headed for the Brie, the Beauce and the Gâtinais, where they hoed the fields before returning to Burgundy in time for the wine harvest. The wheat fields of the Paris Basin also drew huge bands of farmworkers from northern France. Groups of migrant harvesters still appear in late summer and early autumn, travelling in trucks or living in caravans, attaching little suburbs of washing lines and satellite dishes to the edges of vineyards. Occasionally, a family of migrant agricultural workers can be seen walking one behind the other, intent on the road ahead, and moving at a pace that seems slow only at a distance.

These seasonal migrants were once a more obvious presence, in towns as well as in the countryside. On certain days, the main squares of towns and cities filled up at dawn with hundreds of families who had walked through the night with their sickles wrapped in spare clothes. The markets were known as *loues* or *louées*. Harvesters wore ears of corn, shepherds sported tufts of wool and carters hung whips around their necks. Domestic servants wore their best clothes and carried a distinctive bouquet or some foliage to serve as identification. The employer would make them walk up and down to prove that they were not crippled and inspect their hands for the calluses that showed that they were hard workers. A coin placed in the hand sealed the contract. As the day wore on, the crowd of hopefuls became smaller, older and more decrepit. Those that remained at the very end of the day might follow the harvest anyway as gleaners, covering hundreds of miles in a month or two before returning home.

In the highland half of France, the trade in human beings took more dramatic forms. Well into the second half of the nineteenth century, travellers heading east in the autumn would see large bands of little boys – and some girls in disguise – dressed in coarse brown cloth and wearing broad-rimmed hats and hobnail boots, marching towards Paris from Dauphiné, Savoy and Piedmont. Some were only five years old. In the capital, they were known as 'winter swallows' because they appeared in the streets just as the birds were flying south and the weather was turning cold.

A month before, children from different villages had gathered in the plains below the Alps. Their parents gave them a little money, two or three shirts wrapped in a handkerchief, some stony black bread, a passport and sometimes a crude map showing the location of relatives or friends along the route. They walked up to fifty miles a day, sleeping in barns and supplementing the everlasting loaf with stolen eggs and apples. On the long route from Savoy to Lyon and on to Paris and the north, they had time to rehearse their songs and street cries and perhaps some conjuring tricks. The boys from Piedmont often had a triangle or a hurdy-gurdy; others carried a marmot in a cage or a ferret for catching rats. Most of the boys from Savoy were destined to spend the next ten years scraping soot from Parisian chimneys or carrying water up to apartments in tin buckets. Many of them would also work as messengers, boot-blacks and shop-boys.

Child migration came to be seen as a form of slavery and a threat to public order, though there was no effective legislation until the 1870s. To the people themselves, it was a highly organized, respectable and necessary activity. In Dauphiné villages where land and resources were scarce, many children were rented out to employers who paid the parents between fifty and eighty francs a year. The boys had to deliver themselves to the city – Paris, Lyon or Marseille, sometimes Turin or Milan. In Paris, they found their way to the squalid area around the Place Maubert in the Latin Quarter or to the Rue Guérin-Boisseau near the Porte Saint-Denis. There, they were given a bed and instructed in the art of begging. Next morning, they went out with their marmots and begging bowls in groups of three or four. This was their life for the next three or six years, depending on the contract signed by their parents. If they returned at night to the hostel with less than a franc, they were given nothing, but for anything over a franc, they received a commission of 10 or 20 per cent. As part of the deal, every afternoon, they were given reading and catechism lessons. These arrangements were well known to middle-class Parisians who generally considered it the done thing – until immigrant workers became a political issue – to help these little creatures from the furthest corners of France.

The Savoyard chimney sweeps lived under a slightly different regime. On reaching the city, they split up into village groups. Each had its own dormitory and canteen. A spartan building in a particular street might look like a part of Paris when in fact it was a colony of Savoy controlled by a Savoyard sweep-master. The master might also sell pots and pans or rabbit-skins and keep an eye on the boys as they went about the city shouting, '*Haut en bas!*' ('Top to bottom!') If a boy stole money or misbehaved, he was punished according to Savoyard tradition. Boys who fled into the back streets were always found: chimney sweeps knew the city as well as any policeman and better than most Parisians. In severe cases, the culprit was expelled from the community.

A boy who suffered this banishment within exile might be able to find work if he stood with his kneepads and scraping tool in the crowd of unemployed urchins who gathered at the Porte Saint-Denis and the Rue Basse-du-Rempart, on the site of the future Place de l'Opéra. If he was lucky, he might be adopted by a benevolent society and given a proper apprenticeship. If not, he might be trained and dressed by a pimp and turned into one of the hundreds of '*petits jésus*' (rent-boys) who worked on the Champs-Élysées and other parts of the city's perimeter.

The sweeps who avoided asphyxiation, lung disease and blindness, and who never fell from a roof, might one day set up on their own as stove-fitters. Nearly all of them returned home to marry. Their tie to the homeland was never broken. When he emerged from the chimney onto the roof of a Parisian apartment block, a Savoyard sweep could always see the Alps.

*

THE BANDS OF HARVESTERS and the armies of children account for something like 15 per cent of the half million or so people who moved about the land. Theirs was a relatively concentrated and gregarious form of migration. Other migrants, like the pedlars and smugglers mentioned by the army handbook, covered the ground more thoroughly, moving through the labyrinth like sap through a tree.

Every year, until the 1870s, thousands of *colporteurs* (pedlars) left mountain villages with hundred-pound baskets or pine-wood chests strapped to their backs. A stick at the rear allowed them to rest without removing the load. Inside, the merchandise was arranged in smaller baskets and covered with spare clothes. Weight was obviously critical. The pedlars' baskets were masterpieces of packing. One man's basket in 1841 contained 9,800 pins, 6,084 bobbins, 3,888 buttons, 3,000 needles, 36 thimbles, 36 combs, 24 lengths of cotton, 18 snuffboxes, 96 pens and pencils, 200 quills, 40 pairs of scissors and an assortment of hooks-and-eyes, knives, notebooks, suspenders and cakes of soap. Other popular items included religious trinkets, herbal remedies, anything made of silk and, once botanizing tourists had shown there was a market for them, Alpine plants and seeds. A *colporteur* from lower Normandy who died at Longpont in the Perche in 1788 had left his trunk with the curé for safe keeping. It measured three foot by one and a half and was fitted with leather backstraps. The trunk was divided into seven boxes and seven drawers, containing three hundred and eighty-two samples of forty-one different items (two of the drawers were empty), including watch-chains, scissors, seals, earrings, spectacles, razors, knives, ribbons, gloves, stockings and an IOU for a silver watch.

Some of the most profitable merchandise weighed nothing. Long-distance pedlars took advantage of a belief that mountain folk had magic powers. A spell uttered in a strange and incomprehensible dialect could be very convincing. Some pedlars offered medical and veterinary services. They pierced ears, extracted teeth and told fortunes. Even after the practice was outlawed in 1756, Bearnese pedlars in Spain castrated boys whose parents hoped to secure them a place in a cathedral choir. On the return journey, if they followed the routes from Santiago de Compostela to Rocamadour and Le Puy-en-Velay, they could pretend to be pilgrims and beg their way home from one abbey to the next.

Deceit was a particular speciality of pedlars from the Auvergne. A single piece of cloth could be made to last a whole season if it was sold with the promise that a tailor would come the next day and make up the clothes for nothing. The tailor would arrive, measure the customer, take the cloth and never return. The drawback was that a dishonest salesman had to cover vast areas compared to a pedlar who earned the trust of his clientele.

One form of deceit, known as '*la pique*', was a major industry. A sympathetic village priest would sign a letter explaining that the bearer had suffered terrible calamities and was a worthy object of charity: his farm had burned down, his animals were diseased, his wife was on her deathbed and someone had stolen all their money.

The person who wrote the letter took a share of the proceeds. Apparently, old women made the best *pique* writers. A priest who was questioned after the arrest of two pedlars on the *pique* freely admitted that he had signed the bogus document. Even if the details were false, the poverty was real, and a man who was prepared to walk hundreds of miles to make a living from sympathy was at least relieving pressure on village resources.

*

WITH AN ENTIRELY law-abiding population, much of France would have been cut off from the outside world. Smuggling, too, was a major industry that kept the tiny channels of communication open. In some parts, it was practically the only industry. The inhabitants of frontier towns such as Le Pont-de-Beauvoisin, which straddles the France–Savoy border, did little else. Some Provençal villages abandoned agriculture for contraband, and some monasteries had suspiciously large stores of alcohol and tobacco. Nice, which was a separate state until 1860, could export east into Italy and west across the river Var into France.

The frontier between France and Spain was like a sieve. In the west, the hills of the Basque Country were criss-crossed by the smugglers' paths that were later used by guerrillas, Résistants and Basque terrorists. In the east, Catalans and Roussillonnais ran a thriving criminal economy. A report to the Ministry of Foreign Affairs in 1773 complained that 'you can't put one foot in front of the other without running into a band of armed smugglers'. These were not furtive figures creeping about in the undergrowth. They moved in platoons of fifty, with another platoon behind to provide backup. They were fed, paid a salary and divided into ranks like soldiers.

In Brittany, thousands of heavily laden women carrying cakes of salt and over-salted butter poured into Maine, pretending to be pregnant. More than twelve thousand children were tried for smuggling at the salt court in Laval in 1773. This figure included only children who were caught with contraband weighing fifteen pounds or more. When they grew up, some of them would join what was practically an Anglo-French common market. Breton sailors carried brandy to Plymouth while Cornishmen brought tobacco to Roscoff.

The sea lanes used by Gallo-Roman traders and Norman invaders remained as busy as ever, especially when Napoleon imposed the Continental System (1806–13). A smugglers' slang is said to have been in use on both sides of the Channel. Smugglers from Saint-Malo and Granville could converse with Channel Islanders in Norman French. An American visitor to northern France in 1807 found suspicious signs that, despite Napoleon, Calais and Boulogne were still on excellent trading terms with Dover and Hastings:

> Eggs, bacon, poultry, and vegetables, seemed in great plenty, and, as I understood, composed the dinners of the peasantry twice a week at least. I was surprised at this evident abundance in a class in which I should not have expected it. Something of it, I fear, must be imputed to the extraordinary profits of the smuggling which is carried on along the coast.

All this suggests that, while customs barriers stifled trade, they did not necessarily increase isolation. The 'fortress' of France was remarkably porous. Any commemoration of European unity should remember the smugglers and pedlars who helped to keep the borders open.

*

IF THE WELL-BEING of a nation is defined by industrialization and investment, the to-ing and fro-ing and scrimping and saving of half a million migrant workers and petty criminals looks like the feeble activity of a backward economy. But if the entire land mass is taken into account, it seems to indicate a state of health that France has never completely recovered. Maps of the population by *département* seem to show the country entering a new Dark Age in the late nineteenth century. Between 1801 and 1911, when the total population of France increased by more than ten million, the population of nineteen *départements* fell, including several *départements* close to Paris. In another fourteen *départements*, it increased by less than fifty thousand. Today, thirty-six *départements*, representing 40 per cent of the surface of France, have fewer inhabitants than they did a century and a half ago. Seasonal migration may have involved less than 2 per cent of the population but it had a vital effect. It prevented the haemorrhaging of the land by allowing wealth to reach less productive parts.

The results can still be seen in some parts of France: the two-storey *'maisons de lait'* (milk houses) in Burgundy villages that were built with money earned by wet-nurses; the summer villas of retired water-carriers in the remote Cantal; the incongruously grand mansions that began to appear in Barcelonnette and Aiguilles when umbrella salesmen returned to the Alps from South America and when local cheeses began to reach the Mediterranean and even crossed the Atlantic in lead-lined boxes.

The ant-like movements of the migrant minority not only spread wealth but also delayed the growth of the cities. Until permanent migration became the norm in the late nineteenth century, Paris was not the all-consuming gravitational centre of France. The capital was well served by the major rivers of north-eastern France – Yonne, Seine, Marne, Aisne and Oise – but not by the rivers that rise in the Massif Central. The best roads out of the Auvergne all led south. A trade route to Bordeaux, Toulouse, Montpellier or Marseille, busy with mule trains and pilgrims, was preferable to an obscure track that led north into lands where people spoke a different language. Even in the early twentieth century, many villages in the southern Auvergne and Périgord had closer ties with Spain than with the northern half of France. Basque families were just as likely to have relatives in Buenos Aires and, eventually, Manhattan, as in Paris.

If all these routes could have been plotted on a map, the picture would have looked more like Roman Gaul than the Paris-centric road and rail systems of the twenty-first century. Early maps of literacy show the same unexpected pattern. Some regions that were supposed to be far from the light of civilization turned out to have surprisingly high rates of literacy: the Cantal, the Isère, the Drôme, the Alpine *départements* and Savoy. When Balzac described a cultural missionary in *The Country Doctor* (1833), 'improving an uncultivated corner of the world [in the Dauphiné] and civilizing its inhabitants who have been deprived of intelligence', he was transposing his largely illiterate native province of Touraine to the Alps, about which he knew very little. Many Alpine villages had been running their own schools for decades, not to provide a general education but to train the next generation of pedlars. They taught arithmetic, account-keeping and business French. Children in the Oisans region east of Grenoble copied out and memorized model letters. The following example was supposed to be sent by a successful pedlar who had escaped the drudgery of home and was living it up in the capital:

> And so, dear friend, as you can see, we have many more pleasures than at home, where all we do is go from one relative to the next to bid them good day. I strongly urge you to come and live in Paris so that you might taste its delights.

The idea that the salvation of communities depended on small-scale, individual efforts is still apparent in French agricultural policies. Some attitudes that seem parochial and protectionist reflect an accurate perception of French rather than Parisian history. In Victorian Britain, the catastrophic coincidence of urbanization and industrialization created vast polluted zones of misery and disease. In France, most industrial workers were either domestic, like the weavers of Normandy and Lyon, or seasonal, like the mountain people who sweated for six or seven months in the oil-, soap- and perfume factories of Aix and Marseille before returning home to buy a plot of land. Most mills and factories were small enough to ignore the law on child labour that, until 1874, applied only to workshops employing more than twenty people. Unlike British industry, French industry was devoted predominantly to the production of so-called *articles de Paris* – luxury goods such as clocks, jewellery, furniture, fashion accessories, domestic utensils and artificial flowers. As the Larousse dictionary boasted in 1872, France may lag behind Britain and Germany in heavy industry, 'but it has no equal in all industries which demand elegance and grace and which are more concerned with art than with manufacture'.

Apart from a few industrial boom towns like Roubaix and Mont-luçon (pp. 264, 346), French cities remained within their old walls. In 1860, when the boundaries of Paris were extended to include some outlying villages – Montmartre, Grenelle, Vaugirard, etc. – Honoré Daumier published a caricature of a clumpy peasant couple in clogs and smocks standing in a ploughed field with a Paris skyline in the distance, saying, 'To think we're now Parisians!' The suburban ocean of mud and the tiny island-city were just a slight exaggeration. In most parts, a migrant worker entering a town would be announced by the echoing clatter of his hobnail boots on the cobbles. In 1839, Balzac described a sixteen-year-old travelling apprentice arriving one October morning in the town of Provins (Seine-et-Marne). Provins stood on one of the main roads to the east and had mills, tanneries, brickworks and a sugar-beet distillery. It produced roses for nurseries and chemists (the petals were used in cordials and lotions) and had a healthy trade in grain, flour, wine, wool and mineral water. It held four big fairs a year and was just seven hours from Paris on the mail coach.

> He stopped in a little square in the lower part of Provins. At that time of day, he could examine, without being seen, the various houses that stand on the square, which is oblong in shape. The mills along the rivers of Provins were already turning. The sound of their wheels, repeated by the echoes of the upper town, in harmony with the keen air and the sparkling light of morning, only intensified the silence in which it was possible to hear the clanking of a diligence a league away on the high road. . . . There were no signs of commerce, and hardly any of those luxurious carriage-gates of the rich. What few there were rarely turned on their hinges, except those belonging to M. Martener, a doctor who was forced to keep a carriage and to use it.

Most French towns and cities effectively had huge, sparsely populated conurbations of several thousand square miles from which people commuted for several days, weeks or months. Even if the working 'day' lasted several years, it almost always ended with a return to the *pays*. Nîmes and Lyon both drew textile workers from very distant mountain villages. Most migration was rural, and most of the migrants who went to cities were not fodder for satanic mills: they provided services and were self-employed. In 1838, of almost twenty-three thousand Savoyard migrants in France, only two thousand worked in factories, which is to say, from their point of view, in warm, dry places with food and lodging and a steady wage.

Foreigners who go to live in French towns today usually hope to be integrated and accepted by the community. This was not usually a preoccupation of the French inhabitants. By the mid-nineteenth century, half the inhabitants of Paris came from the provinces and most of them did not consider themselves Parisian. Migrants spent as little money as possible while away from home. Mentally, they never left their *pays*. They were insulated from the lands through which they passed and, once they reached the city, they lived, like the chimney sweeps, in miniature versions of home. In certain Paris streets, the sounds and smells of villages and provincial towns drowned out the sounds and smells of the capital. For many, their street cry was the only French they spoke. Tinkers and scrap-metal merchants from a particular valley of the Cantal were concentrated around the Rue de Lappe near the Bastille. Water-carriers and labourers from the neighbouring valley lived in the same *quartier*, divided from their compatriots by a street instead of by the river Jordanne. All the people involved in the conspiracy on which Alexandre Dumas based *The Count of Monte Cristo* came from the same part of Nîmes and lived in the same *quartier* of Paris, between the Place du Châtelet and Les Halles. They met and exchanged news of home in a cafe run by a compatriot in the Place Sainte-Opportune. Traces of these urban villages are still visible, especially near the big railway stations: the name of a cafe or restaurant, a regional dish, a waiter's accent or a photograph of a cow in a mountain meadow.

France itself was like a giant city in which every district had its own speciality. Horse-dealers came from Normandy, mole-catchers and their apprentices from the Orne, lace-makers from Caen and Beauvais. Chambermaids came from Brittany and Guyenne. In the eighteenth century, the sculptural, starched head-dresses of Norman women were a common sight around the Bureau of Wet-Nurses in the Rue Sainte-Apolline in Paris; in the nineteenth century, they were replaced by the black hoods of Burgundian women who followed the timber that was floated down from the Morvan.

Most of these migrants could reach Paris in a few days. Others trekked across the country for weeks: porters and locksmiths (and, supposedly, lock-pickers) from Lyon, second-hand-clothes dealers from Alsace, singers from the Haute-Marne, doormen (known as '*suisses*') from Switzerland, glaziers from Piedmont, cooks from Montpellier, bear-handlers and knife-grinders from the Pyrenees. The Auvergne sent hatters and sawyers from the Forez, rag-and-bone men from Ambert and Le Mont-Dore, and furriers from Oradoux who walked the streets under a mountain of rabbi frightening children and skinning stray cats. The Auvergnat coal merchants called *bougnats* sailed down the Allier and the Canal de Briare. Most of them also sold wine. Some of the best-known cafés in Paris were founded by *bougnats* – Le Flore, Le Dôme, La Coupole, Les Deux Magots. There are still a few coal-selling barkeepers, and almost three-quarters of the *cafés-tabacs* in Paris are still run by Auvergnats and their descendants.

There is no apparent logic to the map of migrations. Once a route had been pioneered, a colony established and a clientele created, these trades had a momentum that ensured their long-term survival. Customers came to associate the product or the service with a particular style of regional dress and a particular accent. But there are few signs of sensitivity to economic change. In the late eighteenth century, cities on the edges of Lorraine – Strasbourg, Troyes and Dijon – were inundated with starving cobblers, most of whom had no raw materials and few skills. Poor regions like the Vercors and the 'pré-Alpes' from Digne to Grasse, which might have benefited from migration, remained cut off until the late nineteenth century, when their populations suddenly began to flow away forever. No one knows why thousands of stonemasons and building labourers left the Limousin every year. There was no shortage of land and their skills were needed in the region. The only obvious reason is that men who had lived away from home made better husbands: they had more money, more prestige and, above all, more interesting stories to tell.

*

THE DESIRE TO DISCOVER the country is usually associated with explorers, scholars and tourists, not with migrant workers. Yet curiosity was clearly one of the main forces behind migration. At a time when most people were afraid to set foot out of doors after dark, the routes forged by migrants provided a comparatively safe passage to the world beyond the *pays*.

The classic example of this organized discovery of France is the apprentice's Tour de France. The expression dates from the early-eighteenth century, though the practice is much older. It was once confined to Provence and Languedoc but eventually included the Loire Valley, Paris, Burgundy and the valley of the Rhône. Avoiding Brittany (apart from Nantes), Normandy, the north and north-east, and the mountains, it described a rough hexagon around the Massif Central. Each trade had its own society with a network of 'Mothers' who provided lodging and employment opportunities in each town on the itinerary.* The apprentice was renamed after his *pays* – 'Libourne', 'Bordelais', 'Landais', etc. He then spent a few weeks or months in the town, working long hours, acquiring local techniques and learning to work with local materials. He also had to learn the secret laws of the Order or 'Devoir' to which his guild belonged. When the time came to leave, a noisy procession with drums and fiddles accompanied him to the edge of town.

A typical tour lasted four or five years, covered more than fourteen hundred miles, usually in a clockwise direction, and included a hundred and fifty-one different towns (to judge by an 'Ordinary Route of the Tour de France' published by a baker from Libourne in 1859). Certain towns were obligatory and, for masons and carpenters, certain works of art in abbeys and cathedrals. During the Tour, the apprentice was inducted into the guild. He then became a 'Compagnon du Tour de France' and was given a second name which reflected his official worthiness: 'Lyonnais-la-Fidélité', 'L'Estimable-le-Provençal', 'Angoumois-le-Courageux', etc. Agricol Perdiguier, a cabinetmaker from the suburbs of Avignon who published his memoirs of the Tour in 1854, was named Avignonnais-la-Vertu. The Compagnon was also presented with a special walking stick festooned with ribbons to make him recognizable on the road. When he completed his Tour and returned home, he was awarded a certificate and remained a Compagnon for the rest of his life.

With the Tour de France, village rivalries and feuds took to the

---

* Apprentices from France and other parts of Europe whose trade involves the transformation of raw material (carpenters, stonemasons, plumbers, bakers, etc.) still undertake a Tour de France and stay in hostels run by 'Mothers'. Football matches have taken the place of pitched battles. There are three orders: le Compagnonnage du Devoir, le Compagnonnage du Devoir de Liberté and l'Union Compagnonnique des Devoirs Unis.

road. Members of the different orders would try to beat each other senseless when they met on the road or when one guild tried to set up a new '*Mère*' in a town. Apprentices quickly learned to use their tools as weapons. A handbook of laws and regulations for workers, foremen and Compagnons published in 1833 devoted seven of its thirty pages to seditious assemblies, insults and defamation, perjury, threats, bodily harm and homicide. When the baker from Libourne interrupted his tour in 1840 to visit the venerable bearded hermit on the Sainte-Baume massif, the hermit understandably had a few sharp words to say on the subject of the Tour de France.* He saw this sectarian aggression as a sign of backwardness and cited the fact that three out of every four Compagnons who had visited his grotto had been unable to sign his visitors' book.

Still, these bloody battles, like the songs that were written by Compagnon poets, created a powerful sense of community. One day, the workforce would be concentrated in factories and cities, confronted with the faceless enemy of economic change and political repression. In those circumstances, solidarity would be a precious weapon. The population in general would come to adopt a view that was once peculiar to police ministers: 'winter swallows' would be seen as aliens and subversives. The village mentality that set one tiny *pays* against another would be applied to entire nations – Italy, Spain, Portugal and Algeria – and some migrant workers would make journeys that would have appalled their nineteenth-century predecessors, crossing the Mediterranean in rowing boats, riding in refrigerated trucks or clinging to the underside of high-speed trains.

*

IT SEEMS TO BE a law of social history that the greater the number of people with a particular experience, the less evidence remains of

---

* One of the three main Orders of Compagnons believed that their founder was a Frenchman who helped to build Solomon's Temple in Jerusalem and retired to the Sainte-Baume. Compagnons still make a pilgrimage to the grotto in July. Relics of their patron saint, Mary Magdalen, are enshrined in the nearby Saint-Maximin basilica, where the graffiti of nineteenth-century Compagnons can still be seen on walls and columns just inside the entrance.

that experience. There are hundreds of pointlessly detailed accounts of banal coach journeys made by tourists, but the odysseys undertaken by migrants have vanished like most of the routes they walked.

The account written by one of the thousands of stonemasons who left the Limousin every year is a priceless exception. Martin Nadaud, who later became a socialist politician, described the gruelling journey to Paris in his memoirs. His account is brief, especially after Orléans, but the scenes he saw along the way can be recreated from other sources.

Nadaud was born in a Limousin hamlet called Martineiche. He was fourteen years old when he left home with his father and uncle. On the day of departure (26 March 1830), his tearful mother dressed him in a top hat, new shoes and a sheep's-wool suit as stiff as cardboard. The suit was made from drugget, which is now used for coarse rugs. Martin was going to walk most of the way to Paris, but he had to look respectable, marching down a main street two hundred and forty miles long.

At the first stopping point, Pontarion, they were joined by other migrants from all over the Creuse. They drank some wine and then the old men who had walked with them on the first part of the journey turned for home, 'telling us always to be well behaved and to keep a fond memory of the *pays*'.

Soon, they lost sight of the 'Druid stones' that stood on a hill behind the village. For Nadaud, these stones stood for his *pays* and the Gallic masons who had 'reconquered the fatherland' from the Romans. Since there was still no road to Guéret, the route ran through the forest on muddy tracks. Raindrops sprang from the branches and soaked them to the skin. By the time they reached Bordessoule on the borders of the *département*, the young masons' feet were sore and bloody: Nadaud's father helped him peel off his stockings and rubbed his soles with fat. The inn was a typical migrants' dosshouse – cheap, hospitable and filthy. The innkeepers along the route put fresh sheets on the beds in November and changed them in March. The trick was to slip into the envelope of grime, fully clothed, and to wrap one's head in a cloth. Sleep came quickly, despite the fleas.

The long march north was an apprenticeship in itself: learning to walk on wet and blistered feet and to keep up with the older migrants, learning to stomach mouldy food when the body was exhausted and above all to defend the honour of the *pays*. As they set off from villages at daybreak, the migrants sang and yelped as though they were at a barn dance. It was their way of keeping their spirits up and warning off the natives. Sometimes, there were pitched battles and the outcome was soon known all along the migration routes and in the masons' colony in Paris. Young Nadaud had often heard about these battles at the village *veillées*, and so, when local peasants shouted at them from the hedgerows, calling them geese and turkeys, 'I was more curious than upset. . . . The boldest in our band grouped together, and you could see from their faces that the insults would not go unpunished.'

On the third day, at Salbris, gendarmes were waiting to escort the migrants to their dosshouse. On the fourth day, after stumbling over the stones and puddles of the cheerless Sologne, they looked across the river Loire and saw the towers of Orléans cathedral. From here, they would travel by coach.

With its forty thousand inhabitants, Orléans was the biggest town the young masons had ever seen. The old story about the peasant who went to Poitiers but never saw it 'because the houses were in the way' might not have seemed so ludicrous to them. For the first time, they would have witnessed the strange phenomenon of a crowd of people all engaged on separate business and moving in different directions. This was part of the new world that the masons were helping to create. At Orléans, there were encouraging signs of a building boom. Town planners had been waging war on the past for forty years. The medieval gates and fortifications had gone, and so had almost every trace of the city's saviour, Joan of Arc. The new Rue Jeanne d'Arc had obliterated a mass of ancient slums, but at least it allowed the cathedral to be seen to full advantage.

The offices of the coach company were filling up with migrants bound for Paris. Liveried employees turned their noses up at the smelly peasants from the south. There were never enough carriages to take them all. Instead, they were piled into tiny coaches known as *coucous* – probably because they looked like giant cuckoo-clocks. The *coucous*, which were also known as 'chamber pots', were notorious for their asthmatic horses and sarcastic drivers. They bumped about so much that passengers were sometimes thrown out. Most of these death-traps raced along the roads near Paris and cluttered up the Place de la Concorde. It was unusual for a *coucou* to make such a long journey. Orléans was seventy-five miles from Paris, and on a good day, the mail coach took eight hours. In a ramshackle contraption like the *coucou*, with a mulish driver who stopped to drink at every inn and refused to be rushed, the masons would be lucky to leave at dawn and arrive before dark.

Like the *matatus* of modern Kenya, a *coucou* was never considered to be full. Extra passengers were crammed onto the driver's seat and attached to the rear of the coach. The former were known as 'rabbits', the latter as 'monkeys'. The Orléans *coucou* was even more accommodating. Four young masons travelled together in the *coucou* equivalent of steerage: a wicker basket slung under the body of the coach, supposed to be used for luggage.

From here on, the view was severely restricted. Through the spray of mud and grit, the seasick human cargo would have seen the walls of Orléans run past for more than two miles. Then the road climbed out of the valley of the Loire to the hamlet of Montjoie and into the Orléans forest. They might have caught a smell of the woodcutters' hamlet at Cercottes but they probably saw no trees since the forest had been cut back a long way from the road to make life hard for highwaymen.

After the forest, for several hours, there were only sandy plains and the windy wheatfields of the Beauce. They rattled across the Roman road from Sens to Chartres. Signs of wealth began to appear: a well-tended orchard, an avenue leading to a château. They passed through Arpajon and Longjumeau, deafened by the clatter of cartwheels in the tunnel of walls, then Antony and Sceaux, where cattle gathered before being driven into the city. When they saw a passenger waiting by the road, the drivers always shouted '*Encore un pour Sceaux!*' (another one for Sceaux) because it sounded like '*Encore un pourceau!*' (another swine). After Bourg-la-Reine with its potteries and Arcueil with its aqueduct, the road surface improved and the traffic increased. At Montrouge, roads from Versailles and the west joined the road from Orléans. Heavy carts with sleepy drivers were leaving Paris for the country.

They reached the edge of the city at the Barrière d'Enfer. It was hardly a triumphal entry. From the basket under the coach, they saw the blur of boots and bare feet, carriage wheels and dog-carts, and the lower part of posters advertising auctions, books, baths and dental treatment. They rattled down the Rue Saint-Jacques, past the Observatory and the Sorbonne, to the Pont Neuf. There was the sudden smell of the river, then skirts and petticoats and patent-leather boots on the more salubrious Right Bank, the cacophony of street cries in a hundred different accents, smells of fried food, and all the multicoloured urban luxury of trash: scraps of paper, bits of bouquet, apple cores and cabbage stalks, and enough horse manure to keep a village for a year.

When they staggered out of the *coucou*, the masons would have been as white as ghosts. Nadaud was to travel on to Villemomble in the eastern suburbs to work on his uncle's building site. First, his father took him down to the sloping strand by the Hôtel de Ville to wash his black hands in the Seine. Tall houses bristling with chimneys ran along both banks as far as the eye could see. Each of those grand, dilapidated buildings contained more people than a Limousin hamlet. From some windows, lights were shining blearily as though a thousand tiny *veillées* were taking place in a thousand tiny rooms.

Across the river, on the hill called the Montagne Sainte-Geneviève, the grey dome of the Panthéon stood out against the clouds. It loomed over the hovels of the Latin Quarter like an unlit lighthouse. Until the Eiffel Tower was completed in 1889, the Panthéon was the highest point in Paris. Every mason who arrived in the capital knew that this impressive, spectral monument was the work of his compatriots. After 1855, its name was familiar from the song that the masons sang like a national anthem:

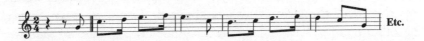

[...]

Les canaux et les ponts	Canals and bridges
De la Seine à la Meuse	From the Seine to the Meuse
Pourraient citer les noms	Could cite the names
Des maçons de la Creuse.	Of the masons of the Creuse.

Voyez le Panthéon,
Voyez les Tuileries,
Le Louvre et l'Odéon,
Notre-Dame jolie:

De tous ces monuments
La France est orgueilleuse,
Elle en doit l'agrément
Aux maçons de la Creuse.

The Pantheon and the palaces
Of the Tuileries and the Louvre,
The Odéon and pretty Notre-
    Dame:

Those monuments are the pride of
    France,
And for every one, she has to thank
The masons of the Creuse.

The Panthéon had started life as a church. It was dedicated to Genevieve, the fifth-century patron saint of Paris, whose prayer campaign had caused Attila the Hun to bypass the city and attack Orléans instead. It had been completed in 1789, just in time for the Revolutionary government to rededicate it to the secular heroes of the modern state. Masons from the Creuse had carved the gigantic letters that proclaimed the fatherland's gratitude to the 'great men' who were buried in its vault: 'AUX GRANDS HOMMES LA PATRIE RECONNAISSANTE.'

From the top of the Panthéon, masons had looked out over slate roofs that ran to the horizon like one row of hills behind the other. At a glance, they could take in a hundred urban hamlets whose inhabitants spoke a hundred different languages and knew little of each other's lives. That vision was filled with painful knowledge of all that lay between Paris and home: the roads intersecting on the edge of the city, the wheatfields of the Beauce and the plains beyond the Loire with their gravelly tracks and hostile tribes, and then, five days to the south, the gentle highlands where Druid stones carved by Gallic masons guarded the view of the Limousin plateaux and the mountains of the Auvergne.

Soon, those distances would be telescoped by trains. The stone-masons, nurses, chambermaids and pedlars would be transported across the country as if by magic, and the little corners of land where saints held sway over tiny kingdoms would vanish from sight. New mysteries, stranger than miracles, would replace the old. Many more people than ever before would leave home on great adventures and never return.

Interlude

The Sixty Million Others

L IKE THE STONE SPIRITS and the fairies (Chapter 7), a huge
population has disappeared almost entirely from daily life. Several species have already made brief appearances in this book; many
others will appear before the end; but without this interlude they
might vanish into the landscape like a herd of chamois in the high
Alps. Sixty million domestic mammals (according to the 1866 census)
and countless wild animals shared the land and the lives of people
and had a profound but incalculable effect on human existence. They,
too, discovered France and made its exploration possible. Many of
them hastened the changes that removed them from French history.

*

THE SCENE IS PÉRONNE, a fortified town on the river Somme,
a few years before the Revolution. In a house on the edge of town, a
small, well-trained band has gathered to make the final preparations
for a long and dangerous journey. Each member of the band has a
tightly packed bale strapped to his back. They know only the law of
blind obedience, not the law they are about to break for the ump-
teenth time. The leader of the band has served an apprenticeship and
is now allowed to make the journey without a load. Responsibilities,
of course, are a burden in themselves. The rules of the business are
few and simple, but they call for skill, experience and courage. In this
respect, the little band would be the envy of a military commander.
Despite the dangers that lie ahead, all the tails are wagging.

The caravan of smuggler dogs sets off to the crack of a whip while
the master goes back indoors to sleep. Somewhere in the night, where

Picardy meets Artois, it will cross one of the frontiers that divide France into zones of taxation. At the barriers, excise duty must be paid on almost everything that humans desire: tobacco, alcohol, leather, salt and iron. Guards patrol the borders. If smugglers are caught, men are sent to the galleys, women and children to prison. Dogs are executed on the spot.

The lead dog sniffs out the route. Human smell means dive into a ditch and stay down until the patrol has passed. Dog smell – it could be an excise hound – means change the route, head out across the marshes or scatter over the moor.

After several hours of excitement and delays, the expedition reaches the other village and the second part of the plan comes into operation. While the carriers lie low in cornfields and hedgerows around the village, the lead dog trots up to a house and scratches softly at the door. The man inside is not alone. Excise officers have been known to visit in the night, to sniff out the contraband and push their noses into every nook and cranny. The door opens. The dog pads across the room like the family pet and curls up in front of the fire. At last, the visitor leaves. A few more minutes pass, then the man looks out into the darkness and gives a whistle. Dogs coated with mud and briars come running in. With their last ounce of energy they leap at the man to congratulate him on another successful mission. Since the humans eat the same food as the animals, there will be a well-earned feast followed by a long and lazy day.

*

SOCIALLY AS WELL AS genetically, the smuggler dogs of northern France are a vanished breed. There are now more domestic dogs per person in France (one for every seven) than in the mid-nineteenth century (one for every seventeen). But for all their physical diversity, twenty-first-century dogs have a tiny sphere of activity. The pre-Second World War canine population was agricultural and industrial, leisured and self-employed. It worked in public service, transport, entertainment, security and crime. With only a slight stretch of the imagination and the normal canine lifespan, a dog might have been the hero of a nineteenth-century education novel, rising from a life of beggary and mange to a position of responsibility in a rural factory or an urban business, and eventually – if the business prospered – attaining the idle luxury of bourgeois retirement, occasionally fetching the newspaper and enjoying a balcony view of the boulevard below, where its former associates pull carts, hold out begging bowls, perform tricks and scavenge at the back doors of restaurants.

In many parts of France, dog-power was vital to the early industrial revolution. In the Ardennes, where nail-making was a major domestic industry, a passer-by who peered into one of the nail-makers' low stone cottages would see a small dog scampering inside a wheel to keep the bellows blowing. In the Jura, villages without a water supply used wheel-spinning dogs to run machines. The usual stint was two hours, after which the dog, slightly singed by flying sparks, went to wake its replacement and could then do as it liked. The humans worked for up to fifteen hours a day and were often stunted, myopic and claw-fisted. The dogs seem to have been better adapted to the work. Like a hired labour force, they took responsibility for their own training. Old dogs taught young dogs the trick. Bitches suckled their puppies as they skittered about inside the wheel and learned the family trade. These working dogs were valued members of the family and were often included in family photographs.

The other main canine industry was carting. Long after dog traction was banned in some *départements*, milk, fruit and vegetables, bread, fish, meat, letters and sometimes schoolchildren were delivered by dog-cart. The dog-cart was the poor man's bicycle and motor car. As late as 1925, well over a thousand dogs in harness were still running about the Loiret *département*, south of Paris. The flatter the terrain, the more dog-carts there were (the practice had spread from the Low Countries), though they also managed to take machine-guns to the trenches and bring back the wounded in the First World War. Like other quiet forms of transport, the dog-cart was driven off the roads by the motor car. The sudden roar of an engine was too much for a responsive dog.

City dogs today are thought of mainly as an excremental menace: over eight million dogs in France – two hundred thousand in Paris –

produce eighty tons of excrement a day and cause thousands of broken limbs. In the days when manure was gold, this was not a major complaint. The dogs themselves were a cheerful part of city life. Even that cat-worshipping aesthete Charles Baudelaire loved the sight of working dogs going about their business, 'driven by fleas, passion, need or duty': 'those vigorous dogs hitched to carts . . . show by their triumphant barking how pleased and proud they are to rival horses.' The 'heroism of modern life' was not peculiar to the human race:

> I celebrate those calamitous canines who wander alone through the sinuous ravines of immense cities, or who say to the abandoned man, with twinkling, intelligent eyes, 'Take me with you, and perhaps we shall fashion a kind of happiness out of our two miseries!'

*

THAT DELICATE KIND of happiness was more common then than it is in the age of production-line livestock. Cows and horses lived next door to their owners. Sometimes large holes were cut in the wall between the stable and the house so that the animal could see what was going on and the humans could converse with their workmates. The tall and bristly pigs of Brittany played with children and were given names. In 1815, in central France, the Scottish writer Sir Archibald Alison was surprised to find in every cottage 'a very motley and promiscuous set of beings': 'The pigs here appear so well accustomed to a cordial welcome in the houses, that when by chance excluded, you see them impatiently rapping at the door with their snouts.'

Animals that were christened, dressed for church and welcomed into the home were, not surprisingly, well treated, or at least treated no more roughly than their owners treated themselves. Many animals that had outlived their usefulness in the fields were fed until they died. Manure, in any case, was more valuable than meat. Their owners talked to them and sang to them. In some parts, a strange chanting could be heard when the fields were being ploughed. To keep the oxen at a steady pace, a good ploughman would sing songs so old they sounded out of tune: each phrase ended with a very long, quavering note that rose a quarter tone.

Though the singing was very similar in different regions, there were many different words for it. None of these words appear in dictionaries: *kiauler, tioler, brioler, hôler, roiler, bouarer, arander*. By the end of the nineteenth century, the singing was confined to 'backward' regions like the Berry and the Morvan, and the word *quiaulin* (from *kiauler*) had come to mean a country bumpkin. All this suggests a very ancient origin. Perhaps these were the last surviving human sounds of pre-Roman Gaul. The popular notion that there was once a time when animals conversed with humans was not as fantastic as it seems.

The most spectacular creature to share the lives of human beings was the Pyrenean brown bear. Visitors to the remote valleys of the Couserans region were often alarmed to see children playing with bear cubs. The cubs were always orphans. The hunter would wrap himself in a triple layer of sheepskins and arm himself with a long knife. When the bear reared up and hugged the woolly human, the hunter pushed its jaw aside with one hand and stabbed it in the kidneys with the other, remaining locked in the embrace until the bear collapsed. The cubs were taken to the village where they grew up with the children and the livestock until they were old enough to be trained. A captive bear never hibernated but it ate surprisingly little and was cheap to maintain.

The bears in the Jardin des Plantes in Paris, having been trained by a cosmopolitan crowd, performed an amazing variety of tricks. The Pyrenean dancing bears had a smaller repertoire. They danced with the aid of a staff and sometimes acted out little scenes: a military parade or a firing squad. The peasants of the Couserans valleys had probably learned from gypsies how to make a bear respond to the sound of a flageolet (the small, high-pitched flute) and then made minor improvements to the original trick. There was even a village school for bears at Ercé, where an older bear acted as 'monitor'. The process lasted about a year. On the day of its graduation, the bear was strapped to a tree while an iron ring was passed through its jaw behind the teeth.

Some of these shambling, muzzled parodies of human beings made horrendously long journeys – to Germany and Britain, and even to

South America. For the people who watched these sad performances, part of the attraction was undoubtedly the handler himself: an example of a primitive species from the edges of France. 'Built like a bear-handler' was a proverbial expression for a weak and shabbily dressed little man.

These one-sided feudal relationships were more important to the humans than the tiny income provided by the bear. In towns and villages that were cut off for part of the year, cowering from the threat of avalanches and the crushing weight of boredom, even a dangerous wild animal was welcome company. An official who visited a mountain village in the Pyrenees was taken to see an old woman in need of charity. She and her husband had raised a dancing bear, but bears are prone to fits of anger and the husband had been mauled to death.

> 'I have nothing, sir, nothing at all – not even a roof for me and my animal.'
> 'Your animal? You mean the one that ate your husband?'
> 'Oh, sir, it's all I have left of the poor man.'

*

A SENTIMENTAL, pet-centred view of the animal kingdom began to prevail in the mid-nineteenth century. With it came the notion that peasants who depended on animals in daily life were always cruel to them. Routine cruelty was certainly common. Hens and geese were used in bloody games of target practice. Poultry in general seems to have been treated as insects are treated today. Some horses were used in coal mines, like those of Rive-de-Gier, in the black valley north-east of Saint-Étienne, which was known as 'the purgatory of men, the paradise of women (because the women stayed at home) and the hell of horses'. The smuggler dogs of Brittany and Maine were not treated as kindly as their Picard counterparts. A family in Maine, where salt was taxed, would leave its dog with a family in Brittany, where salt was free of duty. The dog was tethered, starved and then released with a pack of salt. Only the most intrepid excise man would try to stop an angry, famished dog heading for home. Until 1850, on the Place du Combat in Paris, on the seedy side of the Canal Saint-Martin, every Sunday and holiday afternoon, dogs were pitted against any animal that could be found – bulls, bears, wolves, stags, wild boars, donkeys and other dogs – while savage human beings placed bets and revelled in the gore. At the Saint-Germain market – the roughest of Paris's dog markets – mongrels were bought for experiments at the nearby École de Médecine.

Perceptions of suffering change with every generation and from one country to the next. Many foreign visitors were struck by the gentleness of French coach drivers and sometimes cursed them for not whipping their horses into a gallop. Horses suffered more from stupidity, ignorance and inefficiency than from deliberate cruelty. As long-distance coaches travelled south, the sturdy Percheron horses for which the coaches were designed were replaced by spindly nags who found the lumbering vehicle a cruel burden. The same fate befell the little Cossack horses left behind after the Allied invasions of 1814 and 1815. Horses were expected to share their owners' discomfort. The patient mares of market-gardeners from Roscoff on the Breton coast were known as 'thirty-league beasts' because they carried the cauliflowers and artichokes for thirty leagues (eighty-three miles) without stopping, just as their owners went without food until the load was sold at Rennes or Angers.

The brutal, horse-torturing peasant was more common in bourgeois moral myth than in reality. From the mid-eighteenth century, being kind to animals was a standard injunction in books for children. The object of concern was not the welfare of the animal but the social status of the child. The implication was that a well brought-up child did not behave like a vulgar peasant who slept with his animals and made them work for a living.

The animals themselves were depicted as saintly creatures who existed for the moral benefit of Man. Popular journals like the *Le Magasin pittoresque* published heart-warming tales of philanthropic beasts: 'The Skill of a Goat' (1833), 'Animals' Affection for the Poor' (1836), 'Human Beings Fed By Animals' (1841), 'Maternal Love in Cats' (1876), 'The Language of [Mules'] Ears' (1884), etc. 'To moralize the working classes' was the aim of the Society for the Protection of Animals, founded in 1848, sixteen years before the Society for the Protection of Children. The first law against cruelty to animals, the Grammont Law of 1850, outlawed animal fights in towns and cities, not primarily because the animals suffered but because violent sports were thought to give the proletariat a taste for bloody revolution.

Just as a World Wildlife Fund sticker on a car window does not prevent it from leaving a trail of flattened corpses on the tarmac,* so was sentimental concern able to coexist quite happily with unconscious cruelty. Bourgeois passengers on Mediterranean ships amused themselves by shooting dolphins. Hunters on holiday could be indescribably sadistic in disposing of their prey. The idea that hunters had a special understanding of the animals they killed is extremely dubious. Even at the end of the nineteenth century, some hunters believed that marmots pulled each other along like carts and that chamois and bouquetins (ibex) swung themselves headlong down sheer cliffs by stabbing their horns into the earth. Many of the wild inhabitants of France were no better known than the human inhabitants of the French colonies.

*

ROADKILL AND URBAN SPRAWL are modern innovations, but even two centuries ago there were signs that the discovery and colonization of France would bring devastation and death to animals. Domestic animals in towns were protected by the Grammont Law, but the only protection for animals in the wild was provided by occasional hunting restrictions, and most hunters found that these only enhanced the thrill of the chase.

In the early 1780s, while ominous rumblings were threatening the monarchy, the geologist Horace-Bénédict de Saussure became one of the first people to notice a quiet catastrophe in the animal kingdom. In the 1760s, he had made a series of daring expeditions into the

---

* Deaths caused by speeding vehicles have a significant effect on animal populations. The 600,000-mile-long menagerie-morgue includes some relatively rare or rarely seen species: adders, kites and martens. Larger animals such as boars, deer and of course human beings are removed from the road. A law of 1791, long since repealed, imposed a fine on owners of speeding carriages that ran over animals. The earliest reference to large-scale road-kill appears to be an entry in Jules Renard's diary (8 October 1906): 'The automobile lives on the animals of the road, especially on hens. It consumes at least one hen every fifty kilometres'.

Alpine massifs. Twenty years later, he returned to find that the ubiquitous furry spirit of the mountains was now a rarity:

> Though the profit is small, the people of Chamouni hunt the marmot with passion, and so these creatures are diminishing in number in the most noticeable fashion. On my first journeys, I encountered so many of them that their whistles, echoing around the mountains, their leaping and running away under rocks, were a constant amusement. This year, I heard an occasional whistle at distant intervals but I saw not a single marmot. The hunters of Chamouni have already utterly destroyed or driven away the bouquetins, which once were common on their mountains, and it is likely that in less than a century neither chamois nor marmots will be seen.

This is one of the earliest signs that anyone was saddened by the disappearance of a species. For a long time, the seemingly obvious idea that a species could become extinct, first proposed by Georges Cuvier in a paper on the mammoth in 1796, was an obscure, scholarly notion. In 1825, at the age of twenty-one, George Sand showed no particular concern when she wrote in her Pyrenean diary, 'We are living on bear and chamois, but we see hardly any'. (In fact, she was probably eating disguised goat.) The chamois had played an unwitting role in the exploration of the Alps. In 1844, a chamois disappearing over a distant ridge revealed to a botanist the existence of an unknown pass between the Simplon and the Great Saint Bernard.* A hundred years before, herds of chamois were a common sight. Now, like the izard (the Pyrenean chamois), they were seen only in summer, through telescopes, on the edge of glaciers and snow-fields. The bouquetin was almost extinct in the Pyrenees by the mid-nineteenth century and confined to the slopes of the Maladetta. Sightings of the mouflon – the wild sheep with huge curly horns – were increasingly rare, except in Corsica. Bears were practically extinct in the Jura by 1800. By the end of the nineteenth century, Pyrenean showmen were importing their bears from Russia and the Balkans.

Some sub-species probably died out before they were discovered.

---

* Rion (named Col de Severen: probably the Col de Louvie, north of the Great Saint Bernard).

Shortly before the Revolution, hunters captured a young lynx near Luz-Saint-Sauveur after killing its mother. Until then, few had suspected that lynxes lived as far south as the Pyrenees. The animals were still being shot in the Vercors in 1820 but disappeared before the end of the nineteenth century. Wild cats were rare by the 1830s, though surprisingly common in the Bois de Boulogne on the edge of Paris. Rhône beavers – and home-grown beaver hats – were on the verge of extinction in 1840.

More cunning and determination were deployed in the eradication of species than in the extermination of Protestants in the Cévennes. Eagle hunters had themselves lowered on plank swings until they were level with the eyrie. A blazing torch disposed of the parent and the eaglets were stuffed into a bag. When Chateaubriand reached the foot of the Mont Cenis pass in 1803, he was offered an orphaned eaglet:

> A peasant was holding it by its legs ... it died of the mistreatment it had received before I could set it free. It put me in mind of poor little Louis XVII. . . . How swiftly majesty falls into misfortune!

Edible migrating birds were trapped in nets throughout Gascony and Provence. At the end of September, while flocks of doves from Scandinavia and the Jura were heading for the Basque Country, villagers in the Pyrenees were erecting giant poles. In a tiny crow's nest on top of the tripod of poles, a man scanned the horizon. The other catchers hid behind leafy screens. The man in the crow's nest held a flat piece of wood carved into the profile of a flying bird of prey. When the flock was a hundred yards away, he hurled the wooden bird into the air: the flock dipped and flew into the nets. The job of killing was left to women, who could exterminate several hundred birds in a few minutes by biting their necks.

In Provence, where songbird stew was a popular delicacy, nightingales and warblers, tied together by the beak, could be bought at market. Birds were thought to devour olives and other crops. Until the public-information campaigns of the mid-nineteenth century, and the law against stealing birds' eggs and destroying nests (1862), no one seems to have realized that birds ate harmful insects. Some people planted berry bushes at the door so that they could lean out of the window and kill the birds with a stick. As early as 1764, on a tour through southern France, Tobias Smollett noticed something like an ecological disaster:

> You may pass through the whole South of France, as well as the county of Nice, where there is no want of groves, woods, and plantations, without hearing the song of blackbird, thrush, linnet, gold-finch, or any other bird whatsoever. All is silent and solitary. The poor birds are destroyed, or driven for refuge, into other countries, by the savage persecution of the people, who spare no pains to kill, and catch them for their own subsistence. Scarce a sparrow, red-breast, tomtit, or wren, can 'scape the guns and snares of those indefatigable fowlers.

Most large wild mammals were doomed, long before the human population increased. Deforestation and hard winters drove huge packs of wolves down from forests and mountains, well into the parts of France that were supposed to have been tamed and civilized. They moved in single file, which made it hard to guess their number from the tracks in the snow. The peninsula formed by the winding Seine between Rouen and Jumièges in Normandy was inundated with wolves in the late summer of 1842: they could be heard from the hills above the industrial city.

Tales of werewolves reflected real fears. In *Madame Bovary*, 'wolves running in the fields at night' are one of the reasons why young Emma finds the countryside 'somewhat less than amusing'. A law passed after the Revolution put a price on every wolf, payable to the hunter on presentation of the animal's head to the Prefect: twenty livres for a cub, forty for an adult, fifty for a pregnant wolf, and a hundred and fifty for a known man-killer. In the 1880s, more than a thousand wolves were still being killed every year. Groups of parishes organized *battues*, thrashing through the undergrowth with pikes and staves to chase away the wolves and boars. These beats continued even when the threat was past, and they are still important social events: in autumn in the Jura, the entire male population of some villages can be seen posted at regular intervals on a winding hill road, waiting, gun in hand, for the boar to be flushed from the forest.

*

IN THE MOUNTAINS, the greatest threat to wild animals was not self-defence or sociability but the human propensity for self-destruction. Chamois hunters clearly suffered from a kind of addiction. 'A wild and haggard air makes them stand out in a crowd, even when they are out of costume. It is probably this evil physiognomy that makes some superstitious peasants believe them to be sorcerers' (Saussure). Like the hunters of precious stones and crystals, who scrabbled about in fresh landslides, chamois hunters risked their lives for almost nothing. They started up the mountain after dark, teetered across the groaning glaciers and tried to climb higher than the chamois herds before the sun came up. Some men were gone for days, with just a pocketful of cheese and some bread, drawn further and further into the snowy wastes by the fleeing chamois. Often, the climb was so long and hard that only the skin of the animal could be brought back.

Every year, men fell to their death or perished on the ice. Some were found, years later, perfectly preserved. Most of them expected to die young. Saussure met a hunter from Sixt in Savoy whose father and grandfather had died while hunting and who called his game-bag his 'shroud'. Two years later, he fell off a precipice. Down in the village, frightened wives tried to stay awake because hunters who died on the mountain were thought to appear in dreams to ask their loved ones for a proper burial.

Some wild animals survived because humans wanted them to remain wild or found them too small and troublesome to be worth taming: the black Camargue bulls, which became more lucrative in the mid-nineteenth century when Napoleon III's empress Eugénie lent her support to Spanish bullfighting, and the small, speedy white horses that lived in herds of thirty or forty in the dune-deserts of the Landes, the salt delta of the Camargue and on the plains near Fréjus.

By 1840, when roads, pine plantations and irrigation channels were eating away at the wilderness, only a few hundred wild horses remained in the Landes. Did the threat of extinction sharpen their wits, or was it simply that the most intelligent survived the longest? A horse who was known to the villagers of the Arcachon Basin as 'Napoléon' had spent two years in captivity. He escaped to the land between the sea and the marshes where the fine dune-grass grew and applied the skills he had learned from humans to a herd of his own. Napoléon's horses watched for invaders from the heights of the dunes. When the hunters approached, the herd moved to a higher ridge which the domesticated horses, weighed down by riders and slowed by sand, could never climb. When the humans encircled the sandy fortress, the herd arranged itself into a wedge formation, with foals in front and mares behind, and charged downhill towards the weakest point of the circle.

Nothing more is known about this animal resistance movement. Napoléon may have died in the dunes, or he may have ended his life in a city. By the middle of the century, there were more white horses working in the army and pulling taxicabs in Paris than living free in the Landes.

*

THESE CHANGES OCCURRED so quickly that they made no distinct impression on the human population. Rather than dismay at the extinction of species, there was a gradual, creeping disappointment, a dull awareness that wildness had only to be discovered to disappear. In 1910, when the Tour de France first crossed the high Pyrenees, newspaper reporters imagined, half hoping, that marauding bears might affect the outcome of the race by eating some of the riders. The riders flogged themselves across the mountains on rocky roads long since deserted by the bears.* At Nîmes, on the seventh stage of the Tour, a frisky dog caused a serious accident, but the only lethal animal attack came from a jelly-fish during the rest day at Nice.

As animals collectively played a smaller role in human society, individual animal heroes came to the fore. Sympathetic acquaintance with a separate species was replaced by the projection of human traits onto animals. The movement of human beings to towns and cities was mirrored by the exodus of animals to the countryside. In the mid-nineteenth century, for the first time, thousands of people were being born who would almost never see a living cow.

---

* About fifteen brown bears are thought to survive in the Pyrenees. Most were imported from Slovenia. The last female of pure Pyrenean stock was shot by boar hunters near Urdos in October 2004.

The most famous animal hero produced by this colonization of the animal kingdom was a dog called Barry who worked at the monastery on the Great Saint Bernard Pass. As early as the eighth century, the Saint Bernard dogs had been trained to find travellers who were lost in the fog and snow, which makes their paramedical profession one of the oldest in Europe. All but one were wiped out by an epidemic in 1820. The sole survivor was mated with a breed related to the Pyrenean sheepdog. Unlike most dogs, the Saint Bernards yearned to go outside when a storm was brewing and when drifting snow was reinforcing the grey walls of their fortress. They not only patrolled the pass and sought out helpless travellers, they also took preventive action: they had been known to set off in pursuit of people who passed the monastery and who seemed, in the dogs' estimation, to be unlikely to complete their journey.

Most engravings show the Saint Bernard dogs carrying a neat little brandy-cask on their collar. In fact, they carried a complete survival kit: a basket of food, a gourd of wine and a bundle of wool blankets. They had a precise knowledge of the whole region long before it was accurately mapped by humans and were capable of running for help to the nearest village if the monastery was further away.

Strictly speaking, Barry, whose name means 'bear', was Swiss-Italian, but he was born in the French Empire and became a French national hero. He had saved a monk by warning him of an avalanche; he had rescued a small child by persuading it to climb onto his back and carrying it to the monastery; in 1800, he came close to changing the course of European history by refusing to allow Napoleon's soldiers to pass until they put away their muskets. In 1900, eighty-six years after his death, he was given an impressive memorial at the entrance to the dog cemetery at Asnières-sur-Seine on the edge of Paris. The inscription says, 'He saved the life of 40 people and was killed by the 41st!' The story of this forty-first rescue turned him into a canine martyr. One wintry night, an exhausted man was struggling up the mountain when a huge, powerful animal suddenly bounded towards him through the blizzard. The man managed to crack its skull with his stick, and although Barry was taken to the hospice, he died soon after.

This was the legend of Barry the Saint Bernard. In reality, he retired happily to Berne in 1812 and died of old age two years later. To honour his extraordinary career, he was stuffed and given pride of place in Berne Museum where he stood in a glass cabinet filled with stoats and topped with a spread-eagled owl. Later, his skull was modified to make him look more like a modern Saint Bernard, just as his acts were altered to make him as human as possible. Barry had worked in the wild but after his death he became a hero of the pet age. He showed that, like savages and peasants, animals could be trained to accept the moral values of French civilization.

The Dog Cemetery at Asnières-sur-Seine was created in 1899 when a new law allowed animals to be buried 'a hundred metres from human habitation and under at least one metre of earth'. Barry's monument now towers above all the Fifis, Kikis and Poopys who provided psychological support rather than milk, warmth and manure. These were humanimals rather than creatures of the un-tamed land. By then, wealthy French dogs could travel in special railway carriages. In 1902, the Paris depository for sick animals that had turned into a festering heap of vermin was replaced by a proper hospital on the edge of the city at Gennevilliers. Three years later, the dogs of Paris had their own ambulance. An Anti-Vivisection Society was founded in 1903, and in 1905, one of the proudest symbols of the new relationship between animals and humans appeared in the streets of Paris: dogs wearing special goggles and riding in the passenger seats of automobiles.

*

FAR FROM THE dog-fouled streets of modern Paris, something still remains of the world where humans and animals lived in harmonious independence.

Sixty thousand horses, cows and sheep still migrate in spring to the Pyrenees. In autumn, large flocks can be seen flowing down from the Alps towards the plains of Provence. Transhumance – the movement of livestock to summer or winter pastures – is now seen as a precious reminder of a heroic past. Government funding is available for farmers who move their herds and flocks across the land. But today's

Alpine sheep rarely travel more than five miles downhill. They complete their journey in trucks and often suffer from the sudden change in temperature.

A century ago, some of these journeys lasted for weeks. The length of the journey was determined by the configuration of the land. The high summer pastures of the Jura and the Vosges and the empty plateaux of the Aubrac and the Causses could be reached in a few days from towns and villages. Much longer journeys were made from the southern Landes and northern Spain into the Pyrenees, from Languedoc north into the Cévennes, and from Provence into the Alps.

The main animal watershed was Provence. Ancient routes fanned out from the desert of the Crau like a river system. Some went west to Languedoc, where grassland was rented out after the grape harvest. Others headed up into the Cévennes and the Cantal for more than two hundred miles. Most of the Provençal routes were aimed at the distant Alps: up the Rhône, across the Pont du Gard, then east towards the glaciers of the Oisans; around the north face of Mont Ventoux or up the valley of the Durance towards Gap; east across the wild plains of the Var towards Digne, or further south, within sight of the sea, through Nice and on to Piedmont.

These are probably the oldest routes in France. The *drailles* or drove roads were zones of transit rather than roads. Some were more than a hundred feet wide. In the first century AD, Pliny the Elder observed that 'sheep in their thousands come from remote regions to feed on the thyme that covers the stony plains of Gallia Narbonensis'. The beasts had shaped the landscape and trodden out a network of long-distance tracks long before they were joined by upright apes. Some of the old pilgrim routes probably predate the saints. The annual miracle of fresh growth had drawn creatures in their thousands long before humans visited shrines and spas.

When the sun began to shrivel up the grass, almost a million sheep, goats and cows poured out of the plains of Provence. These enormous caravans created their own travelling atmosphere, filling the air with dust and leaving a trail of half-eaten vegetation. Several thousand sheep and goats, moving at an average speed of less than one mile an hour for two or three weeks, could bring a large part of the country to a halt. Coach companies retimed departures to miss the flocks and herds that might occupy a bridge for half a day or block the narrow corridor along the Rhône.

Tales of transhumance tend to stress dramatic conflicts. There were some hostile villages whose land was laid waste by hungry sheep and trampled by cows, and where *gardes champêtres* were paid to walk alongside the animals until they left the region. When shepherds were prevented by epidemics from making the journey, some farmers ploughed over the drove roads and tried to claim the land. But when, in the early nineteenth century, proposals were made to impose legal restrictions on the herdsmen, very little evidence of animosity could be found. The benefit to communities along these routes is still evident in the hundred and nine place names that contain the word *fumade* (an area on which manure is spread): all these places occur along the drove roads and transhumance zones leading from Langue-doc and Provence, up into the Rouergue and the Auvergne.

Even without the passing tribute of manure, transhumance was not a curse. These land-going ocean liners of livestock were a magnificent sight. The National Museum of Popular Arts and Traditions in Paris has a beautiful display of bells and embroidered collars worn by the leading sheep of a transhumant flock (collected on a mission to the Alps in the early twentieth century). The most prized animals were decorated and dressed when they left for the mountains or when they were taken into church to be blessed. Cows were adorned with headdresses, flowers and flags, and sometimes with little wooden towers containing tiny bells that were thought to protect the herd from lightning.

A few sheep and cows strayed onto fields and gardens, but trans-humant flocks were not a rabble. A strict order was observed. In front went the *menoun* (castrated male goats), then came all the other long-haired goats, the countless troop of sheep or cows and the magnificent white sheepdogs whom, it was said, 'it is an honour to know'. Bringing up the rear were donkeys, carrying the shepherds' belongings and the lambs that were too small to keep up with their mothers.

On the summer pasture, the shepherds lived in *burons* – small chalets or stone huts, most of which were abandoned when irrigation, winter feed and the introduction of more specialized breeds put an end to the prehistoric practice. Many stone *burons* can still be seen, but the commonest type of shepherd dwelling has disappeared entirely: a conical thatched hut on two or three wheels, as long as a man and slightly wider, with a shaft that was propped on a forked stick. This mobile haystack was turned so that the man could watch the animals with his rifle at the ready. Sometimes, a lone sheep was added to a herd in the hope that wolves would make off with the easy prey and leave the cows alone. But the sacrificial sheep was often protected by the herd, which formed a defensive circle when it smelled a wolf. By all accounts, the sheep themselves were not the aimless, skittish creatures of today. They were tough, scrawny, rough-woolled beasts who knew how to defend their mountain territory. In the high passes above Chamonix, opposing flocks of sheep had been known to form battle lines and to launch savage attacks on the enemy flock.

In early autumn, the herds and flocks returned to Provence and brought 'a smile of life to the immensity of the desert' (Mariéton). In the Pyrenees, the shepherds, 'sun-tanned and looking more like Arabs than Frenchmen, walked along in groups in their picturesque costume' (a wide beret, a bright-red vest or belt, a monkish cloak or a bulky sheepskin), 'with ponies or mules transporting their equipment – a few blankets, ropes and chains, and those big gleaming copper kettles in which they collect and curdle the milk' (George Sand).

This descent from the mountains was the only time when chaos threatened the herds. Animals born in the high pastures had their first sight of the human world. As they funnelled into the teeming maze of a hamlet, they broke into a sweat and charged through the streets in a panic. Even Pyrenean sheepdogs, which were known to attack bears, found the discovery of civilization traumatic. In 1788, the scholar and politician Jean Dusaulx was exploring the Pyrenees. One morning, he was about to leave the village of Barèges when he was invited to watch a typical scene. A sheepdog had just been brought in from a remote district:

The owner of this beautiful animal had made it enter the house backwards. It looked as though it had walked into a trap. We saw it digging its nails into the floor in bewilderment, staring in terror at the windows, the walls and all that surrounded it.... Savages are said to experience the same sensations when first they enter our artificial dwellings.

The nomadic instinct was stronger than fear. The declining sun and the lengthening shadows were shepherds that could not be disobeyed. In the Jura and the Vosges, where mountain people rented cows for the cheese-making season, it was often said that the animals knew exactly when to leave. City-dwellers who were accustomed to the feckless herds of northern fields or who had never seen more than half a dozen animals at a time thought this a charming peasant legend, but there are enough detailed descriptions of self-governing herds to suggest that the animals were more familiar with the geography and climate of the land than most human beings.

One October morning, when the air was colder and the grass less tender, a cow would start to amble down the mountainside. The cowherd packed his belongings and hung his bundle from the horns of the most trusted beast. One cow would take the lead and the rest would follow without trying to overtake. When the herd reached the valleys, and tracks began to appear to left and right, some of the animals would wander off towards a hamlet. As the herd thinned out, the cowherd stayed with the animals that came from his own village. And so it went on, until each animal had returned to its home and entered its part of the dwelling, like a farmer after a long day in the fields, to heat up the house for winter and to keep the humans company with its munching and snorting and its mighty smell, settling in for half a year of sloth and rumination, until something told it that the mountains were turning green and luscious again.

PART TWO

9

Maps

O N THE EVENING OF 10 August 1792, a forty-two-year-old man was standing in the belfry of the collegiate church at Dammartin-en-Goële surrounded by various pieces of scientific equipment. He had been working steadily, hoping that no one on the square below would look up and see the glint of glass and metal. There was no time to lose. Like thousands of other monuments to tyranny and superstition, the church at Dammartin had been sold by the state. Any day now, it might be turned into a pile of masonry and antiques.

The man in the condemned belfry attached a blue and curiously lashless eye to his telescope and peered across the space now occupied by the Charles de Gaulle airport at the distant smudge of Paris. By now, his assistant should have left the city and climbed up through the vineyards and quarries to his roof-top observatory among the windmills of Montmartre. At a distance of twenty miles, the hill of Dammartin would appear as a tiny island in the darkening plains. The assistant should now be lighting a flare that would be projected across the intervening space by a parabolic mirror of the kind recently installed in the Cordouan lighthouse at the mouth of the Gironde.

The sky grew dark, but no light appeared. This was not a good start to one of the great expeditions of the new age. Yet there was a light, too reddish and diffuse and too far to the south to be coming from Montmartre. Something was burning in the heart of the city. An army of apprentices, artisans and National Guards, fuelled by rumours of conspiracy and invasion, and encouraged by the support of Citizen Robespierre, had marched from the Faubourg Saint-

Antoine and the ruins of the Bastille to the Tuileries Palace. As the palace courtyard filled up with pikes and red bonnets, shots were fired from the windows and the demonstration turned into a massacre. Eight hundred Swiss guards, palace servants and aristocrats were killed. Fire broke out in the Tuileries, and the red sky sent out its uninterpretable message to the surrounding countryside. In the circumstances, lighting a flare on Montmartre would have been an act of madness. It might be taken as a sign that the invading army of Prussians and Austrians was massing on the hills to the north of Paris.

After ordering his guards to cease fire, the King had walked down the garden steps at the rear of the palace and delivered himself to the Legislative Assembly. To comply with the obvious will of the people, the Assembly suspended him from duty. This 'Second French Revolution' was the end of the ancient monarchy. Five months later, in January 1793, just beyond the bottom of his garden, Louis XVI would be decapitated on the Place de la Concorde.

*

FOURTEEN MONTHS BEFORE, a small group of scientists and mapmakers had gathered in a room at the Tuileries Palace. Louis XVI had known that this might be his last meeting. The coach that was to take him and his family to safety was being secretly prepared by a few trusted servants. They were to leave for Lorraine the next day. But an engrossing hobby has its own sense of time. The King was a skilled watchmaker. He was fascinated by the precision of maps and the modern art of cartography, and he knew the lasting importance of the project.

The scientists had come to explain and seek His Majesty's approval for a truly revolutionary act. One of the scientists, Charles de Borda, had invented a repeating circle – two small telescopes fixed to independently rotating rings – which made it possible to measure the angle between two points with unprecedented accuracy. With this instrument, the meridian of the Paris Observatory was to be remeasured, all the way from Dunkirk to Barcelona. Once the latitudes of the starting and finishing points had been determined by astronomical observation, the size of the Earth itself would be known. A universal standard measurement would exist for the first time in history. This holy grail of the Age of Reason would be France's gift to the world: a single unit of measure which, as Condorcet said, would be 'for all men, for all time'. The metre would measure exactly one ten-millionth of the distance from the North Pole to the Equator. The 'king's foot' and all the other cranky measures that varied from one village to the next would be swept away forever. The free world and all its wares and produce would be measured only by the eternal laws of Nature, not by the length of a man's arm, the appetite of a cow or the arbitrary decision of a despot. Louis XVI gave his blessing to the project and went back to preparing his escape.

The man who stood in the belfry at Dammartin that night in August 1792 was an astronomer from Amiens, which happens to lie close to the meridian. Jean-Baptiste Delambre had been appointed to lead the northern part of the expedition, from Dunkirk to Rodez (seven hundred and fifty kilometres). His colleague, Pierre Méchain, was to survey the shorter but more mountainous and partly uncharted section from Barcelona to Rodez (three hundred and thirty kilometres). They were to determine the meridian by triangulation. The principle is simple: take three clearly visible points – in this case, the Dammartin belfry, a roof in Montmartre and the church of Saint-Martin-du-Tertre. Next, using the repeating circle, find the angles of the triangle. Finally, measure the distance between two of the points using rulers. This provides the baseline, and elementary trigonometry gives the length of the other two sides.* With the first triangle established, sightings taken from a fourth observation point allow the next, adjacent triangle to be calculated. The triangles can than go marching rigidly along the meridian until, at the other end, a second baseline is measured with rulers to verify the results.

Unfortunately, as Delambre discovered, Nature cloaked her immutable laws in change and used human beings to cover her tracks. Variables such as altitude, atmospheric refraction and the contraction and expansion of instruments in heat and cold were small matters compared to the human chaos. Delambre's initial circumambulation

---

* For his baselines, Delambre used the conveniently straight sections of road from Lieusaint to Melun (near Paris) and from Le Vernet to Salses (aligned with the Roman Via Domitia near Perpignan).

of Paris, at a distance of twenty-five to thirty kilometres from the centre, was a sobering glimpse of the struggle ahead. The supposedly unchanging French countryside was in a constant state of flux. Many of the triangulation points set up by earlier expeditions had vanished. Trees had grown up to hide the view; buildings had been moved; staircases in castle towers had crumbled away; churches had been bricked up or demolished.

The biggest obstacle was the fact that few people understood the fraternal and egalitarian nature of the project. At Montjay, Delambre's observation platform was torn down by citizens exercising their new democratic right to destroy anything new. In the Orléans forest, he was able to build his platform only because the local people were busy elsewhere in the forest, demolishing 'a stone pyramid called the Meridian which was built by the former seigneurs as a sign of their greatness'. (It was an obelisk commemorating Cassini's survey of 1740.) Delambre was forced to give impromptu public talks to explain his mission: he was not a Prussian, his spyglass was not for spying and the letters of accreditation bearing the royal seal were not secret messages from Citizen Capet (formerly known as Louis XVI). At Saint-Denis, where the kings of France were buried, a crowd broke into his carriage and discovered the most suspicious-looking collection of objects they had ever seen.

> The instruments were laid out on the square, and I was forced to recommence my lecture on geodesy ... The light was failing and it was almost impossible to see. The audience was very large. The front rows heard without understanding; the others, further back, heard less and saw nothing. Impatience was spreading and there were murmurs from the crowd. A few voices proposed one of those expeditious means, so commonly used in those days, which cut through all difficulties and put an end to all doubts.

Further south, change and decay had swept across the land like a flood. Earlier surveyors had left almost as few traces as Arne Saknussemm in Jules Verne's *Journey to the Centre of the Earth*. Some old people remembered seeing Cassini pass through their village many years before, but the platforms and wooden pyramids he had built as triangulation points had been dismantled for the wood or destroyed as enemy signalling devices. The plains around Bourges had been shorn of every eminence: Delambre was told that a representative of the people had 'demolished all those steeples that elevated themselves arrogantly above the humble dwellings of the sans-culottes'. The Temple of Reason at Rodez – formerly known as the cathedral – was the only original triangulation point that remained in the Aveyron. The more remote the area, the more tenuous the connection with scientific truth. At Bort-les-Orgues, Delambre's signal, placed on the bizarre organ-pipe escarpment above the town, was said to have caused a landslide that sank the streets waist-deep in mud. This happened almost every year, but, for once, the cause was obvious. On the fog-bound summit of Puy Violent above Salers, the wizard's straw-covered house made from three twenty-three-foot tree trunks was blamed for the death of several cows and a spate of minor accidents.

Seven years and thousands of miles later, after suffering atrocious weather, impassable roads and impossible peasants, illness, flimsy platforms that wavered in the wind because the carpenters had skimped on materials, the mental breakdown of Méchain and an attack of wild dogs who scattered the rulers that had been carefully laid along the baseline near Perpignan, Delambre submitted his results at the world's first international scientific conference, held in Paris on 2 February 1799. A metre-long bar of pure platinum was presented to the National Assembly in April. This was to be the permanent standard metre 'for all people, for all time', though it would take another century to persuade the whole country to adopt the decimal system.

Satellite surveys have since shown that the official metre, which was supposed to be one ten-millionth of the distance from the North Pole to the Equator, is approximately 0.23 millimetres short. Ironically, the provisional metre which the Académie des Sciences had been forced to come up with in 1793 is closer by about 0.1 millimetres, though it was an estimate based on earlier surveys. But the metre of Delambre and Méchain had the authority of experience. That bar of platinum was a monument to one of the great expeditions of the age. Like all great expeditions, the journey along the meridian discovered far more than the explorers set out to find. The eternal values on which the republic was supposed to be founded – liberty, equality, fraternity and mathematical precision – had turned out to be extraordinarily elusive. Two men and their assistants had taken seven years to survey a narrow corridor of land. Instead of reducing the country to the size of a map and a table of logarithms, they had shown how much of France remained to be discovered.

*

THE JOURNEY OF Delambre and Méchain was just one episode in a great odyssey which began before they were born and continued long after they were dead. When they returned to Paris in 1799, more than half a century had passed since the young geometer on Cassini's expedition had been bludgeoned to death by the natives of Les Estables, yet the map of France had still not been fully published. Even the published sheets included areas that only seemed to have been charted. This was hardly surprising. Nothing like it had been attempted before. It was the first detailed map of an entire country to be based on extensive, coordinated surveys. As Cassini III* wrote in his introduction to the first sheet (Paris), published in 1750,

> When one considers how many years, journeys, exertions, investigations, instruments, operations and observations are required for the exact description of a country, it is no wonder that a work of such scope, which relies on measurements taken in the field, should progress at such a slow and cautious pace.

The long adventure had begun on a field in Flanders in 1746 during the War of the Austrian Succession. While the French and Austrian armies were laying waste to the land, César-François Cassini de Thury was recording it on beautiful maps of camps and battlefields. To him, this was normal family business. His grandfather and father had surveyed the meridian in 1700. César-François himself had been involved with the work since childhood. He grew up in the Paris Observatory, where his grandfather had discovered four of

---

* The Cassinis are numbered, for convenience, like kings. Cassini I, II, III and IV: Jean-Dominique (1625–1712), Jacques (1677–1756), César-François Cassini de Thury, who took the name of the family château in Normandy (1714–84), and Jacques-Dominique (1748–1845).

the moons of Saturn. At the age of eighteen, he joined the expedition that drew a line perpendicular to the meridian, from Saint-Malo in the west to Strasbourg in the east. At nineteen, he lectured at the Académie des Sciences on the importance of geodesic measurements.

The man who was born at the intersection of the meridian and the west–east line knew the country better than anyone else. No one had undertaken such long journeys across the land, following the invisible line of geometrical truth rather than rivers and roads; no one had surveyed the land from so many vantage points. From scaffolding erected in forests and plains, Cassini had seen views that no one else had seen. He had heard dialects unknown to lexicographers, and he had an unrivalled knowledge of cheese from the Auvergne (unwholesome) to the Jura (delicious).

When Louis XV saw Cassini's battlefield maps, he recognized their military importance. Cassini had been asked to bring along some astronomical instruments to keep His Majesty amused. He not only kept him amused, he also persuaded him to authorize a project so grand and expensive that it makes the seven-year voyage to Saturn of the probe that bears his grandfather's name seem quite modest. Cassini was officially asked to produce a map of the entire kingdom on a scale that would make the smallest hamlets visible.

Now that he had funding for a complete map of France, Cassini could begin to recruit a small team of *ingénieurs-géographes*. They had to be mentally strong, physically fit and, preferably, unattached. They should be familiar with astronomy and trigonometry. They should know how to draw and how to build an observation platform. Since the six-month-long mapping season coincided with the season of military campaigns, they should always be prepared for action. The army's own geometers were expected 'to read and write foreign languages and to be able to swim, so that nothing need prevent them from executing urgent and important reconnaissances'. These athletic scientists were the astronauts of the eighteenth century, with certain obvious differences: they were poorly paid and could expect no personal glory; they would be out of contact for long periods; and they could be quite certain that they would encounter hostile aliens.

*

FOR THE FIRST EXPEDITION (1748–49), Cassini recruited about a dozen young men in their early twenties. They were equipped with miniature instruments that were less accurate than the full-scale instruments but small enough to be carried to the top of a steeple or a mountain. Though some of the provinces had good maps of their own, much of the land that the Cassini team was to explore had never been charted. Until then, most map-makers had simply copied earlier maps and perpetuated old mistakes. There were maps of the Alps that showed a plain in the middle of the mountains near Chamonix and a giant peak called 'La Mont Maudite' (the Cursed Mountain) thirty miles west of its real counterpart, Mont Blanc. Even in 1792, when Savoy was annexed and renamed Département du Mont Blanc, the official government map was more like optimistic science fiction than a record of reality. It showed a road running around the base of Mont Blanc and a carriageway over the 9,068-foot Col de l'Iseran, which was first crossed by road in 1937. Cassini's geometers were starting with a blank sheet of paper.

Their task was far more complicated than Delambre's triangulation of the meridian. On arriving in a new place, the geometer would seek out the curé, the lord or the syndic who represented the local assembly. This could take all day if the man was out in the fields or away at market. After gaining access to the steeple or the tower, he would survey the land and produce a preliminary sketch. The curé, lord or syndic would then be asked to name – in French – the villages, hamlets and farms, the castles and the abbeys, the rivers and the woods, and to point out the location of roads, bridges, fords, locks, windmills, watermills and gibbets. In featureless regions like Champagne or the Landes, tiny landmarks might be noted: a lonely tree, an abandoned tileworks, even the temporary pyramid from which the measurements were taken.

In the evening, the geometer would write the names on his chart and sketch the hills and valleys, trying to keep the vellum clean while the local inhabitants peered over his shoulder or held a meeting to decide what to do about him.

The whole process was a curious mixture of precision and approximation. A priest in the Berry remembered the cartographer's visit in 1756:

He set up three stations in my parish and I accompanied him. He wrote down all the objects he could see: hamlets, farms, main roads, trees, towers, steeples, etc. To confirm his calculations he had his servant measure in common feet the distances of certain objects. I remember that his little pedometer one day gave him the exact number of feet from Issoudun to Graçon [sic for Graçay: fifteen miles]. It is true that for certain things that he was unable to see, such as an estate that lay in a valley, he asked its distance from the steeple . . . If all the engineers were as reliable in their operations as the one I saw at work, their scribes must produce very regular maps.

The naming of all these places and landmarks was a puzzle in itself. There was no complete list of towns and villages, and there were no agreed spellings. Many local names would never be recorded or would survive only in a garbled form. As Cassini explained, some landowners saw the naming process as a splendid opportunity to recreate the landscape in their own image. They saw no reason to identify the obscure farm and the decaying hamlet that were about to be swallowed up by their magnificent new park, or the medieval ruin that would soon be superseded by their new, symmetrical château:

Names had to be given to these new objects, and lords thought that they had the right to name them. Several seigneurs lumped together under the same appellation various estates or fiefdoms which each had their own name and which the local people continue to use.

Despite the King's written orders, some priests refused to unlock the door to the steeple, and some town assemblies refused to cooperate. As the map spread south to Provence and Languedoc, it became apparent that the geometers would have to obtain letters of introduction from authorities more local than a king who lived in Versailles. A man who worked on Sundays and who had nothing to sell might be a tax collector, a spy or a bell thief employed by a rival village. The spidery lines and runic symbols that he etched on his chart did not necessarily explain his purpose. Mountain people who had seen hills and plains spread out at their feet usually had some sense of topography, but to people who lived in lowlands or in closed valleys, the two-dimensional representation of the earth from an imaginary point in space was a complete mystery. The very act of drawing was often an amazing novelty. Well into the nineteenth century, travellers with a sketchbook and an easel attracted crowds from far and wide. Prosper Mérimée instantly became the most famous person in Véze-lay when he began to draw the basilica with the aid of a camera lucida. On a tour of Brittany in 1818, the English artist Charles Stothard asked to draw a girl in local costume.

> Several Bretons seated themselves upon the ground, to watch the motion of Mr. S—'s hand, others pressed around him, and even attempted to touch the pencil he was using, to ascertain, I imagine, what such a magical little implement could be.

In some places, the arrival of a stranger with fantastic tools and an inexplicable plan was a major historical event. In gazetteers and guidebooks published decades later, the only thing worth mentioning in some places was the 'ruins of a pyramid erected by Cassini'. The novelty was too much for some small villages. In 1773, in the heart of the Tarn, a young surveyor from Issoudun was pulled down from the tower of the ruined church of Saint-Martin-de-Carnac near the village of Cuq. Epidemics had passed through the region and left the local people fearful and resentful. His attackers set about him with clubs and knives. Somehow, he escaped. Later that day, a man with bleeding hands and a broken skull was seen staggering along the road from Castres to Lavaur, a mile south of Cuq. No one dared help the fleeing sorcerer. At last, he reached a roadside inn run by 'the Widow Jullia', who sent for a doctor and a surgeon. The surveyor survived but was forced to retire with a pension.

Even before it was finished, it was clear that the map of France, with its standardized spellings and consistent symbols, would be considerably more coherent than the country itself.

*

THE EXPENSIVE DISASTER of the Seven Years War (1756–63) ended Treasury funding for the map of France. With the support of the King's mistress, Mme de Pompadour, Cassini set up a company of fifty shareholders. The first sheet, published in 1750, served as an enticing prospectus. It showed Paris in the centre – just large enough to be divided into *quartiers* – and stretched from Dammartin in the top right to Rambouillet in the bottom left. Like the subsequent hundred and eighty sheets, it measured 3′ 5″ by 2′ 5″ and used a scale of 1 *ligne* for every 100 *toises*, which is equivalent to 1:86,400.* The Paris sheet was more detailed than the others, with forest paths beautifully picked out, partly to attract subscribers and partly because it included the properties of many of the noble sponsors. The epigraph, from the *Natural History* of an earlier explorer of Gaul, Pliny the Elder, sounded a cautiously pessimistic note: 'It is sufficiently honourable and glorious to have been willing to make the attempt, though it should prove unsuccessful.'

No one who sees a well-filled diagram of France in a confident history of the country would guess that it took almost seventy years to publish the Cassini map and that the last sheets (Brittany and the coastal Landes) did not appear until after the fall of Napoleon in 1815. Very few histories even mention the Cassini map, let alone the men who made it. Only about a dozen of the ninety-five surveyors whose names appear on the charts have left any trace. This entry on one of the surveyors, in Michaud's *Biographie universelle* in 1855, is typical:

> Dupain-Montesson [Christian name unknown]: modest and tireless scholar, forgotten until now in all biographies; only fragmentary information could be obtained.

Two of the map-makers had promising careers as painters before they were recruited by Cassini. One man left the Church to join the expedition and another gave up writing plays. Some became teachers and professors; one became a general. The man who left the Church later died of a contagious disease in southern California where he went to observe the transit of Venus in 1769. The 'modest and tireless' scholar taught the future Louis XVI the art of map-making and thus helped to ensure that the meridian expedition of Delambre and Méchain would have royal support.

It is sadly appropriate that the team who put half a million obscure hamlets on the map has been wiped from the record of French

* There were twelve *lignes* in a *pouce* (inch), twelve *pouces* in a *pied* (foot), six *pieds* in a *toise* (just under two metres) and two thousand *pieds* in a *lieue* (league).

history. Their adventures have left no trace other than the map itself. Under a magnifying glass, Cassini I's 1679 map of the Moon turns out to contain a secret message to a woman who was probably his wife: a heart-shaped feature in the Sea of Serenity and a beautiful angelic face with flowing hair formed from the mountains of the Heraclides Promontory. No such secrets are hidden in the map of France. Nothing shows, for instance, that the village of Les Estables was the grave of the man who came to put it on the map.

*

IF ALL THE ADVENTURES of Cassini's surveyors had been recorded, the seventy-year history of his map might have been the *Thousand and One Nights* of French exploration. It might have given a true sense of the size and unpredictability of the country. It would have shown that the provinces were not just the hinterland of Paris, just as the map itself depicted every farm and hamlet on the same scale as the capital and the royal estates.

Not all the stories would have been tales of ignorance and hostility. In the region in which the wild boy Victor de l'Aveyron was discovered in 1799 (p. 11), the 113th sheet of the Cassini map shows a church called Saint Cirice. The tower that represents it is placed on a promontory of hatching and shade between a dark-green wood and a bend of the river Tarn. The busy landscape of farms and villages is deceptive. The effects of the Revocation of the Edict of Nantes were still evident. Most of the Protestant population had fled and more than half the inhabitants of the region lived in isolated cottages and hamlets. If they had been able to decipher the forest of pictograms and read the place names, they would have been amazed to see their home surrounded by so many places of which they had never heard – almost three thousand on this sheet alone.

Some of those hamlets no longer exist, but the cemetery of Saint Cirice is still there, clinging to a cliff between Broquiès and Brousse-le-Château, above an unlit tunnel, built in the late nineteenth century for a railway that was never laid. Here, the river Tarn has dug itself a deep canyon in the limestone. In autumn and winter, a person walking along the north bank would see a misty river as broad as the Rhône flowing softly past the orchards and the vines, but as the sun warmed up the valley and dispelled the mist, a torrent would appear far below. Sometimes, after heavy rain, calcareous rocks came loose and went crashing down to the bottom of the gorge.

On the edge of the chasm, an iron cross with a skull-and-cross-bones stands on top of two gravestones placed back to back. Some of the inscriptions in the little cemetery are misspelt. Even today, for some local people, French is still an awkward, foreign language. But this particular memorial is impeccable. It bears the names of a man and a woman who died within a month of each other in 1843. One of the names is too grand and French to be native to the region. Jacques-François Loiseleur-Deslongchamps came from a family of drapers in the comfortable market town of Dreux, a long day's walk from Paris. He was twenty-two years old when he arrived in the region in the spring of 1769. His journey ended ten miles north of the river Tarn by a small farmhouse at the foot of the Lagast hill.

This remote prominence was well known in the world of geome-ters. From its grassy summit, the volcanoes of the Cantal can be seen to the north, the Montagne Noire to the south and, beyond, the blue haze of a Mediterranean sky. In 1739, when Cassini II was surveying the Paris meridian, a signal had been placed there. Deslongchamps's first job was to build a new one. A reconstruction stands on the summit today – a truncated pyramid of planks on four wooden stilts. It looks like a primitive space rocket. Next to it, the aluminium struts of a radio mast hum with the gales and the static whisper of voices in the ether.

Surveying the area would take several weeks. The village of Saint-Martin-de-Carnac, where one of Deslongchamps's colleagues was savagely attacked a few years later, lay behind the gorse-covered hills, forty miles away in a different *pays*. Here at Lagast, though the original signal had been destroyed, the population was slightly more amenable. A farmer called Boudou, who lived at the farm of Le Vitarel at the foot of the hill, offered the stranger board and lodging. Conversation would be difficult since no one in the region spoke French, but the man from the north might have interesting tales to tell, and an extra hand was always welcome. For Deslongchamps, surveying the Rouergue (as the Aveyron was known before the Revolution) was a journey back in time. He had arrived in a world without clocks and calendars, where the women looked like Joan of Arc with their capes, surcoats and pointed clogs.

During that long summer, Deslongchamps came to know the lie of the land better than any native. He also came to know Boudou's daughter, Marie-Jeanne, who looked after her father's flock of sheep. She watched the lodger taking measurements, tinkering with tools that were never allowed to become dirty, caring for his sheets of paper like a priest. She might have shown him the dolmens that gave shelter from the squalls and how delicious last year's chestnuts were when cooked with salt and fig leaves or mixed in a pot with prunes, dried pears, turnips and potatoes. He told her the names of things that she had known only as the forest, the river or the pile of rocks. A dot on the lens of the telescope was the cathedral at Rodez; the Pole Star indicated the direction in which Paris lay. The hill behind the house where she was born was a milestone on an invisible road that encircled the Earth.

In a land where girls were little more than serfs and even ladies in the towns were separated from their husbands in church, a shepherdess who knew about triangulation and degrees of latitude was a rare and unnatural creature. It was probably just as well that they fell in love. After two seasons of surveying, Deslongchamps, who must have been an able mountaineer, was sent to work in the Pyrenees and then the Alps. He helped to chart the glaciers and the snow-bound valleys. But then, no doubt at his own request, he was sent back to the Rouergue in 1774 to survey the region further up the Tarn, around Nant and Millau. It was close enough to Lagast for an occasional visit to the farm. It seems to have taken him as long to map this area as it took him to map the high mountains on the Italian border.

Five years after first arriving in the Rouergue, Jacques-François Loiseleur-Deslongchamps married Marie-Jeanne Boudou, who had just turned eighteen. They bought a small property ten miles to the south, following the line of the meridian survey, by the banks of the Tarn near the church of Saint Cirice. The name of the property was Puech Cani, which means 'steep hill'. Later, when Marie-Jeanne's father died, her husband became the owner of the farm at the foot of the Lagast hill. The isolated farmhouse is still there, unrestored and uninhabited.

Very little is known of their long life together. Deslongchamps became involved in politics. He survived the Revolution and returned to the Tarn where the winters were long and the summers dry, and vines grew well in the stony soil. When Méchain's assistant on the meridian expedition reached the Lagast hill in 1797, he was delighted to find that the owner of the farm was the fifty-year-old veteran map-maker, Deslongchamps. Any historian would happily give up several years of research to hear the stories that were exchanged that night in the farmhouse.

When Deslongchamps was ninety years old, still living with his wife at Puech Cani, he invented a portable barometer that was presented to François Arago, Director of Observations at the Paris Observatory. Deslongchamps had lived to see the last sheets of the Cassini map appear. The metal plates on which his wife's home had been engraved were almost worn away and other maps were being made. But Deslongchamps knew that the charting of France was still a long way from completion. The barometer measured air pressure, which made it possible to calculate altitude. With a barometer that was portable but accurate, a third dimension could be added to the map: the heights of mountains, which remained as constant as the meridian. Those inaccessible parts of France would at last be mapped for future generations, while the land that was inhabited by people changed with the passing years and turned even the most reliable chart into a picture of the past.

10

Empire

IN 1804, THE HORRORS OF the Revolution were over: the guillotine had been replaced by the machinery of war. Napoleon was
about to crown himself emperor. Most of the colonial empire in North
America and the West Indies was lost between the Seven Years War
and the Louisiana Purchase (1803), but France itself was now expanding to the north, the east and the south. Several new *départements* had
been added to the original eighty-three. Some of the names dreamt
up for these new *départements* made them sound like distant colonies
rather than neighbouring states: Mont Terrible, a misinterpretation
of Mont Terri in Switzerland; Jemmapes, which misspelt the name of
the Belgian town Jumape (in Picard) or Jemappes (in French); and the
unimaginative but picturesque Forêts (Forests), formed from the
Duchy of Bouillon and a densely wooded part of Luxembourg.

At the height of the empire, there were a hundred and thirty
départements stretching from Hamburg (Bouches-de-l'Elbe *département*) to Rome (Tibre *département*). Maps of Europe were out of date
as soon as they were published. Napoleon was well aware that the
land would not conveniently pose while cartographers mapped
it. Cassini may not have shown detail on the same scale as the maps
of cadastral surveys, which established property lines and tax liabil-
ity, but a complete map was better than a patchwork of minutely
embroidered squares and empty spaces. Napoleon wrote to General
Berthier on 26 October 1804:

> The *ingénieurs-géographes* are being asked to make cadastres instead of
> military maps, which means that, twenty years from now, we shall have

nothing. . . . If we had stuck to making maps on Cassini's scale, we should already have the whole Rhine frontier . . . The geometers began a cadastre in Corsica which was considered by people who live there to be a very poor job. . . . Surveyors are left too much to their own devices. All I asked was that the Cassini map be completed. . . . Experience shows that the biggest mistake in general administration is trying to do too much. The result is that one lacks the essential.

Napoleon knew, of course, that Cassini was not infallible and that, while geometers were busy on the battle-scarred frontier, the heart of the empire was still not fully charted. Only a few months before, his wife had confirmed the unsatisfactory state of the national map. That summer, the northern parts of the empire had seemed suffi- ciently safe for Joséphine to take the waters at Aix-la-Chapelle. Since Aix had been Charlemagne's capital, Napoleon was thinking of using it as the venue of his coronation. Joséphine might provide some useful information on the route. He plotted an itinerary for her on the map. It would take her north-east to Sedan, then over the 'Wolf's Back' hill (Le Dos du Loup) and on to Liège through the Forêts *département*.

The nineteenth-century route still exists. A few hundred yards east of the N58 autoroute, the old road crosses the unmarked Belgian border in the forest, then drops down to Bouillon by a hair-raising descent. The Cassini map shows the route as two shaded lines with dots on either side. This was the symbol for a surfaced, tree-lined road. The Emperor's valet remembered the journey for years to come:

In the Ardennes, we ran into danger. The Emperor had planned the route we were to take. Unfortunately, the road existed only on the map. It became so bad that, on a very steep descent, we were forced to restrain the carriages with ropes. In fright, Joséphine decided to abandon the coach, despite the rain and the mud. . . . The carriage in which the first lady-in-waiting Mme Saint-Hilaire was travelling tipped over. She reached Liège a day after the rest of the party. Riders of the escort were sent out to see what was causing the delay and to offer protection, but these attentions appeared insufficient to Mme Saint- Hilaire, who was most offended that the entire court was not thrown into confusion by her absence.

A representative tableau of France in 1804 might show Napoleon at Notre-Dame in Paris, taking his crown from the hands of Pope Pius VII, or the hundred thousand soldiers of the Grande Armée waiting on the coast at Boulogne for the order to invade England, but it would be just as representative if it showed the imperial party wading through a quagmire somewhere north of Sedan.

Long after the country had been mapped, getting lost or stranded in the heart of the French empire was a common experience. Dozens of nightmare journeys can be recreated by comparing Cassini's charts to contemporary accounts. A young army officer called Paul Thiébault, who was in the crowd that stormed the Tuileries in 1792, was travelling from Paris to Millau with two fellow officers in 1795. At this point in his account, they had reached a part where the map showed a 'metalled, tree-lined road':

> Having no paths to follow but the beds of torrents, and finding no habitation, we became lost after passing the spot where our guide informed us that the Beast of the Gévaudan had been killed.* Meanwhile, the light was failing and we were beginning to wonder how we would spend the night among these arid hills when we spotted a house on the far side of a deep gorge.

The house was called La Bastide. It appears on the Cassini map, on an isolated stretch of road, as a little square building marked 'la Bastide – cabaret'. Though the roof was blown off by gales in 2004, the sunken stone vaults of the original ground floor can still be seen. It was here that Thiébault and his comrades spent the night. The inn was deserted apart from two shifty-looking women. After discovering a trapdoor in the floor of their bedroom, the officers barricaded themselves in and slept in their clothes. At daybreak, they asked for the bill and were charged one louis (twenty-four francs) for bed and a stingy omelette. (Twenty-four francs would have bought a cow's milk for a year.)

> 'One louis! Are you mad?'
> 'Faith, you have no cause for complaint. No one did you any harm.'

---

* The Beast of the Gévaudan was never this far south. The guide may have been referring to the Bête des Vaissettes which lived in a pond nearby at Le Bouquet. It made a horrible screaming noise at night and could be heard for miles around.

'Who the devil's talking about harm? I was referring to the price.'

...As we were leaving through the courtyard gate, we found ourselves face to face with two armed men coming along the route we had taken the day before. Behind them, at a thousand paces, were several other men, also armed.... We spurred our horses and set off at a full trot. The walls of the house covered our departure and we were out of range before they could decide what to do.

Despite the map's misleading and potentially lethal depiction of the road system, Cassini was criticized – presumably by people who never left home – for showing only major highways and omitting all the secondary routes. He explained that roads 'changed with the seasons'. A map that claimed to show everything was a public menace, encouraging travellers to venture where none should go without a guide to point out 'the hollow ways and the precipices'. Yet Cassini's own geometers were clearly over-optimistic. People travelling from Toulouse to Bordeaux must have wondered what had happened to the (fictitious) bridges at Verdun and Tonneins, and some travellers in the Alps must have been disappointed when they found that the only way to continue on the road marked 'Grand Chemin de France au Piémont' was to have the carriage dismantled and loaded onto the back of a mule.

*

THIS, THEN, WAS THE visible state of France at the dawn of the nineteenth century: a slightly misleading cartographic masterpiece produced by expeditions that had set off from Paris more than half a century before. Cassini IV was never able to revise the map on which his family had spent part of its fortune. The plates from which it was printed were confiscated by the Revolutionary government and never returned. Cassini was evicted from his home, the Observatory, accused of aiming cannon (telescopes) at the people of Paris and sent to prison, where he described himself as 'an ex-living person'. He might have agreed with Baudelaire that 'nations have great men only in spite of themselves'.

Though it expropriated the map of France, the state showed little interest in charting its domain. The chief concern of the military surveyors was the perimeter of the country. This, however, presented two serious problems. The first was the lack of reliable measurements of altitude. The 1659 Treaty of the Pyrenees defined the frontier between France and Spain as 'the crest of the Pyrenees', but more than two centuries passed before the snowy battlements were measured accurately and the people of the high Pyrenees found out whether they were Spanish or French.

The second problem was a fear that frontier maps would effectively hand the keys of the fortress to the enemies of France. This is why the Cassini map ends abruptly at the old borders, omitting Nice (the homeland of Cassini I), Savoy, Corsica and, because it lay too far off the Vendée coast to fit onto the sheet, the Île d'Yeu. France itself looks like an island. Beyond the borders, apart from a few Notre-Dames floating in space, a tiny spit of land labelled 'Douvres' (Dover) and some loose ends of road, there is nothing. In the Alps, the edge of the world is hemmed with mountains. The only hints of the other side are a few intriguing captions: '[Col de la] Traversette: hole made by human hands which passes through the mountain'. In the Pyrenees, the land drops suddenly into a bottomless abyss and a line of jagged peaks guards the perimeter like a row of fence posts.

However, these shortcomings were trivial compared to those of earlier maps. Despite official interference and lack of funding, the Cassini map was a national treasure. It shed light on the dark domestic interior and had a huge effect on French society. It replaced the Parisian image of a featureless expanse of fields and forests with a Romantic sense of *la France profonde*. It opened up the country to the imagination and provided clues to the worlds that lay beyond the road network. Before Cassini, most maps for travellers covered only a narrow strip of land a mile or two on either side of a river or a road. Most of them, like the 1775 Paris–Reims 'historical and topographical description', showed little more than a traveller would have seen through a carriage window on a rainy day. The idea was simply to provide some instructive entertainment on the long journey. The map was not allowed to speak for itself; it was an illustration of the text:

> Aubervilliers: The inhabitants decided that vegetables would be more profitable than wine, because of the proximity of Paris. Thus,

almost all their land is under cultivation. . . . All the inhabitants are
very hard-working.

Vaubuin [Vauxbuin, a suburb of Soissons]: Its position is somewhat
aquatic as it is surrounded by mountains [sic] on almost all sides.

Sermoise and environs: The eye scarce has time to rest on an object
in the landscape ere it spies another no less worthy of attention.

Typically, the 'eye' had seen very little of what was shown on the
map. Until Cassini, much of what appeared to be known about the
provinces was based on second-hand reports. Even the government
inspector of historic monuments, Prosper Mérimée, was partly
dependent on hearsay when planning his tours of inspection in the
1830s:

> I have often heard tell of a very ancient monument that lies somewhere
> in the mountains to the south-west of Perpignan. Some say that it is a
> mosque, others that it is a church of the Knights Templar. I have also
> been told that it's a hovel in such a ruinous state that no one can tell
> when it was built. Whatever the case, it must be worth an excursion of
> three or four days on horseback.

Thanks to Cassini, Mérimée could at least confirm the existence
and check the location of this mysterious temple. (It was the star-
shaped eleventh-century church at Planès, known locally as 'the
Mosque'.)

Few people actually owned the Cassini map: it was very expensive,*
and only a few hundred copies of each sheet were printed. Map-
reading was a rare skill: no one felt that their intelligence was insulted
if a geographical writer pointed out that two places which lay close
together on the map might in reality be several hours apart. The
important thing was the knowledge that the map existed. Many of
the professional and accidental explorers who appear later in this
book had traced the meandering rivers, spelled out the unfamiliar
names and peered at the little symbols. Some of the sheets were cut
into rectangles and pasted onto a piece of cloth that could be folded
up. They could then be stored in small boxes and kept in a bookcase.

---

* In 1756, the price was four livres for a sheet and five hundred livres for the whole
map. Five hundred livres was the salary of a well-paid village schoolteacher or the
annual income of a successful farmer.

A complete set can be seen in the library of the Château de Vizille near Grenoble, disguised as a row of books. The folded sheets could also be taken on journeys. In his account of a trip to the Rhineland in 1839, Victor Hugo proudly mentions his portable Cassini: 'I took the diligence to Soissons. It was quite empty, which, between our-selves, did not displease me. I was able to spread out my Cassini sheets on the seat of the coupé.'

In a poet's mind, the map itself was a luminous landscape. Without his Cassini sheets, Hugo's account might have lacked some of its picturesque details. The sheet for Soissons gave him the name of the tiny hamlet of La Folie. It also showed the steel-blue bend of the river Aisne and the little clumps of red paint that made Soissons look like an exotic flower head. When he wrote up his account by the light of a candle in the inn, the landscape he had seen through the twilight gloom would rise from the map like a vision:

> As I drew near to Soissons, it was growing dark. Night was already opening her smoke-filled hand in that enchanting valley where the road dives down after the hamlet of La Folie ... Yet through the mists that lumbered across the countryside, one could still make out the clump of walls, roofs and buildings that is Soissons, half-inserted in the steel crescent of the Aisne like a sheaf that the sickle is about to cut.

Cassini's geometers marked the end of the pioneer stage of French exploration and helped to launch the age of mass discovery. Like the fleeing heroine of George Sand's *Nanon*, who memorizes the Cassini map she sees in a house at Limoges before venturing into the wilderness of the Brande, travellers could now strike out across country and know more or less where they were going. Gaps and errors inspired new maps, and by the mid-nineteenth century there were signs of map mania, with popular magazines explaining how to chart one's own little corner of the country. The English custom of wandering about the countryside, getting pleasantly lost among the hedgerows, was catching on in France.

Village steeples were no longer just the totem poles of tiny *pays*. They were coordinates in a network that stretched beyond the horizon, and marked a more lively relationship between the landscape and the mind. The steeple at Illiers, in the plains south-west of Chartres, which had served as a triangulation point in the early 1750s, reappeared in fictional form in Marcel Proust's Combray. Triangulation had drawn new lines across the land and prepared the way for other, less definable explorations:

> At a bend in the road, I suddenly experienced that special pleasure that resembles no other when I saw the two steeples of Martinville lit by the setting sun and apparently being moved about by the motion of our carriage and the twists and turns of the road, and then the steeple of Vieuxvicq which, though separated from the other two by a hill and a valley and placed on higher ground in the distance, appeared to be standing right next to them.
>
> In noticing and registering the shape of their spires, the shifting of their lines and the lighting of their surface by the sun, I felt that I was leaving part of my impression unexplored and that something lay behind that movement and that light – something that they seemed at once to contain and to conceal.

*

UNLIKE THESE TOPOGRAPHICAL journeys into the mind, the great scientific expeditions that followed Cassini's and Delambre's are known only from their findings: maps of agricultural practice in the different *pays* of France, collections of folk songs and tribal lore and catalogues of ethnic types (see p. 316). The Swiss botanist Pyrame de Candolle spent six years (1806–12) studying the flora of France and discovered hundreds of plants that were previously unknown in France and hundreds more unknown anywhere in the world. Charles de Tourtoulon and the Languedocian poet Octavien Bringuier travelled one thousand miles in circles and cul-de-sacs to trace two hundred and fifty miles of the line that divided Oc and Oïl (p. 60), from a hamlet near Soulac on the Atlantic coast, to the region of Guéret, on the masons' route to Paris.

The greatest expedition of all – in size if not in brilliance – was the successor to Cassini's seventy-year-long survey. In 1818, military surveyors started work on the new map of France known as the *Carte de l'état-major* (equivalent to the British Ordnance Survey, which began in 1791). It employed seventy-five officers at a time, plus a small army of draughtsmen, engravers and, eventually, photographers. The first sheet (Paris) appeared in 1821 and the last (Corte, northern Corsica) in 1880, by which time the first sheets were out of date. Army officers working in teams and in a slightly more cosmopolitan world were less vulnerable than Cassini's pioneers, but since many of the officers had never wanted to be assigned to the map in the first place, it was still a heroic undertaking. They braved the heat of the treeless Landes and squinted through the haze at hills of sand that changed position from one month to the next; they bivouacked on freezing mountains, waiting for the clouds to lift; they lay in bed with dysentery and fever in places where nothing ever happened, and devoted months of work to measurements they knew might turn out to be less than accurate. Not all those explorers knew the satisfaction of a job well done.

If enough information had survived, one expedition in particular would deserve a book to itself. It was described in suitably epic terms in 1843, eight years after the ground work was completed:

> Always on foot, heading out across country in all weathers, exposed to every sort of misadventure, following the capricious trail of subterranean strata and unable to devise their itinerary, as ordinary tourists do, according to the availability of accommodation, even the most intrepid mineral hunters were exhausted after a few months of this arduous pursuit. MM. Dufrénoy and Élie de Beaumont, resting only in winter to organize their materials, withstood the ordeal for ten years, from 1825 to 1835. In the course of their minute investigations, they traced out on French soil a route of more than twenty thousand leagues [fifty-six thousand miles]. And they not only studied France to its limits, they tracked the mineral formations that extend across our territory into neighbouring lands – England, Belgium, Germany, Italy and Spain.

The geological map of France had its origins in a faintly disturbing discovery made by the naturalist Jean-Étienne Guettard. In the 1740s, he had noticed that the 'subterranean geography' of northern France appeared to be very similar to that of southern England. Deep down, the Channel was not the great barrier that it seemed. Guettard then formed a bold hypothesis: northern terrains formed 'broad, continuous bands arranged concentrically around the capital': 'If my conjecture was correct, I should find in other provinces, at roughly the same distance from Paris, what I had seen in Lower Poitou and the intervening provinces'.

A series of circular journeys from the capital confirmed his theory. Guettard's *Carte minéralogique* of 1746 was a partial description of this unexpectedly coherent subterranean world. It showed two broad belts labelled 'Bande marneuse' and 'Bande sablonneuse' (marly and sandy) that crossed the English Channel between Bayeux and Boulogne. On Guettard's map, Paris looks like the capital of an underground kingdom with London at the extreme northern tip.

It so happens that Paris really does lie at the heart of concentric bands of sedimentary rocks and escarpments, but it is significant that Guettard formed his Paris-centric hypothesis at such an early stage. It is also significant that the achievements of the Belgian geologist Omalius d'Halloy, who spent six years mapping the subterranean French Empire at Napoleon's request, were largely ignored. Geological formations might have disregarded political boundaries, but the map itself had national implications. The École des Mines in Paris finally agreed to support the project, not because it might show where the valuable coal seams of Belgium and Saarland extended into French Flanders and Lorraine, but because it had become a matter of patriotic pride. In 1822, Britain produced the first reliable geological map of a whole country. It was only then that the eleven-year-old proposal of the Professor of Geology Brochant de Villiers was approved and the fifty-six-thousand-mile expedition could begin.

In the introduction to their twenty-four-foot-square, colour-coded *Carte géologique de la France* (1841) – 'one of the finest scientific monuments on which our country prides itself', according to the Larousse encyclopedia – Dufrénoy and Élie de Beaumont drew some comforting conclusions. The old provinces and *pays* were not arbitrary divisions but ancient, ineradicable truths. To generations that had seen the end of the monarchy and the fall of the empire, it was a consolation to know that France and its capital would always exist:

> The limits of these natural regions remain constant amidst political revolutions, and they may well survive a revolution of the globe that

would shift the bounds of the Ocean and change the course of rivers, for they are profoundly inherent in the structure of the Earth.

As roads and railways spread across the land, 'the suburbs of Paris would extend to the very frontiers of the kingdom' and 'make it possible to gain a firmer grasp of the peculiarities' of each *pays*. This was to be an increasingly common theme in the development of a national identity: the celebration of home-grown diversity and the supreme importance of Paris as the guardian and regulator of that diversity.

*

THE CHARTING OF France had turned out to be a much bigger task than anyone had supposed: seventy years for the Cassini map and then another seventy years to produce a map that was notoriously incomplete. Half a century after the first lines were drawn, the *Carte de l'état-major* still lacked basic information. Railways were drawn onto it in a haphazard fashion, roads were misplaced, missing details were slotted in from cadastral surveys which had followed different conventions. Heights were shown, often inaccurately, with rough hatchings instead of contour lines. By 1865, levelling (the operation that determines the heights of objects and points) had been carried out in only two *départements*: the Cher and the Seine. Civil engineers were forced to conduct their own local surveys, and sometimes, inevitably, chose the wrong course for a new road or railway.

Even when the hexagonal shape of France had become a familiar sight, few people had a clear impression of the topography of the country. In 1837, in an attempt to form a coherent picture in his mind, Stendhal wrote a description of 'the five mountain ranges of France'. 'It was only after writing these pages for myself that I understood the soil of France.' But if his mountain ranges are plotted on a map of France, the result is about as accurate as a medieval chart.

Such was the state of geographical knowledge in 1838 that the Société de Géographie thought it worth sending a learned deputation to no. 8, Chaussée du Maine, on the southern edge of Paris. A retired teacher, M. Sanis, had painstakingly created a three-dimensional model of France on an acre of land. Apart from relief models of the Alps commissioned by wealthy British tourists, nothing like it existed anywhere else. This forerunner of the 'France Miniature' theme park boasted riverbeds carved in stone and a complicated irrigation system. Two flat-bottomed boats holding six passengers each plied the three-foot-deep Mediterranean and sometimes realistically ran aground on the rocks of the Breton coast. There were pieces of apple tree in Normandy and pine tree in the Landes. Geology was represented by thumb-sized cavities into which M. Sanis had pushed a piece of coal, a cube of peat or some other appropriate specimen. The mountains were made of earth and had to be remoulded after rainstorms. As the Society's report rather needlessly pointed out, 'The Vosges, the mountains of the Auvergne, the Pyrenees and the Alps lose their picturesque effects when reduced to miniature proportions'. M. Sanis was intending to remodel them in asphalt and to add roads, boundaries and street plans. The Society suggested that this proliferation of detail might 'obscure the overall picture', but praised him for showing such 'zeal for the advancement of science'.

M. Sanis, whose heroic retirement project now lies somewhere beneath the Gare Montparnasse, showed considerably more zeal than the surprisingly incurious governments of the nineteenth century. The urge to discover seemed to be countered by an equal and opposite force. It was not until 1857 that another epic expedition began to dot the entire country with the circular metal plaques that appear like numerical clues in a gigantic treasure hunt, embedded in the parapet of a bridge, the wall of a church or the plinth of a roadside cross. These were the points required for a complete geodesic survey. The expedition was led by the surveyor of the Suez Canal, Paul-Adrien Bourdaloue. Within eight years, survey points 1,000 metres apart formed a preliminary network of 15,000 kilometres, at which point the French government withdrew 50 per cent of the funding.

Napoleon would not have been surprised to learn that this official indifference to geographical truth had disastrous consequences. On the misty morning of 1 September 1870, French troops commanded by General Ducrot were retreating under heavy fire along the road where Empress Joséphine's coach had come to grief in 1804.

Napoleon III, nephew of Napoleon Bonaparte, had lost the Battle of Sedan even before the first shots were fired. One of the reasons cited for the humiliating defeat of France by Prussia was a shortage of maps and the inadequacy of the *Carte de l'état-major*. It was impossible to tell, for instance, by looking at the map, whether the woods that the Prussian artillery was reducing to a wasteland of mud had once been scrubland or plantation, evergreen or deciduous.

Twelve years later, the lessons had still not been learned. A correspondent of the Bordeaux Geographical Society was walking through the hills of the Entre-Deux-Mers region north of Saint-Émilion. The French army was conducting a training exercise. Through the gun smoke that drifted across the countryside, the geographer could see men in red trousers and képis wandering about in confusion, trying to identify hills and valleys from the map. Only the soldiers who came from the region could find their way. Others were trying to navigate by roads, but years had passed since the original survey, and even a simple training exercise was likely to turn into a journey of discovery. 'In this respect', said the geographer, 'the map is absolutely incomplete. It has not changed at all.'

11

Travelling in France, I:
The Avenues of Paris

E XCEPT FOR FUGITIVES, armies and professional explorers, discovering France – with or without a map – was largely a matter of negotiating the network of roads, rivers, canals and railways. From the distant present, this looks like a tale of steady progress: the speed of travel increased, people and merchandise moved about the country with growing ease and social and economic change arrived by carriage and locomotive instead of on the back of a pedlar or a mule. In the century that followed the Revolution, the national road network almost doubled in size and the canal network increased five-fold. There were fourteen miles of railway in 1828 and twenty-two thousand in 1888. By the mid-nineteenth century, a high-speed goods vehicle could cover fifty miles a day. On well-maintained surfaces, working animals became more efficient by the year: the average load pulled by one horse in 1815 was fourteen hundred pounds; in 1865, it was three thousand.

Roads improved more quickly than at any time since the conquest of Gaul. Tracks that had wandered across country like a peasant returning from a feast were straightened, steep hills were flattened by hairpin bends, violent rivers were tamed or bypassed by imperturbable canals. One day, people would have to travel hundreds of miles to have the thrill of crossing a rickety plank bridge or seeing a carriage wheel skittering on the brink of a precipice. When the poet Alfred de Vigny watched the plume of a steam engine crossing a landscape at more than 10 mph, he dreaded a future of endless, predictable change where 'everyone will run smoothly on a line' and the world would be reduced to a monotonous blur: 'Farewell, slow journeys and distant sounds', 'the twists and turns of varied hills', 'the axle's delays', 'a friend encountered and the hours that slipped away', 'the hope of arriving late in a savage place'.

When Vigny wrote his poem, 'La Maison du berger', in 1844, he was living in a Paris apartment, a few minutes' walk from several omnibus lines, three railway stations* and one of the busiest rivers in France. He had to be careful when crossing the road. The fact that he imagined himself travelling with his mistress in a 'fragrant', four-wheeled shepherd's hut suggests that he had already lost sight of the world beyond the city. He lived in the metropolitan France whose express roads and canals were universally admired as engineering marvels, but not in the other France, which was still recovering from the fall of the Roman Empire.

The changes in French society described in the second part of this book were accelerated by the expanding infrastructure, but the experience of individuals was not arithmetically linked to increasing road length and diminishing journey times. Historical dramas usually show the most efficient technology of the period – healthy horses pulling shiny carriages on slightly bumpy roads – but not the most ordinary scenes of daily life: a cow munching peacefully on a main road near a city; two carriages stuck facing each other for hours on a road so narrow that the doors could hardly be opened; a horse, with wooden planks placed under its belly, being hoisted out of a mud-hole; a farmer ploughing up the road to plant his buckwheat and potatoes.

*

ONE OF THE BEST short guides to the experience of travelling in post-Revolution France is a French–German phrase book published in 1799 by Caroline-Stéphanie-Félicité Du Crest de Saint-Aubin, who is usually known as Mme de Genlis. Her pedagogical bent became apparent when, at the age of six, she delivered a series of lectures to local peasants from the balcony of the family château near Autun. She later became a governess of the future King Louis-

* 124, Rue Saint-Lazare (1837, to Le Pecq), 44, Boulevard Montparnasse (1840, to Versailles) and 1, Boulevard de l'Hôpital or 'Jardin des Plantes' (1843, to Corbeil and Orléans).

Philippe. She was an accomplished seamstress, surgeon, horse rider, harpist and billiards player. Her historical novels are resolutely inaccurate, but her *Traveller's Manual for French Persons in Germany and German Persons in France* is a first-rate historical document. The following phrases are taken from the sections on 'Planning the journey', 'Speaking to postilions during the journey' and 'Talking at staging posts while the horses are being harnessed'. They may sound slightly melodramatic, but similar phrases were used every day on the roads of France.

> Listen, postilion, if you drive at a good speed when the road is good, and slowly on corners and bridges or in towns and villages, then I shall give you a good tip. Otherwise, you shall have only the fare.
>
> Your carriage is heavy and over-loaded.
> Not at all. I assure you that it is neither heavy nor over-loaded.
> This horse is worthless. It is restive. It is skittish. I am decidedly loath to take it. Please give me a different one.
>
> Can one place a harp in its carrying case on the luggage rack?
>
> What kind of road is it?
> It is very sandy.
> It is strewn with rocks.
> It is full of mountains, forests and precipices.
> One must avoid passing through forests at dusk or at night.
>
> Postilion, I do not wish to leave the main road. I am absolutely set against it.
> But the sand is over-tiring my horses.
> I do not wish to leave the main road, and you may not leave it without my permission, for the mail coach must follow the main road unless the passengers agree to leave it.
>
> Postilion, stop; the brakes must be attached.
> The descent is quite steep, I wish the brakes to be attached.
> Please ensure that the trunk is properly attached and that nothing has come undone.
> I believe that the wheels are on fire. Look and see.
>
> Postilion, a man has just climbed onto the back of the coach. Make him get down.
> Postilion, allow this poor man to climb onto the seat.
> He is so tired! Leave him alone. He is an old man!

Climb up, my friend. Climb up, my man.
Do not fall asleep on that seat, my man, you might fall off. . . . Keep
   yourself awake.

The kingpin has fallen out.
The suspension has snapped.
The coach has overturned.

The horses have just collapsed.
Is anyone hurt?
No, thank God.
The horse is badly wounded. It is dead.

The postilion has fainted, administer the eau de Luce.*
Gently remove the postilion from beneath the horse.
There is a large lump on his head. Should we not apply a coin to the
   lump in order to flatten it?
By no means. What you are proposing is very dangerous and one
   should never do such a thing.
I shall simply put salt and water on the contusion or some eau de
   Cologne thinned with water.

Poor man! Be assured that I sympathize with your suffering.

Most of the roads on which these little dramas were acted out had
been created by slave labour. The dreaded *corvée*, instituted in 1738,
was the main road-building scheme until the Revolution. In some
parts, almost the entire male population between the ages of twelve
and seventy – when life expectancy was less than forty years – could
be forced to work on the roads for up to forty days a year. The
national average was one week. The only people who did not have to
break stones, cart rubble and dig ditches were lords, the clergy and
their servants, and a few essential workers: the teacher, the doctor
and the communal shepherd. Invalids were excused but they had to
pay for a replacement if they had any money. If the gang was one
man short, two women took his place. Horses and carts could be
made to travel up to four leagues (eleven miles) to the worksite.
Shirkers were fined, imprisoned, given extra work or driven to the
site by armed guards.

* Oil of amber, caustic ammonia and alcohol.

The blatant unfairness of the *corvée* was a constant irritation. Rich people's carriages came charging along, gouging up the road surface, and went merrily on their way. Many of the road-builders had no idea where the road went and never used it. The main beneficiaries were merchants and nobles. Fenimore Cooper, who travelled through northern and eastern France in 1832, rightly supposed that the *corvée* had often coincided with a visit from the local seigneur:

> Thus, whenever M. le Marquis felt disposed to visit the château, there was a general muster, to enable him and his friends to reach the house in safety, and to amuse themselves during their residence; after which the whole again reverted to the control of nature and accident. To be frank, one sometimes meets with by-roads in this old country, which are positively as bad as the very worst of our own, in the newest settlements.

The effects of aristocratic influence can still be seen: an unexpected detour that takes the road past a château or a seemingly needless cutting that gives a splendid view of a bishop's palace. The châteaux of the Loire Valley are so easy to reach on minor roads partly because their owners knew how to take advantage of slave labour.

It would be hard to exaggerate the inefficiency of the *corvée*. Often, the road was divided up between parishes, which meant it was unusable until every parish had finished its section. Some parishes sub-divided their stretch of road into individual segments and turned it into an obstacle course of tiny worksites. A procrastinating peasant with a persistent pothole and a broken shovel could hold up the traffic of an entire region for years. When the summer's work was done, many villages allowed their work to go to waste. A good road might allow producers from a neighbouring town to come to market and undercut the local farmers. Even if the village had wares and produce to export, the *corvée* was a crippling expense. By vigorous lobbying on behalf of the townspeople, the magistrates of La Souterraine in the Creuse managed to deflect the road from Toulouse to Paris. La Souterraine still lies six miles from the main road and is forced to promote itself with a slightly misleading map as 'the naturally enterprising town at the crossroads of major axes of communication'.

With a few spectacular exceptions, the roads themselves were crudely made – usually flattish rocks between embankments, loaded with stones, then covered with an extra layer of crushed stones or gravel, creating a thick, unstable cake of rubble. The innovation of the Limousin engineer Pierre Trésaguet in 1775, who halved the usual thickness to nine or ten inches, was widely ignored until the 1830s, when it was adopted along with other improvements devised by the Scottish engineer John Loudon McAdam. Most French roads were designed by architects rather than road engineers; many bridges were beautiful works of art until they collapsed into the river. A free national school, the École des Ponts et Chaussées (Highways and Bridges), was founded in 1791, but expertise on a national scale could not be created overnight. Even a century later, the roads lecturer at the École des Ponts et Chaussées could take nothing for granted:

> Setting aside the depths that are covered by the waters of the sea, the surface of the Earth can be seen to have a large number of protuberances, separated by hollow sections called *valleys*. The protuberances are called *mountains*, when they rise more then five or six hundred metres above the surrounding land, and *hillocks* or *hills* when the height is less. These terms are not absolute: a mountain in the Beauce would scarcely be a hill in the Alps. . . .
>
> The road is said to be *en rampe* when it rises, and *en pente* when it descends. These terms are relative to the direction in which one supposes one is advancing along the road. If one turns around in order to pursue the road in the opposite direction, the *pentes* turn into *rampes*, and vice versa.

*

WITH POOR TECHNIQUES, lack of expertise and a self-sabotaging workforce, it is no wonder that road building was so painfully slow. In 1777, in the Généralité of Rouen (equivalent to the Seine-Maritime and parts of the neighbouring *départements*), thirty-seven thousand unpaid workers and twenty-two thousand horses worked for seven days each and produced twenty miles of road. This was fast. In the Landes, where carriages sank in the sand up to their axles, the engineer Chambrelent calculated that once a road had reached a certain length it would be destroyed by the process that built it: 'In travelling to the point where it will be used to prolong the road, one cubic metre of stone or gravel wears out more than one cubic metre of road.' In this case, physical reality was equal to the most perverse superstition: the more work done on a road, the shorter it became.

The main problem was that before the advent of railways, road-builders were dependent on local materials. In the late eighteenth century, carters who brought wine to Paris from Orléans were obliged to carry sandstone slabs on the return journey to help repair the road, but the Paris–Orléans road was exceptionally well maintained. In limestone regions like Burgundy and Languedoc, people and animals coated in dust travelled along blinding white roads. In granite regions like Brittany and the Auvergne, uncrushable, sharp stones made the roads less comfortable than the natural surface. The richer the soil, the worse the road. Rain turned dusty roads into quagmires, carriage wheels carved the quagmires into ruts, which the sun then baked into a chaotic, miniature landscape of ridges and gullies. Sometimes, the only part of the land that was permanently devoid of traffic was the road itself. In 1788, no one would have been mystified by the sight of the equestrian statue of Louis XIV passing through fields and hedges on its way to the main square in Beauvais.

The magnificent system of main roads that eventually came into being was a triumph of administrators and engineers who had worked in conditions usually associated with trench warfare. Baron Hauss-mann, who bulldozed a large part of Paris in the 1850s and 60s and turned it into a hygienic city of broad boulevards and capacious, high-speed sewers, had suffered years of provincial misery as a sub-prefect. He had served in Poitiers, where one part of the town was almost cut off from the other by a steep hill, shoe-piercing cobbles, bad lighting and a lack of taxis. The following year, he left Poitiers for Yssingeaux in the Haute-Loire. It took him six days to reach it, by a series of increasingly antiquated carriages. In 1833, he was sent to take charge of the arrondissement of Nérac, where horses had been known to vanish into mud-holes and the entire road network measured less than thirty miles. 'It did occur to me to go back to Paris and say, "Couldn't I be sent somewhere else?"'

This is why so much of the Roman infrastructure was still in use at the dawn of the industrial age. Some Roman roads had been marked on maps since the seventeenth century, not for antiquarian interest, but because they were the best roads available. Locally, they were known as the *'camin ferrat'* or *'chemin ferré'* (the metalled way), the *'chaussée'* (the surfaced road), the *'chemin de César'* or the *'chemin du Diable'*, since only Caesar or the Devil could have built a road that lasted so long. As the Marquis de Mirabeau observed in 1756, Roman roads had been 'built for eternity', while a typical French road could be wrecked within a year by 'a moderate-sized colony of moles'.

The very large number of places called 'Le Grand Chemin' or 'La Chaussée' shows that the Roman contribution to the development of modern France was not confined to the trade routes through Provence and the Rhône valley. There were long stretches of Roman surface or base layer on the roads from Arles to Aix, Clermont-Ferrand to Limoges, Arcachon to Bordeaux, the old salt route from Saintes to Poitiers, the left bank of the Lot between Aiguillon and Lafitte, and the road that wound up from the Alsace plain to Mont Sainte-Odile with an impressive top layer of nicely squared stones. There were Roman roads in remote parts of Poitou, Champagne and the Morvan. In 1756, a stretch of road from Besançon to Langres was 'so complete and solid, between Chalindrey and Grosses-Saules, that the weight and movement of carriages make no impression on it'. In 1839, Mérimée found the same road quite busy and 'in fairly good condition though it has never been repaired'. In Brittany, the 'chemin de la duchesse Anne' north of Quimper remained in use until the early twentieth century. Popular admiration for 'good old Caesar' was not entirely misplaced.

*

UNTIL THE EIGHTEENTH CENTURY, the best modern roads were those intended for the King: the 'Route du Sacre' (Coronation Road) to Reims and the paved roads from Paris to Versailles and Marly. They were referred to as 'the avenues of the city of Paris'. Louis XIV's chief minister, Colbert, pursued what seemed to be a logical policy of centralization. In 1680, he instructed the intendants of the *pays d'élection* (provinces taxed directly by the state) to 'consider the main route from the provinces to Paris as the principal and most important ... because Paris is effectively the centre of all consumption'. A road that pointed straight at the capital was more likely to be funded than a road that served the nearest town.

The effects of this persistent policy of centralization can be seen on the maps of the developing road and rail network. The lower halves of the maps seem to belong to a different country in a different era: while Paris surrounds itself with vessels like a fertilized egg, the older urban centres – Lyon, Marseille, Montpellier, Toulouse and Limoges – remain almost unchanged. Even in the mid-nineteenth century, a person in Moulins could see the mountains of the Auvergne but be unable to reach any town in the region because all the diligences left from Paris and were usually fully booked. It still takes hours of ingenuity to plot a north–south or west–east route from a Channel port – especially by train – that does not pass through the capital. Paris is the only city in France that cannot be crossed on a long-distance train and the only city that forces all travellers to tread its pavement before continuing their journey. (It is hard to see why so much ridicule was heaped on Ferdinand Lop, the repeatedly unsuccessful presidential candidate of the 1920s and 30s, who was simply following national policy when he proposed extending the Boulevard Saint-Michel to the sea.)

The royal roads, according to an edict of 1607, were at least seventy-two feet wide, which is the same as a modern six-lane autoroute. They ran through great swathes of baldness, extending sixty feet on either side of the road, in which all plant-life was hacked down every six months. There is a good indication of the normal state of these gravelly *routes royales* in the fact that Louis XIV always travelled with his own crew of road-menders. The same edict ordered crosses, posts or pyramids to be erected as signposts at all junctions. Towns usually chose posts; villages preferred crosses. Many of the old stone crosses that stand at junctions and crossroads in the French countryside appeared at this time. Local custom might have turned them into religious monuments, but they began life as road signs and are still quite useful aids to navigation.

The first serious attempt to create an integrated network was made in 1738, when the Finance Minister, Philibert Orry, and the future director of the Ponts et Chaussées (Highways and Bridges), Daniel Trudaine, launched a road-building programme based on the

Principal roads of Roman Gaul

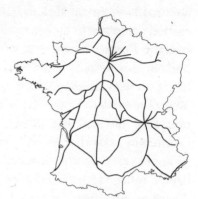

Post-roads, 1643

Post-roads, 1748

Post-roads, 1810

Railways, 1854

Autoroutes, 1986

corvée. Instead of simply patching up the old highways, they created new roads with separate carriageways. In this way, repairs could be carried out without stopping the traffic. Most of the stunningly long, straight French roads that are usually thought to be Roman were built in this period. They were often lined with trees, not, as legend has it, to provide shade for marching troops, but because they looked nice. Trees were impractical: they prevented the road from drying out; they blocked the ditches and gave cover to highwaymen. In Normandy, travellers were often snagged by the straggly branches of apple trees. But the beautiful avenues of elm, ash, sycamore and beech relieved the terrible monotony of an arrow-straight road. These avenues were renewed, and others created, in the nineteenth century, using poplars and plane trees planted ten metres apart. Many of them are now being cut down because cars sometimes crash into them.

Ironically, the great advances that gave France the finest roads in Europe originated in provinces that would later suffer from the increasing centrality of Paris. The provincial government of Langue-doc had already shown that local funding was more effective than slave labour. In Toulouse, between 1750 and 1786, spending on the roads increased from 1,200 livres a year to 198,000 livres. By the end of the century, the elm-lined avenues of Toulouse ran to the foothills of the Pyrenees and the Cévennes. Small grain merchants and their clanking mule trains were replaced by fast, heavy wagons and a commercial mail service that operated up to ninety miles from the city.

Flanders, too, had some lovely smooth roads, partly because tax concessions encouraged the use of vehicles with broad-rimmed wheels. In Alsace and Lorraine, where the economy was largely dependent on haulage, light chariots went racing towards Strasbourg at over 8 mph. But the model for the rest of the country was the Limousin, where the free-trade economist Turgot and his chief engineer Trésaguet created the roads which Arthur Young found 'incomparably fine, and more like the well-kept alleys of a garden than a common highway'. Travellers who passed through the poverty-stricken province were amazed to find themselves skimming along a beautiful road on which even the smallest ruts had been filled with nut-sized bits of marble. In 1789, François Marlin found the contrast exasperating:

> Soon after Bourganeuf, an irksome signpost informs you in great big letters that you are leaving the Généralité of Limoges . . . What is the point of this signpost? The merest carter could hardly fail to notice that he was no longer on a Limousin road.

When he became Finance Minister in 1774, Turgot urged the abolition of the *corvée*. (It was finally abolished throughout the kingdom in 1787.) In 1775, he allowed public coaches – but not private carriages – to use the system of staging posts, which until then had been reserved for the royal mail. The cost of a journey could now be worked out in advance and travellers could be certain that they would never be more than twenty miles from a fresh team of horses. The resulting small increase in the average speed of long journeys was the first significant acceleration since the Middle Ages.

*

BEFORE HE WAS FORCED out of office, Turgot also oversaw the two most telling advances in road engineering. His chief engineer in the Limousin, Pierre Trésaguet, had insisted that a limit should be placed on gradients. Impressively boring in the plain, the relentlessly straight roads of the earlier eighteenth century were a nightmare in the hills. The old road east from Morlaix still includes a needless climb of 15 per cent (1 in 7) because the blundering military Governor of Brittany, the Duc d'Aiguillon, preferred straight lines to the more accommodating curve of the older road that ran alongside. Thanks in part to Trésaguet, it is unusual now to find a climb in excess of 8 per cent (1 in 12). This was thought to be the steepest gradient that a fully laden mule could manage.* British mountain

---

* To judge by the army handbook of 1884, it is fortunate that most road building was left to civil engineers:

> Gradient on which troops can still march in good order: 25 per cent (1 in 4)
> Gradient manageable by mounted horses and light carriages: 33 per cent (1 in 3)
> Gradient manageable by mules: 50 per cent (1 in 2)
> Escarpment that an infantryman can still cross by using his hands: 100 per cent (completely vertical).

roads tend to rise in fits and starts like step pyramids. French mountain roads go much higher, but more steadily, and can comfortably be climbed for hours by a fully laden cyclist.

This simple innovation revolutionized travel. The names of certain hills crop up again and again in travellers' accounts like monsters in *The Odyssey*: 'the famous Reventin slope [near Vienne], which used to stop the big Provençal carts for hours'; 'the terrible Laffrey incline' near Vizille where Napoleon addressed the regiment that was sent to stop him on his return from Elba and which is still marked 'dangerous'; and the fearsome Tarare hill which lay on the shortest of the main routes from Paris to Lyon and the south. It took two hours to climb the Tarare and just as long to descend. Even the smallest carriages had to be emptied out and pulled up the hill by oxen. For centuries, travellers endured a baptism of mud as they entered the Rhône valley. The engineers who flattened these monsters were hailed as national heroes. Though all its seventeen bridges were invisible from the carriageway, the road that zigzagged over the Col de Saverne on the main route from France to Alsace became a tourist attraction in its own right:

> The road that descends from the Vosges to Saverne is one of the masterpieces of man. . . . Snaking skilfully along the dizzying escarpment, its unnoticeably gentle incline seems to mock the rocky steepness and to offer the traveller consolation for the obstacles that Nature tried to place in the way of his pleasure. (Joseph Lavallée, *Voyage dans les départements de la France*, 1792.)

The biggest of these 'obstacles' was the Alps. The route taken by Hannibal and his elephants in 218 BC was one of the commonest subjects of archaeological speculation, for the purely practical reason that, until 1810, the only Alpine crossing for wheeled vehicles was in the far south, over the Col de Tende, where mules and their drivers were sometimes blown over the edge by the howling mistral. In 1800, losing a great deal of equipment on the way, Napoleon had crossed the Alps by the Great Saint Bernard – not on the prancing white charger shown in David's painting (1801) next to a stone carved with the names 'Napoleon' and 'Hannibal', but on a mule borrowed from a local peasant. After the Battle of the Nile, when the Mediterranean ports were blockaded by the British fleet, the main route into Italy was the Mont Cenis Pass. In 1810, a new road was opened and the cavalcade of sedan chairs, stretchers and mules was replaced by carts and carriages. Until the end of war reopened the sea route, about fifty vehicles a day wound their way up to the 6,800-foot summit of Mont Cenis en route from Lyon to Turin – a climb of six miles on a gradient of 7 per cent. The official bulletin, *État général des routes de poste de l'Empire Français*, announced the opening of the pass to encourage merchants to use it:

> In execution of His Majesty's orders, the Mont Cenis pass has been rendered practicable and convenient. Carriages are able to cross the mountain in all seasons and without danger. Twenty-five refuges have been built at various points. They are occupied by *cantonniers* who serve as inn-keepers and who sell comestibles and other items at prices set by the Mayor of Mont-Cenis . . . Some are permanently engaged in walking the road in order to keep it clear and to assist travellers with their needs.

The later painting by Delaroche of a bedraggled mule carrying Napoleon across the Alps (figure 19) is hardly less heroic than David's mythical horse, but an Alpine scene of snack bars and souvenir shops with regulated price lists would have ruined the glamour completely. Napoleon himself knew the economic value of natural beauty and would not have been surprised by the spreading ski-stations of the modern Alps. One of his first instructions to the Prefect of the Hautes-Alpes *département* was 'to have drawings made of the most beautiful views of your Alps for the porcelain factory at Sèvres'. Once the war was over, Italian pedlars and beggars would flow over the pass to pester foreign tourists and thus ensure that commerce kept the arteries of the empire open.

The *cantonniers* or road-menders who patrolled the pass represented the other main innovation of Turgot and Trésaguet. Each road-mender was responsible for about three miles of road. According to nineteenth-century regulations, he had to be present on the road for twelve hours a day from April to September and from dawn to dusk during the other six months. Meals were to be taken on the road at set times. 'Rain, snow and other bad weather' did not excuse absence, though the *cantonnier* was allowed to make himself a shelter 'provided that it not obstruct the public highway and be visible from the road, so that the worker's presence might be registered at all times'. He had to supply his own tools but he was given a special steel ring with which to check that the stones spread on the road had been smashed to the regulation size. The ring had a diameter of six centimetres, which roughly corresponds to McAdam's rule that no stone should be too big to fit inside the mender's mouth.

Apart from its obvious value, the creation of the *cantonnier* had an invigorating effect on daily life in rural France. Like a hermit with shovels and a wheelbarrow, the *cantonnier* was a colonist of remote areas. Little round stone huts and lonely houses marked CANTONNIER in fading paint can still be seen on many roads. As salaried workers, they helped to generate village economies. They served as messengers and relayers of gossip. Bourgeois travellers and social reformers saw the rain-soaked man at the roadside fighting Nature with a bucket and spade as the personification of proletarian misery, but for the road-menders themselves, security and self-respect, not to mention the blue jacket and the brass hat-badge punched with the word 'Cantonnier', were priceless assets. A grenadier from the Vivarais who distinguished himself at the crossing of the Beresina during the retreat from Moscow in 1812 was asked by Napoleon to name his reward. 'Well, sire,' he replied, 'since you have it in your power, after the war I'd like to be made *cantonnier* for life in my *pays*.' Unlike his officers, Napoleon did not find the man's request amusing.

It was Napoleon who consolidated the advances of the eighteenth-century engineers by placing all two hundred and twenty-nine *routes impériales* under the control of central government. Later, in 1836, the state would assume responsibility for the upkeep of the meandering *chemins vicinaux* that ran between villages. There was little fundamental change in this road system until the 1960s. A dynamic map of the network over two centuries would show a gradual thickening of the main inter-city routes and a flickering mass of smaller lines between. Fourteen 'first-class' roads ran from Paris to the frontiers and were numbered clockwise as they radiated from the capital. These were the great 'avenues' that helped Paris to grow more quickly than any other city in France. They spread the Parisian empire through France and the French Empire through Europe. They also helped the Allies to overrun the country in 1814 and to rush the deposed emperor by carriage to the Mediterranean port of Fréjus in exactly seven days. From Fréjus, Napoleon sailed to his tiny island kingdom of Elba, where, shocked to find hills that even mules could barely climb, and determined to turn the island into 'the warehouse of universal commerce' and 'a point of contact for all nations', he immediately launched a sixty-thousand-franc road-building programme.

12

Travelling in France, II: The Hare and the Tortoise

EVEN THE MOST ENTHUSIASTIC road-builders would have been surprised to see how much roads came to dominate and overwhelm the country. Until the advent of railways, the key to national prosperity was thought by many to lie with canals and canalized rivers. In the first century BC, Strabo had written of 'the harmonious arrangement' of the rivers of Gaul. This famous passage of his *Geography* haunted progressive minds. It seemed to describe a super-efficient France of the future, and it suggested that after almost two millennia the country had still not fulfilled its destiny:

> The whole of this country is watered by rivers: some of them flow down from the Alps, the others from the Cemmenus [Cévennes] and the Pyrenees; and some of them are discharged into the ocean, the others into Our Sea [the Mediterranean]. . . . The river-beds are by nature so well situated with reference to one another that there is transportation from either sea into the other; for the cargoes are transported only a short distance by land, with an easy transit through plains, but most of the way they are carried on the rivers – on some into the interior, on the others to the sea.

France had over four thousand miles of navigable river. It also had six hundred miles of canals by the time of the Revolution and over three thousand before the end of the nineteenth century. Another six hundred miles of river were considered navigable at certain times of year, if only in one direction. Much of the wood that was used to build and heat Paris had been floated down from the Morvan by wild-looking *flotteurs* in straw hats and wolfskin coats who spoke a dialect peculiar to the river. From the Auvergne, wood bound for Bordeaux was loaded onto plank boats which were caulked with moss and survived the spring torrents just long enough to reach Libourne, where they were sold as firewood.

Tiny rivers that are now used only by anglers and timid canoeists carried flat-bottomed boats in water so shallow that the boatmen could walk alongside them in the river. A report on the Dordogne *département* in 1810 described the course of thirty-eight rivers but added that there were also five hundred and sixty other 'principal streams' and eight hundred and fifty 'little streams'. Even some scarcely visible *riviérettes* were treated as valuable trade routes and had their banks repaired and strengthened. Many quiet streams in rural parts are still cluttered with brickwork and stone facing, as if they had once flowed through industrial towns. In the Lot and the Tarn, the river was the only lifeline of many villages. Their tiny harbours and landing stages were strung out along the banks like trading posts in the Amazon. Some medium-sized rivers like the Vienne are like the deserted autoroutes of an earlier civilization. Little lanes run down to them like sliproads, leading only to the river and a clutch of houses often called 'Le Port'.

The fact that sixty-one of the original eighty-three *départements* were named after rivers – even if the river was destructive and torrential or obstructed by boulders and cataracts – shows how much importance was attached to water transport. Statistical studies of the new *départements* typically devoted ten times as much space to water-courses as to roads. Great hopes of wealth and vitality were placed in rivers and canals, and there were some astounding examples to inspire the engineers: the Roman Pont du Gard and the aqueduct system that had watered Nîmes until the ninth century, or the unfinished Maintenon aqueduct (1685–88), which was designed to take the waters of the river Eure fifty miles to feed the fountains of Versailles.

With its hundred and twenty miles of water channels, Versailles itself was a showcase of hydraulic marvels. While the townspeople made do with brackish ponds, expensively imported water created glassy parterres that prolonged the mirrors of the Galerie des Glaces, and fountains that decorated the air with musical arabesques. Nature was made to recognize the political centre. The Seine was diverted by the gigantic pump at Marly known as 'the Machine'; the Eure was to be brought from Maintenon. There was even a plan to bring the waters of the distant Loire to Versailles. Statues in the palace gardens represented the great rivers of France as calm, recumbent giants accompanied by cherubic little affluents.*

The grandest project of all was the Canal du Midi, which is now the oldest functioning canal in Europe. It runs for a hundred and fifty miles, through sixty-three locks and under a hundred and thirty bridges, from Sète on the Mediterranean, via Béziers, Carcassonne and the geological gap between the Pyrenees and the Montagne Noire known as the Seuil de Naurouze, all the way to the heart of Toulouse. This beautiful open-air museum of engineering master-pieces was the brainchild of a retired tax-farmer from Béziers, Pierre-Paul Riquet, who spent on it the entire fortune he had made collecting salt tax and died of exhaustion eight months before it was opened in 1681. It employed up to ten thousand men and women at a time and brought forty-five thousand cypresses and plane trees to the Lauragais plain, as well as millions of irises to protect and beautify the banks. This was one of the biggest movements of population and plant life in peacetime history.

Horse-drawn barges carrying oranges, wine and oils from Italy and Spain, grain and cotton from Languedoc, and drugs and spices from the Levant and the Barbary Coast were unloaded at Toulouse onto smaller river boats that negotiated the watermills and shoals of the lower Garonne. At Agen, they took on prunes and other dried fruit for the Atlantic ships at Bordeaux. They returned from Bordeaux with sugar, coffee and tobacco from the Americas. The dream was that, one day, the French isthmus would enjoy the advantages of an island. If the Garonne could be cleared and canalized, ocean-going vessels could sail directly from the Mediterranean to the Atlantic without having to round the Iberian Peninsula. Languedoc and Aquitaine would lie at the centre of a global river of trade and

---

* Seine and Marne, Loire and Loiret, Rhône and Saône, Garonne and Dordogne. Northern bias chose as the Loire's companion the diminutive Loiret, which runs to the south of Orléans for seven miles, rather than the Allier (two hundred and fifty-six miles) or the Cher (two hundred miles), which rise in the Auvergne.

Strabo's description of a naturally efficient, inter-oceanic river system would come true.

Work finally began on the unexcitingly named Canal Latéral à la Garonne in 1839 during the July Monarchy (1830–48), when more canals were built than in all other periods combined. The Canal des Deux Mers – the name given to the entire stretch from Sète to Bordeaux – was completed just as the new Bordeaux–Sète railway opened for business in 1857. The railway company acquired the lease on the Garonne canal and stifled the canal and river trade with extortionate taxes. The Canal du Midi had turned the Lauragais and Toulousain regions into the bread-basket of the south. It had eliminated the devastating annual floods and, in conjunction with the road system, opened up vast new markets. Grain speculators had covered the land with wheat fields and châteaux. But when the railway arrived, wheat from the Paris Basin was suddenly cheaper than the local grain. For centuries, invaders had passed through the Seuil de Naurouze. Now, after the Celts, the Romans, the Visigoths, the Arabs, the Albigensian crusaders, the Black Prince and the Duke of Wellington, came modern capitalism, the unconscious hypocrite, which took away with one hand what it gave with the other.

*

CANALS, WHICH WERE once seen as the highways on which civilization would reach remote parts, came to be associated with sluggishness and constraint. The drunken boat of Rimbaud's poem 'Le Bateau ivre' (1871) begins its adventure only when its haulers have been slaughtered and it leaves the 'impassive rivers' for the open sea. Many tales of the heroic age of canal building and the taming of rivers will never be told. Even the pioneering voyage of Baron Boissel de Monville has passed into almost total obscurity, though he was the first person in history to descend the Rhône from the Swiss border to the point where the river becomes clearly navigable again. He wanted to show that the Rhône could be a major trade link with Savoy and Switzerland. During the Terror, in the autumn of 1794, disguised as a peasant, the Baron passed the cataracts with his iron-clad boat and a jittery crew, who baled out before the boat reached the Perte du Rhône, where the river used to disappear through a fissure into a subterranean cavern. The boat was wrecked and spat out by the resurgent river three hundred and fifty feet downstream. Two weeks later, the Baron rebuilt his boat and sailed it all the way to Surjoux.

This inspiring but ultimately futile exploit* belonged to an age when long-distance travellers took to the water whenever they could and expected the voyage to be an interesting adventure. It was quite usual for a person touring France to make half the tour on rivers and canals: carriage from Paris to Chalon-sur-Saône; passenger boat to Lyon, then down the Rhône to Avignon; post road to Montpellier and Béziers; canal boat to Toulouse, river boat to Bordeaux and another boat to Blaye on the Gironde; diligence or private carriage via Saintes and La Rochelle to Nantes; sailboat or steamer up the Loire to Tours, Blois or Orléans. The tourist could then travel back to Paris by road or by a series of canals to the Seine at Montereau: from there, the daily passenger boat from Nogent-sur-Seine reached Paris in a day and a night. This was the service on which the fifteen-year-old Napoleon first arrived in Paris and on which Frédéric Moreau leaves the city at the start of Flaubert's *L'Éducation sentimentale*. Compared to the jolting road and the clutter of slums and beggars on the edge of Paris, the river was a royal avenue, flowing majestically towards the towers of Notre-Dame.

Better still, the accommodation was cheaper and more comfortable. Diligences – sometimes optimistically called *vélocifères* – were lumbering contraptions composed, like giant beetles, of three sections. The *coupé* in front was protected by thick curtains of foul-smelling, oily leather; the interior was padded and crammed with little pockets and nets for hatboxes and sundry possessions. The *impériale* above the *coupé* was exposed to the wind and the rain, but passengers could at least make sure that the postilion, perched on the nearest horse in his gargantuan jackboots of wood and iron, was still awake. (These were the original 'seven-league boots' of the fairy tale, because seven

---

* The Perte du Rhône was later blown up to allow wood to be floated down the river. The cataract was one of the main tourist attractions of eastern France until 1948, when the waters of the Génissiat dam engulfed the belvedere, the tea-room and the slippery bridge.

leagues was once the common distance between two staging posts.) Suspension was provided by leather thongs nailed to blocks of wood. Even rich travellers who were equipped with inflatable waterproof cushions and lambswool foot-warmers found the diligence an ordeal. The American writer Bayard Taylor described the horrors of the Auxerre–Paris service in his *Views A-Foot, or Europe Seen with Knapsack and Staff* (1846):

> I should not want to travel it again and be paid for doing so. Twelve persons were packed into a box not large enough for a cow, and no cabinetmaker ever dove-tailed the corners of his bureaus tighter than we did our knees and nether extremities. It is my lot to be blessed with abundance of stature, and none but tall persons can appreciate the misery of sitting for hours with their joints in an immovable vice. The closeness of the atmosphere – for the passengers would not permit the windows to be opened for fear of taking cold – combined with loss of sleep, made me so drowsy that my head was continually falling on my next neighbor, who, being a heavy country lady, thrust it indignantly away. . . .
>
> All that night did we endure squeezing and suffocation, and no morn was ever so welcome than that which revealed to us Paris. With matted hair, wild, glaring eyes, and dusty and dishevelled habiliments, we entered the gay capital, and blessed every stone upon which we placed our feet.

The same journey, by the green-painted *coche d'eau* on the river Yonne, offered a large room lined with benches, prettily decorated compartments, better views and more cheerful passengers. Though the Rhône riverboats were more cramped and dirty, people entering Provence by the river usually had nicer things to say about it than those who had entered it by road. The sniffy Countess Gasparin, in her *Voyage of an Ignoramus in the South of France* (1835), found that the lovely views made up for 'the incommodious throng' that blocked the passageways with its luggage and ignored the distinction between first and second class. Boat passengers enjoyed an unfurling tableau of hilltop castles, vineyards, country homes and people waving from the banks. They smelled the warm air of the Mediterranean; they saw the white summit of Mont Ventoux in the east and the towers of the Palais des Papes at Avignon; and when the boat docked beneath the Pont Saint-Bénezet, they invariably sang a chorus of 'Sur le pont d'Avignon'.

On the return journey, though the boat might be held fast by the current for several hours, they had the consolation of knowing that travellers on the road had to face the terrifying carters of Provence, who never gave way to oncoming traffic, unless, according to an ancient custom, the leading horse had four white hooves, in which case it had right of way. 'On two or three occasions', wrote Stendhal, 'my poor little carriage was almost smashed to smithereens by the enormous six-horse carts coming up from Provence. . . . True, I had my pistols, but those carters are quite capable of being afraid of pistols only after they have been fired.'

Boatmen, too, were a law unto themselves, but even the most delicate passengers seem to have entered into the spirit of the river. All over France, whenever one boat passed another, a salvo of abuse was fired at the other boat, referring to its derisory speed, the ugliness of its crew and the profession of the captain's female relatives. The barrage would continue until the boat was out of earshot. The same ritual was performed when the boat passed riverside houses – when masters, wives, children and servants were standing at the windows – if necessary with megaphones.

These boats were the public spaces of a new France, where class barriers were flimsier than before, where people had news and information to exchange, and where – to judge by many accounts of river journeys – chance encounters often led to romantic adventures. The experience of Flaubert's Frédéric Moreau on the steamer to Nogent was not unusual:

> The deck was littered with nutshells, cigar stubs, pear peelings and the remains of meat pies that had been brought on board wrapped in paper. Three cabinetmakers dressed in overalls were standing in front of the canteen. A harpist in rags was taking a rest, leaning his elbow on his instrument. Now and then, there was the sound of the coal in the furnace, a shout, someone laughing. On the bridge, the captain kept walking from one paddle-wheel to the other. To get back to his seat, Frédéric pushed open the gate that led to First Class, disturbing two hunters with their dogs.

It was like a vision:

She was sitting in the middle of the bench, all on her own ... A long shawl with purple stripes was placed behind her back on the brass rail. ... But the fringe was pulling it down and it was about to slip away into the water. Frédéric leapt forward and caught it. She said, 'Thank you, Monsieur.'

Their eyes met.

*

NOT EVERY RIVER JOURNEY, of course, was an undiluted delight. In her bilingual *Traveller's Manual*, Mme de Genlis prepared her readers for the worst. (The first set of phrases is a reminder that road journeys, too, often involved a perilous river crossing.)

Coachman or postilion, stop, I wish to alight before boarding the ferry.
Oh, there is no danger, the horses are gentle ...
I wish to alight, I tell you, and to board the ferry on foot.

How much must I pay to have the little room to myself? And how much must one pay when one is in the large room with all the other passengers?
Are there any women among these passengers?

How shall we be fed?
Quite badly. You shall have only smoked and salted meat, potatoes and cheese. I advise you to take with you some private provisions. This is especially necessary for old people, women and children.

I am suffering greatly. I am going to vomit. Give me the vase.
The smell of tar makes me sick.
Is the wind always so contrary / so bad?
I have toothache.
Shall we soon be there?

The serene river-statues of Versailles were deceptive. Divine providence seemed to have designed the rivers of France to be more picturesque than useful. Some of the stretches of river that carried large passenger boats were not as safe as they seemed. As it corkscrewed its way towards Le Havre, the Seine was full of treacherous currents. Before the passenger steamboat service began (Le Havre–

Rouen in 1821, Rouen–Paris in 1836), some travellers preferred to cut off all the bends between Rouen and Paris and to make a long, disjointed journey by boat, horse, boat, foot, overnight boat to Poissy and carriage to Paris.

On France's eastern frontier, the river Rhine was a model of fluvial efficiency. Raft trains a thousand feet long took construction wood to the Low Countries on three-week voyages. They looked like villages floating down the river with their own anchored landing stages, dining rooms, kitchens, stables and panoramic observation galleries, and enough bread, meat and beer for a crew of five hundred and the owner's party of friends. They were probably the largest vehicles in existence. Crowds gathered on the riverbank to watch them pass. The Rhône by comparison was a fairground ride. The Cassini map shows four hundred and fifty-one tiny islands between Lyon and Avignon. Most people disembarked and walked or rode along the riverbank while the current carried the boat between and sometimes onto the piers of the bridge at Pont-Saint-Esprit.

The Loire, which was supposed to be the cradle of French civilization, disappointed many travellers with its mudflats, its wispy poplars and its monotonous, misty banks. The Renaissance châteaux that appeared every league or so were a welcome distraction and there always seemed to be a tireless expert on anecdotal French history to bring the scene to life. Stendhal's voyage down the Loire was a typical mixture of tedium and adventure. Ten minutes after leaving Tours at 5.30 a.m., his steamboat was sitting on a sandbank, swathed in freezing fog. After several hours, it was pulled off the bank by a boat piloted by a fifteen-year-old boy and into the path of an oncoming ship. The eight horses towing the ship were stopped just in time. For the next few hours, everyone gave their own version of what had happened: 'The ladies in first class had been much more frightened than the peasant women, and so their tales were much more novelistic.' At Ancenis, the metal funnel was lowered to allow the boat to pass under the bridge; it scraped the rotting beams and showered the passengers with splinters.

'My secret reason' for recounting all this, Stendhal explained, was to encourage the reader to take a cheerful view of 'all the little mishaps that often spoil the jolliest expeditions – passports, quarantine, accidents', etc. Modern transport created expectations of comfort and convenience, but a traveller who put his mind to it could avoid ill humour as 'a kind of madness that eclipses the objects of interest that may surround one and amongst which one shall never pass again'.

*

THESE RIVER ROUTES were kept alive by steamboats, but not for long. The low-pressure puffers known as *inexplosibles*, which chugged up and down the Loire until the railway reached Nantes in 1851, moved at the speed of a cart horse. Canals were even slower. The mail boat from Toulouse to Sète took fifteen minutes to pass each lock and the Canal du Midi itself was closed for maintenance for up to two months a year. 'For those who have long been jolted along high roads in Diligences' – and who could bear to spend a night with two hundred members of 'the lower classes' – the mail boat was 'not a disagreeable mode of conveyance', according to Murray's guide. But for merchants and industrialists, it was intolerably slow. Michel Chevalier was a Saint-Simonian reformer who dreamed of steamboats and railways creating a global industrial cooperative, galvanizing snail-like peasants with 'the spectacle of prodigious speed'. In 1838, he pointed out the dismal fact that, until recently, in the time it took a coal barge to reach Paris from Mons (two hundred and twenty miles), a medium-sized sailing ship could cross the Atlantic to Guadeloupe, take on a fresh load, return to Bordeaux, then sail again for the Gulf of Mexico and return to France via New Orleans.

The canal system was already turning into an accessory of the leisure industry in 1876 when Robert Louis Stevenson and a friend canoed along the canals that joined the Sambre to the Oise and Belgium to Paris. At the last lock before Landrecies, they stopped for a smoke:

> A vivacious old man, whom I take to have been the devil, drew near and questioned me about our journey. In the fulness of my heart, I laid bare our plans before him. He said it was the silliest enterprise that ever he heard of. Why, did I not know, he asked me, that it was nothing but locks, locks, locks, the whole way? not to mention that, at this season of the year, we should find the Oise quite dry? 'Get into a

train, my little young man', said he, '. . . and go you away home to
your parents.'

The man at the lock obviously had time to spare for a chat.
Pleasure and prosperity did not have to travel at top speed. Trade
figures suggest an increasingly busy population, but conviviality was
still an essential element of trade. In the early twentieth century, the
wines of Burgundy were still making deliciously slow journeys down
the Canal de Bourgogne and the Canal du Charolais towards the
all-consuming capital.

Time passed slowly on the barges. People who saw those low,
wine-laden boats gliding through a sunny landscape knew that not all
the wine would be incarcerated in bottles and sold in cities. Surprising
quantities of it would filter out along the way and return to the land
that gave it life. In the summer of 1900, disgruntled wine-brokers
at a meeting in Dijon identified one of the happier disadvantages of
transport by canal:

> The boatmen, who voyage for several weeks without supervision,
> surrounded by brimming barrels, indulge in wine-tastings, the size of
> which is directly proportional to the quality of the merchandise. They
> have no hesitation in inviting the riverside people – lock-keepers and
> the like – to join them in depleting the stock, and the navigation
> companies refuse to accept any responsibility in the matter.

*

APART FROM THE LEAVES of plane trees drifting on the brown
surface, a darting dragonfly, a silent racing cyclist on the tarmacked
towpath or a holiday barge with a nervous captain and an idle crew,
there is little movement nowadays on the Canal du Midi. Until the
first signs of the aerospace industry appear on the outskirts of
Toulouse, it is hard to imagine that this was once one of the great
trade highways of Western Europe. Or rather, it is hard to imagine
the canal as one might suppose it should be imagined. Though
commercial traffic is now almost non-existent, the Canal du Midi is
busier today than it was before the railways. The fleet of rental barges
outnumbers the hundred and seventy boats that plied the canal at its
height by more than two to one.

The common experience of a particular age tends to be measured by the fastest transport available at the time. Eighty-six per cent of French people have never flown in an aeroplane and most have never taken a TGV, though both forms of transport will be standard images of early twenty-first-century France in future histories. This distortion by speed is harder to correct for periods that lie beyond living memory. Turgot's reform might have brought Paris closer in time to the twelve hundred towns that lay on the post roads in 1775, but very few people ever took a high-speed coach. In the mid-nineteenth century, many villages to the north of Paris were connected to the outside world for half the year by stepping stones. In many parts, the sound of carriage wheels brought people to their windows. A pastor touring Provence in the 1830s found it hard to get his carriage through the main street of Bédoin at the foot of Mont Ventoux because of the crowd that came to see it.

A journey by diligence was something to be remembered for a lifetime. In 1827, a Lyon newspaper advised heads of families 'to consider making a will as a precautionary measure' before embarking on such a momentous expedition. The newspaper naturally assumed that the diligence traveller was a man of means. A high-speed coach was proportionately as expensive as first-class air travel today. The mail coach from Paris to Calais in 1830 cost forty-nine francs, which was a servant's monthly wage or the cost of dinner in a famous Paris restaurant. The reason why wet-nurses were so often seen in diligences was that their employers paid the fare. The exposed seats on top of the diligence were cheaper, but most of the 'rough and low-bred companions' that Murray's guide warned fresh-air travellers to expect had probably not paid for their seat: postilions were notoriously bribable and often allowed pedestrians to clamber on so they could enter a town after the gates had been closed for the night.

Once the scale of human locomotion was recalibrated to include steam engines and speedy carriages on macadamized roads, every other form of transport looked too slow to be significant. From the window of a diligence or a railway carriage, the rest of France appeared to be rooted to the spot. Walking came to be associated with tortoise-like peasants and leisurely tourists like Robert Louis Stevenson. But Stevenson probably held the record for the slowest journey ever made through the Cévennes. Two years after his canoe trip, it took him and his donkey twelve days to travel from Le Monastier to Saint-Jean-du-Gard – a journey, by his meandering route, of about a hundred and thirty miles. At one point, they were overtaken by a tall peasant 'arrayed in the green tail-coat of the country'. He 'stopped to consider our pitiful advance':

> 'Your donkey', says he, 'is very old?'
> I told him, I believed not.
> Then, he supposed, we had come far.
> I told him, we had but newly left Monastier.
> 'Et vous marchez comme ça!' cried he; and, throwing back his head,
> he laughed long and heartily.

The man in the green tail-coat lived in a world where people thought nothing of walking fifty miles in a day. The simple lesson of the hare and the tortoise was easily forgotten by people who spent their entire travelling life sitting down. By the mid-twentieth century, a whole world of human-powered transport had disappeared from view.

Walking was just one means of locomotion. The swamp dwellers of the Marais Poitevin got about their watery world using fifteen-foot ash-wood poles with webbed feet that allowed them to vault across a canal twenty-six feet wide. The shepherds of the Landes spent whole days on stilts, using a stick to form a tripod when they wanted to rest. Perched ten feet in the air, they knitted woollen garments and scanned the horizon for stray sheep. People who saw them in the distance compared them to tiny steeples and giant spiders. They could cover up to seventy-five miles a day at 8 mph. When Napoleon's empress Marie-Louise travelled through the Landes to Bayonne, her carriage was escorted for several miles by shepherds on stilts who could easily have overtaken the horses. It was such an efficient mode of transport that letters in the Landes were still being delivered by postmen on stilts in the 1930s.

In many parts of France, the usual scale of speeds was turned on its head. In difficult terrain, a horse and carriage were slower than a mule, which was slower than a human being. Tourists on horseback were often accompanied by guides on foot. In the Alps, snow-shoes were used in regions that would never be reached by road or rail. (Skis were not introduced until 1891.) A party of four or five would walk in a little caravan, taking turns at the front to share the effort. Crampons attached to plates of wood and to horses' hooves made it possible to ford glaciers and to farm almost vertical meadows.

In hills and mountains, gravity-assisted forms of transport were vital to the economy. In the forests of the Vosges, strange screeching sounds could be heard up to great distances. Until the 1940s, walkers in the woods occasionally caught sight of a pale-faced forest-dweller running stiffly through the trees, braced against a towering 2½-ton pile of logs. The sledges on which the logs were piled were known as *raftons* in Lorraine and *schlitte* in Alsace. The *schlitteurs'* sledges ran on wooden railways in trains of up to ten. They raced on greased ash soles over wooden viaducts that groaned under the weight, descending by long, gentle slopes that looped across the mountainside until they reached the tributaries of the Rhine, which took the logs on to Strasbourg and Colmar. The *schlitteurs'* legs were the only brakes. Wooden crosses at the side of the railways marked the site of fatal accidents.

Now that brakes are a normal feature of most vehicles, these forms of transport seem more dangerous than efficient, but they were widely used and even enjoyed. Mountain people sat on grassy slopes and turned themselves into human sledges to rocket down to the valley. A botanist visiting the Pyrenees just before the Revolution was persuaded to join one of these gravitational express trains. His only regret was that the botanical specimens flashed past too quickly to be identified:

> We felt as though we were swimming along the even course of a majestic river. At times, we were carried into grass so tall that we lost sight of one another and kept calling out lest we be separated as we tried to avoid the bushes and granite boulders and unforeseen obstacles. We seemed to be sailing among reefs and perils on a stormy sea, and by this means, in a state bordering on delirium, we negotiated at inconceivable speed and quite safely the most precipitous slopes.

Before there were bicycles and skis, these were probably the highest speeds attained by unmotorized human bodies. An estimate of the normal speed can be deduced from an account of the post-pilgrimage descent of the north face of Mont Ventoux. Every year on 14 September, pilgrims climbed 'the Giant of Provence' to visit the chapel on the summit where a hermit had been appointed by the Bishop of Carpentras to guard some fragments of the Cross. It took most of the day to climb the mountain, but the return journey was breathtakingly short:

> They simply slid back down, squatting on a double plank, three spans long and three spans wide. When they were going too fast or approaching a precipice, they stopped abruptly by stabbing a stick into the ground in front of them. In this way, they descended in less than half an hour. (Frédéric Mistral)

Descending over five thousand feet in thirteen miles at an average speed of over 26 mph, a plank-borne pilgrim would have come in only about eight minutes down on a cyclist in the modern Tour de France.

*

WITH A PROPERLY ADJUSTED historical speedometer, the stream-lined view of the age of progress looks as dubious as a nineteenth-century timetable. By the 1830s, Paris was supposed to be only twenty-five hours from the port of Calais and thirty-six hours from London. But these figures are misleading. They were speed records rather than accurate times. Coach-company timetables were designed to attract passengers, not to serve as historical documents. They always assumed perfect conditions, and they excluded the hours spent waiting for horses to be changed and meals to be served. They also referred to the fastest routes. In reality, journey times varied wildly from one part of the country to the next. A map of France that matched time from Paris to distance on the map would show the country contracted to the north and north-east, and pulled up towards Paris along the Rhône Valley, but there would be a gigantic peninsula to the west (Brittany) and a huge, bulging sub-continent in the centre and the south. Large parts of Languedoc and the Mediterranean coast would stretch far away into the ocean. London would be closer than most of the Loire Valley.

Personal accounts of journeys never match the timetables. The following incident took place in 1736, but it could have occurred at any time until the mid-nineteenth century. One day that summer, in the centre of Strasbourg, a young artist-engraver from Germany was waiting to board the express coach for Paris, where he hoped to make his fortune. Johann Georg Wille and a friend had walked a hundred and sixty miles from Usingen on the other side of Frankfurt. They had arrived in Strasbourg with just enough time to register Wille's suitcase at the coach office and to climb the spire of Strasbourg Minster, which was the tallest building in the world. From the top of the spire, they saw the whole Alsace plain and the Vosges mountains where the coach would soon be speeding towards Paris.

The sightseeing and the farewell breakfast went on too long. When they arrived on the square, the coach had gone and was already well on its way to the first staging post at Saverne, twenty-five miles to the north-west.

> What was I to do? The only solution was to run after it. It had been raining and there were still occasional showers. The cobbles were slippery and the only support I had was my feeble sword. Strasbourg is seven leagues from Saverne. I covered the distance, as far as possible, without stopping to eat or drink, and did not catch up with the coach until it was entering the courtyard of the inn at Saverne where it was to spend the night.

In this case, the tortoise was the coach and the hare was the human being. According to a railway engineer who made the journey more than thirty times between 1830 and 1852, the diligence from Lyon to Paris usually took three days and three nights, or four days in bad weather. The mail coach took only forty-two hours and 'one met a better sort of person', but it was twice as expensive and had room for only four passengers. The true average speed of the Paris–Lyon diligence in the mid-nineteenth century, including stops, was therefore less than 4 mph – twice as slow as the speed of Roman emperors travelling in Gaul and just over twice as fast as Stevenson and his donkey.

*

IN 1843, A FRANTIC TRAVELLER who was prepared to spend any amount of money, who was helped at almost every stage by sympathetic people and who was able to take the latest high-speed link to Paris on the final stage, could still suffer terrible delays. On 9 September Victor Hugo was on holiday with his mistress Juliette Drouet. They had sailed from the Île d'Oléron to Rochefort, a busy port on the Atlantic. In a cafe, he picked up a newspaper and learned that five days before, his newly married daughter Léopoldine had drowned in a boating accident on the Seine at Villequier.

For the only time in his life, Hugo was unable to write. However, Juliette Drouet kept an account of the three-hundred-and-fifty-mile journey. According to the 1843 *Annuaire des postes*, the journey should have taken forty hours.

At 6 p.m., Hugo and his mistress left for La Rochelle, where they spent the night. Next day (Sunday), as they boarded the diligence for Saumur, the driver slammed the carriage door, shattering the window pane. At Niort, the carriage crashed into the customs gate because the horses and the driver had fallen asleep. On Monday morning, before crossing the Loire at Saumur, two of the four horses were unhitched and ambled across the bridge in front of the coach. (This was to avoid paying the tax on four-horse carriages.)

They left Saumur at 10 p.m. At Blois, a breakfast of strawberries, melons and half-grilled *andouillettes* was served just as the driver was calling the passengers to reboard. Juliette Drouet suspected a swindle. (Innkeepers often shared the profit on uneaten meals with coach drivers.) At 3 o'clock on Tuesday afternoon, they arrived at Orléans railway station, which had been opened in May:

> At 4 o'clock, we are in the hoists that raise the diligence onto a kind of wheeled floor. The diligence is firmly attached to this floor by chains and iron clamps. . . . We pass through several stations without stopping at most of them. . . . The biggest stations have canteens which are very well stocked and very appetizing.

They reached Paris at 8 p.m. on Tuesday, seventy-four hours after leaving Rochefort, but six days after Hugo's daughter had been buried in the cemetery overlooking the Seine at Villequier.

The last stage – in the body of a diligence strapped to a railway truck moving at 18 mph – was a journey between two ages of travel. Soon, the railways would empty the roads and ruin the roadside inns. They would close off large parts of the country whilst giving passengers the illusion that France was now open to discovery.

Hugo had already witnessed the gradual disappearance of France. He had replayed long journeys in his mind and seen only the horse's rump, the postilion's whip, the arms of a windmill overhead and the uniform of a soldier asking to see his passport. With Juliette Drouet, he had travelled south on the diligence to Bordeaux with its seventeen-arch bridge, its riverside Place Royale and the forest of masts and rigging that seemed to show that economic life began only when France was looking away from itself. 'A hundred and fifty leagues in thirty-six hours and what have I seen? I've seen Étampes, Orléans, Blois, Tours, Poitiers and Angoulême.'

But those inland cities had been reduced to images flashed onto the magic lantern of the diligence window. Orléans was a candle on a table and a thin girl serving thin soup; Blois was a bridge; Tours was a dial marking nine in the morning; Poitiers was a dinner of duck and turnips; Angoulême was a gas lamp and a theatre bill. 'That's what France is when you see it from the mail coach. What will it be like when it's seen from the railway?'

The contraction of space and the gravitational pull of Paris were not just physical and political realities. Writers who set out to discover the country in the age of convenience would have to unravel landscapes that had been wound up tightly in the springs of a clock. In the late 1840s, Gérard de Nerval set off from Paris to visit his friend Alexandre Dumas in Brussels. He spent two hundred francs and eight days travelling along the old Paris–Flanders road. The railway had driven coach companies out of business and left a shattered maze of infrequent, short-distance omnibuses. Once, the journey had taken three days by diligence. Now that the railway had arrived, travel had never been so slow.

Hugo himself had discovered his favourite form of transport in 1821, when he travelled from Paris to Dreux to see the girl he hoped to marry. On the day after arriving, he wrote to Alfred de Vigny to tell him about the vehicle that opened up new vistas and revolutionized his view of the world:

So here I've been since yesterday, visiting Dreux and getting ready to set out on the road to Nonancourt. I walked all the way here under a burning sun, on roads without a shadow of shade. I am exhausted but very proud of having covered twenty leagues on my legs. I cast a pitying glance at every carriage that I saw. If you had been with me, you would never have seen such an insolent biped. When I think that Alexandre Soumet has to take a taxi to go from the Luxembourg to the Chaussée d'Antin, I am tempted to believe myself a superior form of animal. This experiment has proved to me that it is possible to use one's feet for walking.

13

Colonization

T HE NEW ROADS AND RAILWAYS that reached into the heart
of nineteenth-century France were not magical paths to a
timeless world. People who came from monumental cities, where
historical events were marked like the dates on a calendar, found it
easy to imagine, when they visited small, lonely places they would
never see again, that they were discovering a past that had been
miraculously preserved. But the land, too, like Baudelaire's Paris, was
changing 'more quickly than a human heart'.

The tourists who seem to have explored France in all its secret
corners over the last three centuries (Chapters 15 to 17) saw only
part of the land's long history. They 'discovered' the provinces and
'conquered' the Alps by following a few well-established routes. They
observed the advantages and inconveniences of political regimes that
came and went like weather systems. Foreign tourists talked in
general terms about France and 'the French', and forgot how thin a
path they had traced across the country. They saw battlefields and
fortresses but not the endless war that people waged with their
environment.

The physical transformation of France and the stormy relationship
of people, the state and the land are barely discernible in the background
of the tourists' albums and postcards, but, like today's tourists, they
were part of an ancient process of creation and destruction that began
before France or Gaul existed. Before their adventures fill the picture,
that background should be seen without its frames and smiling faces.

*

ON THE NIGHT of 29 April 1832, a chartered steamboat dropped anchor off the deserted coast of the Estaque hills, fifteen miles across the bay from Marseille. A woman wrapped in a man's cape was rowed ashore. She stood shivering in the sea breeze, waiting for day to break and for a messenger to bring the news from Marseille. When he came riding out of the dawn, she expected to hear that her landing had sparked a royalist uprising that would spread through the south of France and, by means that she could imagine but not describe, restore a Bourbon monarch to the throne.

For the last decade, the Duchesse de Berry, the young mother of the Bourbon heir, had travelled all over France, opening charitable institutions, charming people of every political hue and setting the tone for high society. She had caused an invasion of small fishing ports on the English Channel by taking holidays at the new ocean-bathing establishment at Dieppe. Thanks to the Duchess, other resorts were already springing up along the coast. She bestowed on the places she deigned to visit the glamour of French history: in 1820, at the age of twenty-two, she had seen a fanatic with a knife assassinate her husband on the steps of the Paris Opera. Seven months later, she gave birth to the boy who was dubbed by royalists 'L'Enfant du Miracle', the last of the Bourbons, 'the tender flower that rises from a tomb', 'the shoot that shall become a stem' (V. Hugo).

Since then, her country had behaved as though it was blind to its divine destiny. Ignoring the Revolution and the reign of the Corsican usurper, Napoleon Bonaparte, France had been ruled since 1774 by three brothers: Louis XVI, who was guillotined in 1793, Louis XVIII, who dated his reign from 1795, when the little Dauphin had died in prison, and Charles X, the Duchess's father-in-law, who had been forced into exile by a three-day riot of intellectuals and workers. The 1830 Revolution had created a constitutional monarch, Louis-Philippe, who, in the eyes of royalists, was little more than a glorified civil servant. Censorship and the hereditary peerage were abolished, and there were tentative electoral reforms that had increased the electorate to almost 3 per cent of the male population over the age of twenty-one. The Duchess had followed Charles X into exile.

That morning on the cold Mediterranean coast, the news was

conveyed to the leader of the royalist invasion in tactful euphemisms as she sheltered in an inn at the hamlet of La Folie. The promised uprising had taken the form of a feeble demonstration in the streets of Marseille. Despite this disappointment, the Duchess and a small band of supporters and admirers set off into the land that she loved and seemed to know better than anyone else of her class. Four hundred miles to the north, the vast Vendée, hiding behind its natural moats and leafy fortifications, was swarming with the God-fearing, royalist peasants the Duchess had read about in romantic histories and novels. When she was a child, the Vendée had been reconquered by the Revolutionary army from the rebel Chouans after a four-year war during which whole towns were destroyed and the populations of entire *pays* were massacred. The 'Vendée', in fact, was most of the west of France: the war affected eight *départements*, from the Atlantic coast to the heart of the Loire Valley, and from Poitou to the English Channel. The region was still considered a political threat and was still occupied by troops.

The Duchess had toured the Vendée in 1828. She had seen with her own eyes the scars of war and thought of romantic Ireland and the Scottish Highlands. She saw ruined buildings, squalid villages and the orphans of the ten thousand 'martyrs' who had attacked artillery regiments with pitchforks, secure in the belief that their suicidal mission would end in heaven. She had sailed down the Loire to Nantes in the pouring rain and seen the battlements of riverside châteaux thronged with cheering people. She was welcomed with garlands, cardboard *arcs de triomphe*, *fleurs de lys* and choirs of little children. She had met men of rank and talent who were excluded from public office because of their royalist sympathies.

Now, as she travelled west towards Toulouse, at first on foot and then in an open carriage, spurning the advice of the royalists who gave her shelter, the Duchess must have thought of the hated Napoleon, who, seventeen years before, had landed further down the coast, near the fishing village of Cannes. Napoleon had reached Gap and perhaps Grenoble before news of his return from Elba reached Paris. In those days, the telegraph line ended at Lyon; a horseman had galloped with the news all the way from the coast. Now, the spindly arms of the telegraph could be seen in over five hundred places, gesticulating like giant insects from towers and cathedral spires. Since the operators had to distinguish the signals through telescopes, the world's first telecommunications system was still subject to interruptions. Eight years before, because of bad weather over Burgundy, news of her own husband's death had reached Lyon from Paris as though it was written on a torn scrap of paper:

THE MINISTER OF THE INTERIOR TO THE PREFECT OF THE RHÔNE. THE ------- HAS JUST BEEN MURDERED ... IF PUBLIC ORDER MIGHT BE COMPROMISED IN LYON USE THE ------- WITH FIRMNESS AND SAGACITY.

Unfortunately for the Duchess, the April weather was fine. By the time she woke up next morning in a shepherd's hut somewhere north of the coast, people all over France were discussing the interesting news over breakfast.

The Duchesse de Berry reached the Vendée in May and sent out a proclamation to 'the inhabitants of the loyal provinces of the west':

I did not fear to cross France in the midst of perils, in order to keep a sacred promise ... At last I am come among this race of heroes. ... I appoint myself your leader, and with such men I shall surely prevail.

In the event, the civil war in the Vendée consisted of a few desperate attacks on army posts. Small bands of peasants led by old, nostalgic officers, armed only with antique muskets and wishful thinking, were easily shot down by the occupying troops. A few more martyrs were created and a large part of western France was placed under martial law. The Duchess left the lanes and hedges of the bocage and headed for Nantes, dressed as a peasant. The soldiers, she thought, would never look for her in a prosperous modern city of a hundred thousand inhabitants who had no interest in overthrowing the government in Paris. It was market day and people were flowing into the city from all directions. No one noticed the bogus peasant woman, except perhaps when she removed her painful clodhoppers and rough woollen stockings and revealed a pair of perfectly white feet. She quickly rubbed them with black earth and found her way to the home of two royalist ladies in the centre of Nantes.

For five months, she hid in the house at number 3, rue Haute-du-

Château, which overlooked the castle gardens and the meadows by the Loire.

One day at the end of autumn, the building was searched. The Duchess had been betrayed by a double agent. The soldiers failed to find her, but two gendarmes stayed behind to guard the house. They lit a fire in the attic room where the Duchess was wedged into a priest-hole behind the hearth. When the peat burned low, they threw on some old copies of *La Quotidienne*, the royalist daily paper. The Duchess's dress caught fire and she tumbled out.

A few moments later, a telegraph message was heading north from Nantes to Mont-Saint-Michel, then east across Normandy to Montmartre, from where it was relayed to the telegraph station on the roof of the Louvre and transcribed for the Minister of the Interior:

THE DUCHESSE DE BERRY HAS JUST BEEN ARRESTED.
SHE IS AT THE CHATEAU OF NANTES.

Later that year, when the Duchess was moved south to the prison-fortress of Blaye on the Gironde estuary, she was found to be pregnant. During her time in Italy, she had secretly married an obscure Italian count. This effectively ended her claim to be the living incarnation of the Bourbons and made a mockery of the Vendée rebellion. This time, no one attributed the birth of her child to a miracle.

*

FROM ONE POINT OF VIEW, the Duchesse de Berry was a lone heroine trying to save a vanquished people from its oppressors; from another, she was the deluded representative of a feudal dynasty that was prepared to sacrifice thousands of lives to satisfy its thirst for power. In the damp depths of the bocage, it was hard to gain an overall view of the situation, but as the government re-established control over the Vendée in the following months, it became clear that the Duchess belonged to the same Parisian system of power that quashed her attempted coup.

The effect of her invasion was to complete the pacification and colonization of the west of France. The troubles in the Vendée reminded the government that a region with few towns and poor connections with the capital was a political threat. A huge road-building programme was launched: thirty-eight 'strategic roads' with a total length of over nine hundred miles were built. They criss-crossed the region from Poitiers to Nantes and from La Rochelle to Saumur. Forests were felled and the deep lanes filled in. Almost every trace of the Vendée war was expunged within a decade. The only comparable road-building scheme in French history was the web of military routes built along the ridges of the Cévennes in the late seventeenth and early eighteenth centuries. These beautifully engineered war paths, some of which have since been restored as tourist routes, made it possible for artillery regiments to penetrate the chestnut forests and bombard the remote hamlets where the Protestant 'fanatics' hid from their persecutors. Raiding parties could then descend on the hamlets to massacre what remained of the population. Like the military occupation of the royalist Vendée, this was not a religious crusade but a security operation designed to reinforce the central power.

On 6 June 1832, newspaper readers might have noticed a significant conjunction of events. The biggest skirmish in the Vendée uprising, at the village of Le Chêne, had just ended with the defeat of four hundred peasants by a full battalion. That night, in the centre of Paris, eight hundred rioters were massacred by troops in the narrow streets around the church of Saint-Merry. (This was the popular revolt that forms the climax of Victor Hugo's *Les Misérables*.) The government that was supposed to defend the liberal principles of the 1830 Revolution had shown itself to be as ruthless as the former monarchy. The third piece of news concerned the colony of Algiers, which had been conquered in 1830 in the last days of the reign of the Duchesse de Berry's father-in-law, Charles X. On 4 June, battalions of African Light Infantry were formed. All the recruits of the 'Bat' d'Af' had been convicted of serious crimes by civil and military courts. They proved to be brutally effective in stamping out the nationalist revolt of Algerian tribes.

A historian interpreting the broader significance of these events is in the position of a passer-by on a lane in Montmartre, looking up at the twitching arms of the telegraph as it transmits the coded news to the city below. Should they be construed as acts of state violence perpetrated against colonial populations that might otherwise have lived in peace? Or were they a political expression of deep divisions in the population? Were the provinces of France unable to coexist without domestic enemies? Citizens of modern France who have suffered official persecution may find it significant that, after the Vendée uprising, both sides agreed that the true villain was the converted Jew who betrayed the Duchesse de Berry.

Perhaps it was simply that the centralization of power made the nation vulnerable to invasion. France was repeatedly reconquered by French forces. French governments crushed revolutions in 1832, 1848, 1871 and 1968. They conducted coups d'état or, euphemistically, enacted emergency legislation, in 1851 and 1940. The Duchesse de Berry's small invasion was not unique. It seemed ridiculous only because it failed. Eight years later, in August 1840, Napoleon's nephew also made himself a laughing-stock by chartering a pleasure boat in London and sailing to Boulogne-sur-Mer with sixty men and a caged vulture masquerading as an imperial eagle. He proclaimed himself the new head of state, was arrested after accidentally shooting a man in the face and sent to prison at Ham, in the swampy part of the Somme. Yet two years after escaping from prison disguised as a labourer with a plank of wood to hide his face, Louis-Napoléon was elected President of France. Three years after that, he conducted a coup d'état and, as Emperor Napoleon III, founded the Second Empire, thus proving, according to Baudelaire, that 'the first person to come along can, by seizing control of the telegraph and the national printing works, govern a great nation'.

At certain moments, the Duchesse de Berry herself might have glimpsed a pattern of events that stretched far beyond the field of politics and personal ambition. She had slept in the thyme deserts of Provence and hidden in the ditches of the Vendée. She had rubbed the earth of the Loire estuary on her bare feet and seen the weather appear to collude with her plan or to conspire with her enemies. On the scale that was marked by standing stones and transhumance trails as well as cathedrals and highways, the twists and turns of political history were a tiny track in a vast, changing landscape.

*

THE PACIFICATION OF the west of France was part of a much longer process of colonization, both in the political sense and in the original sense of the word (from the Latin *colere*, to till or cultivate). The unruliness of a population was not, on its own, an insoluble problem. Combined with the intractability of the land, it was an obstacle to development that only economics would overcome. Outposts of French power had been set up in the west of France and had fallen prey to climate, terrain and irreversible natural changes. Brouage, on the edge of the Poitevin marshes, had been redesigned by Richelieu in the 1620s to give France a major naval port on the Atlantic and a base from which to besiege the Protestant town of La Rochelle. From its ramparts, Mazarin's niece had surveyed the fleet of warships and the lonely coast, thinking of her sweetheart, the young Louis XIV, who was being forced to marry the Spanish Infanta.

Protestant La Rochelle and its English supporters were defeated and the fortifications were razed to the ground. But all along, a more persistent and devious enemy had been attacking the coast of France, undermining the cliffs of Normandy, blockading the Mediterranean ports and redrawing the map of the Atlantic frontier. The port of Brouage silted up and the salt trade moved away. The citadel from which ships had sailed to Louisiana and Quebec became an island of low white houses in a marshy moor. Later, Brouage was used as a prison. When François Marlin saw Brouage in 1772, the ocean had retreated two miles to the west and left behind a plain of rotting vegetation and a dwindling colony of soldiers who had been bribed to go and live there. According to the local priest, who had banished himself to this Atlantic Siberia for his sins, the inhabitants were old and decrepit by the age of forty, sapped by the pestilential miasma that rose from the mudflats into which the battlements were slowly sinking.

Even Napoleon Bonaparte struggled to make a lasting impression on the west. In 1804, he ordered the capital of the Vendée *département* to be moved from the town of Fontenay-le-Peuple (the revolutionary name of Fontenay-le-Comte) to the paltry settlement of La Roche-sur-Yon, most of which had been eradicated in the Vendée war. A new town called Napoléon or Napoléonville* was laid out and a fresh population of soldiers and civil servants brought in. The idea was that the new, imported ruling class would be unconstrained by any personal loyalty to the region. For the next four years, 'the dullest town in France' (Murray's guide, 1854) slowly rose from the vacant site. Napoléonville was designed to accommodate fifteen thousand people, but the land imposed its own conditions and the population of the bocage refused to coalesce.

Vauban's angular citadel-towns – Gravelines, Maubeuge, Neuf-Brisach, Belfort, etc. – were generally loathed as much as 1960s high-rise housing estates are today, but with its cheap cob houses and faceless public buildings girdled by a treeless boulevard, Napoléon-ville set a new standard in urban ugliness. When Napoleon returned in 1808, he discovered 'the most repulsive spectacle of disorder and filth'. Ducks and geese were puttering about in open drains. The civic monuments consisted of a rain-soaked wooden *arc de triomphe* and a pathetic obelisk. More than a century passed before La Roche-sur-Yon reached its target population. The six main roads that were designed to allow troops to fan out in all directions were the vessels of a lifeless body until the railway arrived in 1866.

These brutal acts of colonization were important events in political and administrative history but tiny specks on the physical map of France. The most dramatic act of colonization in the west – the uprooting and flattening of the bocage – was ecological vandalism on a grand scale, but just a hint of things to come. The towering banks and interminable green tunnels of the bocage survive today only in a few parts of western France, not because of military recolonization, but because the population and its patchwork fields were comman-deered and regimented by large-scale farming. By the mid-nineteenth century, the cosy but inconvenient hedgerows were giving way to a fertile desert of wheat. Winter had become a season of work. Old people sadly remembered the days when they had stayed up to talk into the night instead of going to bed at a reasonable hour.

*

* Renamed Bourbon-Vendée at the Restoration, then, in 1848, Napoléon-Vendée. In 1870, it reverted to its original name, La Roche-sur-Yon.

ELSEWHERE IN FRANCE, the land was colonized by urban development, but at a rate that can be measured more easily in centuries than in years. Of the one hundred and forty-one towns that saw their population increase more than threefold between 1810 and 1910, forty-eight were satellites of Paris. Another thirty-seven belonged to the industrial zones of the Nord and the Pas-de-Calais, Alsace and Lorraine, and the mining and manufacturing centres of Lyon and Saint-Étienne. In 1851, almost one-tenth of the population lived in Paris and its suburbs. By 1911, the rest of the country was occupied by only four-fifths of the population.

Many towns remained within their ancient walls. The mass internal migration that drained the countryside of people was not just a rural phenomenon. Canals and railways enabled some remote settlements to thrive, but they could also suck the life from established towns. Aix-en-Provence demolished its old ramparts and brought in a supply of fresh water (a dam and a new canal were designed by François Zola, the novelist's father). But while its neighbour Marseille doubled in size in less than half a century, spreading along the coast and into the hot, dry hills, Aix retained its size and shape like a preserved fruit. Its population, as demographers say, stagnated: twenty-four thousand in 1807; twenty-five thousand in 1920. Despite campaigning by local businessmen, Aix was ignored by the railway until 1870, when a branch line of the Gap–Avignon railway reconnected it to the Alps and the Rhône. Until 1877, its only link with Marseille was the road that passed through barren hills where the scent of thyme was neutralized by the noxious vapours of soda factories.

The most spectacular example of the railways' power to drain the population of a town was Beaucaire on the Rhône. Since the early Middle Ages, Beaucaire's enormous international fair (21–28 July) had been France's main commercial link with Turkey, Greece and the Middle East. The fair was said to make as much money in a week as the port of Marseille did in a year. By the mid-nineteenth century, this capital of the commercial Mediterranean was in decline. The railway connected it to Lyon, Paris, Marseille and the silk-producing Cévennes and leached away its trade. Beaucaire suffered the paradoxical fate of the twenty other large towns whose population stagnated or shrank during the nineteenth century: eleven of those towns were joined to the railway in the 1850s and all but three had stations before the mid-1860s. The Beaucaire fair was still held every July, but the huge encampment of traders, buyers and entertainers, who had once numbered a hundred thousand, grew noticeably smaller by the year. Soon, the fair was more picturesque than profitable. The broad, brown Rhône itself seemed to become narrower and more sluggish. In *Lou Pouèmo dóu Rose* (*The Poem of the Rhône*, 1896), the poet Mistral looked back a generation as though to ancient times and compared the grooves cut by the barges' cables on the stone embankments to the ruts of chariot wheels on Roman roads. The fairgrounds of Beaucaire are now a long, flat riverbank of weeds and rubbish haunted by dog-walkers and bored teenagers.

Fortunately, economic development is not the only measure of urban health. Now that many large cities are surrounded by Stygian fields of concrete tedium, urban sprawl looks like an obnoxious side effect of prosperity and decline. The oceanic awfulness of northern Paris and the disheartening suburbs of Marseille exact a heavy toll from travellers who come in search of aesthetic pleasure. Yet until the mid-nineteenth century, the suburbs of Marseille were one of the great sights of southern France. The hills that form an amphitheatre behind the city were covered with tiny houses known as *bastidous* or *cabanons*. 'Wherever one looks', said Stendhal, 'one sees a little house of dazzling white that stands out against the pale green of the olive trees'. The low walls that enclosed each property formed a labyrinth as large as a city. There were more than six thousand *cabanons* by the end of the seventeenth century, many of them owned (but not declared for tax) by people who had only a single, sunless room in the city. A Prussian traveller in 1738 counted more than twenty thousand, which was certainly inaccurate but a good indication of the visual effect.

It was fear that first led the Marseillais to discover and colonize their hinterland, just as their ancestors had fled from pirates to hamlet-fortresses above the coast. If a ship suspected of carrying the plague entered the harbour, the population took to the hills. But the terrible epidemic of 1720 had spread far beyond the city and the seven-foot-tall Plague Wall that was built across several miles of the Vaucluse. The main purpose of the *cabanons* was to make life more enjoyable. This was colonization for pleasure, not for gain, and it characterized the urban development of a large part of southern and central France.

The family of Paul Cézanne and their fellow Aixois enjoyed their undeveloped countryside as the Roman founders of Aix had done. Stone cottages, studios and open-air restaurants dotted the landscape around the Montagne Sainte-Victoire. Nîmes had its conurbation of *mazets*, Sète and Béziers their belts of *baraquettes*, Hyères and Toulon their *villas*, *bastidons* and *bastidettes*. Each little house had a table and some chairs and a patch of ground with an olive, fig or almond tree and a few vines for grapes and decoration. Not much else was needed: a musical instrument, a set of *boules* and a gun for shooting birds. During the week, the white walls shone from the hillside like tiny beacons. On Saturday or Sunday, the people of Marseille would leave their stinking port – made more putrid still by the sewage that flowed from the house-covered hills – and walk to the *cabanon* with a donkey carrying food and children in its panniers and an old person on its back.

The same cheerful exodus could be seen along the Rhône, in the Lyonnais hills and in the Auvergne, where traders and shopkeepers from Clermont-Ferrand and Thiers often bought a small vineyard and a one-storey house (called a *tonne* or *tonnelle*). Here, they would celebrate the harvest and spend the profits on a feast for friends and neighbours. According to the Auvergne expert in *The French Portrayed By Themselves* (1840–42), the supposedly stingy Auvergnats were simply saving up for those few glorious days of extravagance: 'The host is never satisfied unless, at the end of the meal, on rising from the table, the locomotive faculties of his guests are seriously impaired'.

*

FURTHER NORTH, the colder climate dictated a different pattern of suburban development. Weekends away from the city were a bourgeois privilege until the late nineteenth century but still a normal part of life for thousands of people. Popular journals published advice on creating a '*maison de campagne*' – a term that was applied to cottages as well as to mansions: how to keep chickens, how to grow chrysanthemums, how to stave off boredom in the countryside. The 'Grand Départ', the mass summer exodus of entomological proportions that creates hundred-mile traffic jams on roads from Paris, has a long history. According to one estimate in the mid-1850s, thirty thousand Parisians left the city every summer.

Before the railways, the spread of summer homes retraced prehistoric paths of settlement, along rivers with high banks and limestone caves. The once deserted banks of the Seine were filling up with villas before the Revolution. The south-facing slopes of the Loire and its tributaries were decorated with luxury cottages, equipped with kitchens and servants' rooms to satisfy the hordes of English tourists who paid a thousand francs for six months' rent and more if they wanted the fruit. By the end of the nineteenth century, the cliff-dwellings of the despised troglodytes were being converted into holiday homes. A cave near Tours was said to contain a suite of rooms in the Empire style with plaster mouldings and period sculptures.

In all this suburban and satellite development, there was little sign of the anxiety that British Victorians felt when they saw towns and cities staining the countryside. Anyone who had reached Paris or left it via the Champagne, the Brie, the Beauce, the Sologne or the fields of northern France had a sense of spaciousness that was not easily forgotten. It was partly because they knew what a depopulated land looked like that so many French people were alarmed at the slow growth of the population. In a land of 'wastes', colonization was a heartening development. When the future Napoleon III devised a plan for 'the extinction of poverty' that would have covered the land with model factories and farms, he cheerfully imagined those 'colonies' taking up all the available space in France and being forced to expand into Algeria and America.

Until the late nineteenth century, there are few equivalents in French literature of the sentiment expressed by William Wordsworth: 'wheresoe'er the traveller turns his steps, / He sees the barren wilderness erased, / Or disappearing' (1814). 'Is then no nook of English ground secure / From rash assault?' (1844). The best-known French elegy on the theme of changing landscape is Victor Hugo's 'Tristesse d'Olympio' (1837). It refers to the gatekeeper's cottage near Bièvres, eight miles south-west of Paris, in which Hugo had rented a room for his mistress. To an English poet, the changes described by Hugo would have seemed barely worth a mention. The steep and sandy road where the beloved left her footprint has been paved, and the milestone on which she sat and waited for her lover has been scuffed by cart wheels. A wall has been built around a spring. But other parts are returning to the wild: 'Here, the forest is missing, and there, it has grown.' 'Our leafy chambers now are thickets.' There is no sign that Bièvres would one day be the home of an industrial bakery, the Burospace technology park, the 'RAID' division of the riot police and the Victor Hugo car park.

> D'autres auront nos champs, nos sentiers, nos retraites.
> Ton bois, ma bien-aimée, est à des inconnus.*

*

INDUSTRIAL COLONIZATION, too, left relatively few traces in French art and literature. Paris was already being deindustrialized in the 1830s as workshops moved out and property speculators moved in. Until quite late in the nineteenth century, mill chimneys and plumes of smoke drifting across the sky were described as interesting novelties. Wizened tribes of factory workers were seen as hellish exceptions rather than the face of the future.

The valley of the Gier, between Lyon and Saint-Étienne, was once a ribbon of black debris dotted with flat, smoky hovels. From Andrézieux, on the other side of Saint-Étienne, horses pulled mining trucks on a railway line that, instead of cutting through the hills, followed every curve of the landscape like a mountain road. (This was France's first railway, inaugurated in 1828 and opened to passengers in 1832.) However, as a well-travelled French tourist observed in 1858, this 'little desolation' was nothing compared to smog-bound Britain and the mining and manufacturing zones of Flanders and the Ardennes. There were more trees than chimneys, more grass than coal dust, and 'the sky is perfectly visible'. Lyon itself, with its sixty thousand chattering looms and its 'rivers of coal-smoke rising into the firmament' (Baudelaire), was constrained by its setting, squeezed

---

* 'Others shall have our fields, our paths and hiding places. / Your wood, my beloved, now belongs to strangers.'

up against the last folds of the Massif Central and the edge of the Dombes plateau, and still largely dependent on family workshops scattered through the countryside.

The great exception was the industrial north, which was practically a separate country straddling the Belgian border (the zone that was sectioned off during the Occupation and directly administered by the Third Reich). The textile towns of Lille, Tourcoing and Roubaix already had a long history of industrial development. They were operating as a single conurbation more than two centuries before they were unified in 1968 under the fetching name of CUDL (Communauté Urbaine de Lille). Thatched houses and unsurfaced roads were already rarities in Roubaix in the early eighteenth century. A dense network of canals joined these tentacular towns to the rest of Flanders, which had the agricultural resources to support a large population of factory workers, almost half of whom were Belgian.

In the rest of the country, industry followed a pattern reminiscent of today's out-of-town *zones industrielles*. Factories were built close to the forests, rivers and coal seams that fuelled them, rather than in long-established towns and cities, which explains why some of the great industrial towns of the nineteenth century are practically unknown in any other context: Le Creusot, Decazeville, Montceau-les-Mines, Rive-de-Gier, etc. On the Cassini maps of the late eighteenth century, most of these places are almost imperceptible, like the first photographs of distant comets. In Alsace, the capitals of the Upper and Lower Rhine *départements* – Strasbourg and Colmar – were quite innocent of manufacturing industry, which settled in the deep folds of the Vosges mountains and benefited from the clan traditions of its rural labour force.

These factories should not be imagined suddenly implanting themselves on a pristine landscape. The thumping cotton mills of Sotteville and Saint-Sever on the outskirts of Rouen and the blast furnaces and silhouette-black villages along the Belgian river Meuse concentrated earlier scatterings of local industries. The countryside in many parts of France became 'unspoilt' only as a result of government-funded conservation projects in the twentieth century. A typical pre-industrial landscape in Picardy or the Ardennes was a mess of smoky forges, stinky black fields where the hemp was laid out to dry and slum colonies of wobbly windmills, compared to which modern wind turbines that seem to cartwheel across the hilltops are an exhilarating sight. Workers in these traditional industries were more likely to die young. For various reasons, it was unusual to find elderly people in the following trades: hemp-carding (stagnant, freezing water), weaving (damp cellars, smoky lamps and long hours), threshing and winnowing (dust), woodcutting (accidents and sweating in the cold) and charcoal-burning (malnutrition and lack of light).

The full horror of industry was hidden away in remote rural areas, where no town had ever existed and which few outsiders ever discovered. In the eighteenth century, the village of Aubin was a row of hovels in the chestnut forest of the Aveyron. Two miles to the north, above the valley of the Lot, was one of the natural wonders of southern France: the Burning Mountain of Fontaygnes. At night, a person peering down into one of the little craters that pocked the mountain would see the glow of a great fire. Coal deposits burned continuously, filling the cellars of the nearest hamlets with smoke. Under its black cloud, Aubin was like an industrial town with no industry. The air stank of sulphur, and the houses, people and pigs were soiled with soot; but the abundance of coal meant that the villagers could stay up after dark without counting the cost, spinning, singing and telling tales of the English invaders who, according to local legend, had set fire to the mountain many years before, or the soldiers who, one day in the 1780s, had come to claim the coal deposits for the King but been driven away by the wine growers and charcoal burners, 'armed only with their ire'.

In 1826, the Duc Decazes, a former Minister of Police, Prime Minister and Ambassador to Britain, bought a mining concession near the hamlet of La Caze, two miles north of Aubin. The river Lot was unnavigable for much of the year and there was no railway, but Decazes had realized that the coal could be used to smelt the iron ore that was also found in the region. Modern industry succeeded where the King's soldiers had failed. Within five years, a workers' town sprouted in the valley. It was named Decazeville, though Decazes himself showed little interest in town planning. Several years passed before Decazeville had 'free schools' (funded by a tax on the workers' wages) and another half a century before it had a hospital.

The miners of Decazeville worked in a maze of collapsing tunnels and burning coal seams. After day-long shifts, they emerged into a landscape of blast furnaces and rolling mills where birdsong and the wind were drowned out by the screech of trucks on iron rails and the incessant pounding of steam hammers. The miners and foundry workers were paid in company tokens stamped with the image of a brick chimney half-obliterating a landscape of hills. With no one to farm the land, stale, overpriced food was imported from distant places. Aubin began to merge along the black valley road with its neighbour Cransac. By the middle of the nineteenth century, there were pawnshops and garish cafes selling beetroot brandy and absinthe to bleary, black-eyed miners and women who were better dressed and worse behaved than their peasant mothers.

In 1865, the company collapsed and Decazeville discovered the modern scourge of unemployment. A new company was founded in 1868 by the Schneider family, which owned the iron foundries of Le Creusot. Its three thousand workers could apparently 'find at Decazeville all the resources that might be necessary from a material, moral and religious point of view' – a phrase which efficiently evokes the misery of a population provided with everything a meeting of shareholders had identified as 'necessary'. In 1869, a strike at Aubin showed that the factories had also been forging a new breed of worker. Fourteen strikers, including one child, were shot dead by troops.

*

THE NEW AGE of industrial slavery and proletarian solidarity has its conspicuous monuments in the giant crater of the 'Découverte' open-cast mine at Decazeville (closed in 1965), the slag heaps of the Pas-de-Calais and the abandoned collieries of Flanders and Lorraine. Some of these industrial monsters have been preserved by eco-museums and will probably have a retirement much longer than their working life. But the other great industrial transformation of France is now almost indistinguishable from the landscape.

The mulberry trees that brighten the countryside all over Provence, the Cévennes and Corsica are picturesque memorials of the agricultural gold rush of the mid-nineteenth century when better communications and the availability of credit made it possible for a peasant to grow a single crop for cash instead of a variety of plants for food and fertilizer. The mulberry trees were stripped of their shiny green leaves every spring to feed the silkworms; the second, tougher growth was fed to goats. The effect, apparently, was hideous: acres of leafless trees that looked like shaggy brooms stuck in the ground. Apart from the overgrown, collapsing terraces that were cut into the hillsides and the almost windowless tenements where the heated silkworms munched the leaves and made the sound of heavy rain, there is nothing in the verdant scenery on either side of the Rhône to show that life in the land of industrial vegetation was just as hard and unpredictable as it was in the foundries and coalfields.

In 1852, a disease called pébrine began to spread among the silkworms. By the time Louis Pasteur discovered the cause and a cure in 1869, the industry had collapsed, the Suez Canal had opened and cheaper silk was being imported from the East. A worm had brought prosperity and a micro-organism took it away. At about the same time, the vines that smallholders had rushed to plant on their plots of rye and wheat were attacked by a peppery mildew called oidium. American vines were imported to replace the diseased stock. Then, in 1863, some wine growers in the Gard noticed the leaves and roots of the new vines turning brown and black. The phylloxera aphid eventually destroyed more than six million acres of vineyard from Nice to Burgundy and from Narbonne to the Loire. For many peasants, it confirmed their belief that they should never have abandoned the old ways. This imported parasite did more than anything else to speed up the French colonization of Algeria. Thousands of people left the country or threw themselves on the mercy of northern industry, leaving behind a stony land that was greener and more pleasant to the eye than ever before.

*

CONCRETE, LEGIBLE EVIDENCE of political and economic change is not hard to find. Many nineteenth-century factories are still in use, and almost every town and village has at least one war memorial, a street named after a general or a battle, and a building bearing the insignia of one of the two empires and five republics.

Far more momentous changes to the face of France occurred in the nineteenth century, but on such a large scale that it is quite possible to travel from one end of the country to the other without noticing them, and without realizing that many of the landscapes that seem typically and eternally French are younger than the Eiffel Tower. Everyone knows that the nineteenth century was an age of change, but for many people of the time, roads, railways, education and sanitation were trivial innovations compared to the complete and irreversible transformation of their physical world. The only obvious points of comparison are the eradication of the Argonne forest in the First World War, the levelling of Normandy in the Second World War and the annual destruction by fire of large parts of the Mediterranean and Atlantic forests. But even these catastrophes belong to a different category of change. Perhaps the people whose experience was closest to that of the nineteenth-century inhabitants of France were the Stone Age people who saw their mountains being remoulded by the volcanoes of the Massif Central.

The transformation had begun with tiny, individual acts of conquest over briar patches and mires. It continued with the creation of monastic domains and royal estates and then the gigantic projects funded by entrepreneurs and the state. By the mid-nineteenth century, huge tracts of land were being reclaimed at a rate of several thousand acres a day. Half the moorland in Brittany disappeared in half a century, dug and fertilized by nomadic gangs of labourers and by colonies of orphans and abandoned children employed by big landowners. To northerners who were used to seeing symmetrical fields crammed with crops and plumbed into the supply lines of cities, a trackless heath dotted with a few mangy sheep looked like a waste of space rather than the shared resource of a pastoral economy. Soon, only a few people would remember that the moorlands themselves had been agonizingly reclaimed from swamps and thickets.

The national obsession with 'wasteland' was reflected in government policy and private initiatives. Watery wastes were drained and arid deserts were irrigated. For thousands of people, the quality of life improved. The Dombes in mid-eastern France was once 'a damp hospital hidden in the fog' where four-fifths of the population suffered from malaria. Twenty years after the draining and forest planting began in the 1850s, average life expectancy had increased from twenty-five to thirty-five years. The sandy Sologne was dredged, drained and forested by big landowners, including Napoleon III. By the early twentieth century, the Solognots, who had once considered themselves healthy if they only had swamp fever, were living longer lives and stood several inches taller than their parents. In the Double, an agricultural black hole of bracken and swamp between the wine-growing Libournais and the pastures of Charente, missionary Trappist monks settled on a hill near the fever-stricken village of Échourgnac in 1868. They drained the land and planted trees. Today, the old Double can only be imagined from the dusty white earth, the well-tended fish ponds and the road subsidence.

Large parts of Mediterranean France were transformed within a generation. The fields of artichokes and strawberries in the Carpentras Plain survive under the summer sun because the old canals of Craponne and Pierrelatte were extended in the mid-nineteenth century, and because there is still a plentiful supply of cheap immigrant labour. It now takes a long, hot ride south to see the original stony desert of the Crau, though a boot scraped across the soil almost anywhere will reveal the underlying steppe, the 'untilled and arid Crau, stony and immense' (Frédéric Mistral). In the Roussillon plain, where medieval irrigation canals were renovated and artesian wells were drilled, the land seems ready to return to its desiccated state within days of the humans' departure. Below the Peira Dreita col, where the Corbières hills drop down to the Mediterranean, clouds of dust sweep across the plain, obscuring Perpignan and the snow-capped Canigou. On the plain itself, in the noise-storm of jet planes and mining trucks, the Catalan Death Valley is still apparent among the ruined barracks of the Rivesaltes military zone where twenty thousand Spanish Republicans, gypsies, Jews and their children were interned by the French authorities in 1941 and spent the last months of their lives helping to fertilize the desert.

The biggest intentional change was the creation of a new geographical zone in the south-west. Less than two centuries ago, most of the Landes was a two-million-acre heath, five days long and three days wide. Almost nothing grew there but gorse, broom, heather, moor grass, helianthemums and lichens. On a clear, dry day, the white line of the Pyrenees could be seen a hundred miles away. In winter, the reflections of clouds sailed over vast stagnant pools of rainwater. With its impermeable layer of sandstone, the Landes was like a flower-pot without a hole, tilted very slightly towards the great barrier of dunes on the Atlantic coast. It took about ten sheep on thirty acres of *lande* to fertilize a single acre of oily black soil. With a hundred sheep, a family of ten could live like castaways in their low wooden houses.

Not a single patch of the original Landes remains. The beautifully preserved village of Marquèze, which stands at the end of a small railway line near Sabres, is an exact, reverse image of the original settlement. Once, it was an oasis of trees in a boundless moor; now, the village is a clearing in the largest artificial forest in Europe. In 1857, a law on 'the Purification and Cultivation of the Landes of Gascony' accelerated the draining and tree-planting that had been carried out in a desultory fashion since prehistory. The bill was championed by Napoleon III, who bought twenty thousand acres of the Landes and created an experimental farming community called Solférino, in honour of his victory over the Austrians. A hundred and sixty-two *communes* in the Landes and Gironde *départements* were forced to turn their common land into pine plantations or, failing that, to sell it to developers. Thousands of acres were sold at auction. All but 7 per cent of the Landes is still in private hands. In the time that it takes for a seed to become a sapling, the agro-pastoral way of life was dealt a fatal blow. Iron foundries, refineries and paper factories sprang up in the forest. The ancient art of collecting resin from pine trees with an *hapchot* (a little axe) and a ceramic cup became a lucrative industry. Rosin, pitch and turpentine flowed from the forest and returned in the form of money, which destroyed the intricate hierarchy of farmers, tenants and labourers.

In 1889, a traveller arriving in Biarritz on the train from Bordeaux was asked by an old man if it was true that the Landes had changed since he last saw them forty years before:

You ask how I found the Landes? ... Well, I didn't. Shortly after leaving Bordeaux, the train entered an interminable forest of pine and oak with an occasional cultivated clearing grazed by some remarkably fine animals. Yet I knew that I hadn't forgotten my geography:

The Landes: *a vast plateau of barren sand, waterlogged in winter and scorched by the sun in summer. Wretched population, debilitated by fevers and pellagra (a disease peculiar to this region). Breeding of a small race of sheep.*

The empty landscapes of the Landes are now known only through the photographs of Félix Arnaudin, a shy ethnologist who gave up a career in the Highways and Bridges to walk and cycle through the Grande Lande (the area north and west of Mont-de-Marsan) from the 1870s to 1921 with his heavy German camera, recording a disappearing way of life. He paid local people, who thought him insane, to recreate the scenes he remembered from his childhood in Labouheyre. 'The forest that blocks the view, narrows the mind', he wrote, as though the Landes was being plunged into the darkness of a fading memory.

Arnaudin's photographs put paid to the myth of a stunted, yellow-skinned tribe of woolly savages that spent all its time on stilts. But nostalgia always has its own tale to tell. Arnaudin was a solitary man with an independent income who chose to remain in his native Landes. He was an explorer in his own land, not a typical Landais. As wealth spread to the countryside, many people moved to the towns or left the region altogether. The largest towns in the Landes more than doubled in size while the population of the whole *département* fell. It continued to fall until after the Second World War. Most Landais were happy not to be stranded with their parents and to be able to choose a wife or husband. They were glad to be able to buy furniture and clothes from Paris, to visit a doctor instead of a faith-healer, to put a new picture on the wall, to take the train to Capbreton or Mimizan on the coast. They preferred to work for an employer in Bayonne or Bordeaux than to be perpetually dependent on the digestive system of a sheep.

The urban Landais has nothing whatsoever in common with the half-wild creature of the Landes: he is a man like any other. He reads *Le Siècle* and *La Presse*, goes to the cafe, takes an interest in the Eastern

Question, and is just as rational or irrational as any town-dweller in any of the eighty-six *départements*.

For the sake of picturesqueness, the author of the 'Landais' chapter in *The French Portrayed By Themselves* ignored the fact that many of those cosmopolitan citizens who talked politics in the cafes of Dax and Mont-de-Marsan were willing refugees from the interminable moor.

*

IN THIS WAR AND PEACE of people and the land, some battles were too large and too remote to make much impression on newspaper readers. The great ecological disaster in the south and east had developed too slowly, over too many centuries, to create a sudden panic. It left few traces in the works of artists and writers. It was not until the terrible floods of 1856, when the Rhône invaded Lyon, and the Loire and the Cher turned Tours into a port on the shores of a great lake, that the situation seized the attention of politicians. General public concern came even later, if at all.

The Revolution seemed to have acted as a catalyst. The old aristocratic and monastic domains had fallen into the hands of a peasantry for whom land clearance was the basis of all agriculture. In regions that were already half-barren, the effects were catastrophic: fields washed away by floods, bare mountains and strange, destructive weather patterns. In the Corbières, the ecological debate took the now-familiar form: obvious individual 'rights' against the not-so-obvious general good. Acres of pasture in place of a lord's hunting forest were a more powerful argument than the complaints of a city-dweller who found the skull-like mountains ugly.

The most eloquent prophets of doom were civil servants. One was Jean-Baptiste Rougier de Labergerie, Prefect of the Yonne, who published several pamphlets on the long-term effects of deforestation. His alarming report on *The Forests of France in their Relations with Climates, Temperature, and the Order of the Seasons* appeared in 1817. He was still being accused of exaggerating the problem in the 1830s when the government sold off thousands of acres of state-owned forest.

The other voice in the man-made wilderness was Pierre-Henri Dugied, who was appointed Prefect of the Basses-Alpes *département* in 1818. Dugied had heard some strange tales of his new *département*, including the claim that more land had vanished in the last thirty years than was ever washed away by floods. Dugied set off on a tour of inspection. All over the *département*, from Castellane to Digne and Barcelonnette, he found 'naked rocks', 'valleys filled with stones, with just a few trickles of water running through them', and 'vast, blackish areas that appear to be formed of vegetable matter but which are simply the result of broken slate being continually eroded by the weather'. The box and broom that grew in cracks in the rock were ripped out for fertilizer. Transhumant flocks were still arriving every year to tug at what remained of the vegetation, exposing the brittle rocks to ice and sun and trampling on the debris. Clouds passed over the treeless summits and when the rain came, it came in storms. It rocketed off the steep slopes, carried the soil away to the Drac and the Durance, flushed it into the Rhône and silted up the Camargue delta.

Like Rougier de Labergerie, Dugied realized that these remote zones were not separate realms but vital organs of the nation. He believed that the deforestation of the Alps had caused the droughts, the late frosts and 'the unknown winds' that had been decimating the olive groves of Provence and the vineyards of Burgundy. Unless the government acted immediately, it would be too late 'to restore the climates'.

The government did not act immediately. Awareness of the ecocidal propensities of the rural population coincided with the first reckless surge of modern industry. In fact, the idea that axe-wielding, pyromaniac peasants erased their own environment because a primeval instinct told them to do so was dangerously simplistic. It was later used to justify the expropriation of land in Algeria: native farmers were blamed for creating the Sahara Desert. Yet the state itself had encouraged land clearance in France by demanding taxes and a steady supply of food for the cities. Industry accelerated the destruction. Glass, paper and porcelain factories, tileworks, limekilns and cloth mills shovelled entire forests into their forges. Picardy and Flanders were losing their woods long before they were turned to muddy plains by the Western Front. In the Pyrenees, eighteenth-century shipbuilders had carved wide tracks through the forests to haul the trees down to the rivers and the coast. Now, the people of the higher valleys lived in semi-permanent disaster zones, talking in whispers when the snow on the peaks began to thicken, removing the bells from their flocks, listening out for the shockwave that would flatten a town before the avalanche itself, unchecked by trees, arrived at the speed of an express train.

The scale of the disaster is obvious in photographs taken by the Restoration of Mountain Terrains service of the Forestry Department between 1885 and the First World War. Many of these photographs are unrecognizable as scenes of Provence. Mountains that had once marked the frontiers of France as though the frontiers would never change seem to have been smashed to pieces by a million road-menders. The bleached, lunar summit of Mont Ventoux and the sharp black stones that trickle down from the summit of the Bonette Pass on Europe's highest road are just tiny remnants of the desert that once covered much of south-eastern France. The tidy little pyramids of northern coalfields are picturesque monuments compared to the titanic slag heaps of the Alps and their foothills.

This ecological disaster drifted into general consciousness only at the end of the nineteenth century, when popular geographers, writing for readers who had studied geography at school, could instil a sense of loss by appealing to national pride: 'The French Alps would be a match for Switzerland and the Tyrol were it not for the fact that their forests have bitten the dust' (Onésime Reclus). Even if the cause was unrecognized, the effects were felt in the rest of the country. People, too, were washed away towards the plains and cities. They flooded the industrial suburbs and left the mountains more sparsely populated than ever.

Some, however, clung to their diminishing plots with amazing tenacity, well into the 1880s and 90s, by which time the people of the Alps had a new collective name for their mountains: 'the ruins'.

*

SOME OF THE MOST tenacious inhabitants of 'the ruins' lived in the heart of the Dévoluy massif. Two cols west of the 4,000-foot Col Bayard on the road from Gap to Grenoble, where Napoleon had passed on his return from Elba, the village of Chaudun was home to more than a hundred people. It had a fifteenth-century church, a small school and a few over-farmed acres of pasture and beech wood. In 1860, when the state had decided to 'restore' the mountains, the Forestry Department offered to buy the badly eroded territory of Chaudun, but the people refused. They stayed on in the shadeless village of their ancestors, watching the face of the mountains age and their soil turn to stone.

One day, they found themselves without a furrow. The fields of oats and rye had been carried off by torrents; most of the forest had gone; a few potatoes grew in earth that had been lugged up from the valleys. When they saw their birthright reduced to rubble, they wrote to the government, begging it to buy their useless acres. The deed of sale was signed in August 1895 and the people of Chaudun left their last, inadequate harvest to the weather. According to the last surviving inhabitant, 'when the people left the village, they all cried. At that moment, they understood the act of betrayal they had just committed'.

Perhaps this was the inevitable end of several millennia of human occupation. But not long after the people had left, the stubble of a new forest began to appear. Millions of seeds sprouted on slopes that had been stabilized by dykes, terraces and drainage tunnels. This time, the colonizing power was the French state and the plants and animals it protected. The homes of the previous occupants fell before the advance of the larches planted by the Forestry Department. Something resembling a virgin forest, complete with deer and mouflons, covered the Cirque de Chaudun. The area is now a ZNIEFF (Zone Naturelle d'Intérêt Écologique, Faunistique et Floristique). To walkers who follow the marked trail, it seems a long way from the polluted Alpine valleys where thousands of visitors in cars and camper vans come to see the shrinking glaciers of the National Parks. If the former inhabitants of Chaudun could return to their ruins, they might think that disaster had been averted. The abandoned village now has a forest lodge, less than two hours' walk from the parking area at the Col de Gleize. The demand for access to the 'cultural heritage' of the region has led to 'the controlled reintroduction of human beings' to the Dévoluy massif. The next invasion has already begun.

14

The Wonders of France

WHILE THE PEOPLE OF the highlands were discovering the plains and valleys, a new migratory type of human had been heading for the mountains. The first individuals had been sighted in the mid-eighteenth century. By the time the village of Chaudun gave up the ghost, they had spread to the rest of the country. In France, they were known as '*touristes*'. The word was borrowed from English to refer to travellers on the Grand Tour, most of whom were bound for Florence, Venice, Rome and Naples.

In the early days, *touristes* were almost exclusively British and were found mainly in the Alps and Pyrenees and at various overnight stops on the three routes south from Paris to Lyon and Italy. In apparent defiance of common sense and physical possibility, the *touriste* travelled for pleasure, edification or health. Unlike explorers, they were not interested in mere discovery. Instead of simply observing and recording, they transformed the objects of their curiosity. They recreated the past, dressed the natives in colours that matched their prejudices and, eventually, constructed their own towns and landscapes.

Almost as soon as it appeared, the new breed of traveller began to proliferate and diversify, growing weaker in the individual and mightier in the mass. However, the original type of *touriste* was still quite prevalent when the philosopher and historian Hippolyte Taine defined it in 1858:

Long legs, thin body, head bent forward, broad feet, strong hands, excellently suited to snatching and gripping. It has sticks, umbrellas, cloaks and rubber overcoats. . . . It covers the ground in an admirable fashion. . . . At Eaux-Bonnes, one of them dropped its journal. I picked it up. The title was *My Impressions*:

3rd August. Crossed the glacier. Tore right shoe. Reached summit of Maladetta. Saw 3 bottles left by earlier tourists. . . . On return, am fêted by the guides. In the evening, cornemuses [bagpipes] at my door, large bouquet with ribbon. Total: 168 francs.

15th August. Leave Pyrenees. 391 leagues in 1 month, by foot, horse and carriage; 11 ascents, 18 excursions. Wore out 2 walking-sticks, 1 overcoat, 3 pairs trousers, 5 pairs shoes. A good year.

P.S. Sublime country; my mind is buckling under the weight of great emotions.

The mock-heroic tale of French tourism had begun a century before, just over the border in Savoy, on 21 June 1741. That afternoon, the prior and villagers of Chamonix were surprised to hear the sound of gunfire and the cracking of whips echoing around their mountains. A few hours later, they noticed an odd procession stumbling inexplicably up the valley of the Arve. Eight English gentlemen and five heavily armed servants were negotiating the torrent with some very tired horses, some of whom had lost their shoes.

The leader of the expedition, William 'Boxing' Windham, had been living in Geneva and was intrigued by the distant white mountains where vast ice-fields known as glaciers were said to lie. Not surprisingly, he had been unable to find anyone rash enough to join him in an expedition to the so-called Montagnes Maudites (Cursed Mountains). But then the explorer Richard Pococke had arrived in town on his way home from Egypt and the Levant. With six other gentlemen who were idling in Geneva, they set off on 19 June. It took them three days to reach Chamonix at the foot of the Montenvers glacier.

Until then, the only visitors to Chamonix had been intrepid tax collectors, touring bishops and the map-makers of the Dukes of Savoy. However, the villagers themselves were well travelled. They sold chamois hides, crystals and honey in Geneva; their shepherds were in demand all over the region as cheese-makers. As travelling salesmen, many of them had walked to Paris by way of Dijon and Langres, from where they claimed to be able to see their mountains on the horizon. At any time, about a third of all Chamoniards lived in Paris.

The band of Englishmen refused the hospitality that was offered and set up camp outside the village. Guards were posted and fires burned all night long. Decades later, old people in Chamonix were still regaling visitors with tales of the English gentlemen who were prepared to defend themselves against stray sheep and inquisitive children. The Chamoniards were excellent impersonators and no doubt exaggerated the precautions of Windham's party. But Windham himself exaggerated the ignorance of his hosts. 'Primitive' people were an essential part of the wildness he had come to see. In the morning, he asked the local people about the glaciers and was gratified but not surprised to hear 'ridiculous' tales of witches holding sabbaths on the ice.

After recruiting guides and porters, and noting what he assumed to be the villagers' admiration of his fearless team, Windham and company scrambled over the 'terrible havock' wreaked by avalanches, teetered on the brink of precipices and followed the hunters' well-trodden path to the summit of the Montenvers. (The same route was followed sixty years later by the ex-Empress Joséphine with sixty-eight guides and her ladies-in-waiting.) At the summit, they saw 'an indescribable sight': 'You must imagine your Lake [Geneva] put in Agitation by a stormy Wind, and frozen all at once.' This Greenland scene was later named – one might almost say captioned – the Mer de Glace (Sea of Ice).

William Windham's great contribution to the development of tourism was not his discovery of the glaciers but his imported Romantic sensibility. His account of the expedition was passed around the salons of Geneva. When it was published in journals all over Europe in 1744, it caused a sensation. Mountains suddenly came into fashion. To most people, icy crags were about as attractive as a filthy village or a decaying Gothic church. 'What did you think of the horrors?' Jean Dusaulx was asked by a lady when he arrived in the Pyrenees in 1788. She was referring to what was later called the scenery. Mountains were wasteland that happened to be vertical. Until the late eighteenth century, few accounts of travelling through Provence even mention Mont Ventoux, which now seems to dominate and coordinate the landscape. Few people knew what a mountain was. In 1792, a priest fleeing from the Terror was amazed to find enormous rocky masses that could scarcely be climbed in half a day: 'I had imagined a mountain to be a huge but isolated prominence.'

To those who gave the matter any thought, mountains – and the people who lived there – were remnants of the primitive world. The Earth, like the human race, was creeping towards a state of perfection 'when gradients shall be such that landslides are impossible and vegetation shall sit peacefully on the corpses of the mountains' (Louis Ramond, *Observations faites dans les Pyrénées*, 1789). 'Such uncouth rocks, and such uncomely inhabitants!' wrote Horace Walpole after spending four days crossing the Alps and seeing his little pet spaniel abducted by a wolf in broad daylight. 'I hope I shall never see them again.'

After the Windham expedition, the Alps of Savoy were invaded by tourists. The Scottish doctor John Moore complained in 1779 that 'one could hardly mention any thing curious or singular, without being told . . . Dear Sir, – that is pretty well; but, take my word for it, it is nothing to the Glaciers of Savoy.' By the end of the century, the Mer de Glace could be reached on horseback and tourists could sleep in a mountain refuge known as 'The Temple of Nature'. There might even have been a proper road if Napoleon had not refused the Chamoniards' request: 'Those people don't understand their own interests. What tales would ladies have to tell if one could reach the Mer de Glace in a carriage?' When the poet Shelley visited that 'desert peopled by the storms alone' ('Lines written in the Vale of Chamouni', 1816), the 'desert' had enough hotels to house the local population several times over. An amazing mixture of tradesmen, teachers, painters, botanists, idle lords and interesting women known as 'adventuresses' sat in excruciating silence around the dining table. Since more than half the tourists were English, English manners prevailed. Some of them came to see the Mer de Glace, others to ascend the mountain that had recently been identified as the highest in Europe: Mont Blanc, which was first climbed in 1786 by a local shepherd and a doctor. A century later, almost every major peak in the Alps and the Pyrenees had been conquered several times. Thanks to diplomatic guides, many people left with the happy impression that they were the first to scale their chosen peak.

*

AT THE TIME OF Windham's expedition, in the flatter parts of France tourism was practically non-existent. There was little to enable a traveller to plan a tour of the country and plenty to encourage him to stay at home. Guidebooks had barely changed since the twelfth-century pilgrim's guide to Santiago de Compostela. Written by a monk at Cluny, it described the main routes and holy sites, the food and accommodation, the time each stage might take and the sort of reception that a pilgrim might expect. The general message was that the further one travelled from the civilized north, the worse things became. Beyond the river Garonne, the language was incomprehensibly 'rustic'; the Landes ('three days on foot') was a region of gigantic flies and sinking sand, where meat, fish, bread, wine and water were unobtainable; the people of Gascony were drunken, lustful, loquacious, sarcastic, badly dressed and – surely a mixed blessing – hospitable.

Seven centuries later, guidebooks were still being written along similar lines. The reader was assumed to be Parisian or at least to have begun the journey in Paris, because, according to *Le Nouveau voyage de France* (1740), 'in order to form one's taste and to gain a sound knowledge of the customs and government of a Province, one should first of all study the Capital and the Court'. For obvious reasons, most books confined themselves to whatever could be seen along the post roads. Jean Ogée's 1769 guide to Brittany was subtitled, typically: 'including all the remarkable Objects that occur Half a League [just over a mile] to the Right and Left of the Road'. The sights themselves were not expected to be the aim of the trip. To make a long journey less boring, the guide would supply the historical details that a traveller might need to lighten the tedium and bore his fellow passengers. John Breval's guide to 'several parts of Europe' (1738) was addressed to that 'set of Readers' who can derive pleasure from 'the barrenest Plain or most uninhabited Village' if they only have a date and a name.

Since geographical information was scarce, most writers took their facts from earlier books, which had been plagiarized from even earlier works. In this way, monuments that had long since ceased to exist were described as though the writer had actually seen them. Many writers clearly never expected anyone to follow their directions and painted detailed pictures of imaginary provincial towns. François Marlin travelled with Robert de Hesseln's compact *Dictionnaire universel de la France* (1771) because it was 'useful to have the whole country in six volumes in the pockets of one's carriage'. Unfortunately, Hesseln's local informers sometimes let him down, as Marlin discovered when he reached the capital of the Lozère *département* in 1790. 'M. Robert went to the trouble of placing Mende on a mountain, giving it a triangular shape and a large population. There are only three errors in this statement.'

Even at the end of the nineteenth century, there were many guidebooks that described the 'eternal snow' on the summit of Mont Ventoux (the 'snow' is white stones). One of those books, published in 1888, also mentioned 'thick clumps of bulrushes growing in a desolate marsh' on the summit of the Gerbier de Jonc, which is completely arid. (Its name comes from two words meaning 'rock' and 'mountain' but, in modern French, suggests a sheaf of rushes.) Most of those authors had never strayed beyond the outer boulevards of Paris, except on a train.

*

BEFORE THE REVOLUTION, the sights of France and neighbouring regions that most people came to see could be summarized in a short list: the squares and monuments of Paris and the nearby châteaux of Fontainebleau, Versailles and Chantilly; a few other cities that were handsome, at least at a distance – Bordeaux and its quays, Lyon and its riverside conurbation, Marseille and its suburbs; and the shipyards of Toulon and Rochefort. Mont-Saint-Michel was already crammed with bars and souvenir shops in the eighteenth century. The main natural attractions were the glaciers of Savoy; the natural amphitheatre of the Cirque de Gavarnie in the Pyrenees; the Perte du Rhône, where the river disappeared underground; the resurgent spring called the Fontaine de Vaucluse; and the source of the Seine, which was unremarkable but conveniently close to a major post road. Modern marvels such as the Canal du Midi, the gardens and pagoda of Chanteloup, near Amboise on the Loire, and the bridge at Tours were tourist attractions in their own right. Cathedrals were remarked on much less than Roman ruins, especially the arches, amphitheatres and temples of Autun, Saintes, Nîmes, Orange and Arles, and the Pont du Gard aqueduct, though one could expect to find the Pont du Gard deserted, even in summer. Little else detained a traveller bound for the wonders of Italy. The *Itinéraire des routes les plus fréquentées* (1783) recommended a year's stay in Paris followed by 'two or three weeks in some of the principal towns, and with a little discernment, you may flatter yourself on knowing France and the French'.

Some of the tourist sights of France had been famous since the Middle Ages and were beginning to show their age. The province of Dauphiné even had an early form of tourist trail called 'The Seven Wonders of the Dauphiné', of which there were fifteen. The Wonders were an assortment of structures and natural phenomena that local legend had identified as miraculous. They included the Winy Fountain, which later made a fortune for a mineral-water bottling company; the Trembling Meadow (a clump of boggy earth in the middle of a swamp); the Inaccessible Mountain (Mont Aiguille), which was known to have been climbed in 1492 on the orders of Charles VIII but was still being depicted in the mid-nineteenth century as an upside-down pyramid; the Manna of Briançon (larch resin); and the Tower Without Venom, on a chilly mountain above Grenoble, where no snake was ever seen.

The 'Tour sans venin', which probably owed its name to Saint Vérin, is now sadly abandoned, not only by snakes. A tour of the sites that were said to be marvellous two hundred years ago makes for a quiet and interestingly disappointing trip. Few people now visit the caves of Bétharram, the slate mines of Angers or the bottomless lake of Signy in the Ardennes. The only miraculous site in the list of the top twenty-five attractions in France in 1996 (excluding ski resorts and casinos) was the Chapel of the Miraculous Medal in the Rue du Bac in Paris, where the Virgin Mary ordered a medallion to be struck in 1830. Early tourists would be amazed at the size of modern, multivolume guides to France and at the absence of some once-famous waterfalls, wells and grottos. For similar reasons, future generations might wonder why early twenty-first-century tourists spent their holidays in the desolate Camargue, on the fly-infested Poitevin marsh or on the sun-scorched beaches of the Côte d'Azur.

The discovery of France was partly the process of determining what was worth discovering and how exactly to appreciate it. The tourists of the late eighteenth and early nineteenth centuries lived between the age of pilgrimage and the age of mass tourism. Apart from a few local attractions like the bogus 'House of Petrarch and Laura' at the Fontaine de Vaucluse, the sights they saw had not been marketed, packaged and explained with brochures and information panels. Readers of the twelfth-century Compostela guide had known exactly what to do when they visited the Roman necropolis near Arles called the Alyscamps or 'Champs-Élysées'. They were to 'intercede there, as is customary, for the deceased with prayers, psalms and alms'. Modern guides had no practical aims such as saving ancient souls. The *Guide pittoresque, portatif et complet du voyageur en France* (1842) simply recommended the Alyscamps as part of 'a walk that is pleasing for the variety of the sites and landscapes'. Another guide saw it as an opportunity to 'use your drawing pencils'. But most Frenchmen who visited Arles were far more zealous in seeking out signs of past glories in the famously beautiful Arlésiennes, who were thought to be descended from the Greeks.

The new generation of travellers was unimpressed by marvels such as magic wells and sacred trees. In 1811, an Alsatian historian, George Depping, published the first comprehensive guide to the 'natural curiosities' of France. He devoted a special section to the Seven Wonders of the Dauphiné. He analysed them 'so as to leave no doubt as to their inanity'. However, he also showed that weird rock formations and volcanic springs were objects of aesthetic and scientific interest. Tourists should admire their beauty, observe the processes of Nature and marvel at the credulity of their ancestors.

*

THE FIRST GUIDEBOOK published in France for the new, enlightened breed of tourist was one of the most passionate, conscientious and useless ever written. Joseph Lavallée's *Voyages dans les départements de la France* began to appear in instalments in 1792. Lavallée was a born-again revolutionary who wanted to show those snooty Parisians that the provinces were just as interesting as their bloated capital. He and his collaborators set out to cover the entire country by tracing an unbroken line through all the *départements* without passing through the same *département* twice.

Apart from its eccentric but theoretically rational itinerary, the book was unusual in several respects. First, Lavallée and his team appear to have actually undertaken the journey. (The drawing of Valenciennes shows the town at a great distance because the artist was in danger of being shot as a spy. The Loire-Inférieure chapter misses out most of the *département* because the roads were impassable and wind prevented the boat from landing at Quiberon.) Second, the book was to be sold all over the country, in every town that had a postmaster. Third, it redefined the sights that a patriotic tourist should want to see. Instead of gloomy old cathedrals, it praised factories, public promenades and new housing developments. The remarks on Nancy are typical:

> The barracks are magnificent, the hospital is beautiful. . . . The other buildings – the churches, for example – are contemptible. The Bishop was better lodged than the God he feigned to honour.

Most unusual of all, the guide was complimentary about provincials, though, even here, Bretons were the exception: those benighted victims of aristocratic oppression were said to drink themselves into a state of suicidal fury, 'and the air oftentimes reverberates with the frenzied blows of a delirious head being bashed against insentient walls'.

Despite the delirious rhetoric, Lavallée's *Voyages* helped to establish a notion that now seems almost synonymous with civilization: the belief that natural beauty and historical interest are part of a nation's wealth. This was still a novel idea when some of the administrators posted to the new *départements* included picturesque sites in surveys of their *département*'s resources. Jean-Baptiste Mercadier's description of the Ariège in 1800 is one of the first official documents to describe the economic potential of tourist attractions.

He mentioned grottos crammed with stalactites, fossil beds, mineral springs and the fountain of Bélesta, which had narrowly escaped being turned into an industrial eyesore by the owner of a sawmill. He also mentioned the ruined castles that stand on the hilltops of the Ariège and in particular Montségur, 'famous for the defeat of the Albigensians [the Cathar heretics], who were massacred there'. This is the earliest sign of the 'Cathar tourism' that is now a vital source of income for the region.

Here again, the nation invariably referred to as 'England' played a vital role. After the fall of Napoleon, curiosity and exchange rates brought huge numbers of British tourists to France. As Morris Birkbeck explained in his *Notes on a Journey through France* (1815), 'twelve years have elapsed since an authentic account has been given of the internal state of France, therefore it is, in some sort, an unknown country'. Foreign accounts were translated into French and revealed a magical world of unsuspected treasures to the people who lived in their midst. For lack of information, Walter Scott had had to invent much of the France he described in *Quentin Durward* (1823), but in France itself the novel created real interest in the Loire Valley. Stendhal hated Brittany but found that Scott's descriptions made it possible for him to enjoy its poverty and ugliness. A pigsty in a swirling mist was suddenly an object of endless fascination.

The effects of this post-war invasion are impossible to quantify but easy to imagine. Those 'buttoned-up clergymen' and 'old ladies equipped with albums' who landed at Calais and Boulogne were a strange enough sight to be noticed by everyone along their route. In the 1820s, the populations of entire villages would have seen the painter J. M. W. Turner sketching scenes along the Seine and the Loire, descending from the diligence to walk the last few miles to town. They would have seen Henry Wadsworth Longfellow striding along the banks of the Loire from Orléans to Tours, talking to peasants in the vineyards and appearing to exist in a different universe:

The peasantry were still busy at their task; and the occasional bark of a dog, and the distant sound of an evening bell, gave fresh romance to the scene. The reality of many a day-dream of childhood, of many a poetic revery of youth, was before me. I stood at sunset amid the luxuriant vineyards of France!

The first person I met was a poor old woman, a little bowed down with age, gathering grapes into a large basket. . . .

'You must be a stranger, sir, in these parts.'

'Yes; my home is very far from here.'

'How far?'

'More than a thousand leagues.'

The old woman looked incredulous.

'More than a thousand leagues!' at length repeated she; 'and why have you come so far from home?'

'To travel; – to see how you live in this country.'

'Have you no relations in your own?'

British and American visitors not only travelled along the trade routes like salesmen with nothing to sell, they also colonized neglected regions. Calais was practically bilingual by the end of the eighteenth century. The population of Tours and the Touraine almost doubled after Waterloo. Pau had been discovered by the British during the Peninsular War. They returned in peacetime to enjoy the bracing air, the view of the Pyrenees and, eventually, their own villas, bowling greens and the first golf course on the Continent. In a country where people from neighbouring *pays* could still view one another as foreigners, tourists who strolled across the entire land as though it was an enormous village green were more effective than patriots like Lavallée in creating a sense of national pride.

*

UNFORTUNATELY, APPRECIATIVE FOREIGNERS were not the first to follow the trail of national treasures. They were preceded by a swarm of scrap merchants and antique dealers who profited from the sale of estates confiscated from the Church and the aristocracy. Collectively, they were known as the 'Bande Noire'. Balzac described one of these parasitic speculators in his novel *The Village Priest* – a hard-working tinker called Sauviat who had once roamed the Auvergne, exchanging pots and plates for old iron:

In 1793, he was able to buy a château that was sold as part of the national domain. He dismantled it and made a profit, and then did the same at several points of the sphere in which he operated. Inspired by his early successes, he proposed something similar on a larger scale to one of his fellow countrymen who lived in Paris. And thus it was that the Bande Noire, so famous for the devastation that it wreaked, was born in the mind of old Sauviat the tinker.

Enterprising wreckers like Sauviat identified the architectural treasures of France as surely as though they had come into possession of a modern guidebook with a list of three-star sites. Meanwhile, French guidebooks were still being written in total ignorance of the treasures that were being destroyed. Carcassonne was cited for its cloth factories but not for its medieval walls. In the Gers, in 1807, a report claimed that priceless sixteenth-century books were being sold as wrapping paper and only English tourists were saving them. 'If this destruction continues, we shall no longer be able to study our nation's literature and history in our country.' In 1827, on a visit to Orange, the novelist Pigault-Lebrun observed, with no obvious sign of concern, that 'one can hardly put one foot in front of the other without trampling on something that once belonged to the Romans'.

The destruction of national treasures is usually blamed on certain groups with well-defined aims: Huguenots, priest-bashing *sansculottes*, Prussian invaders or the scavenging Bande Noire. But the Bande Noire never existed as an institution. Some of its more sophisticated members may even have slowed the process of destruction by finding a market for the treasures. The cloisters of the abbey of Saint-Michel-de-Cuxa near Prades in the eastern Pyrenees can now be seen at the Cloisters Museum of Manhattan, along with those of four other French medieval churches. Without the Bande Noire, they might have gone the way of the saints' heads and carved lintels that adorned the hovels of any local peasants who could be bothered to push a wheelbarrow up the hill. (Evidence of pilfering can still be found. A section of column from the basilica of Saint-Denis, for instance, now serves as a decorative door stop in a nearby cafe-restaurant.)

Most of the damage was caused, not by cynical dealers, but by casual theft, negligence, emergency repairs and ignorant restoration. A blacksmith had his forge in what remained of Mâcon cathedral.

The church at La Charité-sur-Loire was overrun by hens and children. Notre-Dame-de-la-Grande at Poitiers sheltered a salt merchant's store, the residue of which is still eating away at the stone. The walls of the Gothic church of Saint Gengoult in Toul are still encrusted with an estate agent's office, a cobbler's shack and the Marie-Jo boutique.

The Church conspired in its own dilapidation. The canons of Autun demolished the lovely tomb of Saint Lazarus with its marble miniature of the original church and amputated the head of Christ from the tympanum, which is now considered to be a masterpiece of Romanesque sculpture. In 1825, stone figures on the facade of Reims Cathedral were hacked off in case they fell on the King during his coronation. The state itself was a crude and clumsy landlord: it used Mont-Saint-Michel as a prison, the Palais des Papes as a barracks and, after overseeing most of its demolition, the abbey of Cluny as a national stud. Later, it allowed a canal and a railway to smash their way through the ancient necropolis at Arles.

No sooner did poets and art lovers learn of the existence of this magical land than they found it in ruins. However, the ruins had a peculiar charm. For the generation that had grown up in the shadow of the Revolution, cathedrals and châteaux were touched with the mystery of ancient times and the imagined certainties of childhood. They came from the other side of a historical abyss. Charles Nodier, who collaborated on a highly successful series of *Voyages pittoresques** *et romantiques dans l'ancienne France* (from 1820), described himself as 'an obscure but religious traveller through the ruins of the father-land', a 'pilgrim' in search of a god. Each volume contained beautiful engravings of bat-infested, ivy-smothered ruins under stormy skies: the tattered tracery of Jumièges Abbey, which was still being disman-tled and sold piecemeal, seemed to belong to the same forgotten age as the crumbling Roman ruins of Orange.

The book's intended audience was not scholarly but 'artistic': 'This is not a voyage of discoveries but a voyage of impressions.'

---

* *'Pittoresque'* still had its primary sense: related to painting or worthy of being painted.

Thankfully, scholarship prevailed. To Charles Nodier, Victor Hugo and other modern writers, the ruins were not just sounding boards of the Romantic soul, they were clues to the national identity that should be studied and preserved. The saviour of many of the churches and monuments that are now fixtures on the tourist trail was Prosper Mérimée, the author of *Carmen*. In 1834, he was appointed to the recently created post of Inspector General of Historic Monuments. Between 1834 and 1852, Mérimée spent almost three years on the road, discovering what is now called 'the patrimony' and arguing with local authorities who saw demolition hammers as the instruments of progress. He endured long, boring evenings in 'wretched holes' and attended ceremonial dinners that prevented him from appraising the beauties of the local women. He travelled to the Auvergne and Corsica. He badgered politicians in Paris and eventually had almost four thousand buildings classified as historic monuments. Without Mérimée, the bridge at Avignon would have been demolished by a railway company. The basilicas of Vézelay and Saint-Denis, the cathedrals of Strasbourg and Laon and large parts of many medieval towns would have disappeared forever.

Since everyone now agrees with Mérimée, it is hard to imagine what a lonely path he trod. As late as 1870, a popular magazine noted that medieval houses with pointy gables and timber frames could still be seen in many Norman towns but that very few 'merit conservation':

> They no longer suit the needs of modern life. . . . True, they provide relief from the platitude of plaster and the monotony of masonry, but they bring to mind periods of history that were less than happy and lives that were shrivelled and wizened.

Most of those old houses would be destroyed in the Allied bombing raids of the Second World War. The few that remain are objects of almost fetishistic veneration. But some even older buildings identified by Mérimée are still neglected and abused: the ancient stone chambers that look down from the plateaux of the Causses like abandoned sentry boxes are paved with litter; the huge dolmen of Bagneux sits behind solid metal gates like a great caged bear. Prehistoric stones were more popular with Romantic travellers than they are today, perhaps because their beauty lies in a subtle alliance with the landscape rather than in architectural details. In his notes on western France, Mérimée recalled the destruction wrought by the Catholic Church on these symbols of pagan worship, but he also observed a more recent form of iconoclasm which had a long, inglorious career ahead of it:

> The Highways and Bridges department has persecuted them more rigorously than the synods. Since my journey to the Morbihan, the beautiful menhirs of Erdeven have been smashed to pieces so as not to force a road to take a detour of a few metres.

*

AFTER SPENDING so much time in the provinces, lying awake in sleepy towns and pining for Paris, Mérimée could probably have written an equally devastating report on the new industry of tourism and the main obstacles to its development: bad hotels and local food.

There had been huge improvements, of course, since the Revolution: more reliable coach services, faster roads and bridges where none had existed before. Fewer bandits lurked in forests, and their tarred, weather-proofed corpses no longer hung from roadside gibbets to terrify the travellers they had terrorized in life. Barely a generation before, even a member of the royal family had found touring France intolerably irksome. In 1788, the thirteen-year-old Duc de Montpensier was sent on an educational visit to the Trappist monastery in the Perche. Despite being provided with an artist, a botanist and his tutor Mme de Genlis for historical information, he was not a happy tourist:

> We left Versailles at half-past 9 and arrived here [Mortagne] at 6. This evening we saw the whole town, which is horrid. We were made to remark an abominable old well which is supposed to be one of the finest things in the town. We are staying in a very bad inn. However, the beds and the sheets are clean.

For the clean sheets, he probably had to thank his tutor Mme de Genlis, to judge by the section of her phrase book devoted to inns:

> There is a very bad smell in here.

The room must be swept and some sugar or vinegar must be burned. This precaution should be taken whenever one enters a room at an inn.

Bring us some sheets. Some nice, white sheets. I warn you that I shall examine them carefully.

I have my own sheets, but I always take the inn's sheets so that I can place them on the mattress, and then I place my own sheets on top.

Until foreign tourists arrived with their money and expectations, most hotels were simple inns at staging posts. They offered meals at the common table and a spartan room, sometimes just a bunk bed in the kitchen or the dining room. The table was usually occupied by travelling salesmen who helped themselves to the stew before the ladies and appeared to need very little sleep.

Single bedrooms were usually available only in grand hotels. Many travellers found themselves climbing into bed with a member of the innkeeper's family or one of the passengers from the stagecoach. A book on etiquette published in 1728 devoted several paragraphs to this delicate situation: 'If poor lodging oblige one to sleep in the bedroom of a person to whom one owes respect', allow the person to undress first, then slip into the bed and 'sleep without making a sound'. In the morning, do not allow yourself to be seen naked, do not use a mirror and do not comb your hair, especially if the bed is in the kitchen, 'where hair may fly into the plates'.

Away from the main roads, the 'inn' might be nothing more than a farmhouse whose owner had been asked for shelter so often that he had installed a few flea-infested beds in an outbuilding. Well into the nineteenth century, travellers were often forced to accept free food and hospitality and caused great offence if they tried to pay. Tourists – especially French tourists – in the wilder parts seem to have expected their adventurousness to be rewarded and complained bitterly about innkeepers who tried to make a profit. The 'two friends' who published an 'artistic' guide to the Pyrenees in 1835 warned against 'typical mountain people, who are inquisitive, greedy, selfish, crude and ignorant'. To their disgust, the people of Sainte-Marie-de-Campan claimed to be too poor to take them in. The cobbler who kindly let them sleep on the floor of his shop must have been surprised by the growing numbers of people who knocked at his door after the visit of the 'two friends': the guide gives his name and address in the list of hotels, along with Don Farlo at Panticosa, just across the Spanish border, who, 'without exactly being an innkeeper, is generous and hospitable and asks only that visitors pay the cost of their board and lodging'.

When trade and tourism picked up after the fall of Napoleon, the number of tolerable hotels increased. Names such as Hôtel des Alliés, des Anglais or des Américains were usually a sign of comfort (the word 'comfort', in this sense, was borrowed from English). In the larger towns, hoteliers sent servants to meet the coach. As soon as they arrived in Auxerre in 1812, George Depping and his fellow passengers were surrounded by servants singing the praises of their respective hotels:

> Beauty won the day. All the travellers spontaneously placed themselves at the side of the prettiest petitioner, to the vexation of the others, who were still trying to carry off those who lagged behind; but the former, like a good shepherdess, took care to keep them from her flock and successfully led it in its entirety to the Auberge du Léopard.

The innkeeper might also be the postmaster, wood merchant, tobacconist and mayor. Despite these monopolies, prices stabilized remarkably quickly throughout the country, to the irritation of French travellers whose money was worth much less than pounds or dollars. Victor Hugo defined the innkeeper's duties in *Les Misérables*: 'bleed the man, fleece the woman, skin the child'; 'know how much wear and tear a shadow causes the mirror and fix a rate for it.' The usual cost of dinner was three francs, including wine if the hotel was in a wine-growing region; full board was six to eight francs a day at a time when the average daily wage of a worker was one and a half francs.

American and British tourists rarely complained about the cost but were often appalled by the lack of hygiene. 'Fail not to take a piece of soap with you', advised Murray's guide: 'the provisions for personal ablution are very defective'. Meals were commonly served in the bedchamber, the walls and floor of which might be 'black with the accumulated filth of years' and teeming with fleas. Mrs Cradock's maid killed four hundred and eighty in a single room. Dogs were seen wrestling with intestines in the kitchen. In the courtyard of an inn near Lyon, Philip Thicknesse was surprised to see spinach being laid in a flat basket, apparently for the dogs to eat. Later that day, he saw the serving girl deliver it to his table. ('I turned it, dish and all, upon her head.')

For many tourists, the most harrowing expedition was not the crossing of an Alpine pass or a night-time ride on a bad road but the unavoidable visit to the *cabinet d'aisances*. British expectations gradually turned hotels into the efficient, impersonal establishments that the French found soulless and intimidating, but the results were not always to the liking of the foreigners. At Nîmes in 1763, Tobias Smollett found 'the Temple of Cloacina' 'in a most shocking condition':

> The servant-maid told me her mistress had caused it to be made on purpose for the English travellers; but now she was very sorry for what she had done, as all the French who frequented her house, instead of using the seat, left their offerings on the floor, which she was obliged to have cleaned three or four times a day.

Later tourists would be baffled by bidets and daunted by the porcelain footpads on either side of a small dark hole, but even in simpler days there were mysteries to solve. A traveller in Béarn in 1812 who slept on the third tier of a four-tier bunk bed was woken in the night by a smell and a noise of ropes and pulleys. A voice in the darkness whispered, 'Don't worry, sir, it's just the vicar going up.' 'Vicaire' turned out to be a local name for 'chamber pot'. Little fuss was made about the matter in a country which still respects the right to relieve oneself, if necessary, in public. Anyone was welcome to use the designated corner of a farmyard. In villages, sheltered areas such as bridges and covered alleys were 'the water closets of several generations, with the open air as disinfectant' ('Fosse d'aisances', *Grand Dictionnaire universel*).

In towns, public facilities could be surprisingly pleasant. Richard's 1828 guide to Paris made a special point of mentioning 'the *cabinets d'aisances* that are most in vogue'. Some of these *cabinets*, like the toilet at the entrance to the Louvre museum, were cleaner than toilets in private apartments and cost only fifteen centimes. One shining example, in the Rue du Faubourg du Temple, '[deserved] to be seen from a technical point of view'. Doors to conceal the occupant of the *cabinet* became increasingly common, often marked simply '100' (from a feeble pun on '*cent*' and '*sent*', 'smells'). In Provence, town dwellers sometimes opened a convenient little cubicle in the corner of the house and sold the contents to a manure collector. By the 1860s, this mutually profitable arrangement had spread along the stony roads around Nice, Antibes and Saint-Raphaël. Coach travellers who had once had to duck behind bushes found little huts adorned with climbing plants and notices written prettily in French or Nissard by peasants competing for fertilizer: '*Ici on est bien*' ('It's nice here'), '*Ici on est mieux*' ('It's nicer here'), or '*Ma questo è necessario*'.

*

THE OTHER MAIN NECESSITY of life is such a vast subject that an encyclopedia would barely cover it. However, most of that encyclopedia would be devoted to rarities and exceptions. The standard fare was usually too dull to be mentioned, unless it was spectacularly bad, which is why, in early nineteenth-century novels, great meals are usually on a par with outstanding events like orgies, with which they often coincide.

Few people would have guessed that France would one day be the goal of gastro-tourists. Beyond the homes of the rich and a few restaurants, recipes were unusual. The word '*recette*' referred primarily to the preparation of pharmaceutical remedies. Most popular 'recipes' were magical cures – 'Slice a pigeon down the middle; remove the heart; place it on the child's head', etc. – or snippets of peasant wisdom. In Roussillon, ducks were thought to say '*Naps! Naps!*' because they were best served with turnips ('*nap*' in Catalan). Interesting combinations of food appear not to have exercised the minds of people for whom the height of culinary pleasure was a full stomach. A story was told of four young men from Saint-Brieuc in Brittany discussing what they would eat if imagination was the only limit. One suggested an unusually long sausage, another imagined 'beans the size of toes' boiled with bacon, the third chose a sea of fat with a giant ladle to cream it off and the fourth complained that the others had 'already picked all the good things'.

Many towns now promote themselves with a 'traditional' speciality which, more often than not, is a form of *andouille* ('charcuterie composed of pig or boar intestines, chopped, strongly spiced and enclosed in another intestine'). Most modern versions of the *andouille*, like the Scottish haggis, are deceptively refined versions of their rugged ancestors. The pungent *andouille* was a rare treat in any case. For tourists who ventured beyond Paris, the true taste of France was stale bread. The degree of staleness reflected the availability of fuel. A manual of rural architecture published in Toulouse in 1820 stated that the public oven should be large enough to allow the week's bread to be baked in a single twenty-four-hour period. In the Alps, enough bread was produced in a single batch for a year and sometimes two or three years. It was baked, at least once, then hung above a smoky fire or dried in the sun. Sometimes, the 'loaf' was just a thin barley and bean-flour biscuit. To make it edible and to improve the colour, it was softened in buttermilk or whey. Rich people used white wine.

This was bread that had lived through the year with the people who baked it, as hard as stone, immune to the weather and able to travel great distances. The tougher varieties came out of storage as fossilized crisps that had to be smashed with a hammer, boiled five times with a few potatoes and perhaps flavoured with milk. Most travellers quailed at the thought of eating local bread and took their own supply of biscuits. In the Auvergne, rye flour mixed with bran produced a heavy black gloop that was helped down with water and whey. In the south-west, where maize gradually replaced millet, the dough was sliced and fried in fat or cooked under the ashes of a fire. With salted sardines or nettle soup, it was considered delicious, but only by people who ate it every day of their lives.

Tourists in the gastronomically impoverished provinces might have felt deprived as they wolfed down their rabbits and chickens, but they were usually enjoying a far richer diet than the natives. In many parts of France, meat was only for special occasions. A government fact-finding mission to Anjou in 1844 found that despite the tons of meat that were sent from there to Paris, the people of Anjou were practically vegetarian. Dinner consisted of bread, soup (cabbage, potato or onion), a vegetable and a hard-boiled egg. The year's menu might also include an occasional piece of cheese, a few nuts in winter and some salted lard on Sunday to change the taste of the bread.

Meat that was consumed locally did not always come from the farmyard or the paddock. The only large animal that was never eaten, except in times of famine, was wolf, which was known to be repulsive. In Burgundy, some people considered fox a delicacy, 'provided that it be hung out in a garden, on a plum tree, for two weeks during the frosts'. Red squirrels – tame enough to be killed by an old person with a stick – were eaten in the Morvan and the Landes. In the Alps, marmots, which conveniently evacuate their bowels before hibernating, were tugged from their burrows, boiled and sometimes soaked in water for twenty-four hours to remove the musky smell. The flesh had an oily texture and tasted faintly of soot. The fat was rubbed into rheumatic limbs and the grease was burned in lamps. Bears in the Pyrenees sometimes ate humans but were not eaten themselves until tourists created a market for exotic meat. A guide to Toulouse and environs in 1834 advised that 'occasionally, when a bear has been killed, one is served a *beefsteak* [sic] of this meat, which is very good'.

At first, it is hard to tell how anyone survived on the traditional diet. The socialist revolutionary Proudhon, who spent his childhood in Besançon, claims that his family grew 'tall and strong' on a diet of *gaudes* (roasted cornmeal), potatoes and vegetable soup, which would have left them short and sickly. Many diets described in memoirs or in the *'pensions alimentaires'* of wills suggest a fatal lack of vitamins and proteins. In some cases, almost all the calories came from cereals in the form of bread. It turns out, however, that Proudhon also spent much of the day grazing like the cows he tended, filling himself with corn, poppy seeds, peas, rampion, salsify, cherries, grapes, rosehips, blackberries and sloes. In warmer parts of France, the informal diet could be even more nutritious. Near Avignon, Agricol Perdiguier (p. 158) gorged himself on peaches, grapes, apricots and figs, and more varieties of wild fruit than he could name in French. The fact that there were over three million beehives in France in 1862 (one for every thirteen inhabitants) shows that the diet was not always as dire as it sounds. In a plain culinary landscape, a quince crystallized in honey and roasted in the embers of a fire could be an unforgettable feast.

Before industrial agriculture carpeted the country with cereals, edible plant- and animal life was more varied and abundant. The athletic wild man of the Iraty forest seems to have been a vegan. Victor of the Aveyron, who was captured near Saint-Sernin, may have eaten chicken, duck and crayfish, though probably not the other items on the 'Menu de l'Enfant Sauvage' currently on offer at the Saint-Sernin hotel (Roquefort cheese, *soufflé glacé* and walnut liqueur). The feral girl called Memmie who was discovered near Songy in Champagne in 1731 had lived on raw rabbits, frogs, which she ate with leaves, and roots which she grubbed up with a sturdy thumb and forefinger.

Modern tourists who travel through rich agricultural areas only to find themselves confronted with an unapologetic plate of *steak frites* and wilted lettuce galvanized with oil are seeing the results of a process that began over a century ago. As railways rushed tourists to the provinces and produce to the cities, the gastronomic map of France seemed to burst into life. Writers of geographical articles in Paris magazines drooled over the specialities of each region: butter from Isigny, apples from the Pays de Caux, cherries from Montmorency, artichokes from Laon, mustard and *cassis* from Dijon, truffles from Périgord, prunes from Tours and Agen, chocolate from Bayonne. Far from representing the essence of a region, some of these specialties simply reflected the advertising skill of a single grocer. They rarely found their way onto travellers' plates and were not always available in the region itself. The Dijon area was not particularly rich in blackcurrants until an enterprising cafe owner made an exploratory trip to Paris in 1841, noted the popularity of *cassis* and began to market his own liqueur as a regional speciality. Good wine was often hard to find in wine-growing regions. A connoisseur of French wines was better off in London, Paris or Tours (because of the large English community) than in French provinces where people who could afford to drink wine preferred *eau de marc* with their meals (water passed through the mash of grape-skins left by the wine-making process).

Food that was transported to Paris and marketed by caterers and grocers helped to create a fantasy image of the provinces. In the recipe section of Mme Pariset's *Nouveau manuel complet de la maîtresse de maison* (1852), the vital ingredients were obviously a home in Paris and a maid to go shopping at Les Halles. Her recipes called for olive oil from Aix, maize flour from Burgundy, groats from Brittany, Strasbourg bacon and Gruyère cheese, but the sources of the recipes – fairly modest stews and soups with a preponderance of cabbage – were not the French provinces but 'the best tables'.

Nearly all those tables were Parisian. By 1889, there were said to be a hundred restaurants for every bookshop in the capital. 'A nutritional tour of Paris, which would once have been a non-event, would now take almost as long as a voyage around the world.' It was from Paris that many 'provincial' dishes reached the provinces. The Bourbonnais family described by the peasant novelist Émile Guillaumin are shocked (in 1880) to see their visiting Parisian relatives crouching on the edge of ponds and dropping frogs into a bag: 'Since no one knew how to prepare them, the nephew was forced to cook them himself.'

It was only after a century of foreign tourists that large numbers of French men and women began to discover France for themselves. But even then, most food-conscious people preferred to explore the provinces *à la carte*, in a Parisian restaurant. One of the most revealing voyages of discovery made by a Frenchman was Alexandre Dumas's trip to Roscoff on the north Breton coast in 1869. Roscoff was the market-gardening capital of western France. By the 1860s, hundreds of boats carrying onions and artichokes left the little harbour every year for England, apparently because one brave man had once successfully sold his onions in London with a board marked 'The English onion is not good'. But when Dumas settled in Roscoff to write his *Dictionnaire de cuisine*, he was fuelled by imagination more than by food: 'We had fish in abundance, but very little else: bullet-hard artichokes, water-filled *haricots verts* and no fresh butter.' His cook Marie had predicted that nothing good would come of the expedition. She left in disgust and returned to Paris, where all the culinary wonders of France could be discovered and enjoyed.

15

Postcards of the Natives

A CENTURY AND A HALF after Windham's expedition to the glaciers of Savoy, when cyclists were pedalling over the Pyrenees and the first cars were chugging along the dusty roads of France, it would be hard to believe that there was anything left to explore – though the fact that the grandest canyon in Europe somehow escaped attention until 1896, when it was discovered less than twenty miles from a departmental capital (p. 335), suggests that the country was not quite as well known as it seemed to be. In 1869, a daily newspaper pointed out that it would soon be possible to travel 'Around the World in 80 Days' by using the Mont Cenis tunnel and the Suez Canal. Jules Verne read the articles and used the title for his novel *Le Tour du monde en quatre-vingts jours* (1873), in which the journey across France takes up just four lines of Phileas Fogg's notebook:

> Left London, Wednesday 2 October, 8.45 pm.
> Arrived Paris, Thursday 3 October, 7.20 am.
> Left Paris, Thursday, 8.40 am.
> Arrived Turin by the Mont Cenis, 4 October, 6.35 am.

Thanks to the railways, France could be crossed in just over a day, provided that the journey began and ended in a major city. In the 1860s, according to Dumas's collaborator Joseph Méry, Paris was only 'thirty-three cigars from Marseille'. The novelist and travel writer Amédée Achard looked forward to the opening of a branch line that would place the seaside spa of Trouville on the Normandy coast 'at a distance of four cigars from the Boulevard des Italiens'. This represents about one cigar every fifteen miles in a train travelling at a top speed of 38 mph. Migrant labourers measured distances in bread and shoe leather rather than in cigars, but they too began to use the railway when they realized that a few hours in a third-class carriage cost less than five days on the road.

The gentleman who published an anachronistic account of travelling in a restored vintage coach *From Paris to Nice in Eighty Days* (1889) saw himself as a pioneer to the past, a guide to the days when people went on journeys instead of 'transporting themselves from one point to another'. He knew that pleasure and discovery were inversely related to speed. The faster the mode of transport, the less one saw and the more slowly time seemed to pass. People who had once sung songs and told tales in the swaying diligence learned to hate their fellow passengers on the train. The heroic tone of shared discomfort gave way to the peevish impatience of the modern traveller. In 1882, after 'six weeks of constant railway-travel in France', Henry James found himself wondering, as he fitted his body into a carriage on the north-bound express from Marseille, 'laden with Germans who had command of the windows, which they occupied as strongly as they have been known to occupy other strategical positions', whether it was all worth the bother: 'the deadly *salle d'attente*, the insufferable delays over one's luggage, the porterless platform, the overcrowded and illiberal train.' The best a modern traveller could hope for was oblivion. 'Fortunately a railway journey is a good deal like a sea-voyage; its miseries fade from the mind as soon as you arrive.'

Never before had it been possible to cross the country in such a state of blissless ignorance. As early as the 1850s, the great roads from Paris were being drained of traffic by the railways. Travelling east across the plains of Brie was as lonely as it had been before the Revolution. When the Freycinet Plan of 1879 poured billions of francs into the railway system to gee-up the economy, blacksmiths, carters, innkeepers and peasants who made a living from hungry travellers and their horses were forced out of business. Cows and chickens reoccupied the middle of the road. The thin corridors of land covered by earlier guidebooks became narrower still. In the age of steam, the outside world seemed to shrink away and vanish.

Victor Hugo had noticed the effect when travelling by diligence to Bordeaux. Now, it was noticeable even on the rivers. Jean Ogier's guidebook for travellers by rail and river from Lyon to Avignon (1854) wondered what tourists would find to do when their vehicle reached escape velocity and began to cross the space between the cities. As the *Ville d'Avignon* or the *Missouri* steamed out of Lyon, the passengers could observe the tobacco factory, the prison, the hippodrome and the abattoir, but then,

> we reach the point at which it becomes impossible to examine everything in detail, for the speed of the boat is such that towns, hamlets, farms, châteaux, plains and mountains, valleys and ravines all flee before us, vanishing and merging in a single glance. We shall see much, but learn very little.

*

PROGRESSIVE POLITICIANS of the time would have been delighted by modern histories of nineteenth-century France with their streamlined panoramas of blurry landscapes and speeding trains, their statistics of passenger miles and journey times flagging up the progress of the nation like the illuminated kilometre markers in the Mont Cenis tunnel. Most people who witnessed the spread of the railways saw something quite different.

A native returning home after a long absence in the 1860s or 70s would have made more discoveries in the first moments of return than a tourist on an eighty-day tour of France. He might arrive on the railway – not in a carriage but on the track itself, since the flat, well-drained causeway was often the best road in the region, and local trains on branch lines moved slowly enough for people along the line to become familiar with all the faces in the carriage windows.

The scene can be imagined. On either side of the track, the fields are larger and more monotonous, stretching to the horizon instead of huddling around the town. In some parts, they look wilder than before. Fields where cereals used to grow have been given over to cattle to feed the railway workers. The workers have gone, but they leave a scar as deep as their tunnels and cuttings: the memory of their riotous paydays, their rubble of dialects and swear words, their incredible roughness. Hanging from rope ladders, they planted explosives in the rock and pushed off with their feet, far enough,

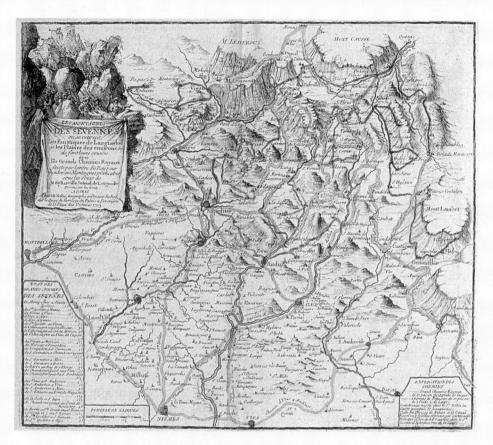

13. 'Les Montagnes des Sevennes ou se retirent les Fanatiques de Languedoc', 1703. The 'Fanatics' hiding in the Cévennes were Protestants persecuted after the Revocation of the Edict of Nantes. Louis XIV's order to turn the 'fox tracks' into highways suitable for cannon launched the biggest road-building programme since the Romans. This map (fifty miles across, west at the top) was used in the military 'cleansing' operation and also served as propaganda. 'Mont Causse' is the Causse Méjean. Robert Louis Stevenson's route through the Cévennes in 1878 ran from the top right (Florac) to the centre (Saint-Jean-du-Gard). The road heading north-west from Nîmes follows the prehistoric Voie Regordane.

14. Jules Breton, *The Song of the Lark*, 1884. The girl holds a sickle of the kind that had been used since the time of the Gauls. The landscape, and a poem by Breton on the same subject, suggest a field near his native town of Courrières (Pas-de-Calais).

15. *Opposite, top*. 'Ex-voto, 22 July 1855.' A votive offering hung in a chapel to thank John the Baptist for saving the victim of a cart accident. The setting is probably the Var in eastern Provence.

16. *Opposite, bottom*. A boy, probably from the Alps, wearing leather shoes instead of clogs for long-distance walking, sells plaster statuettes in a Normandy village. The woman's bonnet is typical of the Pays de Caux, though elaborate headdresses were already rare in 1833. The husband inspects a statuette of Napoleon I; the mother and children prefer the Virgin Mary. The shadowy figure behind the parrot on the right is probably the Wandering Jew. Painting by Joseph-Louis-Hippolyte Bellangé, 1833.

EX-VOTO, LE 22 JUILLET 1855.

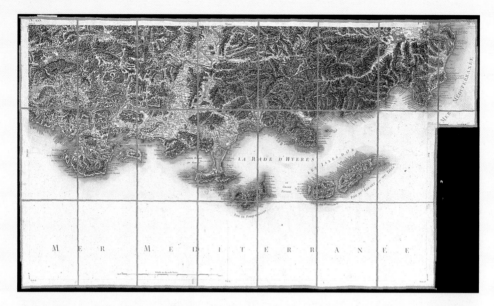

17. Cassini map of France, sheet 131, showing Toulon and the Îles d'Hyères, based on surveys carried out in 1778. The fishing port of Saint-Tropez is in the top right. Some travellers called Toulon 'a northern colony' because it was the only southern town where French was the majority language. When this map was made, parts of the hinterland and its population were practically unknown.

18. 'Le Passage du Mont Cenis' in 1868, three years before the opening of the railway tunnel. During the Napoleonic Wars, this was the main route into Italy. Before the road was opened in 1810, the ascent from Savoy was half as long and twice as steep. Carriages were dismantled and loaded onto mules. Wealthy travellers went up in sedan chairs and descended on sledges.

19. Paul Delaroche, Napoleon crossing the Alps by the Great Saint Bernard Pass on 20 May 1800, with the help of a local guide. The pass was patrolled by the paramedical dogs of the hospice at the summit. The only surfaced track was the vestigial Roman road. Mules were the most reliable form of transport, not only in the mountains. Until the mid-nineteenth century, mules and mule-trains accounted for about two-thirds of all traffic on French roads.

20. Saint-Pierre de Montmartre, the oldest church in Paris, as part of the world's first telecommunications system. Saint-Pierre was built in 1133 on the site of a temple to Mars. It escaped demolition in the Revolution as a 'Temple of Reason' and as a plinth for the telegraph tower. It was the first relay station on the first line (1794), which ran from the roof of the Louvre to Saint Catherine's church in Lille.

21. Carcassonne, c. 1859, at the start of Viollet-le-Duc's restoration. 'The process of converting the place from an irresponsible old town into a conscious "specimen" has of course been attended with eliminations; the population has, as a general thing, been restored away' (Henry James, 1884). There were complaints that Viollet-le-Duc's steep, blue-slate roofs turned the southern citadel into a northern château. The red, Roman tiles and gentler slopes of the local roofs are more typical of the south. The 'chemin creux' (hollow way) is a road fashioned by nature, historical accident and centuries of use. Similar road-ravines were found in Picardy and the west of France.

22. The castle of Pierrefonds, built by Louis d'Orléans (equestrian statue) in the fifteenth century, sold as a ruin after the Revolution, rebuilt by Viollet-le-Duc in the 1860s as a fairy-tale palace. Compiègne (town hall, top left) lay on the other side of the forest, which was landscaped and signposted for Napoleon III's empress, Eugénie. This poster (c. 1895) advertised the Northern railway company's high-speed link from the Gare du Nord in Paris.

23. Gravity-powered transport: a *schlitteur* in the Vosges, on a poster for the Eastern railway company, c. 1895, by which time many *schlitteurs* were carrying tourists instead of logs.

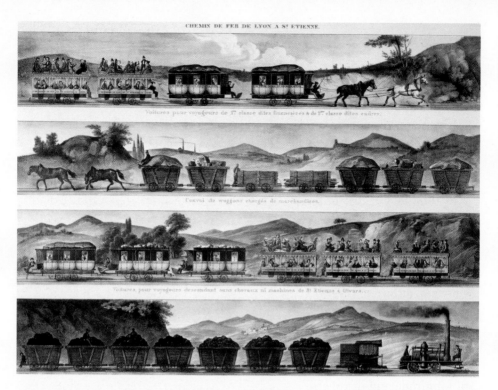

24. The first railway in France, which ran from the coal port of Andrézieux on the Loire, to Lyon, via the manufacturing town of Saint-Étienne. It was opened to passengers in 1832. Horses were replaced by steam in 1844.

ALSACE-LORRAINE.

CHAMPAGNE. LORRAINE. ALSACE.

25. Strasbourg, capital of the 'lost province' of Alsace, after the defeat by Prussia in 1870. From Marie de Grandmaison's *Le Tour de France* (1893), in which two brothers discover France on bicycles. Young Alsatian migrants are saying goodbye to their sisters and girlfriends: 'They are returning to French soil . . . so as to serve one day under the colours of the valiant fatherland.' The picture is a compendium of Alsatian emblems: the girls' black bows, red skirts and large aprons, the tall steeple, the gabled houses and the beer-drinkers. The flower is Alsatian madder, which produced a red dye used for military uniforms.

usually, to escape the blast. The navvies, both men and women, were violent missionaries of a new world in which time was measured in minutes and the worth of a human life in money.

Even at a distance, there are signs of new wealth: the glint of glass windows and iron roofs, the little skyline of limekiln chimneys and a concrete church spire. The place on the edge of town where women used to fetch the water has been deserted since a local man who made a fortune in the coal trade in Paris paid for a safe water supply and a fountain to commemorate his generosity. The old town gates have been removed and anyone can enter the town after dark. In the town itself, a clock face as large as a rose window has been embedded in the west wall of the church. Across the square, the town-hall clock shows a different time – the approximate average of all the nearby village bells that strike the same hour, one after the other, for half an hour or more. Meanwhile, the station clock disagrees with both the town hall and the church. The railway has brought the hour of Paris on the engine drivers' chronometers. The official hour straddles lines of longitude and disregards the march of the sun: Paris time is twenty minutes behind Nice and twenty-seven minutes ahead of Brest, where people regularly arrive at the station to find the train long gone. Portable sundials and clepsydras will soon be collectors' items. Like the decimal system, which is still widely ignored a century after its introduction, standard time is seen as an irritating bureaucratic imposition. At Berthouville in Normandy, the bell ringer upsets the routines of animals and people by changing summer time to winter time in a day, instead of making imperceptible alterations throughout the year.

A new road sign and public notices outside the town hall show that the town itself has been renamed. The old name has been translated into French. In the Alpes-Maritimes, San Salvador (its name in Alpine Gavot) becomes Saint-Sauveur, then Saint-Sauveur-sur-Tinée, to distinguish it from the thirty-nine other Saint-Sauveurs with which it now shares the fatherland. Postal administrators have demanded an end to the confusion. Ironically, the names of some ancient *pays* will be preserved for administrative convenience: Vachères-en-Quint, Rochefort-en-Valdaine, Aubry-en-Exmes, Conches-en-Ouche, etc. Other places, suddenly self-conscious in their national context, have asked to change their names. Worried that outsiders will be reminded of swamp fever and shaking limbs, Tremblevif in the swampy Sologne ('Tremblevif' comes from Latin for 'aspen' and 'village') changes its name to Saint-Viâtre in 1854. Merdogne becomes Gergovie in 1865, because the site of the Gauls' great victory over Julius Caesar is more glorious than a name that sounds like shit.

*

THESE AND OTHER INTERFERENCES with local life are a topic of conversation on the square, on Sundays, when the women are in church. The men still speak the old patois, but their talk is full of fancy French words like top-hatted gentlemen at a village fête: *agriculture, démocratie, économie, salaires*. Politics has arrived with conscripts and migrants, postmen and railway engineers, apostles of socialism sent from the central committee in Paris, and travelling salesmen who sell manifestoes instead of magic spells. In the cafe, pictures of Napoleon and the Virgin Mary, stuck to the walls with a bit of yeast, have been replaced by photographs of political leaders. Some of them will be torn down by the gendarme, acting on orders from Paris. A few of the local citizens voted in the council elections of 1831. Many more cast their vote in 1849, after the February Revolution, and then again, for Napoleon III, in the plebiscite of 1852, swayed by free drinks from the local factory owner, by threats of redundancy, or the belief that Napoleon III was a reincarnation of Napoleon Bonaparte, who was widely believed to have possessed supernatural powers.

When the new Napoleon conducted his coup d'état in December 1851, many towns and villages, especially in the south-east, rose up against the dictator. The savage repression of the uprising and the paranoia of a police state whose spies travel by train and record 'subversive' remarks made by drunken peasants give an appearance of political sophistication to these local conflicts. But to the returning native, the old state of affairs is still obvious despite the socialist slogans and the imperial propaganda. When he registers his presence in the *commune* at the town hall, he finds the eldest son of the wealthiest local farmer sitting in a whitewashed room between a photograph of the emperor and a wardrobe that contains the municipal archives. Democracy – or the semblance of it – has created its own dynastic rulers. Some mayors remain in the post for more than thirty years. Joseph Pic, who presided over the Pyrenean village of Audressein for thirty-six years (1884–1919), and whose hydraulic threshing machine is still its main attraction, was a farmer, a cabinet-maker, a factory owner and a stock-breeder. In the circumstances, corruption is hard to distinguish from tribal honour. The vaudevillist Eugène Labiche defined the *maire* as 'the inhabitant of the *commune* whose dwelling is surrounded by the best maintained roads', and since, for eleven years, Labiche himself was Mayor of Souvigny-en-Sologne, where he owned 2,200 acres or one-fifth of the *commune*, he was talking from personal experience.

In the provinces, politics is not yet the 'heartless science' of ideologues and careerists. The right to vote is the right to strike a blow at the old enemy: meddlesome outsiders, families who grew rich in the Revolution, the neighbouring village, the cagots and the Jews, and even the forces of evil. In the Corrèze, a certain doctor had been revered as a benevolent wizard. Peasants cut splinters from his carriage and the benches in his waiting room to use as talismans. The son was believed to hold the secret of healing from his father and was duly elected to the Conseil Général. In the eyes of voters, political parties are not always what they seem to be in histories of France. In Nîmes, political loyalties were divided into Catholic and Protestant and could be traced back to the Reformation. In the west of France, the old division between the republican 'blues' and the royalist 'whites' lasted well into the twentieth century.

Despite the signs of regeneration, the returning native is unlikely to stay. A few people are employed at the station, the level crossing is controlled by a local woman and another woman runs the post office, but young people are leaving for the cities, where they find better jobs and where the streets are lit at night. In towns and villages all over France, the population is declining and will not begin to recover until the 1960s. By the end of the nineteenth century, two out of every ten French citizens will no longer be living in their native *département*. Even the people who stay behind are beginning to feel like foreigners in their own land.

*

THE ARMIES OF BOURGEOIS travellers who raced across the country in railway trains had set their watches by the station clock. From their point of view, the people of provincial France were relics of the past rather than citizens of a new world.

This class and its culture were overwhelmingly Parisian, whether or not they actually came from Paris. Much of what came to be seen as French was peculiar to Paris or an imitation of something Parisian. A simple analysis of the places of birth and death of five hundred and twenty artists, architects, writers and composers from the late seventeenth to the early twentieth centuries shows that the creators of 'French' culture not only tended to work in Paris and to spend most of their lives there (often retiring to holiday satellites of the capital such as the Normandy coast or the Côte d'Azur), they also tended to be Parisian by birth (more than one third of the total).* Those who came from the provinces left behind only their grey ghosts in the form of statues erected by the local council.

Many provincial cities had lively publishing industries (the bibliography of this book contains titles published in seventy-six different French towns and cities), yet very few prominent writers were ever published outside the capital. Becoming Parisian or making contacts in Paris was a vital step in any career, even for the self-styled 'peasant' Arthur Rimbaud, who moved to Paris just after his seventeenth birthday and tried hard to lose his northern accent. Émile Zola left Aix-en-Provence at the age of eighteen and shed his provincial trappings as soon as he set foot in Paris. In his first letters to his boyhood friend Paul Cézanne, he was already writing as a Parisian, with a condescending view of 'the land of *bouillabaisse* and *aïoli*', the postcard realm of 'pine trees waving in the breeze' and 'arid gorges'. From the heights of Paris, Aix-en-Provence was 'small, monotonous and paltry'.

In lively cities such as Angers, Nantes, Nancy, Strasbourg, Dijon, Lyon, Toulouse, Montpellier and Marseille, the growth of civic pride coincided with a creeping sense of inferiority. A great deal of provincial literature was devoted to assertions of local worthiness and

* Place of birth / death: Paris, 189 / 367; Provinces, 296 / 128; French colonies, 9 / 3; other countries, 26 / 22.

thereby underlined the prestige of Paris. Government policy ensured that the best paintings and artefacts went to the Louvre while provincial museums were left with portraits of local personages and moth-eaten cabinets containing samples of local arts and crafts. Napoleon looted Italy; later governments pillaged the provinces. Provincial literature was represented in the capital by collections of folk songs and legends, tidied up and prettified for the Parisian market by writers who forgot what life was like beyond the outer boulevards. Returning from Paris to 'the land of granite and oaks' he had left as a boy, the Breton poet Auguste Brizeux bought a special 'folkloric costume' in an attempt to fit in. George Sand sponsored some provincial poets but, in order to preserve their provinciality, she purged their work of highfalutin language, fancy images and, in one case, correct spelling. The provinces (which is to say, in 1880, 99.9 per cent of the land and 94 per cent of the population)* came to stand for the homely virtues of simplicity, modesty and authenticity at a time when the most highly prized literary virtues were complexity, arrogance and deliberate artificiality.

Since so much of what was written about France was published in Paris and written for Parisians – or for urban bourgeois who looked to Paris as a model – the state of cultural civil war was never as obvious in books as it was in daily life. A cyclist on holiday in the Vendée in 1892 found that a few disobliging remarks about Parisians ensured cooperation and courtesy from the local peasants, who had 'an instinctive antipathy' to the capital. The word '*Parisien*' is still uttered as an insult in many parts of France, and any visitor with derogatory things to say about Paris is always likely to be treated sympathetically, even by bureaucrats.

*

THE BATTLEFIELDS on which these two cultures clashed no longer look like scenes of social strife. Most spas and seaside resorts are now such pleasant places to visit that it is surprising that more historians and anthropologists have not been inspired to write about them. Spa

---

* These figures refer to the Seine *département*, though, by 1880, some towns in neighbouring *départements* could be considered suburbs of Paris.

towns in particular tend to be quiet, picturesque places full of grand, museumy hotels softened by neglect. Their rates are usually reasonable, thanks to the continued patronage of a health service that values the therapeutic effects of spring water. In the smaller spas, the healing properties of the water are immediately obvious. At Lamalou-les-Bains, which specializes in traumatology, crutch-wielding car-crash victims dodge the traffic. At Eugénie-les-Bains, the sturdy seasonal population braves the apparent irony of signs at either end of the main street proclaiming the spa to be 'France's foremost slimming village'.

The speciality of each spa used to be even more obvious. When the railway network connected the Auvergne and the Pyrenees to Paris and other European capitals, small towns that had seen a trickle of *curistes* since the days of the Roman Empire were suddenly inundated with people who all suffered from the same disease. Barèges, which was famous throughout Europe for its treatment of cripples, lay at an altitude of 4,000 feet in a depressing gorge beneath the Tourmalet, 'which nothing but the hope of recovering health would render endurable beyond an hour or two'. Mutilated soldiers sat in a sunken hall around a basin, smoking their pipes in the sulphurous fumes while their wounds were dressed by local women. Lower down, Bagnères-de-Bigorre was like an infirmary founded by a sadistic joker: half its visitors were suicidal melancholics, the other half were hypochondriacs. Then there was Aulus-les-Bains, a cul-de-sac in the valley of the dancing bears, frequented by 'invalids of love' or 'young people with shameful illnesses' because a syphilitic lieutenant had found some relief in its reddish waters in 1822. (The water seems to have counteracted the effects of the mercury that was administered to syphilis patients.) The lieutenant's regiment spread the word, and by 1849, Aulus had three hotels, a new bridge and an avenue of acacia trees. It survived the discovery of a cure for syphilis and now promotes itself as 'The Cholesterol Spa'.

Under Napoleon III, the vertiginous highway known as the Route Thermale was completed. It coils across the Pyrenees from west to east, joining up the spas that Napoleon's empress Eugénie made fashionable by visiting them on her trips home to Spain. A few Pyrenean towns had witnessed a small-scale gold rush, but nothing like the mineral-water bonanza. Once it was joined to the outside world by the Route Thermale or the railway, a typical spa town with an ambitious mayor would concoct a tale about its popularity in Roman times and petition for 'les Bains' to be added to its name. A local doctor would have himself appointed official Inspector of the Waters and publish a suspiciously enthusiastic pamphlet in which he proved that the spring, whose origins are lost in the mists of time, is the only reliable cure for the injury or disease in which he happens to specialize.

The day on which the waters are pronounced medically sound is the greatest day in the town's history. The new stone fountain in the square is a monument to progress and future prosperity. Instead of bearing a cheerful motto in Latin or French, it is engraved with the results of a chemical analysis conducted by the municipal laboratory: 'The water possesses remarkable organoleptic qualities. It is fresh, light and very pure from the organic and bacteriological point of view ... Tests for pathogenic germs: Negative ... Approved by the Minister of Health'.

Before the sick and dying can be received, wolves and bears are shot or placed in a menagerie, pigs and sheep are barred from the main street, unsightly paupers and lunatics are removed to the municipal hospice. An old coaching inn is refurbished and some houses are knocked together for extra accommodation. If an entrepreneur can be found, a small park with trees and benches will be created and a local woman who speaks some French will be given a white uniform and installed in a booth to collect the money. The baths themselves are a model of the social hierarchy. Titled eminences and industrialists whose names will appear in subsequent editions of the doctor's pamphlet receive their goblets of water and their *douches écossaises* (hot showers alternating with cold) in a marble hall. Lower down the hill, petits bourgeois and soldiers on a state pension bathe in water that has already rinsed the rich.

Soon, carriages are ferrying invalids from the railway station to the hotel and every morning a silent procession makes its way to the marble hall. Saucer-eyed tuberculosis sufferers peer out from sedan chairs carried by mountain people. Those who failed to seek the advice of the spa doctor, who also advises on accommodation, will have to wait their turn. Before long, the walks laid out around the town are dotted with the gravestones of *curistes* who came too late and local people who helped to build the road. Almost everywhere, the population increases by the year: Eaux-Bonnes, the Paris street wedged into a Pyrenean gorge, had three hundred invalids in 1830 and six thousand four hundred in 1856. In the same year, Cauterets, on the road south from Lourdes, had sixteen thousand visitors – almost two hundred for every permanent inhabitant.

Beyond the Pyrenees, new spa cities with theatres and boulevards sprang up almost overnight like the towns and citadels that were said to have been created in a day by the fairy Mélusine. Vichy's population grew almost as fast as that of Paris. Aix-les-Bains, on the banks of the Lac du Bourget, received two hundred and sixty foreign visitors in 1784, and almost ten thousand in 1884, including three thousand Britons and two thousand Americans. Hotel orchestras played 'God Save the Queen' and July 4th was a day of celebration. The key to the success of Aix-les-Bains was the casino, where local people were allowed to work but not gamble. Some doctors noted these developments with dismay. People were taking the waters, not because they were sick but because they liked the spa and its attractions. The doctor who wrote as 'Dr Speleus' was fighting a losing battle when he warned those healthy invalids of the consequences of forsaking showers and mineral water for the giddy round of social events:

> There is a continual mêlée of dressing, spending, follies, conceit, vanity, smugness, trickery and lies. Everyone wants to surpass his neighbour and to eclipse him in body and intellect, birth and fortune, and in this way, each one digs a grave in which he finds disappointment, ruin and regret.

*

A SIMILAR EPIDEMIC of frivolity broke out along the coasts of France. In travellers' accounts, the sea appears to have been stormy and destructive until the early nineteenth century, when the sun came out and sea air was found to have healing properties. The seashore became a civilized refuge from the evils of civilization. Dieppe, which had a regular cross-Channel service to Brighton from 1824, was the first seaside resort to attract large numbers of visitors. Then came Boulogne, Trouville and other more or less fashionable resorts where the pioneering British demonstrated the pleasures and benefits of sea bathing. Many of the scenes painted by the first Impressionists on the Normandy coast were as modern as their paintings of factories and railway stations: parasols and striped awnings on the beach, well-dressed families sitting on straw chairs and playing with fishing nets, the casino flag flapping in the breeze and white mansions which, unlike earlier sea-front properties, faced the sea and had facades as rich and ornate as the patisseries in the shops.

The effect of all this on the local population is easy to imagine but hard to determine. The arrival of mass tourism in a previously unspoilt area – or in an area spoilt only by small-scale activities – was certainly traumatic. In resorts along the Channel coast, land was expropriated, people were displaced and the price of everything went up. Building workers erected their own temporary villages with their own supply of food. Sometimes, while the resort was being built, the only jobs for local people were rubbish collection and toilet cleaning. As in the old days, there were battles between the natives and the migrant workers who despised the peasants and the 'filthy Bretons'. Just as new plants and flowers from other parts of France and Europe were sprouting along the coast and the railway lines, prostitution spread syphilis along the tourist trails.

Some towns were building sites for the best part of a century and were still quite fresh when they were flattened again in the Second World War. Cabourg-les-Bains, founded in 1855, was a cement-and-asphalt wasteland for several years before it acquired its crescent of elegant villas and its gas-lit promenade. New towns such as Berck, Berneval, Deauville and Le Touquet-Paris Plage were developed by speculators, advertised by shareholding journalists and prepared as if for a mass evacuation organized according to social rank. Conty's guide to the Normandy coast (1889) was careful to define the clientele of each resort to avoid embarrassment: Mers was 'an informal bathing-place' for petits bourgeois and their families; Agon-Coutainville was for well-to-do shopkeepers and tradesmen (its beach was called 'the booksellers' beach', where 'booksellers come to forget that they are booksellers'); Landemer-Gréville was for 'artists' and

Étretat for 'famous artists'; Houlgate was the resort of 'aristocratic families', its 'soft, fine sand' being 'worthy of the most elegant and delicate feet'; while Arromanches was 'recommended to bathers who like to live in patriarchal simplicity' (i.e. who don't have much money). Some unfashionable resorts, not mentioned in the guide, received the children of paupers sent to sanatoriums by the Assistance Publique.

Nothing of this magnitude had happened to the coast of Normandy since the Viking invasions and the Hundred Years War. Of all the places mentioned in the previous paragraph, only one – the 'fishing village' of Étretat with its rocky road and its cheap little inn – had appeared in Murray's comprehensive guide of 1854.

When the building crews had gone, the native population found itself in a new world full of strange surprises. Bourgeois families walked into cottages uninvited and poked their noses into the upturned boats in which, they supposed, the fisher folk lived all year round. The model ships and crude paintings that were hung in chapels to thank the Virgin were examined as quaint curios by tourists who treated the chapel as an ethnological museum.

From Brittany to Provence, people who had seen their *pays* modernized and urbanized, who worked in canning factories and understood the tidal effects on their industry of distant markets, were suddenly asked to play the role of primitive stereotypes. No trip to the seaside was complete without a first-hand account of wreckers parading lanterns on the oxen's horns to imitate the lights of ships, luring vessels onto the reef and pulling rings from the fingers of the drowned. Hardy travellers visited the hulks at Brest and Rochefort to watch the convicts being thrashed. Decent families were content with tales of terrible hardship. On a walking tour of Brittany in 1847, the young Gustave Flaubert attended the funeral of a drowned fisherman at Carnac and observed the candlelit features of the widow, 'her cretinous, contracted mouth, shivering with despair, and all her poor face weeping like a storm'. There are dozens of similar accounts of picturesque suffering. In 1837, on the shores of the Arcachon Basin, which is the only sheltered sea along the razor edge of the Atlantic coast, a town councillor on holiday found the recent shipwreck a source of inspiration and edification:

We questioned those noble debris of a disaster which covered these solitary shores in mourning crêpe and brought grief to the surrounding hamlets. They pointed to the immense gulf which not long ago devoured seventy-eight of their unfortunate companions ... We should have liked to stay among them to study their customs and to hear tales of their perilous adventures. It would have completed the emotional *tableau* of our journey.

The Arcachon disaster had occurred on the open sea, out beyond the sandy spit of land called Cap Ferret, where fishermen cast their nets, watching for signs of a storm before rowing smartly back into the basin towards the towering Dune du Pyla. Most ships that sank went down within sight of the shore. Holidaymakers had been known to observe the 'curious and gripping spectacle' from the beach. At Ostend, in 1845, people attending a dance at the bathing establishment watched two ships go down in the harbour. They stood outside in their ball gowns trying to catch the sound of cries of distress on the wind.

A cartoon published in 1906 shows a middle-class couple talking to a Breton peasant woman on the hill above her seaside hovel: 'So you lost your husband and two sons in a shipwreck? How interesting ... You must tell us all about it.' By then, blatant voyeurism was going out of fashion, but scoffing at the natives remained a popular activity at the seaside and in spas. People who felt socially out of their depth at the Grand Hotel could measure their sophistication against the locals. Conty's guide recommended a variety of farcical pilgrimages and *pardons*, and a visit to the beach at Le Tréport, where brawny fishwives pulled the trawlers in on ropes: 'Just imagine the spectacle when the rope breaks!' When picture postcards began to circulate in the late 1880s, photographers came from cities to persuade the locals to act out 'typical' activities. Women would rummage in chests and put on their grandmothers' ancient costumes. Men with wily features and scary hair would sit around a bottle and pretend to be drunk. Peasants in the Auvergne posed in petrified simulation of the lively dance called the *bourrée*. Most of these scenes look so implausible because they depicted a world that was already long dead.

*

No one knows exactly what this condescending interference meant to the people in the postcards. Nosy tourists were probably less irritating than local councils who tried to sanitize the populace and prevent it from frightening away tourists. In Dieppe, women and children were told to wear shoes in public. In Arcachon, once the railway had made it the favourite resort of Bordeaux, men were instructed to wear 'roomy trousers' and women to cover their legs with 'a large gown reaching their heels', which must have made cockle-picking almost impossible. Children were to stop bathing 'immodestly' 'where respectable people walk at all times'. The beach was supposed to be natural, which meant that all signs of work had to be removed, as well as seaweed, dead fish, huts and local humans.

Not all these measures would have been to the liking of the tourists. Staring at naked bodies, sometimes through telescopes sited at strategic points above the beach, was a major attraction of the seaside resorts. Some men went on holiday, not to explore a new part of the country, but to see previously undiscovered parts of the female anatomy. Further down the coast, near the border with Spain, Biarritz was a fishing village of red roofs and green shutters. Basque people came down to bathe in the ocean and to meet their lovers in the grotto called the Chambre d'Amour. For male tourists, the highlights of Biarritz were the ride from Bayonne, when they sat beside a pretty Basque girl (they were always pretty) in a contraption called a *cacolet* (two wicker chairs slung on either side of a horse), and then the sight of shop-girls from Bayonne splashing about in the surf with next to nothing on. Victor Hugo spent one of his happiest days in Biarritz examining the short skirts and tattered blouses.

> My only fear is that Biarritz will become fashionable.... It will put poplars on its hills, banisters on its dunes, stairways on its cliffs, kiosks on its rocks, benches in its grottos and trousers on its bathing women.

Ogling was quite acceptable, but not everyone was content with aesthetic appreciation. Sex tourists were on the prowl long before cheap flights to the Philippines. The Frenchman who repeatedly bought milk and cream from girls in the valley of Chamonix so that he could 'feel his somewhat withered mouth brush against the appetizing lips of those young Alpine nymphs' no longer seems the jolly bon viveur he did to his companions. In 1889, two men from Paris on a walking holiday near the Pyrenean spa of Vernet-les-Bains became excited by the dark eyes and 'delicate smile' of a young gypsy girl and were bitterly disappointed when her parents refused to sell her to them as a living souvenir.

Though fishermen and peasants who left no written record inevitably appear as passive victims, there are signs that local people knew how to defend their honour. At Pont-Aven – a little flour-and-cider port in southern Brittany, which was already famous when Paul Gauguin went there in 1886 in search of 'the primitive' – an Englishman was roughed up by locals and forced to behave in a civilized manner when he refused to remove his hat for a religious procession. Another Englishman, who was being carried by a fisher-woman from his boat to the shore at Boulogne-sur-Mer, decided to test the firmness of her thighs and was dumped into the sea, flat on his back, 'to the great entertainment of all'.

Local people, too, enjoyed making ethnological discoveries. At the Grand Hotel in Cabourg, when electric light flooded the dining room and fishermen and tradesmen, with their wives and children, pressed their noses against the glass and peered at the luxurious scene within, Marcel Proust felt uneasily like an exotic creature in 'an immense, enchanted aquarium'. Comical strangers were not just a welcome distraction, they also provided new jobs: bath attendant, lift boy, chambermaid, shop assistant, waitress and cook. Men and women who had once been dependent on the fickle sea could hire out boats and fishing tackle, deckchairs and donkeys. They could manufacture rustic antiques and sell fake local paintings supplied by a wholesaler in Paris. The ancient profession of begging had never been so lucrative. Tourists bound for the Pyrenean spas were besieged by flocks of girls who sold bunches of flowers through the carriage window, then snatched the flowers away to sell to the next group. In the Ossau valley, Hippolyte Taine was more troubled by beggars than by fleas:

> You see tiny little girls who can scarcely walk sitting on their doorstep eating an apple, and they come tottering up to you with their hand held out. . . . If you are sitting on a hill, two or three children suddenly

descend from a clear blue sky bearing stones, butterflies, curious plants and sprigs of flowers. If you approach a stable, the owner comes out with a bowl of milk and tries to make you buy it. One day, as I was looking at a bullock, the cowherd offered to sell it to me.

To some tourists, this might have seemed the ultimate degradation of a proud and ancient people, but to the cowherd himself, it was a business opportunity. Many of his compatriots had emigrated and some villages were disappearing. A peasant who was lucky enough to live on a tourist route was more likely to be able to stay in the land of his birth.

*

THE MORE SINISTER ASPECTS of this meeting of two worlds were more apparent in laboratories and offices than in spas and resorts. Some anthropologists, misled by postcard photographers with an eye for the outlandish, had noticed what seemed to be Neanderthal types living in rural Picardy and on the Breton coast. Flattened brows, thick lips, dark skin and 'a sinister expression' were unusual, but this only proved – according to an article in the journal of the Paris Anthropological Society in 1872 – that the individuals in question belonged to an ancient race now on the verge of extinction. Perhaps these had been the inhabitants of Europe in the Quaternary period? 'If so, this would be one of the great discoveries of our time. An exhaustive search should be conducted for this extremely rare and sporadic type.'

Some of these early anthropologists could be just as insensitive as the tourists who sauntered into people's houses uninvited. Sixty skulls taken from a cemetery in the Aveyron in the 1870s belonged to corpses that still had living relatives. The scientists, too, were interested in naked bodies and persuaded native people to expose their atavistic features to the camera. While tourists flocked to unspoilt parts of France before they were spoilt by other tourists, scientists rushed to faraway places, such as Provence, Savoy, Corsica and the forested Thiérache near the Belgian border, to buy postcards and to measure skulls, even though, as one researcher warned, 'anthropometrical research may prove difficult and even dangerous'. In this respect, the colonies were better known than France itself. The founder of the Anthropological Society, Pierre Broca, reminded his colleagues in 1879 that, 'until now, anthropologists have described and measured more Negroes than Frenchmen'.

In France, the fledgling discipline was dominated by two contradictory ideas. The first idea was that the suburban savages in industrial cities, the 'dangerous classes' who frightened middle-class people, were dark and stunted, not because of poor living conditions but because they belonged to very primitive races. The second idea was that the vanquished Gauls were the backbone of the nation and that, despite several centuries of invasions and inter-mingling, the population of France embodied something continuous and profound.

Most anthropologists realized that there was no such thing as a 'pure' Frenchman. They also knew that 'Gaul' and 'Celt' were flimsy terms veiling a huge body of ignorance. Unfortunately, some of their premature theories were highly seductive. Napoleon III and, later, Maréchal Pétain and Jean-Marie Le Pen, used the myth of the impetuous, vain but fundamentally decent Gaul to bolster their image of the state: Gauls were the proud antithesis of the sponging, dark-skinned Mediterranean races, but different from the regimented barbarians across the Rhine. It was especially important to show that the people of Lorraine, who lived under the threat and then the reality of German invasion, were essentially Gallic.

It was partly because it told such captivating tales of ancient beings alive in the modern world that the new discipline struck a chord. A science that could identify the man who delivered the coal as a prehistoric relic was bound to find an audience. It also seemed to corroborate the evidence from other disciplines. Statistics had suggested that the 'extremities' of France – which meant almost anywhere that was closer to the sea than to Paris – were effectively a different land. Baron Dupin's celebrated 'Map of France Enlightened and Obscure' (1824) had illustrated the degree of education or 'civilization' in each *département* in several shades, from pure white for the most advanced (Paris and the Île-de-France) to pitch black (the Auvergne). Later versions appeared under the crude title, 'Map of Ignorance'. In 1837, Adolphe d'Angeville's charts of education and illiteracy, tallness and shortness, conformity and criminality, drew a line across the country from Saint Malo to Geneva. It was some time before these geographical differences were shown to be circumstantial and temporary rather than genetic.

When the evidence failed to fit the pattern, it could always be adjusted. Pierre Broca based his conclusions on skulls, divided into brachycephalic (literally, short-headed) and dolichocephalic (long-headed). Parisian skulls supposedly showed that racial superiority was reflected in social class and that, therefore, the Parisian bourgeoisie was at the very apex of the socio-anthropological pyramid: 'The cranium of a modern bourgeois is more voluminous than that of a proletarian.' Basque skulls, however, were worryingly larger than Parisian skulls, despite the fact that the skulls used as evidence had been dug up from the cemetery of an 'ignorant and backward' village that had only recently been roused from its 'vegetative' state by trade and industry. However, as a reviewer of Broca's work added, chortling at the very thought, 'M. Broca is far from concluding that the Basques are more intelligent than Parisians!'

Like most of their academic colleagues, anthropologists marketed their findings with the interpretations attached, but they still managed to amass a great deal of valuable information about life in nineteenth-century France: tools, carvings, devotional objects and love tokens; the ideograms and counting systems used by otherwise illiterate Breton farmers; the linguistic peculiarities of the Basque language, the prehistoric origin of which was demonstrated by the fact that the names of all domesticated animals and cultivated plants were imported from other languages. Some of the arresting traits noted by anthropologists as racial features were the result of a practice that was common throughout much of Europe until the end of the nineteenth century. In some parts, especially Gascony and the Auvergne, babies were strapped into shallow cradles with their heads in a wooden hollow. The skull grew into the shape of its container and by the time the baby could walk, it had a wide head and a high, flat forehead. Since babies instinctively turn to the light on waking, the result was often startlingly asymmetrical. Later, to prevent the growing brain from cracking open the skull (according to midwives interviewed in the 1900s), the head of the child was compressed with a scarf or, in wealthier households in Languedoc, with a band of strong cloth called a *sarro-cap*. Many men and women wore these head-constrictors all their lives and felt naked without them.

Skull-measuring anthropologists recorded a geography of France that has now completely disappeared. More than half the men and women in Rouen hospices in 1833, and nearly everyone in some parts of Languedoc had a modified head and some other deformity: an aquiline nose produced by crushing the cartilage and pulling out the nose, or ears squashed and notched by tight bands until they looked like pieces of crumpled linen that had been severely ironed. Gaits and gestures marked the population just as agriculture coloured the land. The way in which people walked and looked out at the world could reveal their origin as clearly as their accent. A backward elongation of the skull shifts the body's centre of gravity; the neck muscles try to compensate and the angle of the eye is altered, especially when the process has warped the eye socket.

These physical differences disappeared within a generation, but the scientific prejudice that interpreted them as signs of inferiority would survive like the relic of an ancient society.

*

OF ALL THE ARTEFACTS collected for museums and depicted on postcards, the most spectacular were local costumes. Once, it seemed, costumes had varied from one little *pays* to the next, like dialects and domestic architecture. But local styles were already disappearing before the Revolution. The amazing pyramidal headdresses of lace worn by women in the Pays de Caux were a rare sight by the 1820s and are probably more common today in the age of folklore festivals and heritage tourism. 'There are no more national costumes in France', Mérimée wrote in 1834: 'Wesserling dresses everywhere [printed frocks from factories in the Vosges], and bonnets just like those worn by cooks in Paris.' His comment was echoed by hundreds of disappointed travellers who had seen colourful engravings in books. Brittany was still a patchwork of different local styles, but even Bretons were beginning to shed their old clothes as softer, brighter dresses and shirts became available from the shop in the nearest town or a department store in Paris.

Ethnologists hoped that regional dress would provide a magical glimpse of the Celtic and Druidic past. It turned out that even the fashions that seemed indigenous to Brittany had come from Paris. The round hats of the Bretons had once been common throughout Europe and simply lasted longer in parts where time passed more slowly and tailors worked from ancient patterns. The *glazig* ('blue') style of Quimper originated in the sale of blue material that had been used for uniforms in the Napoleonic Wars. The doublets and cocked hats that were worn in parts of the southern Auvergne until the 1820s had been seen in the streets of Paris a generation before. Most local styles were less than a century old. The velvet headdress of the women of Arles had nothing to do with ancient Greek colonists: it dated from the 1830s. The characteristic black butterfly bows of Alsace were only ten years old when they became a patriotic symbol of the lost provinces after the defeat by Prussia in 1870.

Parisians had a chance to see some of these provincial curios at the 1878 Exposition Universelle. The Third Republic was celebrating the nation's recovery from the Franco-Prussian War and the capital's survival of the anarchist Commune. Clothes were a vital part of the Exhibition: they embodied the rich diversity of France and proved that fashion and frivolity were a serious source of wealth. Modern urban fashions could be seen at the Palais du Champ de Mars, near the site of the future Eiffel Tower. Regional costumes were exhibited across the Seine in the Palais du Trocadéro. A new Museum of Ethnography was soon to be installed in the Trocadéro and some of its treasures were already on display.

French explorers had brought back some beautiful examples of tribal dress from North Africa, New Caledonia, the Americas and the Arctic Circle, but traditional French costume had proved surprisingly elusive. A suit from the Montagne Noire had been made for the museum from memory by an old weaver because no authentic example could be found. Five towns and the *département* of Savoie had sent some '*costumes populaires*'. The other five exhibitors were Parisian. One of them was the department store La Belle Jardinière, which had been selling ready-made clothes since 1824. Its regional costumes were more likely to be worn at a fancy-dress ball than in a provincial village, but no one would have accused its tailors of inauthenticity. The role of the costumed dummies was to represent the quaint and colourful world of the provinces – a land that was half remembered and half invented, in which tribal divisions had been marked as clearly as they were in the crowd of black suits and proletarian smocks that flowed through the exhibition halls.

16

Lost Provinces

In 1882, THANKS TO the extraordinary efforts of a thirty-four-year-old primary-school teacher called François-Adolphe Blondel, no one in the little Norman village of Raffetot (population, 650) could possibly be ignorant of the fact that they belonged, not just to a village, a *pays* and a province, but also to a great nation called France. After leaving his native hamlet near Dieppe, M. Blondel had worked hard to qualify as an *instituteur* and took his job as seriously as the Republic expected him to do. Even after the Guizot Law of 1833, which required every *commune* of at least five hundred inhabitants to have a school for boys,* many village teachers had been little more than skivvies: they helped the priest at mass, rang the bells, sang in the choir and were paid the same as a day-labourer, sometimes more if they could read and write. Now, they were properly trained and had salaries and pensions.

M. Blondel was a shining example of the new kind of teacher. He had already won bronze and silver medals for giving free lessons to local adults. Next door to his little classroom in the town hall, he had organized the municipal archives and inscribed on a board of honour the names of all his predecessors since 1668. (Like hundreds of villages all over France, Raffetot had not waited for the dawn of democracy to equip itself with a teacher.) In M. Blondel's classroom,

---

* These schools could be private or public. The dominant role of the Catholic Church was reinforced by the Falloux law of 1850. Primary schools for girls were made obligatory in 1867. The Jules Ferry laws of 1881–82 introduced free, compulsory, secular education for boys and girls from six to thirteen.

the tight horizons of the *pays* seemed to open onto a new dimension: when they looked up from their wooden desks, the pupils could see the flags of foreign countries painted brightly on the ceiling.

One day, M. Blondel had been contemplating the patch of ground that passed for a school garden when he spotted a pedagogical opportunity. He gathered together some rocks, a few clumps of boxwood, some tent pegs and some lengths of rope. Then he set about transforming the garden into a political map of France, as he explained in the local paper, *Le Progrès de Bolbec*:

> I had at my disposal a shrub, which I planted on the site of Paris. On the shrub I hung a flag in the national colours. . . . Another flag, in black crêpe, flies over Alsace-Lorraine and reminds the children and passers-by in the street of one of the greatest losses suffered by our Fatherland.

After carving rivers into the soil with a stick, he completed his interactive landscape with a sea of red sand and boxwood borders. M. Blondel was then able to rehearse his patriotic infant army for the war which, one day, would avenge France and restore Alsace-Lorraine to the fatherland:

> The pupil takes up position in the vicinity of Paris, then heads up the Marne, passes through Châlons and into the Marne–Rhine Canal . . . He reconnoitres Nancy, crosses the new frontier, and, after Sarrebourg and Strasbourg, finds himself on the Rhine. The pupil then returns to Paris by the same route.

Many of those pupils and their children would retrace the route to Strasbourg in reality. Thirty of the names that M. Blondel marked in the register every morning were later inscribed on Raffetot's memorial to the dead of the First World War.

*

THE CHILDREN WHO MARCHED across the school garden at Raffetot were growing up in a republic that used the military defeat of the preceding regime in 1870 as a means of inspiring its citizens with love of the fatherland. The 'lost provinces' and 'lost towns' of Alsace and Lorraine were the missing pieces that would give the new generation a yearning for national unity and, according to the teachers' manuals produced by Ernest Lavisse (Sorbonne professor and former tutor of the imperial prince), 'provide the Republic with good citizens, good workers and good soldiers'. In the new Republican catechism, Jesus Christ, the Virgin Mary and the Holy Ghost were replaced by Vercingetorix, leader of the Gauls, Joan of Arc, Turgot, Vauban and other figures too old to be controversial. 'The fatherland is not your village or your province', wrote Lavisse. 'It is all of France. The fatherland is like a great family.' Compared to similar homilies in British and German schools, French pedagogical nationalism was remarkably untriumphalist, not to say rueful: 'The defeats at Poitiers, Agincourt, Waterloo and Sedan are painful memories for us all.'

In 1907, Professor Lavisse travelled to Le Nouvion-en-Thiérache (this was the *pays* where, not long before, anthropologists had feared to tread) to speak at the annual prize-giving. Lavisse was a native of Le Nouvion but had long since transcended his origins. As he told the children in a confusing mixture of bourgeois prejudice and political rhetoric, they, too, would cease to be stereotypical peasants and become citizens of that vague and glorious thing, the fatherland:

> Little inhabitants of the forests and pastures of the Thiérache, whose minds are quick and practical, who are quarrelsome by nature and whose speech is marked by Picard words and expressions, you are quite unlike the little Bretons who look dreamily on the Atlantic from their rocks and speak the ancient language of the Celts, or the little Provençaux who wave their arms about and shout in a Romance language on the shores of the Mediterranean. The times are gone when Picardy was more foreign to Brittany and Provence than France is to India or America.... Our fatherland, children, is not just a territory. It is the work of man, started centuries ago – a work that we continue and that you shall continue in your turn.

The children would not necessarily remember or understand the lesson in national unity. On the eve of the First World War, about half of all recruits, and quite a few future officers, were unaware that France had lost territory to Germany in 1870. Alsace and Lorraine might as well have been foreign countries.

A sense of national identity was not, in any case, what most people wanted from a school. The need for education had first become apparent in many places as a result of conscription. Parents suddenly felt the burden of illiteracy when their sons left home and letters arrived from the regiment, written by a comrade – with rude words and dirty stories if the comrade had a nasty sense of humour – and were read out on the doorstep by the postman.

But education was not automatically associated with school. Literacy rates were already quite high among Protestants and Jews, who read the Bible, and in regions where boys were trained to become travelling salesmen. Many parents were reluctant to send their sons and daughters to school when they needed them for the harvest. Inspectors often found that girls were kept out of school to work as seamstresses in filthy sweatshops where they spent the day with relatives and neighbours, learning the local traditions and values that their mothers considered to be a proper education. Above all, many parents were afraid that once they had learned to speak and write French like Parisians, their children would leave for the city and never come home.

*

THEIR FEARS WERE JUSTIFIED. A century after the Abbé Grégoire's revolutionary report (p. 50), the Third Republic massed its pedagogical army on the wild frontier of language. The eradication of patois as a first language became a cornerstone of education policy. Schoolchildren were punished for using words they had learned at their mother's knee. A pupil who was heard speaking patois was made to carry a stick or some other token that was then passed on to the next offender. The pupil who had the *signum* at the end of the day was thrashed, given lines or made to clean the toilets. (The same device had once been used in seminaries to encourage the use of Latin instead of French.)

The story of how the majority of French people became French-speakers could be told in a dozen different ways. For the non-French speaker on a school bench, the experience was often traumatic and humiliating. The effects were felt most cruelly in regions where the local tongue least resembled French: Alsace, Brittany, the Basque Country, Catalonia, the Flemish-speaking towns of the north and the island of Corsica. There are Bretons still alive who remember the mortifying difficulty of learning French – 'a language whose words were like half-empty boxes, and you weren't even quite sure what was inside them' – and the endless insults from sneering teachers and patronizing newspaper articles. In Brittany, being patriotic seemed to be the same as denigrating one's *pays*. The popular cartoon character Bécassine, created in 1905, came to represent the outsider's view of Brittany: Bécassine was a Breton maid who worked in Paris and got into all sorts of amusing scrapes because she failed to understand even the simplest French. Her silly round face had no ears and sometimes no mouth. Her costume was more Picard than Breton and her pidgin French had not the slightest connection with the Breton language, but her ethnic characteristics were irrelevant. She was Breton because she was stupid and because her relatives were sly and greedy.

Years later, when education and an ability to speak French were taken for granted, the missionary efforts of the Third Republic's educators would look to some people like a colonial campaign to erase local cultures. The independence movements that formed in the twentieth century saw the patronizing, parochial ignorance of Parisians as part of a system of organized repression. Bécassine herself was afforded the honours of a paramilitary coup. One Sunday in 1939, three Breton 'commandos' entered the Musée Grévin in Paris, where a waxwork statue of Bécassine was on display, and struck a blow for all the Breton maids who had ever been patronized and exploited by Parisian employers by smashing her to pieces.

Ironically, unlike the older, anti-colonial struggles in Corsica and Algeria, these regional independence movements were themselves a product of the Third Republic's education system. Most people who had a sense of being Breton had first learned to think of themselves as French. No separatist was ever monolingual, though he might yearn for the days when most of his compatriots were. 'Breton-speaking Bretons', wrote Pierre-Jakez Hélias in 1975, 'have never been aware of belonging to an entity called Brittany ... They call themselves Bretons when they are outside Brittany, but they aren't quite sure where it begins or ends.' Breton nationalism was only remotely related to earlier, local rebellions against taxation and conscription. It was modelled on a modern image of the state as a cultural and administrative unit, and it owed its violent nostalgia to a concept of the *pays* that was disseminated by the national education system.

In fact, far from being treated as a sign of backwardness, regional pride was widely considered to be a vital aspect of patriotism. Tactful decentralization had been an aspect of official policy since the 1860s. Many teachers were also local historians and were saddened by the disappearance of local languages and dialects. Some taught in dialect as well as French and believed that an ability to speak both languages was an asset. They forced their pupils to use French, not because they wanted to stamp out minority cultures, but because they wanted their pupils to pass examinations, to have the means of discovering the outside world, to improve the lot of their families. Brittany suffered more than most regions, particularly after the anti-clerical laws of 1901 and the subsequent attempt to ban the use of Breton in church services. But the French Republic never led the sort of full-scale linguistic assault on its population that made life so miserable in Alsace-Lorraine after the annexation by Germany in 1870.

The retreat of Basque, Breton, Catalan, Corsican and Flemish before the tide of French belonged to a much older, more compli-cated process of social and material change. Standard French was carried all over the country by conscription, railways, newspapers, tourists and popular songs, which could hardly be sung in dialect without losing the rhymes. The Third Republic may even have prolonged the life of some dialects by promoting the use of French: it presented children with another way of being naughty. In 1887, five years after the introduction of free, compulsory education, a linguistician studying a dialect of the Mayenne noticed a phenomenon that can still be heard today:

> The patois of Montjean is now practically extinct except among old people and children. Old people speak it in earnest and the children enjoy exaggerating their grandparents' pronunciation because they are taught to speak French at school.

*

THE FATHERLAND that children discovered in the classroom can be seen in all its simple variety in the books that were used to teach reading and geography. The main characters were usually children with insatiable appetites for geographical information, accompanied by a pedagogue crammed with uncontroversial facts. In Amable Tastu's *Voyage en France* (1846), a father and his children stand in front of the industrial landscape of Le Creusot: 'You are about to ask me, my children, what a blast furnace and an air furnace are,' says the father. 'I shall try to explain in a few words, with the help of some notes that I took in various books.'

Some of these tales of infant tourists were self-righteously nationalistic, especially after the loss of Alsace-Lorraine. In Marie de Grandmaison's *Le Tour de France* (1893), two young boys explore the entire country on bicycles (this is the first time that the apprentices' expression 'Tour de France' was associated with cycling). They end up in Strasbourg, the capital of Alsace, where they admire the children who are about to escape from 'the odious German yoke' by emigrating to France:

'Come, brother, let us follow their example. It is hard to breathe this air that smells of oppression.'
'Yes,' said Marcel, 'let us leave this beautiful Alsace, but with the hope of returning one day as victors!'

However, the two boys can be quite odious themselves about the French provinces:

'Ah, the Auvergne! Why are the people of this region so gullible?' asked Robert.
'Because of their volcanic terrain,' replied Marcel. 'When Nature herself looks so incredibly strange, the mind can easily accept the most miraculous things.'

This ethnic inanity probably reflects the fact that Marcel and Robert come from a wealthy Paris suburb. Usually, the children came from a province and exemplified the virtues of their *pays*. *Three Months Under the Snow: Journal of a Young Inhabitant of the Jura* (15th edition, 1886) was a lesson in courage and patience. The *petits voyageurs* of P.-C. Briand's 'picturesque description of this beautiful land' (1834) came from the 'little island' of Corsica but felt themselves to be 'true Frenchmen' – which was an improvement on the usual image of Corsicans as hairy bandits permanently embroiled in vendettas.

Best of all was Augustine Bruno's wildly popular *Le Tour de France par deux enfants*, subtitled 'devoir et patrie, livre de lecture courante' (1877). The two boys leave Phalsbourg in German-occupied Lorraine and set off to find their uncle Frantz after the death of their father, a carpenter whose dying wish was to emigrate to France. Their realistic adventures take them south to Marseille, on a boat to Bordeaux via the Mediterranean and the Canal du Midi, across northern France from Brittany to Flanders, then home to lay flowers on their father's grave. From there, they take the train to Paris, whose streets, laid end to end, 'would make a street nine hundred kilometres long, which is longer than the road from Paris to Marseille'. The orphans fend for themselves and learn about the country, not from a pedant with a library in his pockets, but from local men and women who work for a living. The journey ends, not in Paris, but on a farm in the Beauce that has been ravaged by the Franco-Prussian War but which hard work and patriotism will restore to productivity.

Adult historians who are condescending about Bruno's luminous little book should try describing an entire country, along with its people, produce, geography and climate, in a tale that could hold the attention of child. *Le Tour de France par deux enfants*, which had its 386th edition in 1922, gave millions of people a vivid, factual image of France. Some of the experiences and observations of André and Julien Volden were more famous than major events of French history: the shipwreck in the English Channel, the mistreated carthorse, the amazingly sensitive steam-hammer at the foundry in Le Creusot which could tap a cork into a wine bottle, or the hostelry-farmhouse in the Dauphiné:

> The people who entered the inn all spoke patois amongst themselves. The two boys sat in a corner, unable to comprehend a single word of what was being said and feeling quite alone in that foreign farm. . . . Finally, little Julien turned to his big brother and, with a look of affection mingled with sadness, said, 'Why do none of the people of this *pays* speak French?'
>
> 'Because not all of them have been able to go to school. But some

's from now, things will be different, and people throughout France
I be able to speak the language of the fatherland.'

Just then, the door opened again. It was the innkeeper's children,
back from school.

'André!' cried Julien. 'Those children must know French since they
go to a school! What joy! We shall be able to talk to one another.'

*

WHEN THEY LEFT SCHOOL, the generations that had grown up
with these books were encouraged to discover France for themselves by a massive campaign of national self-promotion which is
still going strong in the twenty-first century. Newspapers and magazines urged their readers to visit the unknown parts of France that
were spurned by wealthy tourists and especially the 'lost provinces'
of Alsace-Lorraine. Regions that were practically unexplored until
the 1880s and which few guidebooks had ever mentioned were promoted as holiday destinations: the Ardennes, the Argonne and the
Morvan, the valleys of the Dordogne and the Lot, the roadless
canyon of the river Tarn and the cave-lined Gorges de l'Ardèche,
the Vercors massif with its recent infrastructure of death-defying
roads and tunnels, and the remote Cantal, where Gustave Eiffel's
soaring Garabit Viaduct (1884) was admired as a wonder of the
modern world.

This was the period when people began to say, as they still do, that
'the land least known in France is France itself'. It was as if the loss
of part of its territory had alerted the nation to its untapped treasures.
France had colonized North Africa and Indo-China but had failed to
colonize itself. The rural population was flowing away to the cities,
leaving the countryside exposed to the forces of Nature and foreign
invasion. It was the patriotic duty of every French citizen to go on
holiday to unpopular places, which they would find to be as spectacular as the overrated Alps. The *Magasin pittoresque* imagined a Parisian
holidaymaker, kidnapped and blindfolded and taken to the shores of
Lac Chambon in the heart of the Auvergne. When the blindfold was
removed, he would find himself in a stunning landscape of cloudlike
mountains and glassy lakes and would scarcely believe himself in
France.

The remarketing of France was pioneered by local historians and politicians, provincial academies and geographical societies, railway companies and journalists. Parts of the country were unofficially renamed to make them sound more attractive: the coast of Provence became the Côte d'Azur in 1877. Then came the Côte Émeraude (Emerald Coast) of Brittany, the Côte Sauvage of the Vendée, and the Côte d'Argent (Silver Coast) on the Atlantic between Royan and Bayonne. Little Switzerlands sprang up all over the place, beginning with the unfashionable Morvan and the Limousin. It has since become almost obligatory for any region with rolling pastures to call itself Switzerland. At the time of writing, there are ten French 'Switzerlands', from the 'Suisse Normande' (fifty miles north-west of the 'Alpes mancelles') to the 'Suisse Niçoise' and the 'Suisse d'Alsace'.

In 1874, the geographer Adolphe Joanne and a small group of writers and left-wing politicians founded the Club Alpin Français. Its motto, '*En avant, quand même!*', might be translated 'Forward, come what may!' or, in a less militaristic tone, 'Let's go anyway'. Its aim was 'to discover France for the greater edification of the French'. It sought out local agents to help it in its campaign and claimed to have 'discovered, in the remotest provinces, scholars, writers and artists who didn't even know about themselves'. The following year, the Comité des Promenades in Gérardmer (Vosges), set an example that was followed by tourist offices all over France. These missionary organizations trained guides and porters, persuaded rival villages to work together, laid out signposted walks and organized '*caravanes scolaires*' and '*colonies de vacances*' for schoolchildren. They also encouraged hotels to display their prices and not overcharge tourists. Long before paid holidays for workers were introduced in 1936, a new economic geography of France was taking shape: the Vosges were the Alps of the *petite bourgeoisie*, and the mountains of the Auvergne were the poor man's Pyrenees.*

---

* Relatively poor, that is. In the mid-1880s, a teacher like M. Blondel earned about 1,200 francs a year; women teachers earned half as much as men. The average daily wage of a worker in the Paris region was about seven francs. A single Parisian on a week's holiday to a spa town in the Auvergne might spend the following (in francs): second-class return train ticket: thirty-five; room and board: fifty; excursions, donkey

The touring clubs were pioneers in the tradition of the eighteenth-century map-makers. They not only popularized obscure parts of France, they also discovered them. In 1882, two members of the Club Alpin stumbled on an amazing 'city of stones' in the wild uplands of the Causse Noir. The dolomitic rock formations that tower over the forest of oak and scrub like ruined skyscrapers are visible from a distance of several miles, though nothing on that site had ever been indicated on a map. The uninhabited chaos of columns and ravines was baptized Montpellier-le-Vieux, supposedly because local shepherds had named it after the only city they knew, though this was probably the result of a misunderstanding: the local name, 'Lou Clapas', simply means 'heap of stones', which also happened to be the derisive local name for Montpellier.

The discovery of the Old Heap of Stones was one of the early triumphs of the Club Alpin, a lost treasure reclaimed from the wild provinces. A scale model of 'The Devil's Citadel' was made for the Exposition Universelle of 1889, where it intrigued the crowds who had come to see the Eiffel Tower. A year before, the English writer Matilda Betham-Edwards had seen the real thing when, at the age of fifty-three, she took a carriage from Le Rozier in the Tarn gorges and climbed the almost vertical road on the north wall of the Causse Noir to those 'vast, flower-scented heights, nearly 3000 feet above the sea-level, swept clean by the pure air of half a dozen mountain chains'. She reached the mangy farm of Maubert and was shown around Montpellier-le-Vieux by the farmer, who was already contemplating a new career as an innkeeper.

Fortunately, Mrs Betham-Edwards had some good advice for the farmer and his young wife, who was 'very bright, good-looking, amiable and intelligent', 'but sadly neglectful of her personal appearance, with locks unkempt and dress slatternly'. A French tourist was ensconced in the farmhouse with his guide, eating omelettes. Mrs Betham-Edwards had a vision of the future – a tablecloth spread for breakfast, the dunghill replaced by a flower garden, carpets and armchairs in the best bedrooms and even 'trays, bells and door-fastenings'.

---

hire, tips, etc.: twenty; refreshments and souvenirs: thirty; one map: two; five postcards and stamps: one. Total: 138 francs.

As the Utopia could not be realized this year, I chatted with our hosts upon 'le confort', whilst they brought out one liqueur after another – rum, quince water, heaven knows what! – with which to restore us after our fatigues. Whilst I conversed on this instructive topic: 'Yes', said the handsome, slatternly little mistress of the Cité du Diable, turning to her husband, 'we must buy some hand-basins, my dear.'

*

THE ROCKS OF Montpellier-le-Vieux now bear the gaudy names that were given to them by a Parisian lawyer, Édouard-Alfred Martel: Cyrano's Nose, the Sphinx, the Badger's Eyes, the Gate of Mycenae, etc. The 'Columbus of the nether world' was born at Pontoise near Paris in 1859. After a holiday with his parents in the Pyrenees, Martel became obsessed with the underground world of caves and grottos. Between 1888 and 1913, he made annual expeditions to remote parts of France and eventually to fourteen other countries, including Ireland and the United States. With his trusty assistant, a blacksmith called Louis Armand, he charted most of the caverns and subterranean labyrinths that still attract millions of visitors today: Dargilan, Padirac, the Aven Armand, the Abîme de Bramabiau. He hung from spinning rope ladders, stumbled over rock falls with a canoe on his head and a candle clenched between his teeth, and stood shivering in vast, iridescent caverns wearing a wool suit, a bowler hat and boots with holes to let the water out.

Martel was the popular hero of the new age of domestic exploration. He wrote dozens of books, most of which were bestsellers and only one of which, *Les Abîmes*, is still in print. His true-life tales were just as exciting as the fantasies of his favourite novelist, Jules Verne. This is his description of the descent of the Gouffre de Padirac:

> I was the first to descend. . . . Eight minutes later, I was at the bottom. I detached myself from the ladder and looked up. . . . I seemed to be inside a telescope that was trained on a little circle of blue sky. Daylight fell vertically on the limestone strata of the chasm walls, catching the ridges and sculpted corbels and casting reflections of a kind I had never seen before. . . . Around the rim of the hole I could just make out the tiny heads of my companions: they were lying flat on the ground in order to observe me. How high up and far away they seemed! Long

tufts of shade- and moisture-loving plants hung gracefully down from the tiniest asperities of that colossal funnel. Through the middle of them ran the telephone cable – our connection to the world of the living – like a black thread that a spider had spun across the abyss.

British and American mountaineers had conquered the highest peaks in France; Martel restored some national pride by conquering the deepest depths. He saw himself as a patriotic salesman 'conducting publicity campaigns for compatriots who possess an unexploited source of wealth in the natural beauties of their region'. These compatriots appear in his books as superstitious simpletons while Martel himself is the demystifying missionary, the magician from the Land of Technology who, with dazzling magnesium strips, lights the holes where the Devil used to lurk. An engraving in *Les Abîmes* shows him towering over his companions, standing in a niche like the Virgin of Lourdes, with a candle stuck to the brim of his hat.

A belief in subterranean demons did not prevent farmers from using these holes as waste-disposal chutes. What Martel dreaded most was the repulsive, gluey crunchiness at the bottom of the pits which he called 'carcass soup' and which local people harvested for use as fertilizer and pigment. Tales of quivering peasants warning of vengeful spirits are still trotted out in modern guidebooks. The real response to Martel's explorations was less flattering. Hundreds of people would gather and turn the spectacle into a village fête. Snuffling dogs sent stones flying down the hole while violins and accordions made telephone communication impossible. Old women crossed themselves and wagged their fingers, saying, 'You'll get down there all right, my fine gentlemen, but you'll never get out again', or '*Y o dé nèsci de touto mèno*' ('fools come in all shapes and sizes'). Local men would ask Martel if he and his team had come to measure the hole 'so that they can build one in their own *pays*'. Little did they know that their hole in the ground would one day be more valuable than a gold mine.

*

ANYONE WHO HAS EXPLORED a cavern or a gorge in France has probably walked along a 'Sentier Martel' or admired the view from

one of Martel's 'Points sublimes'. He discovered more than tw
hundred caverns and underground rivers and has had more site.
named after him than most saints. But even Martel was amazed by
the geological monster that came to light in 1905.

Just over a hundred years ago, when Paris had a Métro and the
Eiffel Tower was showing signs of age, one of the natural wonders of
the Old World was known only to a few woodcutters and carvers
who saw no reason to share their knowledge of the local inconvenience with the outside world. The Grand Canyon of the Verdon
runs for thirteen miles through the puzzling limestone landscape of
the Pré-alpes de Castellane. Sixty miles to the south-west lies the
second largest city in France. Many of the boxwood balls that arced
through the air on the dusty malls of Marseille had begun life as
gnarled stumps clinging to the edge of the longest and deepest
canyon in Europe. Men from the hamlets on either side of the canyon
lowered themselves into the chasm to cut the best wood for making
boules while, two thousand feet below, the metallic-green Verdon
rushed through its narrow gorge, scouring the gravel bed and carving
out new caves.

At the eastern end of the canyon, the town of Castellane stands on
a Roman road that joined the Durance to the Mediterranean and the
Via Aurelia to the Via Domitia. Napoleon had passed through
Castellane on his way back to Paris in 1815. At the western end of
the canyon, the village of Moustiers-Sainte-Marie was famous for its
glazed ceramics and the golden star that a crusader returning from
the Holy Land had strung between two cliffs. Both places were
described in guidebooks. Charles Bertram Black's guide to the South
of France in 1885 even mentioned a road between Castellane and
Moustiers that he might have supposed to have existed when he
looked at his map. Meanwhile, the Verdon Gorges remained completely unknown to the rest of the world.

It is almost as interesting to imagine *not* discovering the Verdon
Gorges as it is to explore them. From the road that reaches Moustiers
from the west, a spectacular wall of rock appears to the east. The
evening sun sets a line of silver along its ridge and shows the wall to
be quite thin: something obviously lies behind it. But no one who
climbed up to Moustiers after crossing the wind-blasted Valensole

plain would have felt inclined to prolong the journey and to venture among the cliffs and ravines that slanted off into a poorly mapped region. Most travellers' appetites for grand desolation would have been satisfied to the limit. The entrance to the canyon itself is so narrow as to be invisible even at a short distance, though the scene is now very hard to picture. In 1975, hydroelectric dams created the Lac de Sainte-Croix, submerging fourteen square miles and turning the hillside village of Bauduen into a lakeside resort.

One day in 1896, the people of Rougon, a hamlet near the north-eastern rim of the canyon, were amazed to see a small party of men with a donkey and a dismantled canoe. It was the first boat ever seen in the *pays*. The leader of the expedition, a naval engineer called Armand Janet, claimed to have come from the gorge itself, which seemed impossible. He had negotiated the river as far as the eastern entrance to the gorge, but after a terrifying encounter with the rapids his local guides had refused to continue and he was forced to abandon the attempt.

Nine years later, Édouard Martel was commissioned by the Minister of Agriculture to study the hydrology of the region. It was hoped that the river Verdon could be tamed and used to irrigate the parched fields of the Var and to ensure a supply of drinking water for Toulon and Marseille. Martel, accompanied by Armand Janet, Louis Armand, an agricultural engineer, a local teacher, two road-menders and several porters, sailed the entire length of the Verdon Gorges, naming features, taking photographs with the only camera that survived the torrent and surprisingly remaining alive. Two of the boats were smashed to pieces. It took the party three days to descend ten miles of the river. They finally emerged from the canyon at 10 a.m. on 14 August 1905, near the Roman bridge below Aiguines which has since been swallowed by the lake.

The following year, in the proceedings of the Geographical Society and in a popular magazine called *Le Tour du monde*, Martel described the expedition and revealed this 'American wonder of France' to the world, thirty-seven years after John Wesley Powell's pioneering expedition through the Grand Canyon of the Colorado. His only regret was that this 'new jewel in the rich crown of *la belle France*' scarcely lent itself to tourism. As he suspected, the Verdon Gorges would 'remain for a long time invisible or at least unvisitable'.

A road along the south rim of the gorges, accurately called the Corniche Sublime, was opened in 1947. The north road was completed in 1973. Both roads form an exhilarating circuit of sixty-two miles. The unknown, dangerous region now lies on the other side of the road, away from the canyon, where a valley slopes towards the hills on the blank part of the map. A few dusty tracks lead off into the scrub, across the Grand Plan de Canjuers, a karstic plateau riddled with sinkholes and underground streams. Sometimes, a cloud of dust can be seen rising from the hills, and a traveller who walks a short distance into the bushes, beyond the warning signs, may catch sight of some of the camouflaged denizens of the Canjuers military zone.

*

THE DISCOVERY OF the Verdon Gorges was also a revelation of the nation's ignorance of itself. Until 1906, the most spectacular geographical feature in France might as well have existed in a different dimension; yet, all around the rim of the canyon, Martel and Janet had found farm animals drinking at pools, 'ruins whose history is unknown' and, in the canyon itself, wreckage washed down by the torrent – planks of wood from mills and cabins, and even 'a footbridge from who knows where'.

The 'newly discovered marvel' had been known about for centuries. When the first accurate map was made, it was littered with place names which, like the stratified rocks, trace a long journey back in time. Martel's Jules Verne-inspired names were only the latest layer of colour: the Plateau des Fossiles, the Voûte d'Émeraude (Emerald Vault), the Étroit de la Quille (Skittle Strait). Some of the older names had acquired a modern patina: the farm originally known as Bourogne had turned into Boulogne, and the bridge at the hamlet of Soleis had become the falsely mysterious Pont-de-Soleils (Bridge of Suns).

Despite the French spelling, the original Occitan forms were clearly visible and testified to the long struggle of people with the land: the Baumes-Fères (Wild Caverns), le Maugué (Bad Ford), the

Pas de Vaumale (Bad Valley Pass). A stable in the hills above the eastern entrance to the canyon had once been a sanctuary of the Knights Templar. Its name, Saint Maymes, was derived from the Roman Maximus. Further west, 'Saint Maurice' was probably the Christianized form of a pagan word for 'marsh'. There were few other saints' names, suggesting that human habitation in the gorges predated the Roman roads – if they were indeed Roman – that ran to the west and east of the canyon.

The oldest names of all had been worn away to a few airy vowels. 'Ayen', the name of a pass on the northern rim, has no known origin. It may be the echo of a Gaulish word for 'rock' (*aginn*), used by the Iron Age people whose tombs were later discovered at Soleis, or a lone relic of an unrecorded language that was spoken when the river was still carving out its chasm.

17

Journey to the Centre of France

T HE LAST GREAT geographical discovery made in France was a
spectacular end to the age of tourist pioneers. When the Verdon
Gorges were revealed to the world in 1906, another age of exploration
was already under way, thanks in large part to a miraculous machine
which opened up the depopulated countryside and brought life back
to roads that had been emptied by the railways.

One night in May 1891, just before dawn, a small group of people
had gathered at the top of a hill near Thivars, south-west of Chartres.
They had turned their lanterns to the south to warn of their presence
and were peering down the long, deserted road. Suddenly, a voice
cried, 'Stand back!'

> All at once, three shadows surged out of the darkness, passed like a
> fleeting vision and disappeared into the night. One of us called out,
> 'Who was that?' – 'Mills,' came the reply. – And without a moment's
> delay, we remounted and raced back towards Chartres, to the Hôtel
> du Grand Monarque, where the checkpoint had been set up.

The British amateur, George Pilkington Mills, was on his way to
winning the first Bordeaux–Paris bicycle race. The other two shadows
were cyclists who took turns 'pacing' the competitors (riding close
behind another cyclist reduces wind resistance and increases efficiency
by up to a third). The organizers had laid on refreshments and beds
at towns along the way, but the riders barely stopped to grab the food
and flew on towards the capital. They saw the sun go down over the
plains of Poitou and rise over the Forest of Rambouillet. When Mills
reached the finishing line at the Porte de Saint-Cloud on the edge

of Paris, he had covered the three-hundred-and-fifty-eight-mile course in twenty-six hours thirty-five minutes – an average speed of 13½ mph.

Inspired by the Bordeaux–Paris, the news editor of *Le Petit Journal* organized an even longer race from Paris to Brest and back again. This time, a French victory was virtually certain since only Frenchmen were allowed to compete. On 6 September 1891, thousands of people were on the streets of Paris at 6 a.m. to watch two hundred and six cyclists rolling along the boulevards towards the Arc de Triomphe and the Bois de Boulogne. Out in the Normandy countryside, villagers had set up tables by the side of the road to have the pleasure of seeing their milk, apples, cider and cakes devoured by hungry cyclists. (This still happens in the modern version of the Paris–Brest–Paris, which is open to all well-prepared amateurs.) Some riders stoked themselves with snuff and champagne; others made do with bread and meat broth.

The favourite was the thirty-four-year-old professional cyclist Charles Terront, riding on state-of-the-art, detachable Michelin tyres. He reached Brest on 7 September at 5 p.m. (Paris time), an hour behind the leader, swallowed a pear and some soup and left five minutes later. At Guingamp, he overtook the leader, who was sleeping at the inn, and recrossed the Breton border at noon the next day. At Mortagne, people from all over the *pays* had come to see the riders pass. When Terront hurtled into town after dark he was greeted with thunderous applause and a firework display, and set off again bedecked with flowers. A few miles down the road, he crashed into a fallen branch. Sobbing with exhaustion, he walked to the nearest blacksmith, who repaired his pedal crank and sent him on his way. At five thirty the following morning, ten thousand people saw Terront in the middle of a flotilla of local cyclists cross the line on the Boulevard Maillot with his arm raised in triumph. He had been riding his Humber bicycle for seventy-one hours thirty-seven minutes, averaging 10½ mph for seven hundred and forty-eight miles. He ate four meals, slept for twenty-six hours and then proved his resilience once again by attending eighteen consecutive banquets held in his honour.

*

THESE LONG-DISTANCE exploits were described in Homeric tones by newspaper reporters and are still an inspiration to competitive amateurs, but they give a slightly warped view of common experience. The man who saw George Pilkington Mills flash past on the hill near Thivars was a teacher from Chartres who spent a happy two-week holiday riding sixty-five hilly miles a day ('a distance one should not exceed if one wishes to see and retain something of the journey') from his home to the Pyrenees and back through the Auvergne. He cycled over the mighty Col du Tourmalet (6,939 feet) fifteen years before the self-mythologizing Tour de France made such a meal of it in 1910. Hundreds of other men and women had already pedalled happily over the Pyrenees, but the Tour de France has promoted its own epic history so effectively that it is now generally believed that the first person to cross the Tourmalet on a bicycle was the leader in the 1910 Tour de France who reached the summit covered in sweat and dust, and shouted at the organizers, '*Assassins!*'

The effect of the bicycle on daily life is now drastically underestimated by many historians, who tend to see it as an instrument of self-inflicted torture. Simple truths have been forgotten. As almost everyone knew a hundred years ago, the secret of riding a bicycle as an adult is to pedal just hard enough to keep the machine upright, then to increase the speed very gradually, but without becoming too breathless to hold a conversation or to hum a tune. In this way, with a regular intake of water and food, an uncompetitive, moderately fit person can cycle up an Alp, with luggage, on a stern but steady gradient engineered for an eighteenth-century mule. Descending is more difficult but statistically much safer, to all concerned, than in a car.

To generations unspoiled by automation, hundred-mile bike rides were quite routine. When the teacher from Chartres set off on his thousand-mile holiday in 1895, boneshakers were already a distant memory. His machine was identical in most respects to the modern bicycle. It had ball-bearings and pneumatic tyres. Many velocipedes were lighter and more reliable than the energy-sapping machines that can be seen on city streets today. There were bicycles that folded up into a suitcase and bicycles that pumped up their own tyres. The derailleur, which made it possible to change gear without removing the back wheel, was introduced in 1912. Brakes, however, were still in their infancy. Many cyclists recommended tying a heavy branch to the seat-post before beginning a descent, but only 'in the absence of dust, mud, sudden turns and especially forest guards who may refuse to believe that one has brought one's own branch from Paris' (Jean Bertot, *La France en bicyclette: étapes d'un touriste*, 1894).

As soon as second-hand bicycles and cheap imitations of the well-known models became available, millions of people were liberated from their close horizons by a mechanical horse that could be given fresh limbs and reincarnated by the local blacksmith. A boy with a bicycle could leave his *pays* in search of a job or a bride and be back in time for dinner, which is why the bicycle has been credited with increasing the average height of the French population by reducing the number of marriages between blood relations. It was used by farm workers, urban commuters, postmen, village priests, gendarmes and the French army, which, like many other European armies, had several battalions of cycling cavalry.

Before the First World War, at least four million bicycles were owned in France, which represents one bicycle for every ten people: 3,552,000 were declared for tax, but many more 'feedless horses' must have been hidden in stables. It was now possible to travel long distances at an invigorating speed, with the sort of panoramic view over the hedgerows previously enjoyed only by travellers perched on the roof of the diligence. Bicycles could be hired in most towns and taken on trains for less than a franc. The railway companies accepted responsibility for any damage. The Touring Club de France, founded in 1890 on the model of the British Cyclists' Touring Club, had a hundred and ten thousand members by 1911. There were special maps for cyclists, showing steep hills, danger spots, paved and tar-macked sections and separate bicycle paths in towns. In her *European Travel for Women* (1900), Mary Cadwalader Jones recommended the bicycle as a means of discovering France. Her only word of caution concerned the law on keeping to the right: 'You cannot always be sure: there are right- and left-handed cities and districts, so you must always keep your eyes open if you are bicycling'.

*

THIS OPENING-UP of the domestic frontier was beautifully embodied by the greatest bicycle race of all. The Tour de France was devised as a publicity stunt by a journalist, Géo Lefèvre, and his boss, Henri Desgrange, champion cyclist and editor of the sports newspaper *L'Auto*. The first Tour (1903) covered 1,518 miles and was divided into six stages, each lasting more than twenty-four hours: Paris, Lyon, Marseille, Toulouse, Bordeaux, Nantes, Paris. This was the low-altitude route typically followed by apprentices on their Tour de France: it was perfect for the early Tours, when the stewards' cars were unable to cope with the mountains. Sixty riders started and twenty-one shattered survivors were welcomed back to Paris by a hundred thousand people.

From the very beginning, the Tour de France was a national celebration, the joyful beating of the bounds that millions of people with no interest in sport still enjoy every summer. For those who followed the Tour in newspapers and saw the murky photographs of mud-spattered heroes on the roads of France, from the black grime of the north to the white dust of the south, the 'sacred soil' of France became the setting of an annual adventure story told in the cartoon-epic prose of Henri Desgrange.

As a liberal republican, Desgrange was delighted with the first winner of the Tour de France. Maurice Garin was an Italian by birth. He came from the other side of Mont Blanc in the Aosta Valley. Like thousands of his compatriots, he had left home as a boy and walked all the way to Belgium, where he earned his living as a chimney sweep. Garin had since become a French citizen and settled in Lens in the Pas-de-Calais. 'The Little Chimney Sweep' was as much a symbol of national unity as the French-born Algerian Kabyle, Zinédine Zidane, who captained the World Cup-winning national football team in 1998. Attacks on Italian immigrant workers had been increasing. Poor Italians were employed to do the filthy jobs that no one else wanted and were blamed for driving wages down. But the violence had as much to do with xenophobia as with industrial relations. In 1893, fifty Italians were shot and bludgeoned to death by a mob at the salt works in Aigues-Mortes. The murderous manhunt went on for three days. The perpetrators were arrested, tried and acquitted. In a country that was still divided by the Dreyfus

Affair, national unity seemed a distant dream. Desgrange imagined that his Tour de France would help to heal the wounds and restore national morale. The brawny editorial that he published in *L'Auto* on the first day of the race was almost a peaceful call to arms:

> With the broad and powerful gesture that Zola gave his ploughman in *La Terre*, *L'Auto*, a newspaper of ideas and action, today sends out to all corners of France those unwitting and hardy sowers of energy, the great professional riders.

Unfortunately, the Tour was more catalyst than balm. As a Parisian, Desgrange himself was amazed by what he saw in darkest France: wild faces drawn like moths to the checkpoint's acetylene flares; 'raucous housewives' in a suburb of Moulins, 'who haven't even the decorum to wear a bonnet': 'Just how much further could we be from Paris?' On the second stage of the 1904 Tour, at three o'clock in the morning, 'the Little Chimney Sweep', 'the Butcher of Sens' (Lucien Pothier), 'the Red Devil' (Giovanni Gerbi) and a rider known only by his real name (Antoine Faure) reached the summit of the Col de la République near the industrial town of Saint-Étienne. A mob was waiting in the forest. Faure, the local boy, was cheered on his way while the others were beaten up. The Italian Gerbi later retired from the race with broken fingers. On the next stage, at Nîmes, a riot broke out because the local favourite, Ferdinand Payan, had been disqualified for riding in the slipstream of a car. All along the route, nails and broken bottles were strewn on the road, drinks were spiked, frames were sawn through and hubs quietly unscrewed at night.

The Tour de France gave millions of people their first true sense of the shape and size of France, but it also proved beyond doubt that the land of a thousand little *pays* was still alive.

*

THE TOUR DE FRANCE may have failed to unify the country but it did help to conjure away the feeling that there was nothing left to be discovered. No one could now publish a guide like Charles Delattre's *Voyages en France* (1842), in which the author wrestled with a bear, fled from Spanish smugglers, was sucked into a bog in the Landes and nearly drowned in the *mascaret* tidal wave on the Dordogne.

None of this was true, but at least, in those days, he could expect to be believed. British tourists were already searching for 'undiscovered' places where no other British people would be found. The *Magasin pittoresque* had once bemoaned the 'wasteland' that covered much of the country. Now it bemoaned the cultivation of every little corner. Nature was beginning to look like the Forest of Fontainebleau, with its signposts and log-cabin souvenir shops. The road from Bayonne to Biarritz was filled with traffic and the smell of cheap restaurants. Cliff faces all over the Pyrenees were papered with hotel advertisements.

The mountains described in Desgrange's Tour reports as malevolent giants seemed to be getting lower by the year. A road across the ridge of the Vosges had been completed in 1860. The magnificent Route des Grandes Alpes was opened to civilian traffic before the First World War and made it possible to drive, in summer, all the way from Lake Geneva to Nice. The Côte d'Azur itself was turning into the vast burglar-alarmed suburb that now stretches from Saint-Tropez to the glass-strewn highways of Monaco and into the once-deserted hills where mudslides and the smell of sewage are constant reminders of over-development. Native vegetation was eradicated by Australian mimosa and English shrubs and lawns. A hundred years before, Nice had been a quiet haven for a few travellers waiting for the wind to change before sailing for Genoa. In 1897, Augustus Hare visited Nice and found 'a great, ugly, modern town, with Parisian shops and a glaring esplanade along the sea'.

Despite the rarity of cars compared to bicycles (five thousand cars in 1901, ninety-one thousand in 1913), the destruction they caused was already outweighing the benefits to a small number of people. In 1901, the Dauphiné Automobile Club decided that its race, the Course de Côte de Laffrey, would have to be run in early spring because the road would be 'blocked by the numerous cars that run along it continuously in the summer'. Twenty-five years later, Rudyard Kipling, driving from Cannes to Monte Carlo, found the road clogged with other people's cars: it was '*all* solid traffic': 'The motor car has made the Riviera an Hell – and a noisy smelly one.'

The country that had once seemed so vast was seen to be teeming with life like a fish pond when the water drains away. In this shrinking world, a few remote places and their tiny populations came to play a disproportionate role in the nation's image of itself: the Breton islands of Houat and Hoedic, the almost deserted, waterless Causses, and Saint-Véran, the highest village in Europe, which now has eight hotels and two museums of daily life.

The rapid disappearance of undiscovered France, and the desire to believe that it still existed, contributed to one of the great literary successes of 1913: Alain-Fournier's novel *Le Grand Meaulnes* (translated as *The Lost Domain* and *The End of Youth*). His tale of boyhood longings, set in the rural Bourbonnais, gave a tantalizing sense of *la France profonde* as a distant but familiar place, a little world full of simple things that spoke of another age: the stove in the freezing classroom, the clog-wearing pupils who smelled of hay, the gendarme and the poachers, the beaten-earth floor of the general store, the silence of the countryside. The only strangers who ever appeared in the classroom were gypsies from a travelling circus, 'boatmen caught in the ice on the canal, journeymen and travellers trapped by the snow'.

In *Le Grand Meaulnes*, wickedness and vulgarity were associated with the industrial suburbs of nearby Montluçon and its 'horrible, lisping accent'. Montluçon itself had doubled in size in less than a century. 'The Birmingham of France' was now a sprawling eyesore of factories, railway yards and depots. In the real classroom at Épineuil-le-Fleuriel where Alain-Fournier's father had taught, the stove, the pupils' clogs and galoshes, their leather satchels, some of the books, the furniture and the candles, and the bricks and roof tiles of the school itself would have come from Montluçon by road, rail and canal. But the past of *Le Grand Meaulnes* belonged to childhood, not to history. Exploration was a form of escape. The narrator himself leaves home only to return as an adult to the enchanted land of rural France where the longest journeys were those of the ploughman from one end of the field to the other.

*

A LONG TIME AFTER the disappearance of that enchanted land, on 14 July 2000, the biggest picnic in history took place along the Paris meridian. The French government had decided that the first Bastille

Day of the new millennium would commemorate the line of longitude measured by Delambre and Méchain at the end of the eighteenth century. Ten thousand trees – oaks in the north, pines in the centre, olives in the south – were to be planted along the meridian, turning the imaginary line into a verdant reality. On the day itself, sections of a traditional bistro-style red-and-white-chequered tablecloth six hundred kilometres long were laid across the territory of three hundred and thirty-seven towns and villages between the Mediterranean (Perpignan) and the Channel coast (Dunkirk).

The sky was overcast, and that day's stage of the Tour de France was won by a Spanish rider from Navarre, but nothing could spoil an event that invited citizens to show their patriotic pride by attending a village fête and consuming local produce. More than twelve thousand mayors sat down to a lunch provided by the Senate in the Jardin du Luxembourg. Two thousand homing pigeons followed by a cameraman in a helicopter raced south from Dunkirk and were auctioned for charity. Runners, cyclists, motorcyclists, horse riders and balloonists took part in a twenty-four-hour relay race that ended in the centre of France. Despite the rain, a few million people turned out to enjoy the picnic and to celebrate national unity and cultural diversity 'in a spirit of solidarity and mutual respect'.

Although it had long since been rejected in favour of the Greenwich meridian as the internationally recognized line of zero longitude, the old Paris meridian was felt to be the ideal focus for national celebration. It recalled the birth of the Republic without alluding to the bloodbath in which it was born. Ignoring the fact that the geometers had nearly been lynched by their fellow citizens, the meridian symbolized fraternity and equality. It joined the Flemish-speaking north to the Catalan-speaking south. Of course, Paris was the crucial point, but with a little stretching and pulling, the meridian could also be said to pass through the Gothic cathedrals of Amiens and Bourges and the walled city of Carcassonne. These were the inherited jewels on a necklace that hung from the capital. 'The Incredible Picnic', as it was officially named, reinforced the impression that, despite unemployment, racial conflict and the global market, France was a single nation with a clear sense of direction.

For the purposes of the relay race, the centre of France was defined as the village of Treignat, whose name probably means 'place through which one passes'. On 14 July, the Secretary of State for the Patrimony and Cultural Decentralization was rushed a hundred and fifty miles south from the official Bastille Day military parade on the Champs-Élysées to the town of La Chapelle-Saint-Ursin, to be photographed with the two hundred and thirty mayors of places with 'La Chapelle' in their name, and from there to the village designated as the centre of France. The Minister reached Treignat in the late afternoon, just in time to join the Picnic of the Languages of Oc and Oïl, and to see the runners of the relay race arrive from both ends of the country, covered in the mud of central France.

*

THE MERIDIAN was a relatively uncontentious symbol, but the centre of France was a diplomatic minefield. Three small towns, not including Treignat, currently promote themselves as the exact geographical centre of France. Each of these places has a monument. Vesdun's is an enamel mosaic map of France on a white circular base which has been unkindly compared to a Camembert cheese. Five miles up the road, Saulzais-le-Potier has a little tower of stones topped by a French flag and inscribed with a reference to 'the calculations of the eminent mathematician and astronomer Abbé Théophile Moreux'. Fifteen miles further north, Bruère-Allichamps boasts a third-century milestone that once stood at a *trivium*, the meeting of three roads. In the sixth century, the milestone was converted into a sarcophagus; in 1758 it was dug out of a field, and in 1799 erected at the crossroads in the centre of town, from where it would certainly have been removed – since it stands in the middle of the *route nationale* to Paris – had it not been identified by the popular geographer Adolphe Joanne as the mathematical centre of France.

An ironical postcard that can be bought elsewhere in the region shows these three monuments above the caption 'LES 3 CENTRES DE LA FRANCE'. In fact, there are now too many centres of France to fit on a single postcard. Methods of calculation vary, and so does the definition of France. Some include Corsica and the islands of the Atlantic and the Mediterranean. Some of the earlier calculations were made before Nice and Savoy became part of France in 1860, and others still when the loss of Alsace and Lorraine in 1870 had erased the top-right corner of the hexagon. No one seems to have given the matter much thought until the mid-nineteenth century, when the idea of France as a measurable whole was becoming more familiar. In 1855, during the Crimean War, the Duc de Mortemart built a tall octagonal tower on a hill outside Saint-Amand-Montrond called the Belvédère. His intention was to commemorate the 'immortal glory' of the French army at the Battle of Sebastopol, but the view from the tower was so glorious, and the tower itself so close to the presumed heart of the country, that it was generally agreed to be the centre of France.

Anyone who sets out today to find that semi-mythical place, the centre of France, is in for a long and convoluted journey. The elusive centre is marked in various spots by pointing wooden hands, concrete posts, little flags and a carved silhouette of the country. As coastlines change and islands disappear, the centre of France will continue to dance about the woods and hedges of the Berry and the Bourbonnais.

Meanwhile, the three traditional centres of France have declared a truce. In order to promote the cultural heritage of the region, all are united in homage to their most famous son, Alain-Fournier. The house and classroom that were the model for the school in *Le Grand Meaulnes* are now a museum. A signposted 'Route du Grand Meaulnes' is planned. Alain-Fournier and his novel have come to represent that increasingly nostalgic concept, the *pays*, though the novel itself sites the lost domain in the imagination, not in space. Its coordinates are memories and desires. Its triangulation points are the eminence of age and the distant lights of childhood. The lost domain cannot be discovered with a map. It appears only through the total darkness of the countryside, when the hero's horse has wandered off and he finds himself completely lost, a few miles from home.

*

THE LATEST CENTRE of France, calculated by the National Geographical Institute, happens to lie in a field a few hundred feet from the 'Grand Meaulnes' rest area on the southbound carriageway of the A71 autoroute.

No one could possibly get lost on the A71, which, since the completion of the Millau Viaduct, joins Paris and the north of France to the Mediterranean. In contrast to the homemade signs that mark the nearby centres of France, gigantic illuminated panels obliterate the landscape and connect the users of the autoroute to the data-stream of traffic information and weather reports. When Alain-Fournier published his novel in 1913, few people had ever known that sense of being a moving part in the national machine. Until 1 August 1914, no piece of news had ever reached the entire population on the same day.

That afternoon, in the Limousin, people heard the alarm bells that usually signified a hailstorm and looked up into a clear blue sky. In villages from Brittany to the Alps, firemen rushed out at the sound of clanging bells, looking for the fire. In the little town of Montjoux in the *arrondissement* of Montélimar, a car screeched to a halt in front of the *mairie*. A gendarme jumped out and delivered a package. A few moments later, people in the fields were intrigued to see cyclists whizzing past carrying bundles of posters. Near Sigottier, a man called Albert R . . . met a young lad heading for his village. The boy claimed to be on his way to announce the outbreak of war and round up all the men of the village. On hearing this, Albert R . . . collapsed in tears of laughter and wished him luck with his practical joke.

In places where newspapers were scarce and the main source of news was the weekly market, war came as a complete surprise. According to a survey conducted in 1915 by the rector of Grenoble University, people were 'thunderstruck' and 'stupefied'. The first inkling they had at Motte-de-Galaure, two miles from the busy Rhône corridor, was the order given on 31 July to have all the horses ready to be requisitioned. Some men sang the 'Marseillaise' and looked forward to coming home a few weeks later with tales of glory, but most were silent and dismayed. There was talk of hiding in the woods. At Plan in Isère, 'the men of our peaceful locality who were mobilized did not leave with the same enthusiasm as their comrades from the cities. Rather, they were resigned and went out of patriotic duty.'

In some parts of the Alps, men were making hay in the high summer pastures when messengers brought the news. Some had to leave for the station in the next valley before saying farewell to their families. At the Col de l'Ange Gardien, where the roads from the Col d'Izoard and the villages of the Queyras come spiralling down to join the road to the rest of France, a monument erected after the First World War lists the names of the dead by village: Abriès, Aiguilles, Arvieux, Château-Ville-Vieille, Molines, Ristolas, Saint-Véran. It was here that men and boys from different valleys gathered like the herds returning to their winter quarters. The inscription on the monument says nothing of glory and honour. It evokes the sadness of men whose home was their village, then their *pays* and last of all France:

> From the col that lies close to this mound,
> THEY cast a final farewell glance at their homes . . .
> It was here that they consented to the sacrifice . . .

*

TO JUDGE BY the records of the soldiers whose place of death is known, some of those villagers discovered a France that no living person had ever seen. The Argonne forest is one of the largest remnants of the wooded frontier zones that once divided one Gallic tribe from another. After four years as the front line, the forest had disappeared. Soldiers from all over France found themselves in a land without landmarks, with nothing to guide them but flares and enemy gunfire. They colonized the new land with gun-pits that turned into trenches and tunnels that sometimes intersected the German trenches. They camped in leaf-and-branch huts like ancient Gauls. Horses that had walked the same farm tracks all their lives carried mutilated soldiers across a grassless field. On the hill above Dombasle where Arthur Young had walked in 1789 with a local woman, soldiers trudged through heavy yellow mud towards the scarecrow remains of a church. The *pays* had become a 'sector'.

One of the thousands who lost their lives in that first summer of the Great War was Lieutenant Fournier, whose novel *Le Grand Meaulnes* would soon be read as a prophetic farewell to the France of secret, undiscovered places. On the morning of 22 September, he led a reconnaissance patrol into the woods to the south of Verdun. The men of his platoon came from the Gers in south-western France.

They could hardly have been further from home without leaving the country altogether.

Maps of this sector changed almost every day. Even someone who had spent a lifetime in the forest would have been lost. Without knowing it, Lieutenant Fournier's patrol passed behind enemy lines. A sergeant remembered the moment:

> Suddenly, we heard the crackle of gunfire behind us. The ditch on the edge of the wood gave us some protection while we tried to work out what was going on ... How long did we wait? A minute, maybe two. ... The captain shouted, 'Fix bayonets! Charge!'
>
> As soon as I was on my feet, I saw the enemy kneeling in a ditch ... I noticed a comrade here and there dropping his rifle and falling on his face ... Two of my comrades came up to the beech tree I was using as cover. Both fell dead – one on my back, the other on my feet. All I could think was, they'll get in my way. ... The revolver that Lieutenant Fournier had been firing three metres away from me fell silent ...

The German soldiers buried the bodies in the regulation manner: two rows of ten, head to toe, with the twenty-first laid on top.

The leaves of four autumns fell on the grave, and then the soil was churned up again in the Meuse–Argonne Offensive of 1918. After the Armistice, when old people with long-handled spades were filling in the gun-pits and the trenches, no one knew where to look for the dead of 1914.

*

VISITORS TO THE Argonne once came to see Varennes, where Louis XVI and Marie-Antoinette were arrested and sent back to Paris. Now, they come to see the vestiges of the First World War. Excerpts from the diaries of French, German and American soldiers can be read on information panels. Tunnels and trenches can be explored. But the forest itself exists in several different time zones. Away from the sites of commemoration, it is not always possible to distinguish bomb craters and trenches from the dells carved out by roots and rainwater, the eighteenth-century road embankments and ditches, and the earthworks of more recent foresters who negotiate the craters and the unexploded shells with mechanical excavators and horses for the more difficult terrain.

South of Verdun, the forest is bisected by a Loch Ness Monster of a road: thirteen miles of steep descents followed almost immediately by steep climbs. It gives a cyclist the impression of fleeing, being prevented from flight by the sudden tug of leg muscles, then fleeing again. This is the Tranchée de Calonne, named after the Finance Minister of Louis XVI who built the road to connect his château to the outside world. Between 1914 and 1918, the Calonne Trench was effectively the eastern frontier of France.

Near the bottom of one of the hills, a narrow track leads off into the woods. After five hundred yards, it reaches a small clearing and something that looks like a prehistoric burial protected by a glass pyramid. In the spring of 1991, after a search that lasted fourteen years, a local man who knew the woods as a hunter found some cartridge cases from a French revolver and then some cartridges that had never been fired. Scattered all around the glade was the antiquated equipment of a 1914 reserve regiment: a water bottle made in 1877, boots that were older than the men who had worn them, and the bright-red trouser material that was part of the French uniform until 1915. In a rectangular pit he discovered the bones. The lower part of one of the arms still bore the stripes of a lieutenant.

The site is now marked on the Michelin map with the small black triangle that signifies '*curiosité*'. A French flag flies above the grave. Naturally, there is nothing symbolic about the location itself. The author of *Le Grand Meaulnes* had died close to the road that leads south to the centre of France, but a long way from the magical land of his novel. Almost three hundred miles separate the Argonne forest from the foothills of the Massif Central. But with a favourable wind, the bicycling narrator of his novel could easily have covered the distance in half a week, 'plunging into the hollows of the landscape, discovering the distant horizons of the road that part as one approaches and burst into bloom, passing through a village in an instant and gathering it all up in a glance'. The sense of discovery and escape would have made the long journey home seem all too short.

Epilogue

Secrets

SOME TRAVELLERS NOW GO to France in search of places that lie beyond what can be discovered. The volcanic cone of the Gerbier de Jonc attracts a number of new-age travellers whose sense of mystery would have meant more to the earlier inhabitants of the region than the inexplicable activities of the map-makers. The scaly columns of the Gerbier de Jonc lie at the centre of France's Bermuda Triangle. The magnetic rocks are said to disrupt the navigation systems of aeroplanes. More than twenty planes have crashed or disappeared in the area since 1964. Centuries before, strange crosses appeared in the sky and balls of fire were seen dancing over the grasslands. The demons have changed with the times, but their habitat is almost the same.

The Gerbier de Jonc itself has lost some of its mystique and over five hundred feet in height since the summit collapsed in 1821. A travelling market sometimes materializes at its foot to catch the trade from tourists who come to see the farm that claims to be the 'traditional' source of the Loire, the restaurant that claims to be the source of the Loire according to a cadastral survey and the information panels on which it is explained that, since the Gerbier de Jonc is like a sponge on a bed of granite, there is no single source of the Loire.

These days, the most popular portal to other worlds is the Pech de Bugarach in the south-western Corbières. Like the Gerbier de Jonc, Mount Bugarach is a geological personality with a strangely telephotographic presence. Even at a distance, it seems to belong to another landscape. Its Jurassic limestone reef surges out of the sparsely populated hills like the back of a gigantic dinosaur. From the air, it is thought to resemble a question mark. The Paris meridian passes within a few metres of its summit. The Ark and various trans-dimensional vessels are said to have landed on it, though the summit is such a slender plateau that Pierre Méchain, who spent several days in 1795 sheltering from gales in a farmhouse on its slopes, could barely find room for the buttresses that supported his triangulation signal.

Outsiders live among the small local population, searching the caves inside the mountain for traces of Cathar treasure, the Holy Grail, the last earthly home of Jesus Christ and the underground river that flows either to the Mediterranean thirty miles to the east or, according to some, to the centre of the Earth. An old woman in a miniskirt who lives by begging believes herself to be Mary Magdalene. In villages around the mountain – Rennes-les-Bains, Rennes-le-Château and Bugarach itself – new-age pilgrims and harmless neurotics, infatuated with the ghosts of logical reasoning, pore over scraps of mystical intelligence: local legends taken out of context, misconstrued Latin inscriptions, tales of a greedy priest who was rumoured to have struck a deal with Satan. The people who killed Cassini's geometer two hundred and sixty years ago might have been similarly fascinated by the hieroglyphic calculations in his satchel. Graves in the cemetery at Rennes-le-Château have been disturbed and occasionally dynamited by people in search of ancient secrets. The mayor of the village, a retired paratrooper, has learned to live with the seekers of truth. Their money has paid for new public toilets and there are plans to extend the village down the mountainside. Undiscovered secrets are a vital economic asset.

*

AS THE EIGHTEENTH-CENTURY map-makers knew from painful experience, discovering is not the same as knowing. After the meridian expedition, the exotic name of Bugarach appeared on maps, precisely located on the same line as Paris and traversed by triangulation lines like a busy terminus. Yet the region itself was almost completely unknown to the outside world.

For that matter, how much was known about the other *pays* on the same line of longitude? A century after the Cassini expedition placed the first triangulation signal on Mount Bugarach, on the part of the meridian now occupied by the glass pyramid in the courtyard of the Louvre, a dark, decaying *quartier* of medieval slums lay just below the level of the square. Someone who squeezed past the planks of wood that closed off the *quartier* would find a ruined church, some overgrown gardens and boarded-up doors, an arch from a vanished building and wasteground strewn with blocks of stone waiting to be used for the new Louvre. A few figures might appear amongst the wreckage – squatters and beggars, some of the artists and poets who lived in a small colony or the furtive customers of a homosexual brothel. Few Parisians knew anything about the Quartier du Doyenné. 'Our descendants', wrote Balzac in 1846, 'will refuse to believe that such barbarity existed in the heart of Paris, in front of the palace where three dynasties received the elite of France and Europe':

> When one's carriage passes alongside that dead remnant of a *quartier* and one's eye pierces the gloom of the Allée du Doyenné, the soul turns cold. The mind begins to wonder who could possibly live there and what must go on at night, when the alley becomes a death-trap and the vices of Paris, cloaked in darkness, give themselves free rein.

Thirty years later, when the Louvre had been rebuilt and the Doyenné slums were buried under asphalt, a walk north along the meridian would lead past the Comédie Française and the Bibliothèque Nationale, across the new Boulevard Haussmann to the windmills of Montmartre and then, beyond the fortifications and the customs barriers, to a squalid, windswept perimeter of factories and shacks where the city streets ended before the country roads began. This was the so-called 'Zone', where criminals and degenerates were thought to lurk, plotting the overthrow of the government. Long before the *bidonvilles* of modern France, the suburbs had become a dumping ground.

Most large cities had an underclass and a slum belt, but few were so aware of the 'dangerous classes' on the city's horizon and so reluctant to bring them into the fold. Paris, the cultural and commercial nucleus of the nation, was full of memorials to battles, dynasties and regimes, but while some events were commemorated with blinding brilliance, many others were erased from memory. Even now, scholars of French history can be surprised by obscure catastrophes which, like the Verdon Gorges, lay hidden in a landscape that seemed to have been thoroughly mapped. Very few have heard about the rounding up of the gypsies in 1803, when thousands were separated from their children and sent to work in labour camps. Fewer still have heard of the persecution of the cagots.

Certain regions of French history have come to light only to be reburied. There is now a little Cagot Museum in the Pyrenean town of Arreau, but no one who visits the museum would guess that violent discrimination had ever been a problem in south-western France. The exhibition revives an ancient prejudice in order to equate the supposedly diminutive cagots with the 'little people' of the mountains who were exploited by the 'big people' (lords and clerics). In this view of history, the cagots were not a persecuted caste but the cute, hobbit-like inhabitants of the picturesque Pyrenees.

France has often discovered its own past like a traveller forced to cross a remote and dangerous region without a map. Decades passed before the savage extermination of Paris Communards by government troops in 1871 was recognized as historical fact. It took even longer for the state to acknowledge the fact that the Vichy regime had rounded up Jews even more enthusiastically than the Nazis demanded. While memorials to heroic Résistance members killed by 'the Germans' are a common sight all over France, there is nothing in Vichy to remind a visitor of the genocide.

Now and then, a secret comes to light like an old convict emerging from prison long after the demise of the regime that locked him away. On the night of 17 October 1961, thousands of French Algerians, protesting peacefully against the curfew that had been imposed on them, were rounded up by the Paris police. Though records have disappeared and though official figures still disagree with scholarly estimates, it is certain that many Algerians were tortured, maimed and stuffed into dustbins, and that about two hundred were beaten up by policemen and thrown into the Seine, where they drowned, in the tourist heart of Paris. In 2001, despite the furious opposition of right-wing parties and the Paris police, a discreet commemorative plaque was attached, at knee level, to a corner of the Pont Saint-Michel. Four-fifths of the French population are still completely ignorant of the events of 17 October 1961.

As these pages are being written, towns and cities on the meridian are being discovered by the rest of the country. Cars are burning in the ugly, overpopulated Parisian suburbs of Aubervilliers, Saint-Ouen and Saint-Denis. Amiens and Orléans have been placed under a curfew. A law passed during the colonial war in Algeria in 1955 has been invoked to impose a state of emergency. Newspapers report online conversations from the *terrae incognitae* at the end of the Métro line, with explanatory footnotes to render their form of French comprehensible. A Minister of the Interior calls the rioters *racaille* ('scum'). More insulting names are used in private conversations.

The 'scum' are the children and grandchildren of immigrants. The immediate cause of what the authorities call 'riots' is the death of two boys, who accidentally electrocuted themselves while running away from a group of policemen. Everyone in the suburbs knows that non-whites are routinely harassed and humiliated by the police. The French Republic makes no official distinction between ethnic groups, but many of its citizens do, and most employers prefer white faces. Like earlier immigrants from Brittany, Burgundy, the Auvergne, Savoy, Italy and Spain, Africans and Arabs were encouraged to come and help feed and clean the cities. Once, they lived in shanty towns; now, they live in neighbourhoods dehumanized by cars. They have failed to 'integrate' themselves into the French Republic.

Thirty years ago, the French Arabs I knew carried photocopies of their identity cards because the police would ask to see them and then tear them up. At least they had jobs. Now, the unemployed are blamed for the failures of the state. Two hundred and seventy-four towns have been affected by the troubles and the tourist trade is suffering. In the twenty-first century, many parts of France remain to be discovered.

Chronology

1766   Incorporation of Lorraine.

1768   Genoa cedes Corsica to France.

1774   Accession of Louis XVI.

1775   Public coaches permitted to use staging posts.

1786   *8 August* – First recorded ascent of Mont Blanc.

1789   *14 July* – Fall of the Bastille. *August* – abolition of feudal rights and privileges. *November* – national sale of Church property.

1790   *15 January* – France divided into eighty-three *départements*.

1790   *August* – Abbé Grégoire, 'Report on the Necessity and Means of Exterminating Patois and Universalizing the Use of the French Language'.

1791   *June* – Arrest of Louis XVI and Marie-Antoinette. *August* – Jews granted full citizenship; *September* – annexation of Avignon and Comtat Venaissin (later part of Vaucluse).

1792–8   Meridian expedition of Delambre and Méchain.

1793   *21 January* – Execution of Louis XVI. *16 October* – Execution of Marie-Antoinette.

1794   *28 July* – Execution of Robespierre. *September* – Rhône expedition of Boissel de Monville.

1795–99   Directoire.

1799   *9 November (18 Brumaire)* – Coup d'état: Napoleon Bonaparte First Consul.

1801   First census of the population of France.

1804   Coronation of Napoleon I.

1814   First abdication of Napoleon; first Restoration.

1815   *18 June* – Battle of Waterloo.

1815–24   Reign of Louis XVIII.

1824   Accession of Charles X.

1828   *1 October* – Opening of first railway in France, from Saint-Étienne to Andrézieux (opened to passengers 1832; horses replaced by steam, 1844).

1830   *June* – Capture of Algiers. July Revolution. Abdication of Charles X. Coronation of Louis-Philippe.

1832   *April to May* – Rebellion in the Vendée led by the Duchesse de Berry.

1833   *June* – Guizot's education law: each *commune* of five hundred inhabitants or more to maintain an elementary school for boys (girls from 1836).

1834–52   Prosper Mérimée tours France as Inspector General of Historic Monuments.

1836   The state assumes responsibility for upkeep of minor roads (*chemins vicinaux*).

1841   First complete geological map of France. *June to September* – tax riots.

1848   February Revolution. Universal male suffrage. *June* – repression of popular revolt.

1851   *2 December* – Coup d'état of Louis-Napoléon Bonaparte (Emperor Napoleon III, 1852–70).

1852   Start of pébrine epidemic (disease of silkworms).

1856   Mediterranean joined to Atlantic by the Canal Latéral à la Garonne.

1857–   Forestation of 2.5 million acres of the Landes.

1858   *February to July* – Virgin Mary appears to Bernadette Soubirous at Lourdes.

1860   Savoy and Nice become part of France.

1863   Start of phylloxera epidemic (disease of vines).

1870   *September* – Defeat of France by Prussia at Sedan; Siege of Paris; France loses Alsace and Lorraine. Ligue du Midi founded in Marseille. Proclamation of the Third Republic.

1871   Paris Commune elected (March) and defeated by government troops (May).

1873   Franco-Provençal language identified by G.-I. Ascoli.

1874   Club Alpin Français founded.

1879   Government funding of local railways and canals (Freycinet Plan): 696 stations or halts in 1854; 4,801 in 1885 (6,516 in 2006).

1882   Ethnographic Museum opens at the Palais du Trocadéro in Paris.

1882   *April* – Law for the Restoration of Mountain Terrains.

Chronology

1881–82	Free, compulsory, secular education for boys and girls from six to thirteen (Jules Ferry laws).
1888–1913	Underground explorations of Édouard-Alfred Martel.
1889	Universal Exhibition and inauguration of Eiffel Tower.
1893	*August* – Massacre of Italian immigrant workers at Aigues-Mortes.
1898	*13 January – 'J'Accuse!'*: Zola's letter on the Dreyfus Affair.
1900	*19 July* – Opening of first Métro line in Paris.
1901–4	Anticlerical measures (governments of René Waldeck-Rousseau and Émile Combes).
1903	*1–19 July* – First Tour de France bicycle race (six stages, 1,518 miles).
1904	*8 April* – 'Entente Cordiale' agreements between France and Britain.
1905	*August* – Exploration of Gorges du Verdon.
1909	*April* – Beatification of Jeanne d'Arc.
1911	French protectorate in Morocco.
1914	*1 August* – France orders general mobilization.
1918	*11 November* – Armistice.

Notes

1. THE UNDISCOVERED CONTINENT

5 'out of range of a rifle': Lanoye, 302.

5 'scarcely any accommodation': Murray, 392.

5 hacked to death: Mazon (1878), 271; Reclus (1886), 60; Sand (1860), 228.

6 deliverance from Satan: Devlin, 39–41.

6 considered themselves 'French': 'France' commonly referred to the province of Île-de-France: e.g. Duchesne (1775), 114; Wright, 14.

6 'the locals are no more familiar': Sand (1860), 242 n. 20.

7 'joined and united': Varennes, 2.

8 '*complete isolation*': Stendhal, 190. Rousselan is now Rousseland, between Francheville and Saint-Igny on the N151.

8 La Charité-sur-Loire: Stendhal, 11–12.

8 Paris–Toulouse road: Balzac, IV, 361.

8 internal exile: Cobb (1970), 167.

8 the din of tiny places: e.g. Barker (1893), 27 and 122.

9 Brande region: Sand (1872), 143.

9 'a desolate country': Grandsire (1863), 3.

9 hawthorn bushes: Égron (1831), 305.

9 'Never leave me alone': 'La Maison du berger', v. 279.

10 'dominated by the forces of nature': J. Duval, 198.

10 phantom districts: Assemblée Nationale, IX, 745.

10 wine-merchants: Cavaillès, 16.

10 Julius Caesar: *Gallic War*, VII, 1–4.

11 Rabaut from Nîmes: Peyrat, II, 427; also Rouquette, 4.

11 fleeing the White Terror: Cobb (1970), 337.

11 'capitaines de Bauzon': Riou, in Tilloy, 221.

11 Victor de l'Aveyron: Itard.

11 'wild girl' of Issaux: Buffault, 343.

11 wild man of Iraty: Folin, 73; Russell, 58. Another Pyrenean 'wild girl' was found near Andorra in 1839.

11 Louis Mandrin: Duclos.

12 'enlarged Paris Basin': Barral.

12 Ancien Régime: on this old term: C. Jones, xx.

12 censuses are unavailable: Cavaillès, 277; Foville (1890), 297–98.

12 Young was amazed: Young, 106, 30, 17 and 16.

13 A '*commune*' is not a village: Tombs, 233.

13 recruits from the Dordogne: Weber, 43.

13 towns were half-dissolved: e.g. Merriman, 199 (Perpignan).

14 'no interior towns in France': Pinkney, 142.

14 'those Breton forests': *Quatrevingt-treize*, III, I, 2–3 (Molac misnamed 'Meulac').

15 'no one . . . has ever gone to Brittany': Cambry (1798), I, 53.

15 On a sunny day: Peuchet and Chanlaire, 'Vendée', 16.

15 Openings in the hedgerow: Dumas (1863–84), VII, 97–98. On military consequences: Lasserre, 24.

17 'wild animals': La Bruyère, *Les Caractères*, 'De l'Homme', no. 128.

2. THE TRIBES OF FRANCE, I

19 Goust: Dix, 169–77; also Anon. (1828) and (1840), 206–07; *MP*, 1878, pp. 377–8; Perret (1882), 390–91; and information supplied by Nathalie Barou.

20 high Alpine villages: Fontaine, 17.

20 'Each valley': Chevalier (1837), 627.

21 Chalosse region: *MP*, 1864, 273; on a 'demarcation line' (soil, wine, dress and language) between Poitiers and Châtellerault: Creuzé-Latouche, 24–5.

21 Nitry and Sacy: Restif, 50–51.

22 'no one took her side': Restif, 108.

22 Polletais or Poltese: Conty (1889), 127; Marlin, I, 300; *MP*, 1844, p. 223–4; Turner, I, 9.

22 Le Portel: Lagneau (1866), 634–5; Smollett, letter 4.

22 'floating islands': Gazier, 1879, 54; Hirzel, 325; Lagneau (1861), 377; Lavallée, 'Pas-de-Calais', IV, 22.

22 tribes on the borders of Brittany: Roujou (1874), 252–55.

22 Cannes and Saint-Tropez: Beylet.
23 'some out-of-the-way villages': Topinard (1880), 33.
24 'We had not the slightest notion': Guillaumin, 59.
24 'The people of Périgord': Marlin, II, 137.
24 'The *Lyonnais* acts high and mighty': Marlin, II, 62. Other moral maps: Égron (1830), 11–12; Stendhal, 50–51.
25 Semitic tribes . . . Tibet: Biélawski, 96; Charencey; Girard de Rialle, 185; A. Joanne, *Morbihan* (1888), 28; Mahé de La Bourdonnais.
25 'Franchiman' and 'Franciot': Aufauvre, 153; Boissier de Sauvages, v.
26 games of pelota: Lunemann, 54–5.
26 'France ought not to exist': Le Bras and Todd, 23; Perrot, 127 .
26 zones of ugliness and beauty: Marlin, II, 81 and 97; I, 66; IV, 117; II, 157; IV, 37.
27 'how many pretty women': Marlin, II, 280.
27 priest of Montclar: Barker (1893), 214.
28 'a very fat file' (Lot): Weber, 57.
28 champions were appointed: e.g. Lachamp-Raphaël: Du Boys, 241.
28 Lavignac, Flavignac: Corbin (1994), 58.
28 *pays*: e.g. Planhol, 159–60; Reclus (1886), 454–70.
29 '246 different kinds': *Newsweek*, 1 October 1962.
29 Secret army reports: Weber, 105.
30 heirlooms to the metal: Corbin (1994), 86.
30 recruiting sergeants: Salaberry, 17.
30 dispelled storms: *Feuille villageoise*, 1792–93, 247–8.
30 electrocuted at the end of a bell-rope: Arago (1851); also *MP*, 1888, p. 195.
30 summoned angels: Corbin (1994), 102.
30 countless complaints: Corbin (1994), 99 and 300.
30 *communes* in . . . Morbihan: Augustins.
31 As late as 1886: Levasseur, I, 342.
31 cagot exogamy, 1700–59: Marie Kita Tambourin, in Paronnaud; also Planhol, 207.
32 sophisticated village institutions: Baker; P. Jones (2003), 50–54.
32 Salency: Marlin, II, 346–50.
32 Hoedic and Houat: Bonnemère, II, 445; Laville; Letourneau.
32 La Bresse: N. Richard, 224.
33 Pignou clan: Bonnemère, II, 341–6; Hirzel, 326–7 and 370–84; A. Legoyt, in *Les Français, Province*, II, 209–11.
33 declared independence: P. Jones (1988), 171.
33 measures varied: e.g. Burguburu; Fodéré, I, xxiii; Peuchet and Chanlaire, *passim*; Weber, 30–32.

33 'using Roman numerals': Peuchet, 'Isère', 43.
34 'Chizerot' tribe: Dumont (1894), 444.
34 three meetings: Soulet, in Tilloy, 239.
34 Mandeure thieves: Capt. G. . . .
34 absence of crime . . .: e.g. Pérégrin, 65.
35 illegitimate children: Sussman, 21.
35 'insulting vegetable bombardments': M. Segalen, 49–51.
35 a 'witch' was burned to death: Devlin, 363. Another witch was burned at Tarbes in 1862 (Dix, 326), and a witch's possessions at Rodez, *c.* 1830 (Maurin).
35 French imperial justice: e.g. Corbin (1990).

3. THE TRIBES OF FRANCE, II

36 villages' nicknames: Collet; Labourasse, 198–224.
36 'Faubourg de Rome': Balzac, IV, 359.
38 Foratin people: F. Pyat, in *Les Français, Province*, II, 330; Lagneau (1861), 394–5; Luçay, 70–71; Reclus (1886), 403; Rolland de Denus, 72; Wailly, 330–31.
38 Gavaches or Marotins: Lagarenne, 135; Lagneau (1861), 404; Lagneau (1876); Larousse ('Gavache').
38 confused with 'the English': Barker (1893), 195 and 212.
38 'good old Caesar': Vitu.
38 people of Sens . . . house of Savoy: Marlin, I, 37; Mortillet, in *BSAP* (1865), 200.
39 bards and Druids: Sébillot (1882), I, 27.
39 Colliberts: A. Hugo; Lagardelle; Lagneau (1861), 347 and 365; Saint-Lager, 86.
39 'in the plain': Brune, 136.
39 'Huttiers': Brune, 129–37; cf. Cavoleau.
39 fleet of Marais poitevin: Rabot, 382.
40 Pierre the Collibert: Massé-Isidore, 276–90; also Arnauld; Baugier.
43 cagots (general): Dally; Descazeaux; Keane; Lagneau (1861), 401–4; Magitot; F. Michel; Monlezun, 242; Rochas.
43 dwarfish figure: The little figure carved on the font at Saint-Savin (Hautes-Pyrénées), often said to be a cagot, is a monk.
44 hand was sliced off: Lande, 434.
44 a cagot from Moumour: Descazeaux, 49.
44 curé of Lurbe: F. Michel, I, 133–4.

44 prejudices and persecutions came and went: In the Pyrenees: Anon. (1835), 78; Bilbrough, 99; Bonnecaze, 80; Costello, II, 260–310; C. P. V.; Dix, 243–4; Domairon, XXXIII (1790), 349; Gaskell; H. L.; Haristoy; J. B. J., 286; A. Joanne (1868), lii; Lagneau, in *Dictionnaire encyclopédique*, XI (1870), 534–57; Lande, 444–6; Lunemann, 47; Ramond; Richard and Lheureux, 78; Saint-Lager, 70; F. Michel; Weld (1859), 99. In Brittany: Calvez; Chéruel ('Cagots'); Constantine, 85–119; A. de Courcy, in *Les Français, Province*, III, 33; Lallemand, 133–4; Lande, 446–47; F. Michel, I, 62; Plumptre, III, 232–3; Vallin, 84. Around Bordeaux: Zintzerling, 227–8.

44 'cursed races': F. Michel.

44 cagot mayor . . . Aramits: F. Michel, I, 126–30.

44 at Dognen and Castetbon: F. Michel, I, 136.

44 baker at Hennebont: F. Michel, I, 170; Rolland de Denus, 117.

44 teacher in Salies-de-Béarn: Descazeaux, 67.

45 descendants of Cathars: Cathars: Lagneau (1861), 402; Lande, 438; Le Bas ('Cagot'); *MP*, 1841, p. 295; Perret (1881), 66; Saint-Lager, 71.

45 first Christian converts: Bonnecaze, 79–80; Lande, 436; F. Michel, I, 34; Walckenaer, 'Sur les Vaudois', 330–34.

45 confused with lepers: Descazeaux, 19; Lajard; Lande, 447; cf. Fay.

45 as many Bretons believed: Cambry (1798), III, 146–7.

46 '*A baig dounc la Cagoutaille!*': F. Michel, II, 158.

46 Compostela theory: Descazeaux; Loubès; Paronnaud.

46 perceived as a threat: e.g. Perdiguier (1863).

46 A group of cagots in Toulouse: Saint-Lager, 84.

47 '*Jentetan den ederrena*': F. Michel, II, 150–1; also Webster (1877), 263–4.

48 still tend to intermarry: Marie Kita Tambourin, in Paronnaud.

48 'They have been piled up here': Marlin, I, 47–8.

49 'Saracen': Lagneau (1861), 382–6; Lagneau (1868), 170–73; etc.

49 swore by Allah: Dumont (1894), 445.

49 Val d'Ajol clans: Anon. (1867), 347; *BSAP*, 1874, 704–5; Dorveaux; Hirzel, 389–91; Lévêque.

4. O ÒC Sí BAI YA WIN OUI OYI AWÈ JO JA OUA

50 Abbé Grégoire: Certeau et al. Replies to his questionnaire in Gazier.

51 'flying-buttresses of despotism': Lavallée, 'Ille-et-Vilaine', 35.

51 river Nizonne: Gazier, 1877, 215.

51 Even plants and stars: Gazier, 1878, 244–5.

51 landowner from Montauban: Certeau et al., 261.

51 'only by the Supreme Being': Gazier, 1877, 233.

52 Salins-les-Bains: Gazier, 1878, 256.

52 Lyon was a hive: Certeau et al., 221.

53 later linguistic purges: Vigier, 194–5.

53 forced to use interpreters: Bourguet, 135–8; Romieu, in Williams, 476; Savant.

55 'the language is slow': Larousse, 'Dauphinois'; also X. Roux, 250.

56 manuals for provincials: Anon. (1827), p. ix; Brun; Dhauteville; Gabrielli, 4–5; J.-F. Michel; Molard; Pomier; Sigart, 6. Cf. Callet, 6; Jaubert; Mège, 18.

56 terms such as '*affender*': Larousse ('Picard'); Burgaud Des Marets ('Rochelais').

57 'I was never able': Albert, curé de Seynes: in Certeau et al., 256.

57 'By the time I reached Lyon': La Fontaine et al., 102–3.

60 Oc–Oïl frontier: Gilliéron and Edmont; Lamouche; Plazanet; Terracher, I, 28–31, 62 and 241.

60 'Allobroge': Perdiguier (1854), 381.

61 whistling languages: Arripe (Aas); *BSAP*, 1892, 15–22; *MP*, 1892, 18–19.

61 '*oui*' from Carnac to Erdeven: Lepelletier, 530.

61 fathers ten miles apart: Dempster, 37.

61 As the sun travelled: Beauquier, 232.

62 sub-dialects . . . in a single family: e.g. Dauzat, 288; Sarrieu, 389.

63 'Friends of the Constitution': Gazier, 1874, 426.

63 'Gascon noir': term noted by Arnaudin, 8.

63 'all Gascons understand': Gazier, 1877, 238; on Lorraine dialects: Adam, xliii.

63 '*Maître d'école!*': Boiraud, 105–6; Gazier, 1878, 11; Raverat, 205.

63 '*francimander*': Gazier, 1877, 215; Weber, 98–9.

64 a wider range: Seguin de Pazzis, 48; Gabrielli, 7; Marlin, I, 410–11.

64 farmer . . . from Tréguier: Gazier, 1879, 184–5.

64 language-learning programmes: Peuchet, 'Lys', 21; 'Meurte', 28. On persistence of Flemish: Hurlbert, 332.

65 'French leaves no more trace': www.gwalarn.org/brezhoneg/istor/gregoire.html; see also Raison-Jourde (1976), 357 (Cantal); Stendhal, 294 (Brittany).

65 In the Cerdagne: Weber, 306; also Jamerey-Duval, 118, on his mock-Parisian French.

65 Cellefrouin: Rousselot, 223.

65 Breton soldiers: J. Ian Press, in Parry, 217.

66 'no place for regional languages': Rosalind Temple, in Parry, 194.

67 North of the line, roofs: Brunhes, 308–10; Duby, III, 304.

67 use of the *araire*: Planté.

67 eyes and hair darker: Topinard (1891), 82.

67 frontier zone: Specklin; also Vidal de La Blache, II.

68 carve . . . into *départements*: Assemblée Nationale, especially IX, 698–748; XI, 119–268. Hesseln's proposal to divide France into 9 perfect squares, subdivided into 9 counties, 81 districts and 729 territories, was fortunately abandoned: Dussieux, 176–7; Planhol, 281.

68 to reach the . . . centre in a day: Assemblée Nationale, IX, 744 (11 Nov. 1789).

69 'the most beautiful city in the world': Assemblée Nationale, XI, 122 (8 Jan. 1790).

69 'languages predating Caesar's conquest': Assemblée Nationale, XI, 185 (Saint-Malo); 170 (Basque provinces and Béarn).

69 languages learned from nurses: e.g. Bernhardt, 2; Sand (1844), 53.

5. LIVING IN FRANCE, I

71 stench-laden fug: Blanchard, 32 (Queyras).

72 as soon as they became ill: Hufton, 68; Weber, 170–76.

72 'They wish only for death': É. Chevallier, 77.

72 old people: see Gutton; McPhee (1992), 237.

72 'I wish we knew how long': Guillaumin, 93–4.

72 the soul . . . washed itself: Carrier, 403; Gazier, 1879, 70.

72 'Happy as a corpse': Weber, 14.

73 blessing to the natives: R. Bernard, 152–3; Moore, I, 219; Saussure, II, 488.

73 witch revived the corpse: Devlin, 52; Vuillier, 532.

75 secular holidays: Hazareesingh, *Saint-Napoleon*.

75 'as idle as marmots': Fabre, 7.

75 mountain rodent: Ladoucette (1833), 132; Saussure, II, 153–4.

75 'inhabitants re-emerge in spring': Blanchard, 32.

75 'something like fear': Sand (1856), VIII, 164.

76 'After making the necessary repairs': Thuillier (1977), 206; also Legrand d'Aussy, 280–81.

76 diary of Jules Renard: 16 Jan. 1889 and 24 Dec. 1908.

76 trudged and dawdled: Renard, 6 Mar. 1894; Restif, 192.
76 'dumb idleness': Lavallée, 'Rhin-et-Moselle', 8; Peuchet, 'Pas-de-Calais', 15.
77 'For the remaining months': T. Delord, in *Les Français, Province*, II, 61.
77 'The vital air': Peuchet, 'Pas-de-Calais', 37.
78 'unhygienic' cellars: Audiganne, I, 28–9.
78 son of a Pyrenean peasant: Fabre, 7.
79 'Life and movement': *Eugénie Grandet*: Balzac, III, 1027.
81 'This community is situated': *Cahiers . . . de Cahors*.
81 'On one side': *Cahiers de . . . Rozel*, ed. C. Leroy.
81 '*If only the King knew!*': *Cahiers . . . de Cahors*.
82 parish of Saint-Forget: *Cahier . . . de Saint-Forget* (Yvelines), Service Éducatif des Archives départementales.
82 shift the tax burden: É. Chevallier, 79; e.g. Rousseau's *Confessions*, I, 4.
82 suspiciously repetitive: see P. Jones (1988), 58–67.
83 'We have not yet seen': *Cahiers . . . de Cahors*.
83 poultry feathers: Taine (1879), II, 205.
83 'there is scarce a Village': Breval, 57.
83 layer of clay: Anon., 'Nouvelles' (1840), 374.
84 spontaneous combustion: Yvart, 251–3.
84 Pompey: *Cahier de Doléances*.
84 natural disasters: Braudel, III, 24.
84 forty years after a hailstorm: Guillaumin, 179.
84 almost half the population: Hufton, 23–4.
84 'The people are like a man': Taine (1879), II, 213.
85 'they were convinced': Déguignet, 46 (tr. L. Asher).
87 fairy tales: Darnton, 33–4.
87 'treated as a servant': Martin and Martenot, 495.
87 photograph albums: Weber, 175 n. (quoting P. and M. C. Bourdieu).
87 *tours d'abandon*: Perrot, 144.
87 'angel-makers': Hufton, 327; Perrot, 601.
88 infant overflow: Hufton, 345–6.

6. LIVING IN FRANCE, II

89 'crooked, dirty', etc.: Young, 26, 185, 173 and 63, 60, 26, 33.
89 'superb consolation': Young, 41.
90 'To Combourg': Young, 99.
90 'This M. de Chateaubriand': Chateaubriand, I, 12, 4.

91 how to make a proper haystack: Young, 149.
91 'Chestnut Belt': Braudel, III, 117; Demolins, 79–85 and 428; Durand, 137; Fel; Peuchet, 'Corrèze', 8–9; Taine (1858), 130.
91 'knowing my luck': Haillant, 18, 16 and 17; Dejardin, 287; Weber, 19; Weber, 345n.
92 at Varennes: F. de Fontanges; Valori.
93 political basis of the union: e.g. Gildea, in Crook, 158–62 (on Ligue du Midi and separatism).
93 In 1841, a census: Ploux (1999).
93 When he crossed the country: Fabry; Waldburg-Truchsess.
93 'he'll never be able to do anything': Waldburg-Truchsess, 37–8.
94 three zones: Braudel, III, 127.
95 'every door vomiting out its hogs': Young, 156.
95 'trifling burthens': Young, 90.
96 risk her livelihood: e.g. Lehning, 87–8.
96 at Ry: Price, 151.
97 supply zone of cities: Cobb (1970), 258–9.
97 'destroyed all its bridges': Deferrière, 435 (report by Dupin, Préfet of Deux-Sèvres).
97 the spike of a Prussian helmet: Du Camp. 603.
98 'The man of the fields knows nothing': Jouanne.
98 'amuses the sheep': Carlier, I, 115.
99 Saint-Étienne-d'Orthe: Artigues, 126.
99 mole catchers: Capus.
99 *rebilhous* . . . 'cinderellas', etc.: Weber, 225.
99 judge at Rennes: Hufton, 210–11.
99 'Idle beggar': Déguignet, 70; Hufton, 111.
99 anthropologists of Paris: Privat d'Anglemont, chs 1, 4, 6 and 8.
100 history teacher: Monteil, II, 89–90, 105, 111–14, 136, 177, 209 and 273.
101 Friday was the day: Labourasse, 180.
101 born with the heads of fish: Sébillot (1886), 223.
101 'Lundi et mardi, fête': Sébillot (1886), 219.
102 military recruitment: Aron et al.; Levasseur, I, 385–7.
103 'the face of an old monkey': Pinkney, 36.
103 women . . . the lion's share: e.g. Choules, 168; Greeley, 160; Le Bras and Todd, 179; Morris, 16; Noah, 210 and 224; Perrin-Dulac, I, 207–8; Young, 13.
104 kept house ('badly'): Peuchet, 'Orne', 35.
104 nimble spirits: Bérenger-Féraud, I, 2–5.
104 All along the Atlantic: e.g. at La Teste: Saint-Amans (1812), 196–8.

104 In the Auvergne: Legrand d'Aussy, 284.

104 At Granville: Marlin, I, 215–16.

104 yoked to asses: Peuchet, 'Hautes-Alpes', 18 and 20.

104 beasts of burden: Peuchet, 'Orne', 35.

104 woman born in the Velay: Perrot, 150 and 189.

105 appearance of a girl: Weber, 172–3.

105 'Oats to goats': Haillant, 10.

105 'Marry your daughter far away': Pintard, 109.

105 'A dead wife, a living horse': Strumingher, 136.

105 'A man has but two good days': M. Segalen, 171.

105 'At the well . . . woman comes back . . .': M. Segalen, 152.

106 'No house was ever shamed': M. Segalen, 26.

106 Misinterpretations: Hufton, 38–41; M. Segalen, 173–80.

106 Courting couples: Bejarry; Gennep, I, 264; M. Segalen, 22–3.

106 Vendée peasant: M. Segalen, 23.

106 perpetrated by immigrants: M. Segalen.

107 a woman who walked behind her husband: Hélias, 279.

107 *'laka ar c'hoz'*: Déguignet, 35–6 (tr. L. Asher).

108 questioned . . . by magistrate: Hufton, 321.

108 her wedding night: Sand (1846).

108 'Women give birth after three months': Rolland de Denus, 215.

109 Night Washerwomen: Sébillot (1882), I, 248; Sand (1888), 50.

109 If one of her own babies: Sonnini, 188–9.

109 'A sad country', etc.: Young, 156.

110 Young hears the news: Young, 162.

7. FAIRIES, VIRGINS, GODS AND PRIESTS

112 'olive-planted and fig-bearing': Strabo, *Geography*, IV, 1, 2.

113 shrine at Bétharram: Chausenque, I, 224; J. B. J., 264.

113 cults of the Virgin: Laboulinière, 318; Lawlor, xvi.

114 'The entrance to these grottos': Sand (1856), VIII, 139–40.

114 local chemist: J. B. J., 140–41.

114 its rival, Argelès: Harris, 25.

114 saw a tiny figure: Bernardette's account in Harris, 72.

115 As usual when a Virgin appeared: Joudou, 24.

115 local beauties: Harris, 73.

115 forest fairies: Harris, 77–9; Sahlins, 43–5.

115 Forest Code of 1827: Chevalier (1956), 724–6.

115 'War of the Demoiselles': Sahlins.

116 on common land: Harris, 31.
116 Properties on the road: Harlé, 146–50.
117 'It's a stroke of good luck': Blackburn (1881), 92.
117 places named after a saint: Planhol, 143.
117 Saint-Martin: J.-M. Couderc.
117 Saint-Malo–Geneva line: A. d'Angeville, xxvii; Aron et al.; Dupin, 39; Julia; Nora.
119 Saint Agathe: Sébillot (1882), I, 334.
120 Catholic Reformation: Ralph Gibson, 19.
120 'to give the cross the benefit': Piette and Sacaze, 237.
120 'nail-stone': Marlin, II, 365; IV, 364.
121 two oaks: Bérenger-Féraud, I, 523–4.
121 sharpening-stone: L. Duval.
122 vandalized by passing strangers: e.g. Souvestre, 224–5.
122 Col de Peyresourde stones: Piette and Sacaze; also Sébillot (1882), I, 48–52.
123 'The spirit who inhabits the stone': Piette and Sacaze, 240–1.
124 'Old fool!': Devlin, 7; Ralph Gibson, 144.
124 people of Six-Fours: Bérenger-Féraud, II, 518.
125 diocesan guide: http://catholique-lepuy.cef.fr/pelerinages/
125 Notre-Dame de Héas: Dusaulx, II, 48–53; Saint-Amans (1789), 127–52.
125 Les Andelys pilgrimage: Boué de Villiers.
126 people of Lourdes went somewhere else: Blackburn (1881), 92.
126 pilgrimages expanded . . . areas of trade: e.g. Delvincourt, 4; Depping (1813), 53–4.
126 pilgrimage to Sainte-Baume: Bérenger-Féraud, II, chap. 4.
126 Mont-Saint-Michel: Nerval, II, 957–8 (paraphrase of *Monsieur Nicolas*).
127 very rare breed: Weber, 357.
127 If he refused to ring: Tackett (1977), 155.
127 the curé of . . . Burgnac: Ralph Gibson, 136.
127 walking about during mass: Ralph Gibson, 19.
127 The curé of Ars: Weber, 369.
128 'Sorcerers and sorceresses': Gazier (1876), 31.
128 oath declaring their loyalty: Tackett (1986), 52–4.
128 chaplain at Ribiers: Tackett (1977), 213.
129 Protestant plot: Tackett (1986), 205–19.
129 'showing mutual affection': Certeau et al., 211.
129 converted to Protestantism: Ralph Gibson, 237; P. Jones (1985), 268.

130 saints were still being created: Sébillot (1882), I, 330–33; Largillière, 126–31.

130 Merlin the Enchanter: For example, a prayer left by the stones, unfolded, early on Easter Day 2006, read, 'Dear Merlin, You have made me happy. Please give me some magic spells so I can make others happy too.'

131 'I didn't come here for *him*': Devlin, 8.

131 The Devil: e.g. Bonnecaze, 72–3; Sébillot (1882), I, 177.

131 sidekick Saint Peter: Bladé, 31; Sébillot (1882), I, 310.

131 weird beings: e.g. Agullana, 110; Bladé, 17; Sand (1888), 75; Sébillot (1882), I, 148.

132 Christianity came to an end: Sébillot (1882), I, 79.

132 'There are two "dear Lords"': Ralph Gibson, 137.

132 'Saint Sourdeau', etc.: Chesnel, 128 (Plouradou); Devlin, 10 (Sourdeau); Boué de Villiers, 46–9.

132 new Saint Aygulf: Bérenger-Féraud, III, 515.

133 Saint Greluchon: S. Bonnard; Weber, 348. Also Sand (1866), 17.

133 'You were a just man': Renan, 17.

133 'A blacksmith came too': Renan, 58.

133 If the saint refused: Weber, 347; Bérenger-Féraud, I, 461 and 452–3.

134 took the side of authoritarian regimes: Ralph Gibson, 271.

135 Hedgehogs: Sébillot (1882), II, 97.

135 slice a living white dove: Pineau, 177.

135 magic luminescent herb: Déguignet, 79.

135 list of every folk remedy: Loux and Richard.

136 scraping the mouth: Déguignet, 83.

136 sessions in the smithy: e.g. Vuillier, 511–18.

136 road-mender at Nasbinals: Ardouin-Dumazet (1904); also Mazon (1882), 390.

136 Clermont d'Excideuil: Ralph Gibson, 138.

136 throwing balls of wool: Peuchet, 'Haute-Vienne', 43; Stendhal, 309 (Uzerche).

8. Migrants and Commuters

138 Madrid to Paris: Blanqui, 237–8.

139 'like Robinson Crusoe on his island': Stendhal, 12.

139 art critic Auguste Jal: Jal (1836), I, 35–8.

140 Le Havre heard about the fall: Lefebvre, 79.

140 local tailor: Lefebvre, 82.

140 arrest of the royal family: Braudel, III, 252; Julia and Milo, 470; Ploux (2003), 30.

141 Waterloo: Dumas (1863–84), II, 83–5.

141 'Do not ask . . .': Balzac, X, 1073 (*Les Marana*); see also Ploux (2003), 33 (3.5 hours to Bicêtre).

141 victory at Cenabum: Anon. (1848); Caesar, *Gallic War*, VII, 1; also VI, 3; Cestre. Cf. aerial telegraph: Soulange, 137.

142 Maps of the Great Fear: Lefebvre, 198–9.

142 Massif Central . . . bypassed: Boudin, 348–52; Planhol, 287 and 289; Weld (1850), 57.

143 rumours died out: Lefebvre, 201.

143 suspected a well-organized plot: Hazareesingh, *Legend*, 51.

143 Charlieu: Lefebvre, 86–7.

143 one-fifth of the total surface: Peuchet, 'Finistère', 11; etc.; Assemblée Nationale, II, 7.

144 Beauvais to Amiens: Goubert, 89; also Malaucène: Saurel, I, 57–60.

144 fragile capillaries: Braudel, III, 228–32; Peuchet, 'Calvados', 10.

144 'My road lay through': Stevenson (1879), 56.

144 Voie Regordane: Moch, 49–50. The name may be related to the Gaulish *rigo*, 'king'.

145 Stevenson could have bought: Moch, quoting R. Thinthoin, 49–50.

145 'The little green and stony cattle-tracks': Stevenson (1879), 38.

145 Brownian motion: Planhol, 186–7.

146 south and east of the line: Hufton, 72; Planhol, 242 and 285–9.

146 '*Crabas amont, filhas aval*': Moch, 68.

146 From the . . . Cantal: Weber, 279; Wirth.

146 army handbook: État-major de l'armée de terre, 118.

146 processions of young girls: Dureau de la Malle, 250; also Gildea, 10.

147 *loues* or *louées*: N. Parfait, in *Les Français, Province*, II, 104–5; Masson de Saint-Amand, 129.

147 bands of little boys: Campenon, 64–7; Drohojowska, 128–30; Hufton, 98; Ladoucette, *Histoire*; Peuchet, 'Jura', 14.

148 In Paris, they found their way: A. Frémy, in *Les Français*, I, 145–52, and G. d'Alcy, *ibid.*, *Province*, III, 135; Gaillard; George; Drohojowska, 128–30, 131–3; Perrot, 231; Raison-Jourde (1976 and 1980); Tombs, 238; Weber, 282.

149 pedlars' baskets: Babeau (1883), 80–81; http://montlhery.com/colporteur.htm (May 2002); also Fontaine, 107; Weber, 280.

150 botanizing tourists: Ferrand (1903), 109.

150 Bearnese pedlars in Spain: Hufton, 89.

150 pretend to be pilgrims: Babeau (1894), II, 103; Hufton, 125; cf. Manier, 35.

150 Deceit . . . a speciality: Fontaine, 107; Hufton, 83–4; P. Roux, 211.

151 Smuggling . . . Nice: Pachoud, XLIII, 312.

151 Catalans and Roussillonnais: Hufton, 298–300.

151 pretending to be pregnant: McPhee (1992), 23.

151 More than twelve thousand: Hufton, 291.

152 'Eggs, bacon, poultry': Pinkney, 33.

153 '*maisons de lait*': Martin and Martenot, 489–90.

153 closer ties with Spain: Duroux; P. Girardin, 447; also A. Legoyt, in *Les Français, Province*, II, 214; Moch; Raison-Jourde (1976), 187–8.

153 'improving an uncultivated corner': Balzac, IX, 407.

154 'And so, dear friend': Fontaine, 26.

154 oil-, soap- and perfume factories: Audiganne, II, 242–3.

154 law on child labour (1840): e.g. Simon, 50; Bouvier, 56; A. Frémy, in *Les Français, Province*, I.

154 *articles de Paris*: Larousse, VIII, 726.

155 'He stopped in a little square': Balzac, IV, 29–30.

156 insulated from the lands: Weber, 43.

156 Bureau of Wet-Nurses: Kock, I, 7–16; Sussman.

157 Saint-Oradoux: Clément, 7.

157 starving cobblers: Hufton, 97.

157 Poor regions like the Vercors: Planhol, 390–91.

157 apprentice's Tour de France: Arnaud; Perdiguier (1854 and 1863); also Ménétra; Planhol, 288–89.

158 'Route of the Tour de France': Arnaud, 12–16.

159 laws and regulations: Malepeyre.

159 three out of every four Compagnons: Arnaud, 295.

160 the gruelling journey: Nadaud, 24–39; Tindall. Other details from Cavaillès, 161; Girault de Saint-Fargeau; Grandsire (1863); L. D. M.; Murray; Orlov, I, 24; Peuchet, 'Creuse', 23; Raison-Jourde (1976), 84–5; Sand (1844), 45; Sand (1856), VIII, 6.

161 peasant . . . to Poitiers: Gazier, 1879, 70.

162 *coucous*: Duckett, XVII, 405; Larousse, V, 290.

162 'Encore un pour Sceaux!': Jubinal, 317.

INTERLUDE

165 smuggler dogs of Péronne: Lavallée, V, 'Somme', 23–4; cf. V. Gaillard, in *Les Français, Province*, II, 58. The dogs were 'bergers picards', not directly related to the later breed of that name.

167 nail-makers' dogs: Barberet, IV, 190; Rayeur (illust.); Barker (1893), 113–14; also in Jura: Lequinio, I, 275–6.

167 dog-carts: *MP*, 1908, p. 300; 1911, p. 167.

168 'I celebrate those calamitous canines': 'Les Bons chiens', Baudelaire (1975–76), I, 361.

168 Cows and horses lived next door: e.g. Huet de Coëtlizan, 409.

168 'a very motley and promiscuous set': Alison, II, 22; also Dumont (1890), 426.

168 fed until they died: Perrot, 529.

169 *kiauler, tioler*: Rolland de Denus, 327 and 421; Sand (1846); Weber, 430–31.

169 animals conversed with humans: e.g. Webster (1901), 103.

169 The hunter would wrap himself: Dusaulx, II, 186–7; also Veryard, 111.

169 village school for bears: www.midi-pyrenees.biz/mp/ariege/ariege erce.htm

170 'I have nothing': Montaran, 237–8.

170 'the purgatory of men': Audiganne, II, 100–01.

170 dogs of Brittany and Maine: Hufton, 291–2.

171 Paris's dog markets: Janin, 235–6.

171 percheron horses: Dumas (1847), 28.

171 Cossack horses: Peake ('A Trip to Versailles').

171 'thirty-league beasts': Anon. (1846), 47.

171 being kind to animals: e.g. Fréville.

171 Society for the Protection of Animals . . . Grammont Law: McPhee (1992), 256.

172 shooting dolphins: Busquet; Roberts, 45–6.

172 marmots pulled each other: Lavallée, II, 'Drôme', 25.

172 chamois and bouquetins: Chaix, 200 (quoting Abbé Albert).

173 'Though the profit is small': Saussure, II, 153.

173 'We are living on bear and chamois': Sand (1856), VIII, 131.

173 Russia and the Balkans: Planhol, 388.

173 young lynx near Luz: Dusaulx, II, 13–14; Saint-Amans (1789), 75; also Brehm, I, 302.

174 Eagle hunters: Ladoucette (1833), 33.

174 'A peasant was holding it': Chateaubriand, II, 14, 6.

174 flocks of doves: Weld (1859), 225–9.

174 public-information: Anon. (1851); also *MP*, 1883, p. 407 and 1887, p. 114.

174 stealing birds' eggs: Anon. (1851); *MP*, 1862, p. 402; 1868, p. 366; 1884, p. 303.

174 berry bushes at the door: Mazon (1878), 192.

175 'You may pass through the whole South': Smollett, letter 20; also *MP*, 1868, p. 366.

175 Deforestation and hard winters: e.g. Crignelle, 225–37.

175 Normandy . . . inundated with wolves: Brehm, I, 482.

175 price on every wolf: Deferrière, 435 (report by Dupin, Préfet of Deux-Sèvres); Sonnini, 167.

176 a kind of addiction: Leschevin, 326–27; Saussure, II, 152.

176 his game-bag his 'shroud': Saussure, II, 151.

176 black Camargue bulls: Brehm, II, 665–6.

176 A horse . . . 'Napoléon': Brehm, II, 324; *MP*, 1841, pp. 250–51.

178 Barry . . . the Saint Bernard: Brehm, I, 406–7; *MP*, 1846, p. 200.

178 epidemic in 1820: Brehm, I, 404–6.

179 special railway carriages: McPhee (1992), 256.

179 Transhumance: F. Bernard; J.-E. Michel, 198–206; Peuchet, 'Bouches-du-Rhône', 10.

180 'sheep in their thousands': Pliny, *Natural History*, XXI, xxxi, 57.

181 'it is an honour to know': Blackburn (1881), 239.

182 conical thatched hut: Baring-Gould (1894), 112 (drawing).

182 lone sheep: e.g. Maupassant (1884), 77.

182 sheep . . . form battle lines: Bourrit, 335.

182 'a smile of life': Mariéton, 401.

182 'looking more like Arabs': Sand (1856), VIII, 136.

182 'The owner of this beautiful animal': Dusaulx, I, 159–60.

183 knew exactly when to leave: Lequinio, I, 384–5; also Peuchet, 'Jura', 9; Legrand d'Aussy, 281; Mariéton, 401.

9. MAPS

187 evening of 10 August: Meridian expedition: accounts in Delambre and Méchain; researched and recounted by Alder.

187 Dammartin-en-Goële: Alder, 26–7.

188 Tuileries Palace: Alder, 21.

189 cranky measures: Burguburu; Peuchet, *passim*; etc.

190 'a stone pyramid called the Meridian': Alder, 109.

190 'The instruments were laid out': Delambre, I, 33–4.

191 'demolished all those steeples': Delambre, I, 73–4.

191 Bort-les-Orgues: Delambre, I, 80.

191 Puy Violent: Coudon.

191 attack of wild dogs: Alder, 241.

192 Cassini's expedition: Cassini de Thury (1750 and 1754); G. de Fontanges; Gallois; Konvitz; Pelletier; Pelletier and Ozanne.

192 'When one considers': Cassini de Thury (1750), 9.

193 knowledge of cheese: Konvitz, 14.

193 army's own geometers: Konvitz, 39 (in 1762).

194 government map: *Département du Mont Blanc (cy-devant Savoie). Décrété par la Convention Nationale le 27 novembre 1792*; Reverdy, 123.

195 'He set up three stations': Pelletier, 97–100.

195 Many local names: Ronjat; Whymper, 21.

195 'Names had to be given': Cassini de Thury (1750), 10.

196 a camera lucida: Mérimée (1941–64), I, 309–10.

196 'Several Bretons seated': Bray, 225; see also Brune, 149.

196 Saint-Martin-de-Carnac: Cazals, 162; Dainville, 134.

198 map of the Moon: Launay. However, paths around the family château at Thury-en-Valois are picked out in green and seem to form a masonic symbol.

199 Loiseleur-Deslongchamps: Cosson; Delambre, I, 305; etc.

200 looked like Joan of Arc: Monteil, I, 149.

200 last year's chestnuts: Monteil, II, 37.

10. EMPIRE

203 'In the Ardennes': Wairy, 148–50; see also Argenson, 198 (Marie Leczinska in 1725); Beauchamp, I, 181 (Napoleon to Montier-en-Der).

204 'Having no paths to follow': Thiébault, II, 11–13.

205 'changed with the seasons': Pelletier, 108. The first road maps date from the early eighteenth century: Arbellot (1992), 775; Konvitz, 114; Reverdy, 7.

205 'Grand Chemin de France': e.g. Fodéré, I, 158.

205 'nations have great men': Baudelaire (1975–76), I, 654.

206 most maps for travellers: e.g. Coutans; Ogée.

206 Aubervilliers: Coutans.

207 'I have often heard tell': Mérimée (1941–64), I, 288–9 (2 July 1834).

207 places . . . close together: Dupain-Triel, 3–4; Peuchet, 'Hautes-Alpes', 16.

207 could be folded up: Pacha, 37.

208 'I took the diligence to Soissons': V. Hugo, 'Voyages', p. 32.

208 memorizes the Cassini map: Sand (1872), 122.

208 signs of map mania: Anon. (1855); Anon. (1856).

209 'At a bend in the road': M. Proust, I, 177–8.

209 Pyrame de Candolle: C. Malte-Brun (1810), 240; also Bentham's expeditions in 1820 and 1825.

209 Charles de Tourtoulon: Plazanet.

209 *Carte de l'état-major*: Coraboeuf; G. de Fontanges; V.-A. Malte-Brun (1858 and 1868).

210 'Always on foot': Anon (1843), 206; also Anon. (Nov. 1835); P. Buache, *Carte minéralogique* (1746); *Tableau d'assemblage des six feuilles de la Carte géologique*.

210 'broad, continuous bands': Anon. (1843), 27–8.

211 'limits of these natural regions': Anon. (1843), 208.

212 lacked basic information: Ardouin-Dumazet (1882); Josse, 471; Webster (1901), 343.

212 'five mountain ranges': Stendhal, 60.

212 M. Sanis: Barbié du Bocage.

213 relief models of the Alps: e.g. H. d'Angeville, 7–8.

213 geodesic survey: Bourdiol.

214 Bordeaux Geographical Society: Ardouin-Dumazet (1882), 103–4.

11. TRAVELLING IN FRANCE, I

215 high-speed goods: Cavaillès, 245.

215 load pulled by one horse: Price, 270.

216 wooden planks: Duby, III, 183.

218 the *corvée*: Babeau (1878), 236–8; Cavaillès, 87–96; Flour de Saint-Genis, 11; Martin and Martenot, 415–16; Robillard de Beaurepaire, 24–5; Sonnini, 79–80; Vignon, 14–24.

219 'Thus, whenever M. le Marquis': Cooper, 313–14.

219 châteaux of the Loire Valley: Hufton, 189–90 and n. 3.

219 undercut the local farmers: Cavaillès, 120; also the Cahier de Doléances of Maron, Meurthe-et-Moselle, no. 23.

219 vigorous lobbying: Peuchet, 'Creuse', 38.

220 innovation of . . . Trésaguet: Cavaillès, 90.

220 Most French roads: Robillard de Beaurepaire, 14.

220 'Setting aside the depths': Durand-Claye, 90.

220 Généralité of Rouen: Robillard de Beaurepaire, 14.

220 'In travelling to the point': Cavaillès, 282.

221 sandstone slabs: Marlin, I, 274.

221 The richer the soil: e.g. Duchesne (1762), 208; Pradt, 106–7.

221 statue of Louis XIV: Goubert, 90.

221 Baron Haussmann: Haussmann, 52 (Poitiers); 67–71 (Yssingeaux); 90–91 (Nérac).

221 'Couldn't I be sent': Haussmann, 91.

221 Roman roads had been marked: e.g. G. Delisle.

222 'moderate-sized colony of moles': Mirabeau, 183.

222 stretches of Roman surface: Lavallée, 'Bouches-du-Rhône', 10 (Arles); Legrand d'Aussy, 36–37 (Clermont); Saint-Amans (1812), 214 (Arcachon); Bizeul (Saintes), 259; Saint-Amans (1799), 22 (Aiguillon); Grad, 614–15 and Reinhard (Sainte-Odile); Jourdain, 191 and Mérimée (1941–64), II, 253 (Chalindrey); Peuchet, 'Deux-Sèvres', 36; Abgrall (Quimper).

222 'the avenues of the city of Paris': Cavaillès, 57.

222 'consider the main route': Cavaillès, 54 and 58.

223 a person in Moulins: Weld (1850), 54.

223 edict of 1607: H. Gautier, 194; also Assemblée Nationale, II, 7.

223 travelled with his own crew: Goubert, 90.

223 crosses, posts or pyramids: H. Gautier, 194; Veuclin.

223 Orry and . . . Trudaine: Arbellot (1973), 766–9.

225 lined with trees: Lecreulx, 8–10; Marlin, II, 135.

225 branches of apple trees: Duchesne (1762), 208.

225 In Toulouse: Forster, 67.

225 Flanders: Barbault-Royer, 93; Lavallée, V, 'Jemmapes', 23.

225 'incomparably fine': Young, 25.

226 Soon after Bourganeuf: Marlin, II, 141–2.

226 Governor of Brittany: Trévédy, 5.

226 army handbook: État-major de l'armée de terre, 161.

227 Reventin slope . . . Laffrey incline: Stendhal, 147 and 395.

227 Tarare hill: e.g. Bouchard, 95.

227 flattened these monsters: Cavaillès, 198; Lavallée, V, 'Rhône', 3–4.

227 route taken by Hannibal: e.g. Whymper, 52 (elephant inn sign at Ville-Vieille).

227 Col de Tende: J. Black, 31.

228 'In execution of His Majesty's orders': Cavaillès, 188–9.

228 'to have drawings made': Ladoucette, 'Anecdotes', 73.

228 Italian pedlars and beggars: Fortis, I, 371.
228 nineteenth-century regulations: Préfecture du Calvados.
229 grenadier from the Vivarais: Volane, 154–5.
230 'warehouse of universal commerce': Pons, de l'Hérault, 292 and 298.

12. TRAVELLING IN FRANCE, II

231 'the harmonious arrangement': Strabo, *Geography*, IV, 1, 2.
232 plank boats: also the Loire: Barker (1894), 147–8; Hufton, 121; Leca.
232 Tiny rivers: Cavaillès, 264; Cobb (1970), 283.
232 report on the Dordogne: Peuchet, 'Dordogne', 8.
234 first person . . . to descend the Rhône: Boissel; Peuchet, 'Ain', 5.
235 Perte du Rhône . . . blown up: Reclus (1886), 328.
235 daily passenger boat (Yonne and Seine): Restif, 274; L. Bonnard, 77; Cobb (1975 and 1998); Frye, 97.
235 Diligences: e.g. Carr, 32–3; Murray, xxv–xxvi.
236 waterproof cushions: Bayle-Mouillard, 249–51.
236 'I should not want to travel': Taylor, 362–3.
236 'the incommodious throng': Gasparin, I, 30.
237 four white hooves: Mistral (1906), 189.
237 'my poor little carriage': Stendhal, 135; also Assemblée Nationale, XXXVI, 310 (22 Dec. 1791).
237 salvo of abuse: Courtois, 45; Cradock, 260; Fleutelot, 11; Masson de Saint-Amand, 92.
237 'The deck was littered with nutshells': *L'Éducation sentimentale*, part I, ch. 1.
239 between Rouen and Paris: Roland de La Platière, 13.
239 Raft trains: Lavallée, V, 'La Roër', 8–9; Peuchet, 'Rhin-et-Moselle', 5–6.
239 Pont-Saint-Esprit: e.g. Coulon, 162; Smollett, letter 9; Thicknesse, I, 59; etc.
239 voyage down the Loire: Stendhal, 219–26.
240 mail boat from Toulouse: Mercier-Thoinnet, 24.
240 'For those who have long been jolted': Murray, 455.
240 Saint-Simonian reformer: Chevalier (1838), 215.
240 'A vivacious old man': Stevenson (1878), 'To Landrecies'.
241 wine-laden boats: Martin and Martenot, 411.
241 hundred and seventy boats that plied the canal: Forster, 69–70.
242 stepping stones: Hubscher, 376 n. 77.
242 pastor touring Provence: Frossard, I, 80.

242 'consider making a will': Weber, 198 n. (quoting G. Garrier).

242 'rough and low-bred': Murray, xxv.

242 notoriously bribable: Barbault-Royer, 170–72; Blackburn (1870), 239.

243 'arrayed in the green tail-coat': Stevenson (1879), 14.

243 swamp dwellers of the Marais Poitevin: Lagardelle, 210.

243 shepherds on stilts: Saint-Amans (1812), 35 and 66; also
Administration centrale des Landes, 2; Best, 354; Lawlor (1870), 545;
Tastu (1842), 297.

243 snow-shoes . . . Crampons: Saussure, I, 479; Chaix, 77; Ladoucette
(1833), 140.

244 *schlitteurs*: Grad, 23–6; Robischung, 88; Valin.

244 'We felt as though we were swimming': Saint-Amans (1789), 29–30;
other accounts: Dusaulx, I, 171–2 (Pyrenees); Thévenin (Vosges),
76–7.

244 bicycles and skis: skis were introduced to the French Alps in 1891 by
Henri Duhamel, who had acquired a pair, with no instructions, at the
Paris Exhibition of 1878.

245 'They simply slid back down': Mistral (1906), 222.

245 speed records: Arbellot (1973) (times from Paris); Aynard; Chevalier
(1838), 305–7 (diligences); Viard (mail timetables). E.g.: in 1721,
Saint-Simon (127–37) went from Paris to Bayonne in seventeen days;
in 1815, Théodore Aynard (117) went from Lyon to Paris in six days;
in 1843, letters took five days to reach Paris from Finistère, parts of
the Auvergne and all the Mediterranean and Pyrenean provinces, six
days from parts of the Basses-Alpes and between six and nine days
from Corsica.

246 'What was I to do?': Wille, I, 50; also Maclean, 180: 'some of us,
having set off on foot before the diligence, walked the whole stage
[nine miles, from Cavignac to Saint-André-de-Cubzac], and had
breakfasted before the others arrived.'

246 railway engineer: Aynard.

246 emperors travelling in Gaul: L. Bonnard, 12.

247 Drouet kept an account: V. Hugo, 'Voyages', pp. 990–93.

247 profit on uneaten meals: Bernhard, 56; A. Duval, 43 n.; etc.

248 Orléans was a candle: V. Hugo, 'Voyages', p. 751.

248 Nerval set off: Nerval, III, 'Voyage au Nord'.

249 'So here I've been': Hugo to Vigny, 20 July 1821.

Notes

13. COLONIZATION

250 'more quickly than a human heart': 'Le Cygne', *Les Fleurs du Mal*.

251 ocean-bathing . . . at Dieppe: Duplessis, 321; Perrot, 302.

252 toured the Vendée: Nettement; Walsh.

253 'THE MINISTER OF THE INTERIOR': Ploux (2003), 33.

253 sent out a proclamation: Nettement, III, 127–8.

255 road-building programme: Cavaillès, 184 and 202–3; H. Proust; Weber, 196.

255 military routes . . . of the Cévennes: Cavaillès, 60; Dainville, 78; Foville (1894), II, 95; map *.

256 'the first person to come along': *Mon cœur mis à nu*, xxv: Baudelaire (1975–76), I, 692.

256 Brouage in 1772: Marlin, IV, 295.

258 Napoléonville: Anon. (1856); Savant, 43, 74 and 61 (on Pontivy-Napoléonville).

259 mass internal migration: e.g. Cleary, 11–12; A. Joanne (1869), I, lx; Moch, 22.

260 grooves cut by the barges' cables: Mistral (1896), 3.

260 tiny houses: Audiganne, II, 150–51; Jordan, 33–4; Lavallée, I, 'Bouches-du-Rhône', 60; Marlin, I, 94; Michot de La Cauw, 31; Pachoud, XLIV, 162–3; Plumptre, II, 194–5.

260 'Wherever one looks': Stendhal, 713.

260 labyrinth as large as a city: Coyer, I, 109.

260 more than twenty thousand: Pöllnitz, IV, 103.

261 *mazets*, *baraquettes*, etc.: Audiganne, II, 150–51; Aufauvre, 147; Moch, 86; S. Papon, 10.

261 'The host is never satisfied': A. Legoyt, in *Les Français, Province*, II, 223.

262 thirty thousand Parisians: Perrot, 301.

262 deserted banks of the Seine: Smollett, letter 6.

262 cliff-dwellings: Baring-Gould (1911), 39.

262 cave near Tours: Capitan, 581.

262 'the extinction of poverty': Bonaparte.

263 France's first railway: Caron, 85; Blerzy, 656–7.

263 'the sky is perfectly visible': Tonnellé, 514.

263 'rivers of coal-smoke': 'Paysage', *Les Fleurs du Mal*.

264 clan traditions: Audiganne, I, 163–8.

264 pre-industrial landscape: e.g. Planhol, 240.

264 Sotteville and Saint-Sever: Audiganne, I, 55.

265 elderly people: C. Malte-Brun (1823), 269.

265 Aubin: Monteil, I, 63–5.

265 Burning Mountain: Peuchet, 'Aveiron', 4; Monteil, I, 58.

265 its neighbour Cransac: Barker (1893), 337–8.

266 'find at Decazeville': Larousse, VI, 218.

267 phylloxera aphid: e.g. Bouvier, 56; McPhee, in Crook, 143; Moch, 47.

268 tracts of land . . . reclaimed: McPhee (1992), 223; Sutton.

268 colonies of orphans: Anon. (1849).

268 'a damp hospital': Reclus (1886), 76–7.

269 swamp fever: F. Pyat, in *Les Français, Province*, II, 236.

269 the Double: Barker (1894), 246–7.

269 Craponne and Pierrelatte: Duby, III, 195.

269 'untilled and arid Crau': Mistral (1859), VIII, 25.

269 Rivesaltes: see Grynberg, 202–7.

270 flower-pot without a hole: About, 107.

270 tree-planting . . . since prehistory: Mortemart de Boisse.

270 'You ask how I found the Landes?': Guignet, 140–41.

271 yellow-skinned tribe: e.g. Rosenstein, 347–54; Saint-Amans (1812); V. Gaillard, in *Les Français, Province*, II, 113–15.

271 'The urban Landais': V. Gaillard, in *Les Français, Province*, II, 120.

272 In the Corbières: McPhee (1999).

272 effects of deforestation: Dugied; McPhee (1999); Museon Arlaten; P. Chevallier; also Fauchet, 11–13; Grangent, 21.

273 tour of inspection: Dugied, 3 and 17.

273 Picardy and Flanders: Duby, III, 197.

274 In the Pyrenees: Buffault, 343 (the 'chemin de la mâture').

274 talking in whispers: Dusaulx, I, 108.

274 Restoration of Mountain Terrains: Museon Arlaten.

274 'The French Alps': Reclus (1886), 88.

274 'the ruins': O. Reclus (1886), 89.

274 Chaudun: Museon Arlaten.

275 'when the people left the village': M. Chabre, www.retrouvance.com/histoire.htm

276 'controlled reintroduction': *Bois-Forêt.Info*, 26 Sep. 2002.

14. THE WONDERS OF FRANCE

277 borrowed from English: e.g. Égron (1830), 17, where the word is explained in a note.

277 routes south from Paris: described by Leduc.

277 'Long legs, thin body': Taine (1858), 282–3.

278 21 June 1741: Windham (1744).

278 visitors to Chamonix: Durier, 52; Ferrand (1912), 6; Windham (1879); Bruchet.

278 Dijon and Langres: Durier, 52; La Rochefoucauld d'Anville, 31.

279 excellent impersonators: Leschevin, 326; Saussure, II, 165–6.

279 'terrible havock': Windham (1744), 6–7.

279 'You must imagine': Windham (1744), 8.

279 'What did you think of the horrors?': Dusaulx, I, 57; also L. Bonnard, 59; Fortis, I, 111; Jourdan, 141; Peuchet, 'Hautes-Alpes', 6.

280 'I had imagined a mountain': Desnoues, 16.

280 'corpses of the mountains': quoted in Orlov, II, 90–91.

280 'Such uncouth rocks': letter to Richard West, Turin, 11 Nov. 1739.

280 'one could hardly mention': Moore, I, 186.

280 'Those people don't understand': Fortis, II, 237.

280 excruciating silence: Achard (1850), 281–2.

281 the first to scale: e.g. a wooden cross on the Pic de Rochebrune in 1819: Ferrand (1909), 41.

281 Santiago de Compostela: Melczer, 90–91.

281 'to form one's taste': Piganiol de La Force, I, vi. Cf. Louette.

281 'the barrenest Plain': Breval, 1–2.

282 monuments that had . . . ceased to exist: e.g. Piganiol de La Force; J.-P. Papon.

282 'M. Robert went to the trouble': Marlin, III, 65 and 148; Hesseln, IV, 369–70; also J.-P. Papon.

282 'eternal snow': Barron, *Rhône*, 224–5; also Flaubert, 355; Girault de Saint-Fargeau, 490; Murray, 444; Peuchet, 'Vaucluse', 7; Pigault-Lebrun, 44.

282 'clumps of bulrushes': Barron (1888), 23.

283 Pont du Gard . . . deserted: e.g. Richard and Lheureux, 12–13; Thicknesse, I, 63.

283 a year's stay in Paris: Dutens, 17.

283 Seven Wonders of the Dauphiné: e.g. Chorier, I, ch. 12; Saugrain, 125; Wraxall, I, ch. 7.

284 'intercede there, as is customary': Melczer, 97.

284 'a walk that is pleasing': Girault de Saint-Fargeau, 72.

284 'use your drawing pencils': Briand, x.

284 'natural curiosities' of France: Depping (1811), 606–14. Other lists in Girault de Saint-Fargeau, p. xiii ff. and La Roche, the first to use a star system for 'those Articles one would most regret missing'.

285 Valenciennes . . . Quiberon: Lavallée, 'Nord', 18; 'Loire-Inférieure', 3.

285 'The barracks are magnificent': Lavallée, III, 'Meurthe', 12.

285 'the air oftentimes reverberates': Lavallée, I, 'Côtes-du-Nord', 8.

285 Ariège in 1800: Mercadier de Bélesta, 60–65.

286 'Cathar tourism': Mercadier de Bélesta, 64.

286 'twelve years have elapsed': Birkbeck, 3.

286 *Quentin Durward*: Warrell, 18–19.

286 Scott's descriptions: Stendhal, 282.

286 'buttoned-up clergymen': Hallays, VIII, 85.

286 J. M. W. Turner: Warrell, 115.

286 'The peasantry were still busy': Longfellow, 94–6.

287 Calais . . . bilingual: Lavallée, IV, 'Pas-de-Calais', 25.

287 population of Tours: Holdsworth; Orlov, I, 64.

287 'In 1793, he was able': Balzac, IX, 643.

288 'If this destruction continues': Peuchet, 'Gers', 1.

288 'one can hardly put': Pigault-Lebrun, 39.

289 'This is not a voyage of discoveries': Nodier, 'Ancienne Normandie', 5.

290 Between 1834 and 1852: Mérimée (1835, 1836, 1838 and 1840); Raitt, 139–46.

290 appraising the beauties: Mérimée (1941–64), I, 327.

290 bridge at Avignon, etc.: Raitt, 154.

290 'They no longer suit': Thérond, 31.

291 'The Highways and Bridges': Mérimée (1852).

291 'We left Versailles': Bader, 9.

291 'There is a very bad smell': Genlis, 49–50.

292 'If poor lodging': Courtin, 202–3.

292 the 'inn' . . . a farmhouse: e.g. Bailly, 7.

292 'typical mountain people': Richard and Lheureux, 23.

293 list of hotels: Richard and Lheureux, 103–4 and 136.

293 'Beauty won the day': Depping (1813), 277–8.

293 innkeeper's duties: *Les Misérables*, II, 3, 2 and 9; also Dumas (1863–84), VII, 106–7.

293 'Fail not to take a piece of soap': Murray, xxix.

294 killed four hundred and eighty: Cradock, 260.

294 'I turned it, dish and all': Thicknesse, II, 106–8.

294 'the Temple of Cloacina': Smollett, letter 12.

294 'Don't worry, sir': Depping (1813), 261–2.

294 1828 guide to Paris: Audin, 61, 191 and 206; cf. Hughes, 158.

295 '*Ici on est bien*': Karr, 232–5.

295 'Slice a pigeon': Haan, 127.

295 '*Naps! Naps!*': Perbosc, 281.

295 young men from Saint-Brieuc: Sébillot (1886), 327–8.

296 'charcuterie composed': *Grand Dictionnaire universel.*

296 manual of rural architecture: Saint-Félix, 26.

296 smashed with a hammer: Lefebvre d'Hellancourt, 9–10.

296 fact-finding mission: Anon. (1844).

297 wolf . . . repulsive: Crignelle, 278; Weld (1869), 208.

297 fox a delicacy: Restif, 215.

297 Red squirrels . . . were eaten: Saint-Amans (1812), 15; Weld (1869), 212–13.

297 marmots . . . flesh: Saussure, II, 153; Montémont, I, 137; Windham and Martel (1879), 58.

297 'when a bear has been killed': Dagalier, 208.

297 a diet of *gaudes*: Proudhon, 26.

297 '*pensions alimentaires*': Gutton, 64–75; R.-J. Bernard; Thuillier (1965).

297 gorged himself on peaches: Perdiguier (1854), 62–3.

297 three million beehives: Girard.

297 a quince crystallized: Barron, *Garonne*, 296; Marmontel, 50.

298 Victor of the Aveyron: Itard.

298 Memmie: La Condamine.

298 specialities of each region: e.g. MacCarthy; for an earlier example, Reichard ('carte gastronomique').

298 connoisseur of French wines: Planhol, 231–2.

299 'A nutritional tour of Paris': Barberet, VI, 166.

299 'Since no one knew': Guillaumin, 250.

299 trip to Roscoff: Dumas (1878), 116–26.

299 'The English onion': Dumas (1878), 1059.

15. POSTCARDS OF THE NATIVES

300 'Around the World in 80 Days': Anon. (1869).

300 Mont Cenis tunnel: Chérot, 323; Saint-Martin.

300 'thirty-three cigars from Marseille': Merson, 210.

300 Boulevard des Italiens: Achard (1869), 86.

301 a third-class carriage: Anon. (1842), 96.

301 *From Paris to Nice*: Gauthier de Clagny, 2.
301 'six weeks of constant railway-travel': James, 250; on railway manners: Siebecker, 119–21.
301 drained of traffic by the railways: L. Bonnard, 135; Cavaillès, 225 and 276–7; Marmier, 2; *MP*, 1854, p. 21; Lenthéric, 291; Murray, 505; Weber, 210 and 218.
302 'we reach the point': Ogier, 19; see also Demolière; Mazade.
302 illuminated kilometre markers: Saint-Martin, 393–4.
302 on the track itself: Égron (1837), 223.
302 faces in the carriage windows: Guillaumin, 268.
302 planted explosives: Weld (1850), 268.
303 The navvies: e.g. Le Play, 104.
303 old town gates: e.g. Poitiers: Favreau.
303 The official hour: Arago (1864); Nordling; Thuillier (1977), 206; time differences: e.g. Anon. (1792), 115; Miller, 26–7; older means of telling the time: S. Papon, 95; Davis, 19.
303 Berthouville: Corbin (1994), 113.
303 names of some ancient *pays*: Soudière, 70–72.
304 Tremblevif: Reclus (1886), 133.
304 Merdogne: Reclus (1886), 32; *MP*, 1903, p. 491; Conseil d'État, 3 Feb. 2003, no. 240630.
304 Politics has arrived: Agulhon; Berenson, 127–36.
304 photographs of political leaders: Berenson, 131 and 149.
304 supernatural powers: Hazareesingh, *Legend*.
304 especially in the south-east: Judt.
305 dynastic rulers: Audiganne, II, 223 (Villeneuvette); P. Jones (1988), 255; Singer, 40; Weber, 539.
305 Labiche defined the *maire*: Laudet, 152; also Hamerton, 58.
305 the 'heartless science': Baudelaire (1973), I, 579.
305 In the Corrèze: Vuillier, 507.
305 In Nîmes: Audiganne, II, 165–68; Moch, 105–06; É. de La Bédollière, in *Les Français, Province*, II, 54–6.
305 level crossing: Home, ch. 1.
305 runs the post office: Viard's list (1843) shows that 1,092 of the 1,938 post office directors were women, though only one was director in a departmental *chef-lieu*.
306 'the land of *bouillabaisse*': Zola, I, 96.
307 provincial museums: Babeau (1884), II, 338; Chennevières; Georgel, 109; E. Pommier in Nora.
307 collections of folk songs: Thiesse (2001).
307 'folkloric costume': Williams, 483.

307 George Sand sponsored: especially correspondence with Charles Poncy.

307 'an instinctive antipathy': Brochet, 43.

308 Barèges: Bar; Dusaulx, I, 206–8; Leclercq, 23; Saint-Amans (1789), 122.

308 'which nothing but the hope': Murray, 230.

308 Bagnères-de-Bigorre: Dagalier, 214.

308 Aulus-les-Bains: Labroue, 164.

309 a typical spa town: Anon. (1867); Frieh-Vurpas; Maupassant (1887); Monnet.

309 'The water possesses': from the fountain at Saint-Martin-Vésubie.

309 silent procession: e.g. J. Girardin; Taine (1858): on Eaux-Bonnes.

310 gravestones of *curistes*: J. Girardin.

310 Aix-les-Bains: Fortis, I, 80–85; Frieh-Vurpas, 11 and 28.

310 'There is a continual mêlée': Speleus, xv.

310 the sea: Corbin (1988); Garner, 80.

311 arrival of mass tourism: Corbin (1988); Brittany: Céard; Warenghem; Dieppe: Perrot, 302; Royan: *MP*, 1891, p. 252.

311 new plants and flowers: Blanchet, 61–4.

311 Conty's guide: Conty (1889).

312 Bourgeois families: Garner, 109, 113, 140.

312 wreckers parading lanterns: e.g. Mangin, 13.

312 'her cretinous, contracted mouth': Flaubert, 111.

312 Arcachon Basin: Garner, 68–70.

313 'We questioned those noble debris': Garner, 97–8 (and translation).

313 'curious and gripping spectacle': Corbin (1988), 235 (quoting Émile Souvestre) and 245.

313 'So you lost your husband': Huard.

313 'Just imagine the spectacle': Conty (1889), 342.

313 picture postcards: Garner, 176.

314 wear shoes in public: Duplessis, 321.

314 'roomy trousers': Garner, 109.

314 Biarritz was a fishing village: e.g. Russell, 1–15.

314 a *cacolet*: Doussault, 98; Lagarde, 74–8; Longfellow, 163.

314 'My only fear': V. Hugo, 'Voyages', p. 775.

314 'his somewhat withered mouth': Montémont, I, 57–8.

315 young gypsy girl: Gratiot, 16–17.

315 At Pont-Aven: Champney, ch. 16.

315 at Boulogne-sur-Mer: Garner, 107.

315 'immense, enchanted aquarium': M. Proust, II, 41.

315 rustic antiques: Conty (1889), 27.

315 snatched the flowers away: Blackburn (1881), 35.
315 'You see tiny little girls': Taine (1858), 133.
316 Neanderthal types: Roujou (1872 and 1876).
316 cemetery in the Aveyron: Durand, 421.
316 'anthropometrical research': Fauvelle, 958.
317 'more Negroes than Frenchmen': Broca (1879), 6.
317 the vanquished Gauls: Marchangy; Thierry, I, v; Thiesse (2001).
317 a 'pure' Frenchman: e.g. Broca (1859–60); Lagneau (1859–60, 1861 and 1867).
317 a prehistoric relic: e.g. Edwards, 39–41; Lagneau (1867); Roujou; Thierry, I, lxx.
318 Pierre Broca based his conclusions: Broca (1862), 580–82.
318 'ignorant and backward' village (in Guipuscoa): Broca (1862), 580.
318 'M. Broca is far from concluding': Broca (1862), 588.
318 counting systems: Landrin.
318 a practice that was common: Bonald, 259; F. Delisle; Gélis; Guérin; Lagneau (1861), 337 and 361; Lunier (1852 and 1866).
319 local styles . . . disappearing: Babeau (1883), 44; Lavallée, III, 'Marne', 45; 'Moselle', 27; Masson de Saint-Amand, 2; Orlov, I, 309; S. Papon, 101; Peuchet, 'Creuse', 35; Piédagnel, 192–3.
319 'no more national costumes': Mérimée (1941–64), I, 332.
319 Brittany was still a patchwork: e.g. Quellien and V. Segalen, 95 (the Bigouden *pays*).
319 dresses and shirts: Hélias, 277; Martin and Martenot, 491–2.
320 round hats of the Bretons: Planhol, 297 and 311.
320 *glazig* style: Planhol, 302.
320 women of Arles: Weber, 231.
320 butterfly bows of Alsace: Planhol, 310.
320 Regional costumes were exhibited: *Exposition universelle*, 460–70.
320 Museum of Ethnography: Hamy; Thiesse (2001), 197–207; also Quimper: Watteville Du Grabe; Anon. (1886).
320 Montagne Noire: Thiesse (2001).

16. LOST PROVINCES

322 extraordinary efforts: Blondel; on M. Blondel: G. Turquer and D. Raillot: http://perso.wanadoo.fr/dieppe76/personnages.html
324 'The fatherland is not your village': Weber, 108.
324 'The defeats at Poitiers': Lavisse (1888), 315.
324 'Little inhabitants of the forests': Lavisse (1907), 35.

324 eve of the First World War: Weber, 110.

325 result of conscription: Forrest, 44–50. Sample letters: 119–20.

325 nasty sense of humour: Guillaumin, 205.

325 read out on the doorstep: Dondel, 177.

325 kept out of school: Strumingher, 134–6.

325 pedagogical army: see Gildea.

325 the *signum*: Baris, 45–6; Serbois, 214.

325 Latin instead of French: Sigart, 25.

326 'like half-empty boxes': Hélias, 339.

326 Bécassine . . . Breton language: M.-A. Couderc, 10.

326 think of themselves as French: Planhol, 324.

326 'Breton-speaking Bretons': Hélias, 341.

327 regional pride . . . patriotism: Thiesse (1997).

327 Tactful decentralization: Hazareesingh (1998).

327 ability to speak both languages: Baris, 47 and 65.

327 to pass examinations: Hélias, 148.

327 ban the use of Breton: Press, in Parry. The signs in buses that forbade spitting and speaking Breton are a myth: Broudic.

327 losing the rhymes: Rousselot, 223.

327 'The patois of Montjean': Dottin.

328 'You are about to ask me': Tastu (1846), 23.

328 tales of infant tourists: e.g. Consul; Delattre (1846); Desarènes; Labesse.

328 *Three Months Under the Snow*: Porchat, 6.

329 'true Frenchmen': Briand, i.

329 usual image of Corsicans: e.g. Forester; Lemps; Liodet.

329 'The people who entered the inn': Bruno, 165–6.

330 'lost provinces': e.g. P. Joanne (1883), 13, and Alsace-Lorraine volumes in Ardouin-Dumazet's series: *Les Provinces perdues*; retitled *Les Provinces délivrées* in 1919.

330 death-defying roads: Ferrand (1904); A. Joanne (1860), 385–7.

330 'the land least known in France': e.g. Armaignac, 361, quoting Martel; Dujardin, 510.

330 kidnapped and blindfolded: *MP*, 1846, p. 8.

331 Little Switzerlands: Beauguitte; Grandsire (1858), 67; Philipps, 12; Reichard, 8; *Les Français, Province*, II, 365.

331 'discovered, in the remotest provinces': Larousse, XVI, 549.

332 Montpellier-le-Vieux: Betham-Edwards, 279–99; also Armaignac, 374–5; Gourdault, 193–5.

333 'As the Utopia': Betham-Edwards, 298–9.

333 'Columbus of the nether world': Baring-Gould (1894), 27.

333 'I was the first to descend': Martel, 'Le Gouffre', and (1894), 262–3.

334 'conducting publicity campaigns': Martel, *Les Cévennes*.

334 engraving in *Les Abîmes*: Martel (1894), 327.

334 Snuffling dogs: Martel (1898).

334 Old women crossed themselves: Martel (1894), 14.

335 Grand Canyon of the Verdon: Martel (1906); Reclus (1899), 355.

335 road between Castellane and Moustiers: C. Black, 166.

336 'American wonder of France': Martel and Janet, 596.

17. JOURNEY TO THE CENTRE OF FRANCE

339 'All at once, three shadows': Briault, 5.

340 Paris to Brest and back again: Dargenton.

340 Charles Terront: Gendry, 1–10.

341 'a distance one should not exceed': Briault, 17.

341 Col du Tourmalet: e.g. Conty (1899), 309.

341 bicycles that folded up: Marcadet, 285 (picture).

341 pumped up their own tyres: *MP*, 1909, 184.

342 heavy branch: Bertot, 92; Rougelet, 53.

342 railway companies. M. C. Jones, 71; also Curtel.

342 Touring Club de France: L. Bonnard, 147–8.

342 maps for cyclists: Baedeker (1903), xxxviii.

342 'You cannot always be sure': M. C. Jones, 16.

344 'With the broad and powerful gesture': Ejnès, I, 20.

344 'Just how much further': Ejnès, I, 26.

345 Forest of Fontainebleau: Mangin, 6.

345 Bayonne to Biarritz: *MP*, 1858, p. 160.

345 hotel advertisements: Gratiot, 141.

345 ridge of the Vosges: Grad, 431.

345 Route des Grandes Alpes: *À travers le monde*, XVII (1911), 169–70; Giraut, 300; J.-P. Martin, 35.

345 The Côte d'Azur (population growth): Bernoulli, III, 6; Nash, 153; Rességuier, 5; Young, 215.

345 Native vegetation: Hare, 28 and 31.

345 'a great, ugly, modern town': Hare, 51.

345 Course de Côte de Laffrey: J.-P. Martin, 41.

345 'The motor car': Kipling (2003), 85.

346 'boatmen caught in the ice': Alain-Fournier, part II, ch. 3.

346 'horrible, lisping accent': Alain-Fournier, part II, ch. 5.

346 biggest picnic in history: *L'Humanité*, 14 July 2000; *Le Monde*, 16 July 2000; http://www.culture.gouv.fr/culture/actualites/

communiq/pique-nique.htm; http://14juillet.senat.fr/banquet2000/
piquenique.html

348 geographical centre of France: pictures by J. Zeven and E. Wertwijn:
   http://www.kunstgeografie.nl/centre.mich.htm
349 the Belvédère: A. Joanne (1869), 58; P. Joanne (1890–1905), VI, 4034;
   Reclus (1886), 4–5.
350 rector of Grenoble University: Becker, 34–7.
350 hiding in the woods: Bonnet; Weber, 43.
350 'the men of our peaceful locality': Becker, 37.
351 wooded frontier zones: Planhol, 13–14; Strabo, *Geography*, IV, 3, 5.
352 'Suddenly, we heard the crackle': Denizot and Louis, 45–6 (Sgt
   Bacqué).
352 filling in the gun-pits: Kipling (1933), 42.
353 In the spring of 1991: Denizot and Louis; also Robert Gibson, 304–5.

EPILOGUE

354 summit collapsed: Baedeker (1901), 53; Du Boys, 243.
354 Bugarach . . . Pierre Méchain: Delambre, I, 69–70; Alder, 202–5.
356 'Our descendants': *La Cousine Bette*: Balzac, VII, 100.
357 rounding up of the gypsies: Lunemann, 47–8; Walckenaer, 'Sur la
   diversité', 74–5.
357 commemorative plaque: Stevens.

Works Cited

*The place of publication is Paris, London or New York, unless otherwise noted.
Publishers' names are given only where interesting or necessary.*

Abbreviations:

AV: *Annales des voyages*

BSAP: *Bulletins de la Société d'anthropologie de Paris*

BSG: *Bulletin de la Société de géographie*

EF: *Ethnologie française*

MP: *Le Magasin pittoresque*

NAV: *Nouvelles annales des voyages*

RLR: *Revue des langues romanes*

TM: *Le Tour du monde*

Abgrall, Jean-Marie. 'Étude de la voie romaine et du chemin de pèlerinage des Sept Saints de Bretagne'. *Association bretonne*, XXX (1912), pp. 202–30.

About, Edmond. *Maître Pierre*. 1858.

Achard, Amédée. *Une saison à Aix-les-Bains*. 1850.

Achard, A. *La Vie errante*. 1869.

Adam, Lucien. *Les Patois lorrains*. Nancy and Paris, 1881.

Administration centrale des Landes. *Description du département des Landes*. Year VII (1799).

Agulhon, Maurice. *La République au village*. 2nd ed. 1979.

Agullana, Rosa. 'Mon enfance'. In *Archives de Gascogne* (1993), pp. 107–19.

Alain-Fournier. *Le Grand-Meaulnes*. 1913.

Alder, Ken. *The Measure of All Things*. 2002.

Alison, Sir Archibald, et al. *Travels in France During the Years 1814–15.* 2 vols. 2nd ed. Edinburgh, 1816.

Angeville, Adolphe d'. *Essai sur la statistique de la population française.* Ed. E. Le Roy Ladurie. 1969.

Angeville, Henriette d'. *Une excursion à Chamouny en 1790.* Bourg, 1886.

Anon. *Journal d'un voyage de Genève à Paris, par la diligence.* Geneva and Paris, 1792.

Anon. *Glossaire genevois, ou Recueil étymologique des termes dont se compose le dialecte de Genève: avec les principales locutions défectueuses en usage dans cette ville.* 2nd ed. Geneva, 1827.

Anon. 'Hameau de Goust, dans les Pyrénées'. *NAV,* XXXVII (1828), pp. 109–13.

Anon. *Un voyage d'artiste: guide dans les Pyrénées par deux amis.* Paris and Toulouse, 1835.

Anon. 'Notice sur la carte géologique générale'. *Comptes rendus hebdomadaires des séances de l'Académie des sciences,* I (30 November 1835), pp. 423–9.

Anon. *De la Loire aux Pyrénées.* Lille, 1840.

Anon. 'Nouvelles agricoles'. *Annales agricoles et littéraires de la Dordogne* (Périgueux), 1840, pp. 372–5.

Anon. *Petit almanach national pour Paris et les départements, ou Ce que les Français ont besoin de savoir.* 1842.

Anon. 'La Carte géologique de France', *MP,* 1843, pp. 26–8 and 205–8.

Anon. 'Nourriture des cultivateurs'. *MP,* 1844, pp. 66–7.

Anon. 'Les Jardins de Roscoff'. *MP,* 1846, pp. 47–8.

Anon. 'Sur les signaux des Gaulois'. *MP,* 1848, pp. 190–1.

Anon. 'Colonies bretonnes d'orphelins'. *MP,* 1849, pp. 279–80.

Anon. 'Contre la chasse aux petits oiseaux'. *MP,* 1851, pp. 35–6.

Anon. 'Les Meilleurs atlas'. *MP,* 1855, pp. 21–3, 389 and 173–5.

Anon. 'Documents sur la fondation de la ville de Napoléon-Vendée'. *Revue des provinces de l'Ouest* (Nantes), 1856, pp. 170–79.

Anon. 'Manière de lever la carte du pays que l'on habite'. *MP,* 1856, pp. 355–8.

Anon. 'Plombières et ses environs'. *TM,* XV (1867), pp. 337–52.

Anon. 'Le Tour du monde en 80 jours'. *NAV,* CCIII (1869), p. 239.

Anon. 'Le Musée ethnographique de Quimper'. *MP,* 1886, pp. 216–18.

Arago, François. *Astronomie populaire.* I. 1864.

Arago, F. 'Du danger de sonner les cloches pendant les orages'. *MP,* 1851, pp. 206–7.

Arbellot, Guy. *Autour des routes de poste: les premières cartes routières de la France.* 1992.

Arbellot, G. 'La Grande mutation des routes de France au milieu du XVIIIe siècle'. *Annales*, XXVIII, 3 (1973), pp. 765–91.

Ardouin-Dumazet, Victor-Eugène. *Voyage en France. XXXV. Rouergue et Albigeois.* 1904.

Ardouin-Dumazet, V.-E. 'À travers l'Entre-deux-Mers et le Bazadais'. *BSG commerciale de Bordeaux*, 1882, pp. 102–8.

Argenson, René-Louis, marquis d'. *Mémoires et journal inédit.* Vol. I. 1857.

Armaignac, H. 'Les Cévennes et la région des Causses'. *BSG commerciale de Bordeaux*, 1890, pp. 361–85.

Arnaud, J.-B.-E. *Mémoires d'un compagnon du tour de France.* Rochefort, 1859.

Arnaudin, Félix. *Contes populaires recueillis dans la Grande-Lande, le Born, les Petites-Landes et le Marensin.* Paris and Bordeaux, 1887.

Arnauld, Charles. *Histoire de Maillezais.* 1840 (?).

Aron, Jean-Paul, P. Dumont and E. Le Roy Ladurie. *Anthropologie du conscrit français.* 1972.

Arripe, René. *Les Siffleurs d'Aas.* Pau, 1984.

Artigues, Baron F. d'. 'Pierre, le métayer'. In *Archives de Gascogne* (1993), pp. 125–40.

Assemblée Nationale. *Archives parlementaires de 1787 à 1860.* Première série, 50 vols.

Audiganne, Armand. *Les Populations ouvrières et les industries de la France.* 2 vols. 2nd ed. 1860.

Audin, Jean-Marie-Vincent. *Le Véritable conducteur parisien, ou le plus complet, le plus nouveau et le meilleur guide des étrangers à Paris.* 'Par Richard'. 1828; 1970.

Aufauvre, Amédée. *Hyères et sa vallée: guide historique, médical, topographique.* 1861.

Augustins, Georges. 'Mobilité résidentielle et alliance matrimoniale dans une commune du Morbihan'. *EF*, 1981, 4, pp. 319–28.

Aynard, Théodore. *Voyages au temps jadis en France, en Angleterre [. . .].* Lyon, 1888.

Babeau, Albert. *La Province sous l'Ancien Régime.* 2 vols. 1894.

Babeau, A. *La Vie rurale dans l'ancienne France.* 1883.

Babeau, A. *Le Village sous l'Ancien Régime.* 1878.

Babeau, A. *La Ville sous l'Ancien Régime.* 2 vols. 1884.

Bader, Clarisse. *Les Princes d'Orléans à La Trappe en 1788.* La Chapelle-Montligeon, 1895.

Baedeker, Karl. *Le Nord-Est de la France.* Leipzig and Paris, 1903.

Baedeker, K. *Le Sud-Est de la France,* 7th ed. Leipzig and Paris, 1901.

Bailly, Dr Émile. *Les Vacances d'un accoucheur. Trois semaines d'excursions en Velay et en Vivarais.* 1881.

Baker, Alan. *Fraternity among the French Peasantry.* Cambridge, 1999.

Balzac, Honoré de. *La Comédie Humaine.* 12 vols. 1976–81.

Bar, A. de (illust.; text anon.). 'Barèges (Hautes-Pyrénées)'. *MP*, 1879, p. 124.

Barbault-Royer, Paul-François. *Voyage dans les départemens du Nord, de la Lys, de l'Escaut, etc.* 1800.

Barberet, Joseph. *Le Travail en France.* 7 vols. 1866–90.

Barbié du Bocage, A.-F., et al. 'Rapport [sur la carte en relief de M. Sanis]'. *BSG*, II, X (1838), pp. 280–88.

Baring-Gould, Sabine. *Cliff Castles and Cave Dwellings of Europe.* 1911.

Baring-Gould, S. *The Deserts of Southern France: An Introduction to the Limestone and Chalk Plateaux of Ancient Aquitaine.* I. 1894.

Baris, Michel. *Langue d'oïl contre langue d'oc.* Lyon, 1978.

Barker, Edward Harrison. *Two Summers in Guyenne: a Chronicle of the Wayside and Waterside.* 1894.

Barker, E. H. *Wanderings by Southern Waters, Eastern Aquitaine.* 1893.

Barral, Pierre. 'Depuis quand les paysans se sentent-ils français?' *Ruralia*, 3 (1998).

Barron, Louis. *La Garonne.* 1891.

Barron, L. *La Loire.* 1888.

Barron, L. *Le Rhône.* 1891.

Baudelaire, Charles. *Correspondance.* 2 vols. Ed. C. Pichois. 1973.

Baudelaire, Charles. *Œuvres complètes.* 2 vols. Ed. C. Pichois. 1975–76.

Baugier, M. 'Le Marais de la Sèvre, ses aspects, ses habitans'. *Mémoires de la Société de statistique du département des Deux-Sèvres* (Niort), 1839–40, pp. 140–50.

Bayle-Mouillard, Élisabeth-Félicie. *Manuel des dames, ou L'Art de l'élégance.* 1833.

Beauchamp, Alphonse de. *Histoire des campagnes de 1814 et de 1815.* 4 vols. 1816.

Beauguitte, Ernest. 'Au cœur de l'Argonne'. *MP*, 1901, pp. 642–6.

Beauquier, C. 'Vocabulaire étymologique des provincialismes usités dans le département du Doubs'. *Mémoires de la Société d'émulation du Doubs* (Besançon), 1880, pp. 221–429.

Becker, J. J. 'L'Appel de guerre en Dauphiné'. *Le Mouvement social*, 49 (1964), pp. 32–44.

Bejarry, A. de. 'Mœurs et usages du Bas-Poitou'. *Bulletin de la Société archéologique de Nantes*, I (1859–61), pp. 529–36.

Bentham, George. *Catalogue des plantes indigènes des Pyrénées et du Bas*

Languedoc, avec des observations sur les espèces nouvelles ou peu connues. 1826.

Bérenger-Féraud, Laurent-Jean-Baptiste. *Superstitions et survivances étudiées au point de vue de leur origine et de leur transformation.* 5 vols. 1896.

Berenson, Edward. *Populist Religion and Left-Wing Politics in France, 1830–1852.* Princeton, 1984.

Bernard, François. 'Transhumance'. In *Nouveau Dictionnaire d'économie politique,* II (1900), pp. 1050–51.

Bernard, Richard Boyle. *A Tour Through Some Parts of France, Switzerland, Savoy, Germany and Belgium.* 1815.

Bernard, R.-J. 'L'Alimentation paysanne en Gévaudan au XVIIIe siècle'. *Annales,* XXIV (1969), pp. 1449–67.

Bernhard, Carl Gustaf. *Through France with Berzelius. Live Scholars and Dead Volcanoes.* 1989.

Bernhardt, Sarah. *Ma double vie: mémoires.* 1907.

Bernoulli, Jean. *Lettres sur différens sujets, écrites pendant le cours d'un voyage par l'Allemagne, la Suisse, la France méridionale et l'Italie.* 3 vols. Berlin, 1777–79.

Bertot, Jean. *La France en bicyclette: étapes d'un touriste.* 1894.

Best, Adolphe, et al. (illust.; text anon.). 'Landes de Gascogne'. *MP,* 1835, pp. 353–4.

Betham-Edwards, M. *The Roof of France, or the Causses of the Lozère.* 1889.

Beylet. 'Demi-sauvages de la Provence'. *BSG,* II, VI (1836), pp. 56–60.

Biélawski, Jean-Baptiste-Maurice. *Récits d'un touriste auvergnat.* Yssoire, 1888.

Bilbrough, E. Ernest. *Twixt France and Spain, or A Spring in the Pyrenees.* 1883.

Birkbeck, Morris. *Notes on a Journey Through France.* 1815.

Bizeul, Louis-Jacques-Marie. 'Voie romaine de Nantes vers Limoges'. *Annales de la Société académique de Nantes,* 1844, pp. 258–308.

Black, Charles Bertram. *The South of France, East Half.* Edinburgh, 1885.

Black, Jeremy. *The British Abroad. The Grand Tour in the Eighteenth Century.* Stroud, 1992; 1997.

Blackburn, Henry. *The Pyrenees: a Description of Summer Life at French Watering Places.* 1881.

Blackburn, H. *Normandy Picturesque.* 1870.

Bladé, Jean-François. 'Quatorze superstitions populaires de la Gascogne'. *Revue de l'Agenais* (Agen), 1883.

Blanchard, Raoul. 'L'Habitation en Queyras'. *La Géographie,* XIX (1909), pp. 15–44.

Blanchet, Dr. 'Plantes nouvellement découvertes dans les départements des

Landes et des Basses-Pyrénées'. *Bulletin de la Société de Borda à Dax*, VII (1882), pp. 61–7.

Blanqui, Adolphe. *Voyage à Madrid*. 1826.

Blerzy, H. 'Études sur les travaux publics. Routes, chemins et tramways'. *Revue des Deux Mondes*, 1 June 1878, pp. 628–58.

Blondel, François-Adolphe. 'Carte en relief de la France'. *Société normande de géographie. Bulletin* (Rouen), 1882, pp. 387–9.

Boiraud, Henri. *Contribution à l'étude historique des congés et des vacances scolaires en France*. 1971.

Boissel, T. C. G. (Boissel de Monville). *Voyage pittoresque et navigation exécutée sur une partie du Rhône, réputée non navigable. Moyens de rendre ce trajet utile au commerce*. Year III (1795).

Boissier de Sauvages, Pierre-Augustin. *Dictionnaire languedocien–français*. Nîmes, 1785.

Bonald, Jacques de. 'En Morvan'. *MP*, 1902, pp. 257–60.

Bonaparte, Louis-Napoléon. *Extinction du paupérisme*. 1848.

Bonnard, L. *Le Voyage en France à travers les siècles*. Touring-Club de France, 1927.

Bonnard, Sylvestre. 'Le Culte de Saint Greluchon'. *L'Intermédiaire des chercheurs et curieux*, 15 March 1933, pp. 221–6.

Bonnecase, Julien. 'L'Institution de l'"Héritière" dans le Béarn moderne'. *Revue philomathique de Bordeaux et du Sud-Ouest*, 1920, pp. 1–6.

Bonnecaze, Jean. 'Moeurs et génie des Béarnais (1786)'. *Bulletin de la Société des sciences, lettres et arts de Pau*, 1910, p. 69–98.

Bonnemère, Eugène. *Histoire des paysans depuis la fin du Moyen âge jusqu'à nos jours*. II. 1856.

Bonnet, René. *Enfance limousine*. 1954.

Bouchard, Jean-Jacques. *Les Confessions de Jean-Jacques Bouchard, parisien*. 1881.

Boudin, Jean-Christian-Marc. *Traité de géographie et de statistique médicales*. 1857.

Boué de Villiers, Amaury-Louis-R. *Le Pèlerinage de la Fontaine Sainte-Clothilde aux Andelys*. Paris and Rouen, 1870.

Bourdieu, P. and M. C. 'Le Paysan et la photographie', *Revue française de sociologie*, 1965.

Bourdiol, H. 'Importance d'un nivellement général de la France'. *BSG*, V, X (1865), pp. 177–96.

Bourguet, Marie-Noëlle. *Déchiffrer la France: la statistique départementale à l'époque napoléonienne*. 1988; 1989.

Bourrit, Marc-Théodore. *Itinéraire de Genève, Lausanne et Chamouni*. Geneva, 1791.

Bouvier, Jeanne. *Mes mémoires [. . .] 1876–1935*. 1983.

Braudel, Fernand. *L'Identité de la France*. 3 vols. 1986.

Bray, Anna Eliza (Mrs Charles Stothard). *Letters Written During a Tour Through Normandy, Britanny [sic], and Other Parts of France*. 1820.

Brehm, Alfred Edmund. *L'Homme et les animaux: description populaire des races humaines et du règne animal*. 2 vols. 1869–85.

Breton, Jules. *Œuvres poétiques. Les Champs et la mer. Jeanne*. 1887.

Breval, John Durant. *Remarks on Several Parts of Europe, Relating Chiefly to Their Antiquities and History*. 1738.

Briand, Pierre-César. *Les Petits voyageurs en France, ou Description pittoresque de cette belle contrée*. 1834.

Briault, C. *Les Pyrénées et l'Auvergne à bicyclette*. Chartres, 1895.

Broca, Paul. *Instructions générales pour les recherches anthropologiques à faire sur le vivant*. 1879.

Broca, P. 'Recherches sur l'ethnologie de la France'. *BSAP*, 1859–60, pp. 6–15.

Broca, P. 'Sur les caractères des crânes des Basques'. *BSAP*, 1862, pp. 579–91.

Brochet, Régis. *En bicyclette au bocage vendéen*. Fontenay-le-Comte, 1893.

Broudic, Fanch. ' "Il est interdit de cracher par terre et de parler breton" '. *Bulletin de la Société archéologique du Finistère*, 2001, pp. 363–70.

Bruchet, Max. *La Savoie d'après les anciens voyageurs*. Annecy, 1908.

Brun, Marie-Marguerite. *Essay d'un dictionnaire comtois-françois*. Besançon, 1753.

Brune, Guillaume-Marie-Anne. *Voyage pittoresque et sentimental dans plusieurs des provinces occidentales de la France*. London and Paris, 1788.

Brunhes, Jean. *La Géographie humaine*. 1956.

Bruno, G. (Augustine Bruno). *Le Tour de France par deux enfants: devoir et patrie*. 1877.

Buffault, Pierre. 'Forêts et gaves du pays d'Aspe'. *BSG commerciale de Bordeaux*, 1903, pp. 341–56 and 361–71.

Burgaud Des Marets, Henri. *Glossaire du patois rochelais; suivi d'une Liste des expressions vicieuses usitées à La Rochelle*. 1861.

Burguburu, Charles. 'Le Système métrique en Lot-et-Garonne'. *Revue de l'Agenais* (Agen), 1927, pp. 302–5.

Busquet, Alfred. *Poésies*. 1884.

Cahiers de doléances de la paroisse du Rozel. Ed. C. Leroy. 1999. http://perso.orange.fr/ch.leroy/cahiers.htm

Cahiers de Doléances de la Sénéchaussée de Cahors pour les États-Généraux de 1789. Ed. V. Fourastié. Cahors, 1908.

Callet, Pierre-Moïse. *Glossaire vaudois*. Lausanne, 1861.

Calvez, Marcel. 'Les Accusations de contagion comme argument d'exclusion: l'exemple des caqueux de Bretagne'. *EF*, 1992, 1, pp. 56–60.

Cambry, Jacques. *Description du département de l'Oise*. 3 vols. Year XI (1803); 2 vols, ed. J. Gury.

Cambry, J. *Voyage dans le Finistère, ou État de ce département en 1794 et 1795*. 3 vols. Year VII (1798).

Campenon, Vincent. *Voyage à Chambéry*. 1797.

Capitan, Louis. 'Dessins d'habitations dans le rocher'. *BSAP*, 1892, pp. 581–2.

Capus, G. 'Études sur la taupe'. *MP*, 1884, pp. 303–6.

Carlier, Claude. *Traité des bêtes à laine, ou Méthode d'élever et de gouverner les troupeaux aux champs et à la bergerie*. 2 vols. 1770.

Caron, François. *Histoire des chemins de fer en France*. I. *1740–1883*. 1997.

Carr, John. *The Stranger in France*. 1803.

Carrier, J. 'Folklore ou vieilles coutumes des habitants de la paroisse de Saint-Amand-de-Coly'. *Bulletin de la Société historique et archéologique du Périgord* (Périgueux), 1893, pp. 396–404.

Cassini de Thury, César-François. *Avertissement ou Introduction à la Carte générale et particulière de la France*. 1750 (?).

Cassini de Thury, C.-F. *Introduction à la seconde feuille occidentale de la Carte de la France*. 1754.

Cavaillès, Henri. *La Route française, son histoire, sa fonction*. 1946.

Cavoleau, Jean-Alexandre. *Description abrégée du département de la Vendée*. Fontenay-le-Peuple, year IX (1800).

Cazals, Rémy, ed. *Histoire de Castres, Mazamet, la Montagne*. Toulouse, 1992.

Céard, Henry. *Terrains à vendre au bord de la mer*. 1906.

Certeau, Michel de, D. Julia and J. Revel. *Une politique de la langue. La Révolution française et les patois: l'enquête de Grégoire*. 1975.

Cestre, A. 'Les Vigies celto-romaines établies le long du Rhin pour la transmission des dépêches'. *NAV*, CCVI (1870), pp. 131–40.

Chaix, Barthélémy. *Préoccupations statistiques, géographiques, pittoresques et synoptiques du département des Hautes-Alpes*. Grenoble, 1845.

Champney, Benjamin. *Sixty Years' Memories of Art and Artists*. 1899; 1977.

Charencey, Hyacinthe de. *Ethnographie euskarienne*. 1889.

Chateaubriand, François-René, Vicomte de. *Mémoires d'outre-tombe*. 2 vols. Ed. J.-C. Berchet. 1989–92.

Chausenque, Vincent de. *Les Pyrénées ou Voyages pédestres dans toutes les régions de ces montagnes*. 2 vols. Agen, 1854.

Chennevières, Philippe de. 'Les Musées de province', *Gazette des Beaux-Arts*, February 1865, pp. 118–31.

Chérot, A. 'Circulation des voyageurs et des marchandises dans le Tunnel du Mont-Cenis'. *Journal des économistes*, May 1875, pp. 322–4.

Chéruel, Adolphe. *Dictionnaire historique des institutions, moeurs et coutumes de la France*. I. 7th ed. 1899.

Chesnel, Adolphe de. *Coutumes, mythes et traditions des provinces de France.* 1846.

Chevalier, Michel. *Des intérêts matériels en France: travaux publics, routes, canaux, chemins de fer.* 1838.

Chevalier, M. 'La Vallée de l'Ariége et la République d'Andorre'. *Revue des Deux Mondes*, 1 December 1837, pp. 618–42.

Chevalier, Michel. *La Vie humaine dans les Pyrénées ariégoises.* 1956.

Chevallier, Émile. *De l'assistance dans les campagnes.* 1889.

Chevallier, Pierre and M.-J. Couailhac. *L'Administration des Eaux et Forêts dans le département de l'Isère au XIXe siècle.* Grenoble, 1983.

Chorier, Nicolas. *Histoire générale de Dauphiné.* 1661–72; 2 vols. Valence, 1869–78.

Choules, John Overton. *Young Americans Abroad, or Vacation in Europe.* Boston, 1852.

Cleary, M. C. *Peasants, Politicians and Producers: the Organisation of Agriculture in France since 1918.* Cambridge, 1989.

Clément, Henry. *La Désertion des campagnes en pays limousin.* 1909.

Cobb, Richard. *The Police and the People. French Popular Protest, 1789–1820.* Oxford, 1970; 1972.

Cobb, R. *Paris and its Provinces, 1792–1802.* Oxford, 1975.

Cobb, R. *The French and Their Revolution.* Ed. D. Gilmour. 1998.

Collet, Vital. 'Sobriquets caractérisant les habitants de villages lorrains'. *Le Pays lorrain* (Nancy), 1908, pp. 442–49.

Constantine, Mary-Ann. *Breton Ballads.* Aberystwyth, 1996.

Consul, Sylva. *Les Petits touristes: premier voyage de vacances.* 1892.

Conty, Henri A. de. *Côtes de Normandie.* 1889.

Conty, H. A. de. *Les Pyrénées occidentales et centrales et le sud-ouest de la France.* 1899.

Cooper, James Fenimore. *A Residence in France.* 1836.

Coraboeuf, Colonel. 'Levée de la carte de France'. *BSG*, I, VIII (1827), pp. 239–40.

Corbin, Alain. *Les Cloches de la terre.* 1994. (Tr. M. Thom: *Village Bells*, 1999.)

Corbin, A. *Le Territoire du vide.* 1988. (Tr. J. Phelps: *The Lure of the Sea*, 1994.)

Corbin, A. *Le Village des cannibales*. 1990. (Tr. A. Goldhammer: *The Village of Cannibals*, 1992.)

Cosson, Jean-Michel, et al. *Les Mystères de l'Aveyron*. Clermont-Ferrand, 1999.

Costello, Louisa Stuart. *Béarn and the Pyrenees*. 2 vols. 1844.

Couderc, Jean-Mary. 'Les Toponymes "Saint-Martin" dans nos campagnes'. *Mémoires de la Société archéologique de Touraine*, LXII (1997).

Couderc, Marie-Anne. *Bécassine inconnue*. 2000.

Coudon, Gilbert. 'Quand Jean-Baptiste Delambre arpentait le Cantal'. http://gilbert.coudon.chez-alice.fr/delambre.htm

Coulon, Louis. *Le Fidèle conducteur pour les voyages de France, d'Allemagne, d'Angleterre et d'Espagne: montrant exactement les raretez et choses remarquables qui se trouvent en chaque ville, et les distances d'icelles, avec un dénombrement des batailles qui s'y sont données*. Troyes and Paris, 1654.

Courtin, Antoine de. *Nouveau traité de la civilité qui se pratique en France parmi les honnestes gens*. 1728.

Courtois, Jacques. *Voyage de M*** en Périgord*. 1762.

Coutans, Dom Guillaume. *Description historique et topographique de la grande route de Paris à Reims*. 1775.

Coyer, Gabriel-François. *Voyages d'Italie et de Hollande*. 2 vols. 1775.

C. P. V. 'Cagots'. *L'Intermédiaire des chercheurs et curieux*, 10 December 1901, pp. 845–6.

Cradock, Anna Francesca. *Journal de Mme Cradock: voyage en France*. 1896.

Creuzé-Latouche, Jacques-Antoine. *Description topographique du district de Chatelleraud*. Châtellerault, 1790.

Crignelle, Henri de. *Le Morvan, a District of France: its Wild Sports, Vineyards and Forests*. Tr. Capt. Jesse. 1851.

Crook, Malcolm, ed. *Revolutionary France, 1788–1880*. Oxford, 2002.

Curtel, Georges ('W. Quick'). *En bicyclette à travers l'Engadine, la Valteline, le Tyrol et l'Italie du Nord*. Saint-Étienne, 1893.

Dagalier (bookseller). *Guide des étrangers dans Toulouse et ses environs*. Toulouse, 1834.

Dainville, François de. *Cartes anciennes du Languedoc*. Montpellier, 1961.

Dally, Eugène. 'Sur les cagots des Pyrénées'. *BSAP*, 1867, pp. 111–14.

Dargenton, Michel. 'Paris–Brest–Paris'. www.memoire-du-cyclisme.net/pbp_livre

Darnton, Robert. *The Great Cat Massacre, and Other Episodes in French Cultural History*. 1984; 1985.

Dauzat, Albert. 'Glossaire étymologique du patois de Vinzelles'. *RLR*, LVI (1913), pp. 285–412.

Davis, I. B. *The Ancient and Modern History of Nice*. 1807.

Deferrière, Alexandre. *Archives statistiques de la France*. 1804–5.

Déguignet, Jean-Marie. *Mémoires d'un paysan bas-breton*. Ed. B. Rouz. Ar Releg-Kerhuon, 1998. Tr. L. Asher: *Memoirs of a Breton Peasant*. 2004.

Dejardin, Joseph and J. Stecher. *Dictionnaire des spots ou Proverbes wallons*. Liège, Paris and London, 1863.

Delambre, Jean-Baptiste and Pierre Méchain. *Base du système métrique décimal, ou Mesure de l'arc du méridien compris entre les parallèles de Dunkerque et Barcelone*. 3 vols. 1806–10.

Delattre, Charles. *Curiosités naturelles de la France*. Limoges and Paris, 1842 (?); also published as *Voyages en France*.

Delattre, C. *Le Jeune industriel, ou Voyages instructifs de Charles d'Hennery avec sa famille*. 1846.

Delisle, Fernand. 'Sur les déformations artificielles du crâne dans les Deux-Sèvres et la Haute-Garonne'. *BSAP*, 1889, pp. 649–59.

Delisle, Guillaume. *Carte des comtéz de Haynaut, de Namur et de Cambrésis*. 1706.

Delvincourt, J. *Impressions sincères d'un touriste sur le pèlerinage de La Louvesc*. Montpellier, 1884.

Demolière, Hippolyte-Jules, et al. *De Paris à Bordeaux*. 1855.

Demolins, Edmond. *Les Français d'aujourd'hui: les types sociaux du Midi et du Centre*. 1898.

Dempster, Charlotte Louisa Hawkins. *The Maritime Alps and Their Seaboard*. 1885.

Denizot, Alain and J. Louis. *L'Énigme Alain-Fournier*. 2000.

Depping, Georges Bernard. *Merveilles et beautés de la nature en France*. 1811.

Depping, G. B. *Voyage de Paris à Neufchâtel en Suisse*. 1813.

Desarènes, Paul. *La Famille de Blanzac ou Promenades en Limousin*. Paris and Limoges, 1849. Later ed. attr. l'abbé Jouhanneaud. 1856.

Descazeaux, René. *Les Cagots: histoire d'un secret*. Pau, 2002.

Desnoues, abbé. *Mon Émigration: journal inédit d'un voyage en Savoye (septembre 1792)*. Orléans, 1899.

Devlin, Judith. *The Superstitious Mind. French Peasants and the Supernatural in the Nineteenth Century*. Yale, 1987.

Dhauteville, I. *Le Français alsacien: fautes de prononciation et germanismes*. Strasbourg, 1852.

Dictionnaire encyclopédique des sciences médicales. 10 vols. 1869–89.

Dix, Edwin Asa. *A Midsummer Drive Through the Pyrenees*. 1890.

Domairon, Louis. *Le Voyageur françois, ou la Connoissance de l'ancien et du nouveau monde*. Vols XXIX–XLII. 1788–95.

Dondel Du Faouëdic, Noémie. *Le Journal d'une pensionnaire en vacances*. Vannes, 1905.

Dorveaux, P. 'Opinion de quelques médecins sur les rebouteurs du Val-d'Ajol'. *Le Pays lorrain* (Nancy), 1911, pp. 562–7.

Dottin, Georges. 'Notes sur le patois de Montjean (Mayenne)'. *Revue des patois gallo-romans*, 1887, pp. 172–6.

Doussault, E. 'Fontarabie (Espagne)'. *TM*, XXIX (1875), pp. 97–112.

Drohojowska, Antoinette-Joséphine-Anne. *Une saison à Nice, Chambéry et Savoie*. 1860.

Du Boys, Albert. *Album du Vivarais*. Grenoble, 1842.

Duby, Georges, et al., eds. *Histoire de la France rurale*. 4 vols. 1976.

Du Camp, Maxime. *Souvenirs littéraires*. 1892; 1994.

Duchesne, Antoine-Nicolas. *Voyage de Antoine-Nicolas Duchesne au Havre et en Haute Normandie, 1762*. 1898.

Duchesne, A.-N. 'Relation d'un voyage à Reims à l'occasion du Sacre de Louis XVI'. 1775; *Travaux de l'Académie nationale de Reims*, 1902, pp. 21–140.

Duckett, William. *Dictionnaire de la conversation et de la lecture*. 27 vols. 2nd ed. 1853–8.

Duclos, Jean-Claude, et al. *Louis Mandrin*. Grenoble, 2005.

Dugied, Pierre-Henri. *Projet de boisement des Basses-Alpes présenté à S. E. le Ministre Secrétaire d'État de l'Intérieur*. 1819.

Dujardin, Victor. *Voyages aux Pyrénées. Souvenirs du Midi par un homme du nord*. Céret, 1890.

Dumas, Alexandre. *Impressions de voyage: de Paris à Cadix*. 1847; 1989.

Dumas, A. *Grand Dictionnaire de cuisine*. 1878.

Dumas, A. *Mes mémoires*. 10 vols. 1863–84.

Dumont, Arsène. 'Étude sur la natalité dans le canton de Fouesnant'. *BSAP*, 1890, pp. 415–46.

Dumont, A. 'Uchizy: une colonie de Sarrazins en Bourgogne'. *BSAP*, 1894, pp. 444–9.

Dupain-Triel, Jean-Louis. *La France connue sous ses plus utiles rapports, ou Nouveau dictionnaire universel de la France, dressé d'après la Carte, en 180 feuilles, de Cassiny*. 1785.

Dupin, Charles. *Forces productives et commerciales de la France*. 1827.

Duplessis, Arthur. 'Paris à Dieppe'. In *Paris, ou Le Livre des Cent-et-Un*. XV (1834).

Durand, Joseph-Pierre. 'Sur l'action des milieux géologiques dans l'Aveyron'. *BSAP*, 1868, pp. 135–47.

Durand-Claye, Charles-Léon. *Cours de routes: professé à l'École des Ponts et Chaussées*. 1895.

Dureau de la Malle. 'Fragmens d'un voyage en France'. *NAV*, XXIX (1826), pp. 249–57.

Durier, Charles. *Le Mont Blanc*. 1877.

Duroux, Rose. *Les Auvergnats de Castille*. Clermont-Ferrand, 1992.

Dusaulx, Jean. *Voyage à Barège et dans les Hautes-Pyrénées*. 2 vols. 1796.

Dussieux, Louis. *Géographie historique de la France*. 1843.

Dutens, Louis. *Itinéraire des routes les plus fréquentées*. 4th ed. 1783.

Duval, Amaury. *Souvenirs (1829–1830)*. 1885.

Duval, Jules. 'Sol agricole de la France', *MP*, 1867, p. 198.

Duval, Louis. *Gargantua en Normandie*. Alençon, 1880.

Edwards, William Frédéric. *Des caractères physiologiques des races humaines considérés dans leurs rapports avec l'histoire*. 1841.

Égron, A. 'Des voyages en France'. *NAV*, XLV (1830), pp. 5–29.

Égron, A. 'Essai statistique sur une partie des départements de la Marne et des Ardennes'. *NAV*, LII (1831), pp. 304–26.

Égron, A. 'Coup d'œil général sur les chemins de fer en France'. *NAV*, LXXIII (1837), pp. 223–31.

Ejnès, Gérard, et al. *Tour de France, 100 ans, 1903–2003*. 3 vols. L'Équipe, 2002.

État-major de l'armée de terre. *Aide-mémoire de l'officier d'état-major en campagne*. 1884.

Exposition universelle internationale de 1878, à Paris. Catalogue officiel. II. 1878.

Fabre, Daniel, J. Lacroix and G. Lanneau. 'Des lieux où l'on "cause"'. *EF*, 1980, 1, pp. 7–26.

Fabry, Jean-Baptiste-Germain. *Itinéraire de Buonaparte, depuis son départ de Doulevent, le 29 mars, jusqu'à son embarquement à Fréjus*. 1815.

Fauchet, Joseph. *Description abrégée du département du Var*. Year IX (1800).

Fauvelle, Charles. 'Photographies de criminels'. *BSAP*, 1890, pp. 957–9.

Favreau, Robert, ed. *Histoire de Poitiers*. Toulouse, 1985.

Fay, H.-M. *Lépreux et cagots du sud-ouest*. 1910.

Fel, André. 'Petite culture, 1750–1850'. In H. Clout, ed. *Themes in the Historical Geography of France*, 1977, pp. 215–45.

Ferrand, H. *L'Oisans et la région de la Meidje, du Pelvoux et de la Barre des Escrins*. Grenoble, 1903.

Ferrand, H. *Le Pays briançonnais, de Briançon au Viso*. Grenoble, 1909.

Ferrand, H. *Le Vercors, le Royannais et les quatre montagnes*. Grenoble, 1904.

Ferrand, H., ed. *Premiers voyages à Chamouni*. Lyon, 1912.

La Feuille villageoise: adressée, chaque semaine, à tous les villages de France, pour les instruire des loix, des évènements, des découvertes qui intéressent tout citoyen. 1790–95.

Flaubert, Gustave. *Par les champs et par les grèves. Voyages et carnets de voyages.* 1973.

Fleutelot, Jean-Baptiste. *Journal manuscrit d'un voyage de Dijon en Provence.* Marseille, 1905.

Flour de Saint-Genis, Victor. *Cahier de doléances du tiers-état de la paroisse de Saint-Beury [Beurizot] en Auxois.* 1901.

Fodéré, François Emmanuel. *Voyage aux Alpes Maritimes.* 2 vols. 1821.

Folin, Léopold-Alexandre-Guillaume de. 'Une excursion à la forêt d'Iraty'. *BSG commerciale de Bordeaux*, 1878, pp. 68–74.

Fontaine, Laurence. *Le Voyage et la mémoire: colporteurs de l'Oisans au XIXe siècle.* Lyon, 1984.

Fontanges, François de. *La Fuite du Roi (20 juin 1791).* 1898.

Fontanges, Guillaume de. *Le Service géographique de l'Armée.* 1938.

Forester, Thomas. *Rambles in the Islands of Corsica and Sardinia.* 1858.

Forrest, Alan. *Napoleon's Men: The Soldiers of the Revolution and Empire.* 2002.

Forster, Robert. *The Nobility of Toulouse in the Eighteenth Century.* Johns Hopkins, 1960.

Fortis, François-Marie, comte de. *Amélie, ou Voyage à Aix-les-Bains et aux environs.* 2 vols. Turin and Lyon, 1829.

Foville, Alfred de. *Enquête sur les conditions de l'habitation en France.* 2 vols. 1894.

Foville, A. de. *La France économique: statistique raisonnée et comparative.* 1890.

Les Français peints par eux-mêmes. Encyclopédie morale du dix-neuvième siècle. 10 vols. 1840–42.

Fréville, Anne-François-Joachim. *Histoire des chiens célèbres, entre-mêlée de notices curieuses sur l'histoire naturelle, &c.* I. 1796.

Frieh-Vurpas, Geneviève. *Aix-les-Bains.* Grenoble, 1998.

Frossard, Émilien. *Tableau pittoresque, scientifique et moral de Nisme et de ses environs.* 2 vols. Nîmes, 1834–35.

Furet, François and W. Sachs. 'La Croissance de l'alphabétisation en France'. *Annales*, XXIX (1974), pp. 714–37.

Frye, William Edward. *After Waterloo, Reminiscences of European Travel, 1815–1819.* 1908.

G . . ., Capt. 'Notice sur le village de Mandeure'. *AV*, XXIII (1814), pp. 367–72.

Gabrielli, C.-F.-J.-B. de. *Manuel du provençal ou les Provençalismes corrigés.* Aix and Marseille, 1836.

Gaillard, Jeanne. 'Les Migrants à Paris au XIXe siècle'. *EF*, 1980, 2, pp. 129–36.

Gallois, L. 'L'Académie des Sciences et les origines de la Carte de Cassini'. *Annales de géographie*, 1909, pp. 193–204 and 289–310.

Garner, Alice. *A Shifting Shore: Locals, Outsiders, and the Transformation of a French Fishing Town*. Ithaca and London, 2005.

Gaskell, Elizabeth. 'An Accursed Race'. *Household Words*, XII (1855).

Gasparin, Valérie de. *Voyage d'une ignorante dans le midi de la France et l'Italie*. 2 vols. 1835.

Gauthier de Clagny, Prosper. *De Paris à Nice en quatre-vingts jours*. 1889.

Gautier, Henri. *Traité des ponts où il est parlé de ceux des Romains et de ceux des modernes*. 1716.

Gazier, A. 'Lettres à Grégoire sur les patois de France'. *Revue des langues romanes* (Montpellier), 1874–79.

Gélis, Jacques. 'Refaire le corps. Les Déformations volontaires du corps de l'enfant à la naissance'. *EF*, 1984, 1, pp. 7–28.

Gendry, E. *Sport vélocipédique. Les Champions français*. Angers, 1891.

Genlis, Mme de (Caroline-Stéphanie-Félicité Du Crest de Saint-Aubin). *Manuel du voyageur, ou Recueil de dialogues, de lettres, etc.* Berlin, 1799.

Gennep, Arnold van. *Manuel de folklore français contemporain*. 9 vols. 1937–58.

George, Jocelyne. 'Les Varois de Paris: évolution et fonctions d'originaires'. *EF*, 1986, 2.

Georgel, Chantal, ed. *La Jeunesse des musées*. 1994.

Gibson, Ralph. *A Social History of French Catholicism, 1789–1914*. 1989.

Gibson, Robert. *The End of Youth: The Life and Work of Alain-Fournier*. Exeter, 2005.

Gildea, Robert. *Education in Provincial France, 1800–1914. A Study of Three Departments*. Oxford, 1983.

Gilliéron, Jules and E. Edmont. *Atlas linguistique de la France*. 1902–10.

Girard, Maurice. *Les Abeilles: organes et fonctions*. 1887.

Girard de Rialle, Julien. *Les Peuples de l'Asie et de l'Europe: notions d'ethnologie*. 1881.

Girardin, J. *Souvenirs des Pyrénées*. Rouen, 1838.

Girardin, Paul. 'Voyage en France, par Ardouin-Dumazet'. *La Géographie*, IX (1904), pp. 445–9.

Girault de Saint-Fargeau, Eusèbe. *Guide pittoresque, portatif et complet du voyageur en France: contenant les relais de poste, dont la distance a été convertie en kilomètres*. 1842.

Giraut, Charles. *Carnets de route*. Châlons-sur-Marne, 1914.

Goubert, Pierre. *Beauvais et le Beauvaisis de 1600 à 1730*. 1960.

Gourdault, Jules. *La France pittoresque*. 1893.

Grad, Charles. *L'Alsace, le pays et ses habitants*. 1909.

Grandmaison, Marie de. *Le Tour de France*. 1893.

Grandsire, E. (illust.; text anon.). 'Les Bords de la Creuse'. *MP*, 1858, pp. 67–70.

Grandsire, E. (illust.; text anon.). 'La Sologne'. *MP*, 1863, pp. 3–6.

Grangent, Stanislas-Victor, et al. *Description abrégée du département du Gard*. Nîmes, year VIII (1799).

Gratiot, Maurice. *Deux parisiens dans le Val d'Andorre*. 1890.

Greeley, Horace. *Glances at Europe, in a Series of Letters from Great Britain, France, Italy, Switzerland, &c.* 1851.

Grégoire, Abbé Henri. 'Rapport sur la nécessité et les moyens d'anéantir les patois et d'universaliser l'usage de la langue française'. In Gazier (1879), pp. 193–217.

Grynberg, Anne. *Les Camps de la honte: les internés juifs*. 1999.

Guérin, Jean. 'Les Nourrissons'. *MP*, 1890, pp. 131–4.

Guignet, Charles-Ernest. 'À travers les Landes'. *MP*, 1889, pp. 140–3.

Guillaumin, Émile. *La Vie d'un simple*. 1904; 2001.

Gutton, Jean-Pierre. *Naissance du vieillard*. 1988.

Haan, Paul. 'Pratiques empiriques des Flandres'. *BSAP*, 1897, pp. 125–7.

Haillant, Nicolas and A. Virtel. 'Choix de proverbes et dictons patois de Damas'. *Annales de la Société d'émulation du département des Vosges* (Épinal), 1903, pp. 1–28.

Hallays, André. *En flânant à travers la France*. 9 vols. 1903–23.

Hamerton, Philip Gilbert. *Round My House, Notes of Rural Life in France in Peace and War*. 1876.

Hamy, Ernest-Théodore. *Les Origines du Musée d'ethnographie*. 1890.

Hare, Augustus J. C. *The Rivieras*. 1897.

Haristoy, abbé. 'Les Paroisses du pays basque: Ciboure'. I. *Études historiques et religieuses du Diocèse de Bayonne*, 1895, pp. 273–88.

Harlé, Édouard. 'Le Pont de la Basilique de Lourdes'. *Revue philomathique de Bordeaux et du Sud-Ouest*, 1922, pp. 145–55.

Harris, Ruth. *Lourdes: Body and Spirit in the Secular Age*. 1999; 2000.

Haussmann, Georges-Eugène. *Mémoires du Baron Haussmann*. I. *Avant l'Hôtel de Ville*. 1890.

Hazareesingh, Sudhir. *From Subject to Citizen: The Second Empire and the Emergence of Modern French Democracy*. Princeton, 1998.

Hazareesingh, S. *The Legend of Napoleon*. 2004.

Hazareesingh, S. *The Saint-Napoleon: Celebrations of Sovereignty*. 2004.

Hécart, Gabriel-Antoine-Joseph. *Dictionnaire rouchi-français*. Valenciennes, 1834.

Hélias, Pierre-Jakez. *Le Cheval d'orgueil: mémoires d'un Breton du pays bigouden*. 1975. Tr. J. Guicharnaud: *The Horse of Pride: Life in a Breton Village*. Yale, 1978.

Hesseln, Robert de. *Dictionnaire universel de la France*. 6 vols. 1771.

Hirzel, Hans Caspar. *Le Socrate rustique, ou Description de la conduite économique et morale d'un paysan philosophe*. 2nd ed. Zurich, 1764.

H. L. 'Cacous et cagots'. *L'Intermédiaire des chercheurs et curieux*, 15 August 1899, pp. 267–8.

Holdsworth, J. H. *Memoranda on Tours and Touraine: Including Remarks on the Climate [. . .] also on the Wines and Mineral Waters of France*. Tours, 1842.

Home, Gordon. *Normandy, the Scenery and Romance of its Ancient Towns*. 1905.

Huard, Charles. *Paris, province, étranger: cent dessins*. 1906.

Hubscher, Ronald H. *L'Agriculture et la société rurale dans le Pas-de-Calais*. 2 vols in one. Arras, 1979.

Huet de Coëtlizan, Jean-Baptiste (?). *Recherches économiques et statistiques sur le département de la Loire-Inférieure*. Nantes and Paris, year XII (1803).

Hufton, Olwen H. *The Poor of Eighteenth-Century France*. Oxford, 1974.

Hughes, Rev. W. *A Tour Through Several of the Midland and Western Departments of France*. 1803.

Hugo, Abel. *La France pittoresque*. 2 vols. 1835.

Hugo, V. *Œuvres complètes*. 15 vols. 1985–90.

Hurlbert, William Henry. *France and the Republic: A Record of Things Seen and Learned in the French Provinces During the 'Centennial' Year 1889*. 1890.

Itard, Jean-Marc-Gaspard. *De l'éducation d'un homme sauvage*. 1801.

Jal, Auguste. *De Paris à Naples: études de mœurs, de marine et d'art*. 2 vols. 1836.

Jamerey-Duval, Valentin. *Mémoires. Enfance et éducation d'un paysan au XVIIIᵉ siècle*. Ed. J.-M. Goulemot. 1981.

James, Henry. *A Little Tour in France*. 1884; 1900.

Janin, Jules. 'Le Marchand de chiens'. *In Paris, ou Le Livre des Cent-et-Un*. VIII (1832).

Jaubert, Hippolyte-François. *Glossaire du Centre de la France*. 2nd ed. 1864.

J. B. J. *Guide du voyageur aux bains de Bagnères, Barèges, St-Sauveur et Cauteretz*. 1819.

Joanne, Adolphe. *Atlas historique et statistique des chemins de fer français.* 1859.

Joanne, A. *Dictionnaire géographique, administratif, postal, statistique, archéologique, etc. de la France, de l'Algérie et des colonies.* 2 vols. 1864; 1869.

Joanne, A. *Géographie du département de [. . .]* (separate monographs). 1874–93.

Joanne, A. *Itinéraire général de la France: Les Pyrénées.* 3rd ed. 1868.

Joanne, A. and É. Reclus. 'Excursions dans le Dauphiné'. *TM,* II (1860), pp. 369–418.

Joanne, Paul. *Dictionnaire géographique et administratif de la France et de ses colonies.* 7 vols. 1890–1905.

Joanne, P. *Vosges, Alsace et Ardennes.* 1883.

Jones, Colin. *The Great Nation: France from Louis XV to Napoleon.* 2002; 2003.

Jones, Mary Cadwalader. *European Travel for Women.* 1900.

Jones, Peter. *Liberty and Locality in Revolutionary France.* Cambridge, 2003.

Jones, P. *The Peasantry in the French Revolution.* Cambridge, 1988.

Jones, P. *Politics and Rural Society: the Southern Massif Central.* Cambridge, 1985.

Jordan, Claude. *Voyages historiques de l'Europe: qui comprend tout ce qu'il y a de plus curieux en France.* I. 1693.

Josse, H. 'Construction, révision et vulgarisation de la Carte de France'. *BSG commerciale de Bordeaux,* 1878, pp. 469–73.

Jouanne, P. 'Maison rurale d'enfants, fondée à Ry'. *La Science sociale. Journal de l'école sociétaire,* 16 December 1867, pp. 298–300.

Joudou, Jean-Baptiste-Marie. *Guide des voyageurs à Bagnères-de-Bigorre et dans les environs.* Tarbes, 1818.

Jourdain, Dom. 'Mémoire sur les voies romaines dans le pays des Séquanais'. *NAV,* CLXXV (1862), pp. 174–210.

Jourdan, Justin. *Excursions dans Toulouse et le département de la Haute-Garonne.* Toulouse, 1858.

Jubinal, Achille. 'Le Conducteur de coucou'. In *Paris, ou Le Livre des Cent-et-Un.* XIV (1834).

Judt, Tony. *Socialism in Provence, 1871–1914.* Cambridge, 1979.

Julia, Dominique and D. Milo. 'Une culture passante'. In A. Burguière and J. Revel. *Histoire de la France. L'Espace français.* 1989.

Karr, Alphonse. *De loin et de près.* 1862.

Keane, A. H. 'Cagots'. *Encyclopaedia of Religion and Ethics.* III. Edinburgh and New York, 1910.

Kipling, Rudyard. *Souvenirs of France.* 1933.

Kipling, R. 'Motoring Diaries'. Ed. J. Barnes. *Areté*, 12 (Autumn 2003), pp. 63–85.

Kock, Paul de. *La Grande Ville: nouveau tableau de Paris*. 2 vols. 1844.

Konvitz, Josef W. *Cartography in France, 1660–1848*. Chicago, 1987.

Labesse, Édouard Decaudin. *Notre pays de France: le Roi du biniou (Bretagne)*. 1893.

Laboulinière, P. *Annuaire statistique du département des Hautes-Pyrénées*. Tarbes, 1807.

Labourasse, Henri-Adolphe. 'Anciens us, coutumes, légendes, superstitions, préjugés, etc. du département de la Meuse'. *Mémoires de la Société des lettres, sciences et arts de Bar-le-Duc*, 1902, pp. 3–225.

Labroue, Émile. 'À travers les Pyrénées: Aulus'. *BSG commerciale de Bordeaux*, 1884, pp. 161–70.

La Condamine, Charles-Marie de. *Histoire d'une jeune fille sauvage, trouvée dans les bois à l'âge de dix ans*. 1755.

Ladoucette, Jean-Charles-François. *Histoire, topographie, antiquités, usages, dialectes des Hautes-Alpes*. 2nd ed. 1834.

Ladoucette, J.-C.-F. 'Mœurs et usages des Hautes-Alpes'. *BSG*, I, XX (1833), pp. 131–43.

Ladoucette, J.-C.-F. 'Anecdotes sur Napoléon'. In *Paris, ou Le Livre des Cent-et-Un*. XV (1834).

La Fontaine, Jean de, et al. *Voyages des poètes français (XVIIᵉ et XVIIIᵉ siècles)*. 1888.

Lagarde, Prosper de. *Voyage dans le Pays Basque et aux bains de Biaritz*. 1835.

Lagardelle, Firmin. 'Notes anthropologiques sur les colliberts, huttiers et nioleurs des marais mouillés de la Sèvre'. *BSAP*, 1871, pp. 202–14.

Lagarenne, Pierre. 'Notice sur le patois saintongeais'. *RLR*, VII (1875), pp. 134–44.

Lagneau, Gustave. 'Les Gaëls et les Celtes'. *BSAP*, 1859–60, pp. 514–19.

Lagneau, G. 'Notice-questionnaire sur l'anthropologie de la France'. *BSAP*, 1861, pp. 327–406.

Lagneau, G. 'Sur l'incurvation lombo-sacrée comme caractère ethnique'. *BSAP*, 1866, pp. 633–37.

Lagneau, G. 'De l'anthropologie de la France'. *BSAP*, 1867, pp. 389–99.

Lagneau, G. 'Sur les habitants de l'Aveyron et les Sarrasins de France'. *BSAP*, 1868, pp. 168–73.

Lagneau, G. 'Sur les Gavaches'. *BSAP*, 1876, pp. 38–39.

Lajard, J. and F. Regnault. *De l'existence de la lèpre atténuée chez les cagots des Pyrénées*. 1893.

Lallemand, Léon. *Histoire de la charité*. IV. 2 parts. *Les Temps modernes*. 1910–12.

Lamouche, Léon. 'Note sur la classification des dialectes de la langue d'oc'. *RLR*, XLIII (1900), pp. 351–63.

Lande, Lucien-Louis. 'Les Cagots et leurs congénères'. *Revue des Deux Mondes*, 15 January 1878, pp. 426–50.

Landrin, Armand. 'Écriture figurative et comptabilité en Bretagne'. *Revue d'ethnographie*, 1882, pp. 369–80.

Lanoye, Ferdinand de. 'Voyage aux volcans de la France centrale'. *TM*, XIV (1866), pp. 289–304.

Largillière, René. *Les Saints et l'organisation chrétienne primitive dans l'Armorique bretonne*. Rennes, 1925.

La Roche, Jean de. *Voyage d'un amateur des arts en Flandre, dans les Pays-Bas, en Hollande, en France, en Savoye, en Italie, en Suisse*. 4 vols. Amsterdam, 1783.

La Rochefoucauld d'Anville, Louis-Alexandre de. *Relation inédite d'un voyage aux glacières de Savoie en 1762*. Club Alpin français, 1894.

Larousse, Pierre. *Grand Dictionnaire universel du XIXᵉ siècle*. 17 vols. 1866–79.

Lasserre, Bertrand. *Les Cent jours en Vendée*. 1906.

Laudet, Fernand. 'Monsieur le maire'. In *Archives de Gascogne* (1993), pp. 151–52.

Launay, Françoise. 'La Dame de la Lune'. *Pour la Science*, 307 (May 2003).

Lavallée, Joseph and Louis Brion de La Tour. *Voyage dans les départements de la France*. 5 vols. 1792–1802.

Laville, André, et al. Article by Jho Pale on Hoedic and Houat. *BSAP*, 1909, pp. 5–9.

Lavisse, Ernest. *Discours à des enfants*. 1907.

Lavisse, E. and François Picavet. *Instruction morale et civique*. 1888.

Lawlor, Denys Shyne. *Pilgrimages in the Pyrenees and Landes*. 1870.

L. D. M. *Itinéraire complet de la France, ou Tableau général de toutes les routes et chemins de traverse de ce royaume*. 2 vols. 1788.

Le Bas, Philippe. *France. Dictionnaire encyclopédique*. III. 1841.

Le Bras, Hervé and E. Todd. *L'Invention de la France. Atlas anthropologique et politique*. 1981.

Leca, Colonel. 'La Loire navigable'. *Société de géographie commerciale de Nantes* (1897), pp. 57–84 and 161–213.

Leclercq, Jules. *Promenades dans les Pyrénées*. Paris and Tours, 1888.

Lecreulx, François-Michel. *Description abrégée du département de la Meurthe*. Year VII (1799).

Leduc, Pierre-Étienne-Denis. *Maître Pierre ou Le Savant de village. Entretiens sur la Géographie de la France*. 1833.

Lefebvre, Georges. *La Grande Peur de 1789.* 1932.

Lefebvre d'Hellancourt, Antoine Marie. *Le Voyage de Dhellancourt en Oisans (1785).* Grenoble, 1892.

Legrand d'Aussy, Pierre Jean-Baptiste. *Voyage d'Auvergne.* 1788.

Lehning, James. *Peasant and French: Cultural Contact in Rural France During the Nineteenth Century.* Cambridge, 1995.

Lemps, Abbé de. *Panorama de la Corse.* 1844.

Lenthéric, Charles. *La Grèce & l'Orient en provence.* 1910.

Lepelletier, Almire. *Voyage en Bretagne [. . .] avec [. . .] l'iconographie des principaux types de forçats.* 1853.

Le Play, Frédéric. *Les Ouvriers des deux mondes.* I. 1857–85.

Lequinio, Joseph-Marie. *Voyage dans le Jura.* 2 vols. Year IX (1800).

Leschevin, Philippe-Xavier. *Voyage à Genève et dans la vallée de Chamouni.* Paris and Geneva, 1812.

Letourneau, Charles. 'Le Clan primitif'. *BSAP*, 1889, pp. 265–73.

Levasseur, Émile. *La Population française: histoire de la population avant 1789.* 3 vols. 1889–92.

Lévêque, Louis. 'Une famille de rebouteurs lorrains'. *Le Pays lorrain* (Nancy), 1909, pp. 65–78.

Liodet, Louise. *La Corse à vol d'oiseau.* 1873.

Longfellow, Henry Wadsworth. *Outre-Mer: a Pilgrimage Beyond the Sea.* 1835; Boston, 1882.

Loubès, Gilbert. *L'Énigme des cagots: histoire d'une exclusion.* Bordeaux, 1995.

Louette (printer). *Itinéraire complet de la France.* 2 vols. 1788.

Loux, Françoise and P. Richard. 'Recettes françaises de médecine populaire'. *EF*, 1981, 4, pp. 369–74.

Luçay, Jean-Baptiste-Charles Legendre. *Description du département du Cher.* Year X (1801).

Lunemann. 'Le Pays des Basques'. *NAV*, XLIX (1831), pp. 30–71.

Lunier, Ludger. 'Recherches sur quelques déformations du crâne'. *Mémoires de la Société de statistique du département des Deux-Sèvres* (Niort), 1852, pp. 73–89.

Lunier, L. 'Sur quelques déformations du crâne'. *BSAP*, 1866, pp. 139–42.

MacCarthy, O. (illust.; text anon.). 'Productions gastronomiques de la France'. *MP*, 1847, pp. 267–70.

Maclean, Charles. *An Excursion in France, and Other Parts of the Continent of Europe.* 1804.

McPhee, Peter. *Revolution and Environment in Southern France: Peasants, Lords and Murder in the Corbières, 1780–1830.* Oxford, 1999.

McPhee, P. *A Social History of France, 1780–1880.* 1992; 1993.

Magitot, Émile. 'Moulages de doigts recueillis sur des cagots'. *BSAP*, 1892, pp. 553–72.

Mahé de La Bourdonnais, A. *Voyage en Basse-Bretagne chez les Bigouden de Pont-l'Abbé [. . .] Affinités des Bigouden avec les Lapons, les Mongols-Kalkhas [. . .] et autres peuples d'origine mongolique des monts Himalaya et de l'Indo-Chine.* 1892.

Malepeyre, Léopold. *Code des ouvriers.* 1833.

Malte-Brun, Conrad. 'Rapports sur deux voyages [. . .] par M. Decandolle, professeur de botanique'. *AV*, VI (1810), pp. 240–50.

Malte-Brun, C. 'Population du département de l'Aisne'. *NAV*, XX (1823), pp. 266–73.

Malte-Brun, V. A. 'Esquisse historique des grandes cartes topographiques'. *BSG*, IV, XV (1858), pp. 182–93.

Malte-Brun, V.-A. 'État d'avancement et réduction de prix de la Carte de France'. *NAV*, CXCIX (1868), pp. 201–6.

Mangin, Arthur. *Le Désert et le monde sauvage.* Tours, 1866.

Manier, Guillaume. *Pèlerinage d'un paysan picard à Saint-Jacques de Compostelle.* Montdidier, 1890.

Marcadet, Jules. 'Les Étapes de la bicyclette'. *MP*, 1894, pp. 283–5.

Marchangy, Louis-Antoine-François de. *La Gaule poétique.* 8 vols. 1815–17; 2nd ed., 1819.

Mariéton, Paul. *La Terre provençale.* 1894.

Marlin, François. *Voyages d'un français, depuis 1775 jusqu'à 1807.* 4 vols. 1817.

Marmier, Xavier. *Les Mémoires d'un orphelin.* 1890.

Marmontel, Jean-François. *Mémoires.* 1999.

Martel, Édouard-Alfred. *Les Abîmes.* 1894.

Martel, É.-A. 'Le Gouffre du puits de Padirac'. *TM*, LX (1890), pp. 401–6.

Martel, É.-A. *Les Cévennes et la région des Causses.* 1890.

Martel, É.-A. 'Dans les cavernes des Causses (dixième campagne souterraine)'. *TM*, n.s., IV (1898), pp. 301–12.

Martel, É.-A. 'La France inconnue: Fontaine-l'Évêque et les avens de Canjuers; le grand cañon du Verdon'. *La Géographie*, XIII (1906), pp. 473–5.

Martel, É.-A. and A. Janet. 'L'Exploration du Grand Cañon du Verdon'. *TM*, n.s., XII (1906), pp. 577–600.

Martel, Pierre, *see* Windham.

Martin, Germain and P. Martenot. *Contribution à l'histoire des classes rurales en France au XIXᵉ siècle: la Côte-d'Or.* Dijon and Paris, 1909.

Martin, Jean-Pierre. *La Traversée des Alpes.* Grenoble, 2000.

Massé-Isidore, Charles. *La Vendée poétique et pittoresque.* Nantes, 1829.

Masson de Saint-Amand, Amand-Narcisse. *Lettres d'un voyageur à l'embouchure de la Seine*. 1828.

Maupassant, Guy de. *Mont Oriol*. 1887.

Maupassant, G. de. 'En Bretagne'. *La Nouvelle Revue*, 1 January 1884, pp. 70–86.

Maurin, E. 'Une sorcière en Rouergue'. *Revue du traditionnisme français et étranger*, 1911, pp. 187–9.

Mazade, Étienne-Laurent-Jean. *Itinéraire ou Passe-temps de Lyon à Mâcon, par la diligence d'eau*. Lyon, 1812.

Mazon, Albin ('le Dr Francus'). *Voyage autour de Privas*. Privas, 1882.

Mazon, A. *Voyage aux pays volcaniques du Vivarais*. Privas, 1878.

Mège, Francisque. *Souvenirs de la langue d'Auvergne*. 1861.

Melczer, William, ed. *The Pilgrim's Guide to Santiago de Compostela*. 1993. (Book V of *Codex Calixtinus*.)

Ménétra, Jacques-Louis. *Journal de ma vie*. 1982.

Mercadier de Belesta, Jean-Baptiste. *Ébauche d'une description abrégée du département de l'Ariège*. Foix, year IX (1800).

Mercier-Thoinnet, M. and Mme. *Souvenirs de voyage*. 1838.

Mérimée, Prosper. *Correspondance générale*. Ed. M. Parturier. 17 vols. 1941–64.

Mérimée, P. *Notes d'un voyage dans le Midi de la France*. 1835.

Mérimée, P. *Notes d'un voyage dans l'Ouest de la France*. 1836.

Mérimée, P. *Notes d'un voyage en Auvergne*. 1838.

Mérimée, P. *Notes d'un voyage en Corse*. 1840.

Mérimée, P. 'Des monuments dits celtiques ou druidiques'. *L'Athenaeum français*, 11 (Sept. 1852), pp. 169–71.

Merriman, John M. *The Margins of City Life: Explorations of the French Urban Frontier*. Oxford, 1991.

Merson, Ernest. *Journal d'un journaliste en voyage*. 1865.

Michaud, Louis-Gabriel. *Biographie universelle*. 85 vols. 1811–62.

Michel, Francisque. *Histoire des races maudites de la France et de l'Espagne*. 2 vols. 1847.

Michel, Joseph-Étienne. *Statistique du département des Bouches du Rhône*. Year XI (1802).

Michel, J.-F. *Dictionnaire des expressions vicieuses, usitées dans un grand nombre de départemens, et notamment dans la ci-devant province de Lorraine*. Nancy, Metz and Paris, 1807.

Michelet, Jules. *Le Peuple*. 1846.

Michot de La Cauw. *Voyage philosophique, politique et pittoresque, nouvellement fait en France*. Amsterdam, 1786.

Miller, William. *Wintering in the Riviera*. 1879.

Mirabeau, Victor Riqueti, marquis de. *L'Ami des hommes, ou Traité de la population*. Avignon, 1756.

Mistral, Frédéric. *Mes origines: mémoires et récits*. 1906.

Mistral, F. *Mirèio*. 1859; 1978.

Mistral, F. *Lou Pouèmo dóu Rose*. 1896; 1995.

Moch, Leslie Page. *Paths to the City: Regional Migration in Nineteenth-Century France*. 1983.

Molard, Étienne. *Le Mauvais langage ou Recueil, par ordre alphabétique, d'expressions et de phrases vicieuses usitées en France, et notamment à Lyon*. 4th ed. Lyon and Paris, 1810.

Monlezun, Jean-Justin. *Histoire de la Gascogne depuis les temps les plus reculés jusqu'à nos jours*. I. Auch, 1846.

Monnet, Antoine-Grimoald. *Les Bains du Mont-Dore en 1786*. Clermont-Ferrand, 1887.

Montaran, Marie Constance Albertine. *Mes pensées en voyage: excursions dans les Pyrénées*. 1868.

Monteil, Amans-Alexis. *Description du département de l'Aveiron*. 2 vols. Rodez, year X (1801).

Montémont, Albert. *Voyage aux Alpes et en Italie*. 2 vols. 1821.

Moore, John. *A View of Society and Manners in France, Switzerland, and Germany*. 2 vols. 1779; 1789.

Morris, William. *Letters Sent Home. France and the French, or How I Went to the Paris Exhibition, and What I Saw by the Way*. Swindon, 1870.

Mortemart de Boisse, François-Jérôme-Léonard de. *Voyage dans les Landes de Gascogne*. 1840.

Murray, John, et al. *A Handbook for Travellers in France*. 1854.

Museon Arlaten. *Restaurer la montagne*. 2004.

Nadaud, Martin. *Mémoires de Léonard, ancien garçon maçon*. Bourganeuf, 1895.

Nash, James. *The Guide to Nice. Historical, Descriptive and Hygienic*. 1884.

Nerval, Gérard de. *Œuvres complètes*. 3 vols. Ed. J. Guillaume and C. Pichois. 1984–93.

Nettement, Alfred. *Mémoires historiques de S. A. R. Madame, duchesse de Berry*. 3 vols. 1837.

Noah, Mordecai Manuel. *Travels in England, France, Spain and the Barbary States*. 1819.

Nodier, Charles, Baron Taylor and A. de Cailleux. *Voyages pittoresques et romantiques dans l'ancienne France*. 18 vols. 1820–78.

Nora, Pierre, ed. *Les Lieux de mémoire*. II. 1986.

Nordling, Wilhem de. 'L'Unification des heures'. *BSG*, VII, XI (1890), pp. 111–37.

Ogée, Jean. *Atlas itinéraire de Bretagne*. Nantes, 1769.
Ogier, Théodore. *Voyage de Lyon à Avignon par le chemin de fer et le Rhône*. Lyon, 1854.
Orlov, Grigorii Vladimirovitch. *Voyage dans une partie de la France*. 3 vols. 1824.

Pacha, Béatrice and L. Miran. *Cartes et plans imprimés de 1564 à 1815*. 1996.
Pachoud. 'Tournée en Provence en 1828'. *NAV*, XLIII and XLIV (1829), pp. 295–322 and 147–73.
Papon, Jean-Pierre. *Voyage littéraire de Provence*. 1780.
Papon, S. *Voyage dans le département des Alpes Maritimes*. Year XII (1804).
Pariset, Mme [M. Gacon-Dufour and É. Marie Bayle-Mouillard]. *Nouveau manuel complet de la maîtresse de maison, ou Lettres sur l'économie domestique*. 1852.
Paronnaud, Jean-Claude. 'Les Cagots'. http://cgpa64.free.fr/cagots/index.htm
Parry, M., et al., eds. *The Changing Voices of Europe*. Cardiff, 1994.
Peake, Richard Brinsley. *The Characteristic Costume of France; from Drawings Made on the Spot*. 1819.
Pelletier, Monique. *La Carte de Cassini*. Pont et Chaussées, 1990.
Pelletier, M. and H. Ozanne. *Portraits de la France: les Cartes, témoins de l'histoire*. 1995.
Perbosc, Antonin. 'Le Langage des bêtes'. *Revue du traditionnisme français et étranger*, 1907, pp. 280–85.
Perdiguier, Agricol. *Mémoires d'un compagnon*. 1854; Ed. A. Faure. 1977.
Perdiguier, A. *Question vitale sur le compagnonnage et la classe ouvrière*. 1863.
Pérégrin. *Excursions pyrénéennes: une flânerie aux Pène-Taillade et Pourry*. Tarbes, 1886.
Perret, Paul. *Le Pays Basque et la Basse-Navarre*. Poitiers, 1882.
Perret, P. *Les Pyrénées françaises*. I. *Lourdes, Argelès, Cauterets, Luz, Saint-Sauveur, Barèges*. Poitiers, 1881.
Perrin-Dulac, François. *Description générale du département de l'Isère*. 2 vols. Grenoble, 1806.
Perrot, Michelle, ed. *Histoire de la vie privée*. IV. *De la Révolution à la Grande Guerre*. 1987.
Peuchet, Jacques and P.-G. Chanlaire. *Description topographique et statistique de la France*. 3 vols. 1807.

Peyrat, Napoléon. *Histoire des pasteurs du désert*. 2 vols. Paris and Valence, 1842.

Philipps, Dr. *Vacances en Limousin*. 1886.

Piédagnel, Alexandre. *Jadis, souvenirs et fantaisies*. 1886.

Piette, Édouard and J. Sacaze. 'La Montagne d'Espiaup'. *BSAP*, 1877, pp. 225–51.

Piganiol de La Force, Jean-Aymar. *Nouveau voyage de France, avec un itinéraire et des cartes faites exprès*. 2 vols. 1740.

Pigault-Lebrun and V. Augier. *Voyage dans le midi de la France*. 1827.

Pineau, Léon. 'Les Remèdes populaires'. In *Archives d'Auvergne* (1993), pp. 173–80.

Pinkney, Ninian. *Travels Through the South of France, and in the Interior of the Provinces of Provence and Languedoc [. . .] by a Route Never Before Performed*. 1809.

Pintard, Eugène. 'Proverbes du Vexin'. *Revue du traditionnisme français et étranger*, 1909, pp. 109–11.

Planhol, Xavier de. *Géographie historique de la France*. 1988. (Tr. J. Lloyd: *An Historical Geography of France*. Cambridge, 1994.)

Planté, Paul. 'Les Matériels aratoires du Midi méditerranéen au XIXe siècle'. Doctoral thesis. Montpellier, 1997.

Plazanet, Général. 'Essai d'une carte des patois du Midi'. *BSG commerciale de Bordeaux*, 1913, pp. 166–85 and 208–27.

Ploux, François. *De bouche à oreille: naissance et propagation des rumeurs dans la France du XIXe siècle*. 2003.

Ploux, F. 'Politique, rumeurs et solidarités territoriales'. *Cahiers d'histoire*, 1999, 2, pp. 237–65.

Plumptre, Anne. *A Narrative of a Three Years' Residence in France*. 3 vols. 1810.

Pöllnitz, Karl Ludwig von. *The Memoirs of Charles-Lewis, Baron de Pollnitz*. 4 vols. 1738.

Pomier, Émile. *Manuel des locutions vicieuses les plus fréquentes dans le département de la Haute-Loire et la majeure partie du midi de la France*. Le Puy, 1835.

Pons, de l'Hérault. *Souvenirs et anecdotes de l'île d'Elbe*. 1897.

Porchat, Jacques. *Trois mois sous la neige: journal d'un jeune habitant du Jura*. 15th ed. 1886.

Pradt, Dominique de. *Voyage agronomique en Auvergne*. 1828.

Préfecture du Calvados. *Livret de cantonnier*. Caen, 1842.

Price, Roger. *The Modernization of Rural France*. 1983.

Privat d'Anglemont, Alexandre. *Paris anecdote*. 1860.

Proudhon, Pierre-Joseph. *Mémoires sur ma vie*. Ed. B. Voyenne. 1983.

Proust, Henri. 'Le Progrès agricole dans le Bocage'. *Revue des Deux Mondes*, 15 April 1861, pp. 1034–46.

Proust, Marcel. *À la recherche du temps perdu*. 4 vols. Ed. J.-Y. Tadié. 1987–89.

Quellien, Narcisse. 'Quelques particularités de certains costumes bretons'. *Revue d'ethnographie*, 1885, pp. 354–5.

Rabot, Charles. 'Les Marais du Bas-Poitou'. *La Géographie*, X (1904), pp. 377–85.

Raison-Jourde, Françoise. *La Colonie auvergnate de Paris au XIXᵉ siècle*. 1976.

Raison-Jourde, F. 'Endogamie et stratégie d'implantation professionnelle des migrants auvergnats à Paris au XIXᵉ siècle'. *EF*, 1980, 2.

Raitt, Alan. *Prosper Mérimée*. 1970.

Ramond, Louis. *Observations faites dans les Pyrénées*. 1789.

Raverat, Baron Achille. *À travers le Dauphiné*. Grenoble, 1861.

Rayeur, I.-A. 'À travers l'Ardenne française'. *TM*, LXVIII (1894), pp. 161–92.

Reclus, Élisée. *Nouvelle géographie universelle: la terre et les hommes*. II. *La France*. 1885.

Reclus, Onésime. *France, Algérie et colonies*. 1886.

Reclus, O. *Le Plus beau royaume sous le ciel*. 1899.

Reichard, Heinrich August Ottokar. *Guide des voyageurs en France*. Weimar, 1810.

Reinhard, Aimé. *Le Mont Sainte-Odile et ses environs*. Strasbourg, 1888.

Renan, Ernest. *Souvenirs d'enfance et de jeunesse*. 1883; 1983.

Renard, Jules. *Journal, 1887–1910*. 1960.

Rességuier, Fernand, Comte de. *En wagon de Toulouse à Rome*. Toulouse, 1879.

Restif de la Bretonne, Nicolas-Edmé. *La Vie de mon père*. 1778. Ed. G. Rouger. 1970.

Reverdy, Georges. *Atlas historique des routes de France*. Ponts et Chaussées, 1986.

'Richard' *see* Audin.

Richard, Ambroise and A. A. Lheureux. *Voyage de deux amis en Italie par le Midi de la France*. 1829.

Richard, Nicolas-François-Joseph. 'Coutume de la Bresse'. *BSG*, I, XVIII (1832), pp. 221–26.

Rion, J.-A. 'Découverte du col de Severen'. *NAV*, CIX (1845), pp. 106–12.

Roberts, Emma. *Notes of an Overland Journey Through France and Egypt to Bombay*. 1841.

Robillard de Beaurepaire, Charles de. *Les Ponts-et-Chaussées dans la Généralité de Rouen*. Rouen, 1883.

Robischung, François-Antoine. *Mémoires d'un guide octogénaire, échos des vallées d'Alsace et de Lorraine*. Tours, 1886.

Rochas, V. de. *Les Parias de France et d'Espagne (Cagots et Bohémiens)*. 1876.

Roland de La Platière, Jean-Marie. *Voyage en France, 1769*. Villefranche, 1913.

Rolland de Denus, André. *Dictionnaire des appellations ethniques de la France et de ses colonies*. 1889.

Ronjat, Jules. 'Restitution de quelques noms de lieux dans l'Oisans'. *RLR*, LI (1908), pp. 60–63.

Rosenstein, M. 'Promenade sur les côtes du Golfe de Gascogne [. . .] par M. J. Thoré'. *AV*, XVI (1811), pp. 346–54.

Rougelet, Albert. *Zigzags folâtres. Vers les rives du Bourget, raid cyclofantastique*. Lyon, 1901.

Roujou, Anatole. 'Sur quelques types humains trouvés en France'. *BSAP*, 1872, pp. 768–82.

Roujou, A. 'Sur quelques races ou sous-races locales observées en France'. *BSAP*, 1874, pp. 249–55.

Roujou, A. 'Quelques observations anthropologiques sur le département du Puy-de-Dôme'. *BSAP*, 1876, pp. 330–50.

Rouquette, Jules. *Jean Cavalier, le héros des Cévennes*. 1892.

Rousseau, Jean-Jacques. *Les Confessions*. 2 vols. 1782; 1980.

Rousselot, Pierre-Jean. 'Les Modifications phonétiques du langage étudiées dans le patois d'une famille de Cellefrouin'. *Revue des patois galloromans*, 1892 (Supplément), pp. 9–62.

Roux, Paul. 'Les Riches colporteurs'. In *Archives d'Auvergne* (1993), pp. 211–15.

Roux, Xavier. *Les Alpes, histoire et souvenirs*. 1877.

Russell, Henry. *Biarritz and Basque Countries*. 1873.

Sahlins, Peter. *Forest Rites: The War of the Demoiselles in Nineteenth-Century France*. Harvard, 1994.

Saint-Amans, Jean-Florimond Boudon de. *Description abrégée du département de Lot et Garonne*. Agen, Year VIII (1799).

Saint-Amans, J.-F. B. de. *Fragmens d'un voyage sentimental et pittoresque dans les Pyrénées*. Metz, 1789.

Saint-Amans, J.-F. B de. 'Voyage agricole, botanique et pittoresque, dans une partie des Landes'. *AV*, XVIII (1812), pp. 5–220.

Saint-Félix, Armand-Joseph-Marie de. *Architecture rurale, théorique et pratique*. Toulouse, 1820.

Saint-Lager, Jean-Baptiste. *Études sur les causes du crétinisme et du goître endémique*. 1867.

Saint-Martin, Viven de. 'Achèvement du tunnel du Mont Cenis', *L'Année géographique*, 1870–71, pp. 379–97.

Saint-Simon, Louis de Rouvroy, duc de. *Papiers inédits*. Ed. É. Drumont. 1880.

Salaberry, Charles-Marie d'Irumberry. *Mon voyage au Mont d'Or*. Year X (1802).

Sand, George. *Histoire de ma vie*. 8 vols. 1856.

Sand, G. *Jeanne*. 1844; 1986.

Sand, G. *Légendes rustiques*. 1888; 1987.

Sand, G. *La Mare au diable*. 1846.

Sand, G. *Le Marquis de Villemer*. 1860; 1988.

Sand, G. *Nanon*. 1872; 1987.

Sand, G. *Promenades autour d'un village*. 1866.

Sarrieu, Bernard. 'Le Parler de Bagnères-de-Luchon et de sa vallée'. *RLR*, XLV (1902), pp. 385–446.

Saugrain, Claude-Marin. *Nouveau voyage de France, géographique, historique et curieux, disposé par différentes routes*. 1720.

Saurel, Ferdinand and A. Saurel. *Histoire de la ville de Malaucène et de son territoire*. 2 vols. Avignon and Marseille, 1882–83.

Saussure, Horace-Bénédict de. *Voyages dans les Alpes*. 4 vols. Neufchatel and Geneva, 1779–96.

Savant, Jean. *Les Préfets de Napoléon*. 1958.

Sébillot, Paul. *Coutumes populaires de la Haute-Bretagne*. 1886.

Sébillot, P. *Traditions et superstitions de la Haute-Bretagne*. 2 vols. 1882; 1967.

Segalen, Martine. *Mari et femme dans la société paysanne*. 1980.

Segalen, Victor. 'Journal de voyage'. *Œuvres complètes*. I. Ed. H. Bouillier. Laffont, 1995.

Seguin de Pazzis, Maxime de. *Mémoire statistique sur le département de Vaucluse*. Carpentras, 1808.

Serbois, L. de. *Souvenirs de voyages en Bretagne et en Grèce*. 1864.

Siebecker, Édouard. *Physiologie des chemins de fer*. 1867.

Sigart, Joseph. *Glossaire étymologique montois ou Dictionnaire du wallon de Mons et de la plus grande partie du Hainaut*. Brussels and Paris, 1870.

Silhouette, Étienne de. *Voyages de France, d'Espagne, de Portugal et d'Italie*. 4 vols. 1770.

Simon, Jules. *L'Ouvrière*. 1861.

Singer, Barnett. *Village Notables in Nineteenth-Century France*. Albany, 1983.

Smollett, Tobias. *Travels through France and Italy*. 1766; Oxford, 1979.

Sonnini de Manoncourt, Charles-Nicolas-Sigisbert. *Manuel des propriétaires ruraux et de tous les habitans de la campagne*. 1808.

Soudière, Martin de la. 'Lieux dits: nommer, dé-nommer, re-nommer'. *EF*, 2004, 1, pp. 67–77.

Soulange, Ernest. *Inventions et découvertes*. 12th ed. Tours, 1880.

Souvestre, Émile. *En Bretagne*. 1867.

Specklin, Robert. 'Études sur les origines de la France (fin)'. *Acta geographica*, 50 (1982), pp. 37–43.

Speleus, Dr. (pseud.). *Çà et là dans les Pyrénées*. Toulouse, 1870.

Stendhal. *Voyages en France*. Ed. V. Del Litto. 1992.

Stevens, Mary. 'Commemorative Fever? French Memorials to the Veterans of the Conflicts in North Africa'. *French Studies Bulletin*, Winter 2005, pp. 2–4.

Stevenson, Robert Louis. *An Inland Voyage*. 1878; 1904.

Stevenson, R. L. *Travels with a Donkey in the Cévennes*. 1879.

Strumingher, Laura. 'Rural Parents, Children and Primary Schools; France 1830–1880'. In *Popular Traditions and Learned Culture in France*. Ed. M. Bertrand. Stanford, 1985.

Sussman, George. *Selling Mother's Milk: The Wet-Nursing Business in France*. Illinois, 1982.

Sutton, Keith. 'Reclamation of Wasteland During the 18th and 19th Centuries'. In H. Clout, ed. *Themes in the Historical Geography of France*. 1977. Pp. 247–300.

Tackett, Timothy. *Priest and Parish in Eighteenth-Century France*. Princeton, 1977.

Tackett, T. *Religion, Revolution, and Regional Culture in Eighteenth-Century France*. Princeton, 1986.

Taine, Hippolyte. *Les Origines de la France contemporaine. L'Ancien Régime*. 2 vols; 1879; 1901–4.

Taine, H. *Voyage aux Pyrénées*. 1858.

Tastu, Amable. *Voyage en France. Paris and Tours*, 1846.

Tastu, A., et al. *Alpes et Pyrénées: arabesques littéraires*. 1842.

Taylor, J. Bayard. *Views A-Foot, or Europe Seen with Knapsack and Staff*. 1846.

Terracher, Adolphe-Louis. *Les Aires morphologiques dans les parlers populaires du nord-ouest de l'Angoumois*. 2 vols. 1912–14.

Thérond, Émile (illust.; text anon.). 'Bernay (Département de l'Eure)'. *MP*, 1870, pp. 31–2.

Thévenin, Évariste. *En vacance: Alsace et Vosges*. 1865.

Thicknesse, P. *A Year's Journey Through France and Part of Spain*. 2 vols. Dublin, 1777.

Thiébault, Paul. *Mémoires*. 5 vols. 1893–5.

Thierry, Amédée. *Histoire des Gaulois: depuis les temps les plus reculés jusqu'à l'entière soumission de la Gaule à la domination romaine*. 3 vols. 1828.

Thiesse, Anne-Marie. *La Création des identités nationales*. 2001.

Thiesse, A.-M. *Ils apprenaient la France: l'Exaltation des régions dans le discours patriotique*. 1997.

Thuillier, Guy. *Pour une histoire du quotidien au XIXe siècle en Nivernais*. 1977.

Thuillier, G. 'L'Alimentation en Nivernais au XIXe siècle'. *Annales*, XX (1965), pp. 1163–84.

Tilloy, M., et al., eds. *Histoire et clandestinité du Moyen-Age à la Première Guerre Mondiale*. Albi, 1979.

Tindall, Gillian. *The Journey of Martin Nadaud*. 1999; 2000.

Tombs, Robert. *France 1814–1914*. 1996.

Tonnellé, Alfred. *Trois mois dans les Pyrénées et dans le Midi*. Tours, 1859.

Topinard, Paul. *L'Homme dans la nature*. 1891.

Topinard, P. 'Discussion sur les moyennes'. *BSAP*, 1880, pp. 32–42.

Trévédy, Julien. *Voyages dans le département actuel des Côtes-du-Nord: 1775–1785*. Saint-Brieuc and Rennes, 1890.

Turner, Dawson. *Account of a Tour in Normandy*. 2 vols. 1820.

Valin, Pierre [Edmonde Travers]. *Le Vosgien*. 1889.

Vallin, Édouard. *Voyage en Bretagne. Finistère*. 1859.

Valori, François-Florent. *Précis historique du voyage entrepris par S. M. Louis XVI, le 21 juin 1791*. 1815.

Varennes, Claude de. *Le Voyage de France, dressé pour la commodité des françois et des estrangers*. Paris, 1687.

Verne, Jules. *Le Tour du monde en quatre-vingts jours*. 1873.

Veryard, Ellis. *An Account of Divers Choice Remarks [. . .] Taken in a Journey Through the Low-Countries, France, Italy and Part of Spain*. 1701.

Veuclin, Ernest. *Les Croix des grands chemins*. Bernay, 1889.

Viard, C. *Annuaire des postes pour 1843, ou Manuel du Service de la poste aux lettres*. Paris: Hôtel des postes, 1843.

Vidal de La Blache, Paul. *Tableau de la géographie de la France*. 2 vols. 1908.

Vigier, Philippe. 'Diffusion d'une langue nationale et résistance des patois en France au XIXe siècle'. *Romantisme*, 25–26 (1979), pp. 191–208.

Vignon, Eugène-Jean-Marie. *Études historiques sur l'administration des voies publiques en France*. III. 1862.

Vigny, Alfred de. *Les Destinées: poèmes philosophiques*. 1864.

Vitu, Auguste. 'Voyage en France. Le Puy-de-Dôme'. *Musée des familles*, 1851–52, pp. 233–9.

Volane, Jean. *En Vivarais*. I. Paris and Nancy, 1897.

Vuillier, Gaston. 'Chez les magiciens et les sorciers de la Corrèze'. *TM*, n.s., V (1899), pp. 505–40.

Wailly, Léon de. *Curiosités philologiques, géographiques et ethnologiques*. 1855.

Wairy, Constant. *Mémoires de Constant, premier valet de chambre de l'Empereur*. III. 1830.

Walckenaer, Charles-Athanase. 'Sur les Vaudois, les Cagots et les chrétiens primitifs'. *NAV*, LVIII (1833), 320–36.

Walckenaer, C.-A. 'Sur la diversité des races d'hommes qui habitent les Pyrénées'. *NAV*, LX (1833), 64–84.

Waldburg-Truchsess, Friedrich Ludwig von. *Nouvelle relation de l'itinéraire de Napoléon*. 1815.

Walsh, Joseph-Alexis. *Suite aux Lettres vendéennes, ou Relation du voyage de S.A.R. Madame, duchesse de Berry*. 1829.

Warenghem, Léon. *En Bretagne: Trébeurden, ses îles, ses grèves, son climat, ses légendes*. Lannion, 1899.

Warrell, Ian. *Turner on the Loire*. 1997.

Watteville Du Grabe, Oscar-Amédée, *Rapport adressé à M. le Ministre de l'Instruction Publique sur le Muséum ethnographique des missions scientifiques*. 1877.

Weber, Eugen. *Peasants into Frenchmen: the Modernization of Rural France, 1870–1914*. Stanford, 1976; 1988.

Webster, Wentworth. *Les Loisirs d'un étranger au pays basque*. Châlons-sur-Marne, 1901.

Webster, W., ed. *Basque Legends*. 1877.

Weld, Charles Richard. *Auvergne, Piedmont, and Savoy: a Summer Ramble*. 1850.

Weld, C. R. *Notes on Burgundy*. 1869.

Weld, C. R. *The Pyrenees, West and East*. 1859.

Whymper, Edward. *Escalades dans les Alpes de 1860 à 1869*. Tr. A. Joanne. 1873.

Wille, Johan Georg. *Mémoires et journal*. 2 vols. 1857.

Williams, Heather. 'Writing to Paris: Poets, Nobles and Savages in Nineteenth-Century Brittany'. *French Studies*, LVII, 4 (2003), pp. 475–90.

Windham, William and Pierre Martel. *An Account of the Glacieres [sic] or Ice Alps in Savoy*. 1744.

Windham, W. and P. Martel. *Relations de leurs deux voyages aux glaciers de Chamonix*. Geneva, 1879.

Wirth, Laurent. *Un équilibre perdu: évolution démographique, économique et sociale du monde paysan dans le Cantal au XIXe siècle*. Clermont-Ferrand, 1996.

Wraxall, Nathaniel William. *Voyage en France*. 2 vols. 1806.

Wright, Edward. *Some Observations Made in Travelling Through France, Italy, &c.* 1764.

Young, Arthur. *Travels in France and Italy During the Years 1787, 1788 and 1789*. 1792; 1977.

Yvart, Victor. 'Observations de l'embrasement spontané d'un tas de fumier'. *Bibliothèque physico-économique instructive et amusante*, 1789, II, pp. 251–4.

Zintzerling, Justus ('Jodocus Sincerus'). *Voyage dans la vieille France*. Tr. T. Bernard. Paris and Lyon, 1859.

Zola, Émile. *Correspondance*. 10 vols. Ed. B. H. Bakker. Montreal and Paris, 1978–95.

General Index

Geographical Index

Channel Islands 81, 152
Chanteloup pagoda, Amboise (Indre-et-
 Loire) 283
Chantilly (Oise) 12, 282
La Chapelle-Saint-Ursin (Cher) 348
Charente region 269
Charente river 68, 138
La Charité-sur-Loire (Nièvre) 8, 289
Charlieu (Loire) 143
Charolais, canal 241
Charost (Cher) 37
Chartres (Eure-et-Loir) 130–1, 162, 209,
 339, 341
Château-Ville-Vieille (Hautes-Alpes)
 351
Châteauroux (Indre) 8–9
Châtelet, Paris 156
Chaudun, Cirque de 275
Chaudun (Hautes-Alpes) 275–6, 277
Chaussée d'Antin 249
'La Chaussée' (place name) 222
'Chemin de la duchesse Anne' 222
Le Chêne, nr Saint-Philbert-de-Bouaine
 (Vendée) 255
Cher *département* 34, 212
Cher river 233n, 272
Cherbourg (Manche) 24, 26
'Chestnut Belt' 91
Cheylard-l'Évêque (Lozère) 145
Clermont d'Excideuil (Dordogne) [del: 4],
 [del: 68,] 136
Clermont-Ferrand (Puy-de-Dôme) 4, 12,
 68, 89, 117, 222, 261
Cloisters Museum, Manhattan 288
Cluny, Abbaye de (Saône-et-Loire) 281,
 289
Colmar (Haut-Rhin) 95, 244, 264
Colombey-les-Belles(Meurthe-et-Moselle)
 36
Combourg (Ille-et-Vilaine) 90
Comédie Française, Paris 356
Compostela *see* Santiago de Compostela
Conches-en-Ouche (Eure) 303
Corbeil (Essonne) 216n
Corbières hills 269, 272, 354–5
Cordouan lighthouse 187
Corniche Sublime, Verdon Gorges 337
Cornwall 151
Corrèze *département* 305

Corsica 53, 60, 65, 73, 103, 173, 203, 206,
 210, 266–7, 290, 316, 326, 329, 348
Corte (Haute-Corse) 210
Côte d'Argent 331
Côte d'Azur 22, 61, 124, 284, 306, 331,
 345
Côte Émeraude 331
Côte Sauvage 331
Cotentin peninsula 104, 119
Côtes-du-Nord *département* (now Côtes-
 d'Armor) 68
Couserans region (Ariège) 169
Couvin, Belgium 27
Cransac (Aveyron) 266
Craponne canal 269
Crau plain 112, 180, 269
Creuse *département* 160, 164, 219
Le Creusot (Saône-et-Loire) 264, 266,
 328, 329
Croissant language zone 60, 67–8
Croisset, nr Rouen (Seine-Maritime) 97
CUDL (Communauté Urbaine de Lille)
 264
Cuq (Tarn) 196
Cure river 22
Cyrano's Nose, Montpellier-le-Vieux 333

Dammartin-en-Goële (Seine-et-Marne)
 187, 189, 196–7
Dargilan, Grotte de (Lozère) 333
Darnac (Haute-Vienne) 136
Dauphiné, province 63, 147, 148, 153,
 283, 329
Dax (Landes) 272
Deauville (Calvados) 311
Decazeville (Aveyron) 264, 265–6
Découverte mine, Decazeville 266
Deux Mers, Canal des 234
Devil's Citadel, the *see* Montpellier-le-
 Vieux
Dévoluy massif, French Alps 275–6
Dieppe (Seine-Maritime) 22, 23, 94–5,
 251, 310–11, 314, 322
Digne-les-Bains (Alpes-de-Haute-
 Provence) 157, 180, 273
Dijon (Côte-d'Or) 89, 140, 157, 241, 278,
 298, 306
Dive river 40
Dognen (Pyrénées-Atlantiques) 44

Acknowledgements

This book began and ended with the friendliness and expertise of Andrew Kidd and Sam Humphreys at Picador, Starling Lawrence at W. W. Norton, Gill Coleridge and Peter Straus at Rogers, Coleridge & White, and Melanie Jackson. Along the way, I incurred debts of gratitude to many people (some will have to remain nameless and others are acknowledged only by the frequency with which their names appear in the notes): Morgan Alliche, Jean-Paul Avice, Nathalie Barou, Nicholas Blake, Alain Brunet, Wilf Dickie, Camilla Elworthy, Laurence Laluyaux, Molly May, Claude and Vincenette Pichois, Raymond and Helen Poggenburg, Chas Roberts and team, Stephen Roberts and Morgen Van Vorst. I am especially grateful to the staff of the following institutions: the Social Science Library of Oxford University, the Taylor Institution Modern Languages Faculty Library, the Bodleian Library, the Bibliothèque Nationale de France, the Musée Dauphinois, the Musée National des Arts et Traditions Populaires, the Bibliothèque Historique de la Ville de Paris and the Musée d'Aquitaine.